Eiríhr Magnússon

National Life and thought of the Various Nations throughout the World

A series of Addresses

Eiríhr Magnússon

National Life and thought of the Various Nations throughout the World
A series of Addresses

ISBN/EAN: 9783744757683

Printed in Europe, USA, Canada, Australia, Japan

Cover: Foto ©Suzi / pixelio.de

More available books at **www.hansebooks.com**

NATIONAL LIFE

AND

THOUGHT

OF THE VARIOUS

NATIONS THROUGHOUT THE WORLD

A Series of Addresses

BY

EIRIKR MAGNUSSON, M.A.; Prof. J. E. THOROLD ROGERS
J. THEODORE BENT; F. H. GROOME;
Mrs. CUNNINGHAME GRAHAM; Prof. PULSZKY;
W. R. MORFILL, M.A.;
AND OTHERS.

NEW YORK

FREDERICK A. STOKES COMPANY

MDCCCXCI.

PREFACE.

THE Lectures contained in this Volume were delivered on Sunday afternoon, at South Place Institute, during the Session 1889-90, and were designed to give information, in a popular form, with regard to the national development and modes of political action among the different nations throughout the world, by means of sympathetic and trustworthy accounts of their history, national aspiration, and modes of government, it being thought that a general dissemination of such knowledge would not only improve our Institutions, but, by stimulating our interest in foreign countries, tend to promote international amity.

The Committee take this opportunity of expressing their obligations to the different Lecturers for the willingness with which they have made it possible to carry on this work, and trust that the general public, to whom this Volume is now offered, will appreciate the information therein contained as highly as did the audiences to whom the Lectures were originally addressed.

WM. SHEOWRING, } *Hon. Secretaries,*
CONRAD W. THIES { *Institute Committee.*

SOUTH PLACE INSTITUTE.

CONTENTS.

THE ARMENIANS, ARMENIA, AND THE ARMENIAN QUESTION.

M. SEVASLY.

WHEN Mr. Wm. Sheowring, the Honorary Secretary of the South Place Institute, requested me to lecture on the Armenians and on the Armenian Question, he invited my attention to a statement that appeared in the *Diplomatic Fly Sheet*, in which the Armenians are classed by C. D. Collett as a *religious* community, and not as a nation. To refute the assertion will constitute the subject-matter of the first part of this paper.

The Armenians are a nation, and one of the oldest nations in the world. Descended from the great Aryan race, they are as ancient as the Jews, the Assyrians, the Babylonians, the Persians, and the Greeks. The antiquity of the Armenian nation is attested by ancient writers. Thus we find that Alexander Polyhistor, a Greek writer (75 B.C.), affirming that the Armenians were known as a nation twenty centuries before Christ ; and in support of this assertion, he says that the Armenians made an expedition against that powerful maritime people, the Phœnicians, whom they defeated, and that among the prisoners captured was the nephew of Abraham the patriarch. Again we find the name of Armenia and Ararat designated in the Bible, in Herodotus, in Strabo, and others. Moreover, cuneiform inscriptions on the celebrated Rock of Van also attest the antiquity of the Armenian people.

According to Armenian chronology, the foundation of the first Armenian kingdom dates so far back as 2540 B.C. As with the history of other ancient countries, that of Armenia begins with legend : " Haïg, a local chief, who lived in the country of Ararat, migrated with his sons and daughters to Senaar in Mesopotamia. While they lived in those regions the Tower of Babel was erected, and the Babylonian Empire was ruled by Belus. Haïg, unwilling to submit to the authority of Belus, returned with his family of about three hundred persons to the fatherland, where he incorporated himself with the earliest settlers.   Belus marched against him with his warriors all clad in iron armour, and supplied with powerful spears and bows and arrows.   Yet destiny was about to found a great nation and a vast empire.   The small band of Haïg proved victorious, and Belus fell by an arrow from the bow of Haïg.

Victory and the spoils of war inflaming their breasts, the Haïgs (or Armenians) went on conquering, until a territory stretching from the Caspian Sea to the east of Cilicia on the Mediterranean, on the west ; and from the borders of the Pontus on the north to the confines of Assyria at the south, formed one vast and powerful *Haiasdan* or *Armenia.*

The name of Armenia[1] was derived from Aram, the sixth successor of Haïg, who became so renowned by his exploits that from his time the surrounding nations designated the country as *Aramia,* after his name, which, in course of time, has been corrupted into the modern nomenclature of "Armenia."

The height of glory was only attained during the reign of Tigranes.   "It is but a few days' journey from the country of the Cabiri or Sebastia, present Sivas, into Armenia," says Lucullus, "where Tigranes, King of kings, is seated surrounded with that power which has wrested Asia from the Parthians, which carries Grecian Colonies into Media, subdues Syria and Palestine."

Again, Cicero, alluding to the same King Tigranes the Great, tells us that he made the Republic of Rome tremble before the prowess of his arms.

Unfortunately, the country became the prey of neighbouring nations.   Persians, Greeks, Romans, Tartars, each and all overran the country.   All by turns have contended for mastery.

Three dynasties maintained power in Armenia proper.

---

[1] There is a controversy on the origin of the word "Armenia."   Some also attribute it to *Arameen,* which signifies *High Land* in Armenian.   But it is most likely that the country has been called after Aram, one of our greatest kings, and who achieved fame among his neighbours.   Semiramis the great Assyrian queen waged war against Ara, the son of Aram, the brave and handsome Armenian chief, in consequence of his stern determination to resist the offers of the mighty Assyrian sovereign.   (Read *Sarchedon,* by G. T. Whyte-Melville.   Ward, Lock, & Co., Salisbury Square, E.C.)

[2] The first dynasty begins with Haig, 2540 B.C., and ends on or about 150 B.C.   The second, or Arsacidian dynasty, under which Armenia reached the height of its glory, from 150 B.C. to 428 A.D..   The third, or Pagradounian dynasty, closes in the year 1080 A.D.

In the early part of the eleventh century, after the fall of the Pagradounian Dynasty, flying before the Mongolian invader, thousands of Armenians left the seat of their sires to take refuge in the inaccessible fastnesses of the Taurus, and transformed Cilicia into an Armenian Kingdom under the Rupenian Dynasty, whose last King, Leo VI.,[1] after a heroic struggle with Egyptian invaders, was captured in 1375, from which dates the extinction of the Armenians as an independent nation.

The Cilician Kingdom lasted three centuries; and this really is marvellous, for the Armenians had to contend not only with Moslem foes, but with the Byzantine Greeks, whom they defeated and worsted on more than one occasion. While in Cilicia the Armenians rendered eminent service to the cause of Christendom and civilisation by helping the Crusaders in their wars against the Saracens. The claim of the Armenian people as a Christian people upon the support of Christian Europe may be said to date from the time of the Crusades.

The Armenians have been the first people who have abandoned their former religion, which was that of the Magi, to embrace Christianity. In fact, the introduction of Christianity among them was coeval with Jesus Christ, or soon after. Thaddeus, one of the seventy, was sent to Edessa, then the capital of Armenia (for the capital of Armenia has often changed), to instruct the King Abkar in the new faith, which he did. He baptized him and the citizens of that metropolis.

The seeds of Christianity were consequently sown; but it was not until some three centuries later, when appeared Gregory of Cæsarea, that a revival of the faith was created by him. Hence the appellation given to him by the Armenians of "Gregory the Illuminator."

It is, in truth, this form of national Christian Church that has so far kept the Armenians together.[1]

There are about 200,000 Armenians belonging to the Romish Church, and 60,000 to the Protestant, out of 6,000,000 of Armenians.[2] But the spirit of nationality is deeply rooted in them all.[3]

---

[1] Leo died at Paris on the 29th November 1393. His remains are interred at St. Denis, which has become a place of pilgrimage for the Armenians. There the Armenians of Paris resort every Easter, and appropriate speeches are delivered on the tomb of the last Armenian king.

[2] *L'Arménie,* by J. Broussali (*Revue Française,* June 1886).

[3] The Spiritual Supreme Head of the Gregorian Armenians is the

The Armenians have all the good qualities to make them the champions of civilisation and progress in Asia Minor. There is, indeed, no other Asiatic race so capable of appreciating the civilisation of Europe, or so worthy of European support and sympathy.

And as to their qualities and virtues, they can appeal to an areopagus of historians, poets, statesmen, travellers.

Gibbon's *Roman Empire* bears testimony to the mercantile genius, religious fervency, and valour and prowess of the Armenians in the third and fourth centuries.

" It is difficult," says Byron, " to trace in the annals of a nation less crime than in the Armenian, whose virtues are those of peace, and whose vices the outcome of oppression."

An exampled oppression—" The helpless nation," says Gibbon, " has seldom been permitted to enjoy the tranquillity of servitude. From the earliest period to the present hour Armenia has been the theatre of war. Under the rod of oppression the zeal of the Armenians is fervent and intrepid ; they have often preferred the crown of martyrdom to the white turban of Mahomet."

Lamartine styles the Armenians the Swiss, while Dulaurier gives them the appellation of the Dutch of the East. Lord Carnarvon, in a speech in the House of Lords, equalled them to the Greeks in intellectual power. Mr. James Bryce, in his *Transcaucasia and Ararat*, tells that " when there meets you a keener or more restless glance, you may be sure that it comes from an Armenian eye."

They have given statesmen and men of action to famous nations. Nubar Pacha, the brilliant Egyptian Minister ; Melikoff, the Russian General who captured Kars, are there to bear one out. Some 30,000 Armenians at Zeythoun, in Cilicia, the representatives of those who formed the Cilician Kingdom, have, to a score of years ago, maintained their independence.

Catholicos of Echtmiadzin, whose seat is in Russian Armenia, near Erivan. The patriarch of Constantinople exercises spiritual and some sort of temporal power over the Gregorian Armenians of Turkey. He is assisted by a civil and ecclesiastical council, and is responsible to an "assembly of representatives," in virtue of a Charter granted by the Porte in 1862, in amplification of the privileges and rights conferred by Sultan Mahommed II., on the first Armenian Patriarchate he instituted in Constantinople after the capture of that capital. The powers of the said body end where those of the state begin. It has a voice in the management and control of the educational and ecclesiastical affairs of the community ; but it cannot remedy any of the evils under which the Armenians are now groaning.

Armenian literature is rich and varied, and history, philosophy, and poetry are amply represented.

Armenia is now partitioned among three Powers : Russia, Turkey, and Persia. Her limits cannot be easily defined, and have undergone many a change in the course of her historical vicissitudes. Armenia in older days extended from the Caucasus to Mesopotamia, and to Western Asia Minor, and occupied an area of about 150,000 square miles. The country is of a mountainous character. Its plains are high, but fertile, yielding corn of the finest quality, and in abundance ; as also tobacco, flax, rice, and cotton ; its pasture lands sustain breeds of horses ; its valleys produce the grape, the apple, and other fruits ; trees such as the poplar, oak, olive, carob, and fig thrive.

Armenia is the source of several important rivers, such as the Euphrates, which springs from the mountains of Erzeroum (Garin), and flows into the Persian Gulf, after joining the Tigris below Bagdad ; the Tigris, the second river of Armenia, falls into the Persian Gulf ; the Araxes, after the Armenian King Aramays (the Gihon of the ancients), which runs into the Caspian Sea ; and the Tchorouk, or the Phison of the Scriptures, which takes its source near the Baïbourt mountains, and flows into the Black Sea. Where the territories of Persia, Turkey, and Russia meet in North-east Armenia, Ararat (the Massis of the Armenians, after Amassia, the grand-nephew of Haïg, and upon which tradition says that the Ark of Noah rested), with its summit covered in perpetual snow, rises above the plain at its base, to the height of 14,320 feet.

Again, the Taurus and Ante-Taurus chain cover an extensive area, from Armenia proper to the South-western Armenia (Cilicia).

These mountain chains contain mines of rock-salt, nitre, naphtha, sulphur, iron, and copper, as also lead, silver, and even gold, zinc, and other metals. The traces, however, of the gold-mines have now been lost, although these were known to exist in olden times.

The zoological kingdom of the country is also extremely rich. On the Erzeroum plateau more than 170 kinds of wild birds are known to exist. The crane and stork are the favourite birds of the Armenians, and frequently form the subject of their folk-poesy. Wild animals abound, and the bear, lynx, wolf, hyena, leopard, tiger, buffalo, bull, wild ass and wild sheep, and others cover that immense country. The domestic animals, the sheep, of which more than a million are exported ; the horses and camel, while the rivers and the lakes Van, Ourmiah, and Sevan (three principal lakes of Armenia, situate in Turkish, Persian, and Russian Armenia respectively) abound in multifarious fishes of various colours.

The climate of Armenia is essentially cold. Though in the same parallel of latitude as Greece, Italy, and Spain, and parts of Asia-Minor, nevertheless the severity of her winter is even greater than that of the north of France and that of Germany.

The country was rich in the distant past in large and important cities, such as Ani, the ruins of which attest its ancient splendour and magnificence, Armavir on the Araxes, Vagharshabad, and Digranakuerd. Van, Erzeroum, were then, as they now are, important centres.

The Armenian Question.—Armenia is, as above stated, divided among Russia, Persia, and Turkey. In the beginning of the seventeenth century she was partitioned between Persia and Turkey.

Towards the end of the eighteenth century the province of Karabag, a fertile and mountainous country, peopled by 200,000 Armenians and 100,000 Tartars and Persians, and governed by Armenian chiefs, under the nominal domination of Persia, was conquered by Russia, and thus ever since the beginning of this century Armenia is ruled by three Powers. Russia subsequently, in 1828 and in 1829, extended her conquests in Persian and Turkish Armenia. The Treaty of Turkmen-Tchaï of 5th March 1828 delimitated the Russo-Persian frontiers, while the Berlin Treaty of 1878 fixed those of Turkey and Russia in Asia Minor.

The Armenian grievances, or the Armenian Question, became one of immediate international concern ever since the insertion of a special Clause in the Berlin Treaty of 1878 in favour of the Armenians occupying the provinces of Van, Erzeroum, Diarbekir, Kharpoot, and Dersim, in *Turkish Armenia*, and numbering about two millions. The Clause referred to, which is but a modified form of Article 16 of the Treaty of San Stefano, runs thus: "The Sublime Porte undertakes to carry out, without further delay, the improvements and reforms demanded by local requirements in the provinces inhabited by the Armenians, and to guarantee their security against the Circassians and Kurds. It will periodically make known the steps taken to this effect to the Powers, who will superintend their application." This Clause, coupled with Article 62 of the same instrument, place the civil and religious liberties of the Armenian people under the express guarantee of the International Law, and under the supervision and control of the Powers, parties to the Treaty. Article 62 enacts that "The Sublime Porte having expressed its intention of maintaining the principle of religious liberty, and giving it the widest scope, the contracting parties take note of this spontaneous declaration. In no part of the Ottoman Empire shall difference of religion be alleged against any person as a ground for exclusion from or incapacity for the discharge of civil and political rights, and admission to public functions. All persons shall be admitted without distinction to give evidence before the tribunals. The freedom and exercise of all forms of worship are assured to all."

The *raison d'être* of Article 61 of the Berlin Treaty may be explained in a few matter-of-fact sentences thus classified :—

I. The absence of Civil and Political Equality.

II. The non-admission or non-appreciation of Armenian evidence in the Turkish Courts of Justice (in cases where the Armenian is the wronged party and the Moslem the delinquent).

III. The systematic pillage and destruction of Armenian villages ; the sacking of convents ; the perpetration of all kinds of crimes and oppressive acts by new-imported Circassians, and especially by the Kurds—not unfrequently also by the police and by the local officials.

IV. The venality of justice.

V. The systematic efforts to crush and ruin the peasant classes (1) by heavy and arbitrary taxes, and (2) by dispossessing them of their holdings.

These grievances exist down to the present day as they did when the Berlin Treaty was signed. It would occupy too much space to explain in detail the evils complained of, and bring out minutely the consequences resulting therefrom. I shall principally deal with Grievance II.

The positive prescriptions of Imperial Hatts and Imperial Firmans issued from time to time by reigning sovereigns of Turkey, ever since the reign of Sultan Abdul-Medjid, to their Christian subjects promising them liberty of conscience, and equality before the law, equality of taxation, and assurances of reform, are mere idle words. Whatever the letter of the law may say, the testimony of the Christian is not received, or if received, not appreciated, with what result it will be easy to understand. The attention of the civilised world has been lately absorbed by the prevalence of slave trade in the Dark Continent, and international conferences and a congress held to devise the most efficacious means for the suppression of that immoral traffic. Now in Armenia—and, I may add, in Turkey in general—slavery exists and is rampant in one of its worst forms, and is connived at and supported by the Moslem judges. The polygamous Kurdish or Turkish Beys and Aghas, whose hitherto regular supply of Circassian girls from the Caucasus has been cut off from them since the annexation of the province by Russia, have recourse now to a bold system of rape. They swoop down upon an Armenian village, with their armed acolytes, and carry off to their harems, by main force, as many good-looking girls and women as they can lay hands on. This is permitted to them; and the *modus operandi* by which the abduction of Armenian girls is rendered legal by the Moslem judges may be summed up as follows :—When the relatives present themselves in court to claim the abducted victim, the ravishers are ready with a brace of Moslem witnesses (a hundred could be produced if wanted), who declare on oath that the kidnapped woman pronounced in their presence the regular formula of the Moslem faith : "There is no God but God, and Mahomed is His Prophet," Christian evidence to the contrary being invariably rejected.

The judge thereupon dismisses the case, on the ground that the stolen and ravished girl has by that profession abjured her former faith and embraced Mohammedanism. And the verdict of these upright judges is not to be set aside. The victims protest; but their protestations avail them nothing. They invoke in vain the positive prescriptions of the Imperial Hatts, and the distinct stipulations of solemn treaties, promising liberty of conscience and equality before the law. The Turkish Solon is not to be moved. His invariable reply is, that the Koran—source of all human and Divine legislation—is the supreme law of the land, and it would be blasphemy to admit or suppose that any subsequent enactments could in any way have modified its sacred teachings.

Hundreds of Armenian girls are thus lost to their homes and imprisoned in Turkish harems; they are never set free, and if one ever succeeds in escaping, the chances are ten to one that sooner or later she will be murdered.[1]

Again, in consequence of the non-appreciation of Christian

---

[1] A custom prevails in Turkey whereby a Moslem is exempted from military service if he elopes with a Christian girl and keeps her in his *harem* for a time long enough to warrant the presumption that she embraced Mohammedanism.

evidence, Mahometans commit all sorts of crimes and misdeeds on the Christian population, who cannot obtain justice, through their evidence being ignored and contemned, and Mahometans seldom coming forward to give evidence against a coreligionist. Moreover, through the non-admission of Christian testimony, Mahometans, Turks or Kurds, or Circassians, find the most efficacious means to dispossess the Armenians from the lands they inherited *ab antiquo.* Kurds or Circassians settle or encamp in the vicinity of Armenian villages, and cultivate the lands belonging to Armenians. Should a dispute arise, a number of Moslem witnesses are produced in Court, who testify to the lands having been owned by the Kurds from time immemorial. Armenian evidence to the contrary is seldom accepted. And thus, under the ægis of the law, the Armenians are gradually dispossessed of lands they inherited from their forefathers for the benefit of predatory and wild tribes. The Kurds were known in the time of Xenophon, who pelted his army with stones in the famous retreat. They have not crystallised into a "nation" ever since. They possess no literature and no learning, and most have no fixed abode. They usually have recourse to Armenian or Persian alphabets whenever they wish to express their thoughts in writing. In olden times they inhabited the country south of the province of Van, in the Hekkeari district, in close proximity to the present Nestorians. The policy of the Sublime Porte, especially since the Crimean War, has been to gradually replace the historic, peaceful, and laborious Armenian by the predatory Kurdish element, with a view, on the one hand, to radically stamping out the "Armenian Question;" and, on the other, in the event of a war with Russia, to utilise the Kurds in arresting the Muscovite legions from a further advance in Asia Minor. As soldiers the Kurds are useless, and they amply proved it during the last Turko-Russian War. They are not a brave people, nor have they any high or manly qualities. Their robberies, their crimes, and their misdeeds are dastardly affairs. They seldom attack armed travellers, except in very superior numbers. They assault more commonly peaceful caravans, or defenceless villages. Feuds and quarrels are frequent among them. Mutual confidence is almost unknown. All the villages from Erzeroum to Bitlis, and from Van to Salmaste, in Persia, are more or less exposed to Kurdish raids and plunder. Thus it will be seen that the Kurds [1] are, on the one hand, the

---

[1] Through the continual usurpation of the lands the Kurds have elevated

usurpers of the lands of the Armenians, with the connivance of the
Turkish Government; and, on the other, they are brigands, and
high-robbers and raiders, well armed and equipped with modern
rifles, and left unrestrained to commit all sorts of excesses on
defenceless populations.

"The Kurds," says Mr. C. Wilkinson, who visited Armenia
and Asia Minor about a hundred years ago, and whose evidence
testifies that Armenia is to-day what she then was; "the Kurds," [1]
says the traveller, "are constantly on the watch for an opportunity
of plundering the caravans. If a good guard is not kept in the
tents, they come privately and pull out bales of goods with hooks,
without being perceived; and if the bales are fastened together
with cords, they are seldom without a good razor to cut them. As
caravans generally set out before daybreak, the rogues mix with
the drivers, and turn out of the way a few miles laden with goods,
which they easily carry off in the dark; and they seldom choose
the worst, for they know the bales of silks as well as the owners.
These people own no masters, *and the Turks never punish them,
even when they are taken up for murder and robbery.*"

And Mr. Wilkinson's assertions are true to the present day.
The case of the notorious Kurdish chief, Moussa Bey, is an illustration of what has been said above as to the futility of Turkish
promises to mete out justice to Christians where they are wronged
by a Mahometan; it shows that, notwithstanding all the pompous
Imperial enactments, Christian evidence is still either not
admitted or not appreciated. It shows, moreover, the tacit, if
not overt, encouragement given by the "Authorities" in Turkey
to the Kurds to pillage, burn, and slaughter the Armenians.
Who is Moussa Bey, whose name has now become almost a
"household" word in Europe? This is what an impartial writer,
during the troubled times of the Turko-Russian war, said of
Moussa Bey, on whom the Turks have bestowed the palm of
martyrdom:—"Mr. C. B. Norman, Correspondent of *The Times* at
the seat of war in Armenia in 1877, in his work entitled 'Armenia
and the Campaign of 1877,' says: 'In the neighbourhood of
Moosh, one Moussa Bey, a son of Mirza Bey, a Kurd from Wear

---

themselves, in some districts, in Bitlis in particular, to the position of feudal
chiefs, and make the Armenians pay them tribute. Should the Armenian
refuse to pay, the Kurd ravages and pillages his village.—Dr. Grigor, Artzruni,
editor of the *Mschag* (Tiflis).

[1] "A Tour through Asia Minor and the Greek Islands." By C. Wilkinson.
London: Printed by Darton & Harvey, Gracechurch Street.   1806.

Van, has been ravaging the country at the head of a small body of cavalry. The villages of Moolah Akjam, Hadogan, and Kharkin, having been first pillaged, were set on fire. At Ardork he extracted £60, and at Ingrakam £40 from the head men of the village, under pretence of sparing them from destruction, and straightway set the places on fire. He then proceeded to a Mussulman village called Norashen, and, hearing that an Armenian merchant of Bitlis was passing through, robbed him of all his goods, to the value of 30,000 piastres, and then ordered his men to murder him. At Khartz this monster entered the house of the Armenian priest, who had lately brought his bride to his father's home. Binding the old man and his son together with cords, this inhuman scoundrel ravished the poor girl before their eyes, and then gave orders for the murder of the three. I can write no more. A bare recital of the horrors committed by these demons is sufficient to call for their condign punishment. The subject is too painful to need any colouring, were my feeble pen enabled to give it.' "

Moussa Bey was, these crimes notwithstanding, appointed a *Mudir*, or a petty governor, in one of the districts of Moosh. He subsequently, three years ago, perpetrated other crimes of an equally atrocious nature, setting fire to and destroying barns, extracting money from inoffensive peasants, killing some and wounding others, not sparing American missionaries. While, in the spring of 1889, he committed a series of outrages, which the readers will find recorded in the Blue Book, No. 1, of 1889 (Turkey). They may be summed up thus : He carried off women, massacred villagers, seized a notable, and flung him on faggots, and burned him alive in presence of his followers. An outcry was raised. The cry of the suffering Armenians, of outraged women, of desperate humanity, the cry of desolation and ruin reached the ears of Europe. Public opinion was agitated, and the Turks saw that something had to be done. Moussa was " invited " to proceed to Constantinople, not as a criminal, but as an honoured guest. He is first conducted to Bitlis in triumph, escorted by the head of the Moslem religious community, and a train of functionaries, soldiers, zaptielers, softas, and cavaliers. On leaving Erzeroum, Moussa is escorted for some miles by the governor of the province and a strong body of cavalry. At Constantinople the ceremony is still more formal ; and as soon as the steamer conveying the truculent brigand is signalled, two generals proceed on board to receive him. In the

Turkish metropolis he is comfortably quartered, surrounded with servants and attendants, and frequently entertained and feasted by friends in authority. More than forty witnesses and complainants travelled all the way from Armenia to Constantinople to give evidence, and to substantiate the charges preferred against him. The trial of three of the principal counts was concluded on 2nd December last, and the hearing of the other adjourned *sine die.* Moussa was acquitted by a majority of Mussulmen judges, notwithstanding most direct and conclusive evidence. Those who saw the trial described it as a virtual farce all through. The Public Prosecutor, who represents the State and the Law, and whose duty it is to protect the suffering people, bullied the witnesses, and overtly acted as a counsel for Moussa Bey. "Suffice it to say," writes Sir William White, Her Britannic Majesty's Ambassador at Constantinople to the Marquis of Salisbury (*vide* Blue Book, Turkey No. 1, 1890, page 100), "that the position taken up by the Public Prosecutor savoured rather of that of a lawyer for the defence than of a prosecutor on behalf of the Government, and it is generally considered *unprecedented in the judicial annals of this country.*" Thus ended one of the most scandalous trials on record. The case of Moussa Bey is but an instance, a specimen, and serves to illustrate how justice is prostituted in Turkey, even in her very metropolis, at the very gates of Europe.

After the scandalous proceedings in connection with this now celebrated trial, the following report from Van, which gives a graphic description of the present condition of the country, explains itself : " Every Armenian village is compelled, notwithstanding its extreme poverty, to provide food almost daily for the army of tax-gathering officials, who on their part treat the inhabitants with absolute inhumanity. The peasant, reduced now to the last extremity, must either sell his oxen and plough, his house and fields, and clear out ; or go to distant provinces in quest of work, with no prospect of returning ; or emigrate ; or start out and beg from door to door. Thanks to this policy, many of the southern and eastern districts of Vasbouragan (Province of Van) are nearly depopulated of their Christian element, whose place has been taken by Kurds, Turks, Yezidis, &c. Even the educational expenses of the Turks are provided out of the taxes paid by the Armenians. As for the Kurd, he is under no restraint of law, under no burden of taxes, and has no regular military service to undergo. A chartered outlaw, he devastates, plunders, burns, and kills; and no man calls him to account. Robberies and outrages are committed without number; but the Government neither sees nor hears, for its own officials are too often the perpetrators. Forced marriages, forced conversions to Mohammedanism are common, always and everywhere. In a word, civil rights, justice, order, and tranquillity have, as it were, bidden their last farewell, and departed from the land of the Armenian subjects of Turkey.

" Corruption reigns supreme among the officials without distinction, from the highest to the lowest. It has become a law. Every official, even the Governor himself, obtains his office from the Central Government by bribery, and by this alone; and throughout all the official world plunder is the great business of life. In all the courts of law, cases are kept pending until the litigants have been sucked dry; and as often as not an unjust judgment is given in favour of the suitor who has lumped down the biggest bribe. But woe to the non-suited should he venture to question the judge's decision! Imprisonment for life, or, at the least, perpetual exile, is apt to be his answer. It is absolutely forbidden to draw up public memorials. The Press is gagged, till there is nothing left for it to print but flatteries of the persons by whom the gags have been applied. Numerous houses are everywhere searched on the flimsiest and most impudent pretences. Private detractors and calumniators are rewarded with honours and offices. Young men are exiled for indefinite periods; and their defenceless and helpless families are left to shift as they may. The prisons are filled with Armenians (many of whom clergymen) who have been flung there without rhyme or reason."

No account of the present condition of Armenia would be complete without a comprehensive statement on the numerous irregularities committed and the vexatious measures adopted by the fiscal officials in connection with the collection and assessment of taxes. The Armenian Christian subjects of the Sultan are exempted from military service in consideration of a poll-tax, named *bedelaskerie* (military exemption tax), the amount of which is not properly and equitably assessed. Thus the aforesaid tax, which applies only to persons fit for service, is demanded from the relatives of people who are dead, who have emigrated, or who are infirm. In many cases the tax is levied on newly-born persons and on old men. Again, with respect to the fixed taxes levied upon property (*emlak*) and upon professions (*temettu*), the local officials carry on unjust assessments, without regard to the value of the property, to its resources, or to the capabilities and earnings of the person assessed for the "professions" tax. Moreover, the assessing officials, contrary to imperial orders, undervalue the properties owned by Mahometans. Thus the property tax falls more heavily upon Christians than upon Mahometans. Cases can be quoted where lands belonging to Armenians have been registered for taxation at ten times their real actual value. The *temettu* tax (tax on professions), which should by law be levied on artisans and shopkeepers, is arbitrarily extended to farmers, and even to women who exercise no such profession. The tax-gatherers in collecting taxes infringe the existing laws of the empire by seizing and selling the most necessary household goods, trade implements, wearing apparel, and bedding of the debtor. They invariably, when the taxpayer is not able to satisfy the State, seize objects indispensable for the proper working of any immovable property, such as animals attached to cultivation, agricultural implements, seed corn, etc. The proprietor, entirely stripped of all movable capital, has nothing remaining but the bare land, denuded of those accessories without which it can yield nothing.

Tithe farming, which does not exist in theory since the promulgation of the Hatts Houmayoun of 1856, is still in full force in the Armenian provinces. It may be remembered that one of the principal causes which led to the Herzegovinian insurrection was due to the excesses of the tithe farmers in the Nevesinje district. The tithe farmers in the Armenian provinces are generally the beys or local functionaries, who, in order to avoid an overt breach of the law, rent the tithes through their sons, relatives, or servants. The tithes of a given province are farmed out to the highest bidder. The farmers, in collusion with the governor of the province, never hesitate to bid an elevated price. They calculate the price they are willing to pay on the basis of more than forty per cent. minimum profit for themselves. They have nothing to fear in the way of incurring losses; for where the value of tithe is affected by a sudden fall in the produce markets, the farmers (*multezims*) are allowed *carte blanche* to recoup themselves by vexatious exactions, or by over-estimating the quantity of the produce. The tithe farmers compel the peasants to pay in specie, although the tithe is due in kind. Should the cultivator display reluctance to pay the tithe in money in lieu of in kind, the *multezim* refuses to assess his crops, thus exposing the agriculturist to severe losses, for until the tithe is assessed he is not allowed to remove his produce, which stands out in the open air, exposed to rain, hail, etc. The unfortunate peasant in despair appeals to the tithe farmer, who assesses the crops after payment of double the amount he demanded before. Even the produce of gardens attached to dwellings, and used for home consumption, is subjected to taxation, contrary to the existing laws of the Empire. Where the tithe is paid in kind, the producer is bound to deliver it. The peasants wait day after day at the doors of the Government stores, in order that their crops may be measured and stored. It is, moreover, a subject of complaint that the *multezims* do not assess the crops at harvest time, often on account of the farming out of the tithes being delayed until that season, although the law prescribes that they should be farmed out in spring. The crops are consequently left out in the fields and threshing-floors, where they not unfrequently decay and perish. But the *multezims* compel the peasants to pay for the damaged produce as if it were sound. Should the peasants refuse to pay, they are subjected to all kinds of vexation. They are dragged into the law courts, ill-treated, and imprisoned. The officials, in secret league with the tithe farmers, only serve the interests of the latter, and the poor agriculturist has to sacrifice all he possesses. The villager is bound to provide the *multezim* and his agents food and lodgings without remuneration for such time as they may choose to remain in the village. Not unfrequently the *multezim* beats the villager and sullies the honour of his wife and daughter. The tithe farmers commit multifarious other abuses, in the way of levying fresh taxes, assessing produce exempt from taxation, etc. The complaints are more grievous in districts where there are beys, agas, or Kurdish chiefs who have friends in authority to cover their systematic misdeeds. Under the aforesaid circumstances the peasant, unable to satisfy the State, has recourse to usurious loans, and he thus becomes the bondsman or serf of the usurer, who in time dispossesses him of all his goods, movable and immovable. He finally has to emigrate and seek a mode of living in distant climes.

Such are the unredressed Armenian grievances twelve years after the passing of Article 61 of the Berlin Treaty. To remedy existing evils, it is not necessary to create an independent or autonomous Armenia, nor do the Armenians aim either at independence or at a distinct political existence. All they ask for are civil liberties and the establishment of institutions calculated to guarantee their personal safety, the security of their property, the honour of their wives and daughters, their rights, in fact, as men and civilised beings. The fulfilment of Article 61 of the Berlin Treaty, as explained by the Collective Note addressed to the Porte in 1880 by the great Powers, will afford satisfaction, and will avert a crisis which is assuming menacing proportions. To check the incessant plunder and raids of the Kurds and Circassians, a *gendarmerie* recruited among the natives and commanded by native officers should be instituted. To eradicate corruption and venality, the present administration of Armenia, which is essentially Turkish, should be entrusted to the aborigines of the land, who constitute the vital forces of the country. The provinces of Van, Erzeroum, Diarbekir, Bitlis, Karpout, and Dersim, to be grouped in one province, with an Armenian governor at its head, sitting at Erzeroum, whose duties it will be to enforce the laws of the empire, and under whose command the established *gendarmerie* is to be placed for the maintenance of security and order. The *desiderata* of the Armenians may be therefore defined thus: *An Armenian administration in Armenia.*

Cast a glance on the map and see where Armenia lies, and what a commanding position she holds, and what grave consequences would result through a Russian occupation of that country through its being allowed to seethe with discontent and disaffection. Indeed, a Russian occupation of Turkish Armenia means the practical supremacy of the whole of Western Asia. In the words of the author of *Greater Britain*, "Russia could reach Constantinople through Asia Minor, not so directly, but more surely and more safely than through Europe."[1] Military authorities testify to the Armenia plateau of Erzeroum being the key of Western Asia. Erzeroum, moreover, the capital of Turkish Armenia, is the point where converge the roads from the Caucasus and of those leading into Syria, Anatolia, and the Persian Gulf. If the Muscovite legions were allowed to become masters of such a commanding position, they would intercept the whole overland trade to India and Persia; they may become a Mediterranean Power—with Alexandretta as their commercial port —and menace England in Cyprus and Egypt. The commercial interests of England in those regions would be placed in jeopardy by a further Russian advance; for, to quote Lord Salisbury's own words, "the existing European trade which now passes from Trebizonde to Persia would be liable to be arrested at the pleasure of the Russian Government, by the arbitrary barriers of

---

[1] *Present Position of European Politics* (p. 161), by Sir Charles Dilke.

their commercial system." Lord Salisbury's views are shared by Sir Charles Dilke, who adds : "There is one loss by a Russian occupation of the remainder of the Turkish dominions which no British Government would willingly face. It is the loss of trade. In Asiatic provinces acquired by Russia at the end of the last war, where there was formerly a considerable British trade, there is now none ; it has been killed by protection duties."

I have alluded to the natural wealth of the country, to its valuable mineral resources, which remain unexplored and dormant through want of security and safety. What an immense opening for the industrial and enterprising classes of England if they would devote their attention to my unhappy country instead of spending millions for the exploration of the Dark Continent, under guise of suppressing slave trade !

I have endeavoured to bring out the past, the brilliant past, of the Armenians, their services to civilisation and Christendom, their rights, and how these rights are trampled under foot, and how the distinct stipulations of treaties have remained a dead letter. I have endeavoured, moreover, to show of what interest it is to England—an interest commercial, strategical, and political —to bring about the solution of the long-pending Armenian Question. I now make a solemn appeal, on behalf of outraged humanity, to the people of this country, and ask them to use their legitimate influence for the amelioration of the condition of a suffering nation, groaning under a most odious tyranny. I may here remind England's responsibilities. Subsequent to the last Turko-Russian War, Russia reserved to herself, in the 16th Article of the Treaty of San Stefano, the sole Protectorate of the Armenians. England refused to admit such a stipulation ; and a Convention was signed between England and Russia, on May 30, 1878, wherein it was agreed that the Protectorate should be jointly shared by the two contracting states. On the 4th June of the same year England signed with Turkey the so-called Cyprus Convention, which increased her responsibilities, for under that instrument she actually *guaranteed* the introduction of reforms in Armenia. In fact, by the Cyprus Convention, England is co-responsible with Turkey for the effective amelioration of Armenia, and she shares with that country the right of exercising a constitutional prerogative in Asia Minor.

It is now high time that something should be done by this nation, which has been rightly styled the protector of the weak and oppressed, in the interests of humanity and justice, to say

nothing of interests already dwelt upon other than of pure sentiment; and it would thereby be echoing and confirming the words
of a great orator, John Bright, who, in a speech delivered in
Birmingham prior to the Turko-Russian hostilities, said of the
people of Great Britain that the lover of freedom always looks to
them; the oppressed everywhere turn their eyes to ask for
sympathy, and wish for help from them; they feel that they make
this upon them—a free people. They do not deny that claim,
but they freely acknowledge it.

Armenians have a claim upon England, Scotland, and Ireland,
and they are confident of the result.

II

AUSTRIA.

DR. S. SCHIDROWITZ.

A FEW weeks ago I was reading in the newspapers a notice to the effect that the ballet girls of Vienna are the handsomest and the best performers in any theatre in Europe. This is almost the only favourable notice about Austria which I have seen in an English newspaper for many a year ; and I certainly would not have ventured to mention it, if it had not struck me as a very peculiar thing that such a small matter should be almost the only one mentioned in a great London paper. But it is so. Austria, though a very great country in Europe, is very little known in England, much less known than many countries in Africa and Asia, and perhaps the cause of it is this. One of the greatest and most illustrious British statesmen said publicly a few years ago, "Show me a spot on earth where Austria has done any good." Of course, such a statement from the lips of one of the greatest Englishmen does perhaps prejudice peoples' minds ; and editors, who know how to take their cue, do not occupy themselves or their readers very much with a country of which such a great statesman made such a disparaging remark. Another very great Englishman, an historian, in all his writings has hardly a good word to say about Austria, but always to the contrary ; in fact, he does not acknowledge Austria at all. He says there is an archduchy of Austria, and there is a house of Hapsburg, but he really does not know Austria. Therefore the people who read his books cannot know anything about Austria either.

It is a very remarkable circumstance that with some people history only commences very recently. With some, let us say, only in 1830 with the Reform Bill ; with others perhaps only in 1867, or at some other period. If politics alone constituted the life, the principal mainsprings of the life of a people, then perhaps that great illustrious statesman and the historian might in some degree be right in saying that Austria, in comparison with a great many other nations of the world, would play a very small, perhaps a very poor, *rôle* amongst them ; but the political life, the political phases of a people, do not constitute the main interest of ninety-nine out of a hundred of the people of a nation. Election for Parliament only occurs on an average about once in every four or five years. Then, of course, the free citizen can vote, can do as he wishes in political matters, and so forth. But the ordinary pleasures and enjoyments of life, these are shared alike by every one, by the poorest as well as the richest, not once during five years, but every day, in the morning, at noon, and in the evening ; and in these enjoyments of life, in the civil enjoyments of life, in the enjoyments of all liberties, the people of Austria are certainly not behind any other people, and indeed in many respects perhaps they enjoy the pleasures of life much more than other nations.

The rich in Austria are not so rich as the English rich, as " Milor," for instance, who is supposed on the Continent to be a kind of angelic being who discovers gold ; but, on the other hand, the poor in Austria are not so poor, not so destitute, not so badly off as they are here. I have never in my life seen in an Austrian newspaper a notice headed " Died of Starvation." The Austrian papers have no occasion to mention, as is unfortunately too often the case in other countries, that such and such a man or woman had been found dead of starvation. Furthermore, I have never seen or read in an Austrian paper (and more particularly as regards Vienna) of drunken women fighting in the streets. I have never seen in Austria drunkenness to the extent that one sees in other countries. I have never seen the disgraceful scenes that are to be witnessed daily in countries where, according to the newspapers, a much higher degree of civilisation exists than in poor benighted Austria. The Austrians, and especially the Viennese, have always had the reputation of being an easy-going, pleasure-loving people, so much so, that Schiller, one of the greatest of German poets, spoke of Vienna as the "lotus-eating town." The common belief in Germany and other countries was, that the people of Vienna did not care about anything but pleasure and enjoying life as much as they could. But this is a very great error. I have remarked before how it was stated of Austria, "Show me a place on earth where she has done any good."

It may be true, that in the history of Austria, during, say, the last fifty or sixty years, nothing very great, or stirring, or interesting as compared with other nations has happened, but history does not commence either in 1830 or in 1848. But Vienna and Austria were for hundreds and hundreds of years the bulwark, the shield of Christian Europe, of Christianity, against the inroads of the Mussulmans ; and to say that Austria has never done any good to the world, can certainly not be quite correct, when we consider that for many hundred years the people of Austria have had to shield and to protect, I may say, Europe from the attacks and inroads of the most savage enemies of civilisation which Europe and Christianity ever knew. The very name of Austria should show you the origin and scope of the history of that country. Austria means the Eastern country or Eastern Marches, a country which was specially created for the very purpose of protecting Germany and Western Europe against the inroads of the people who at the time of the exodus from Asia in the sixth century commenced to overrun that part of Europe. The Eastern Marches, which were created by the Emperor Charlemagne, were meant to be a barrier against Vandalism. And as at that time Christianity had only commenced to be propagated, and had no very deep hold in the country, the work which Charlemagne had laid for this people was certainly a very important and a very difficult one.

And now let us see how this people who, according to the present common saying, did nothing but enjoy themselves in going to the theatre. Let us see how they proceeded. On the Danube there had been erected for a great many years a fortified castle ; but, as had happened in other countries, as had happened in England, the Roman legions, valorous though they were, could not stand against the native element, and they had to leave. On the very spot where Vienna to-day stands Celtic tribes were living. Therefore a thousand years ago Great Britain and Austria had a common nation—the Celts. Celtic tribes were living where Vienna now stands, in the same way that Celtic people inhabit the North of Scotland and Ireland. These tribes were also subject to the attacks of the nations which advanced from the south in the fifth and sixth centuries. But Vienna always managed to keep her own. We have authenticated statements how at that time, and especially later on in the eleventh century, the people of Vienna always defended themselves most valiantly against the inroads and the attacks of these people, but the real object and the real purpose for which Austria had been created commenced only in the twelfth century.

Well, the people of Hungary came up, and at that time the German Emperor made the family of the Babenbergers Dukes of Austria, and with the Babenbergers commenced the real origin of Austria and of

Vienna.   You will see at once what spirit these Babenbergers were
of, when I tell you the very first thing the greatest of the Babenbergers did—his name was Heinrich—was to lay the foundation
of the noblest church in Europe—the Stephen's Kirche.   He knew
that if he wished to make Vienna a town of the future, one which
would last and not be ruined by barbarous invaders, he would
have to invoke the help of the Church, and he did that by laying
the foundation stone of the Stephen's Kirche.   It is certainly one
of the finest domes in Europe, if not in the world.   It took over
two hundred years to finish this most wonderful church dome,
and now this very dome is considered by all Austria, and especially by the Viennese, as the very centre of their life.

Seven hundred years had passed, when a very great danger
threatened the whole of Europe.   It was at the time when the
Turks under Sultan "Solyman the Magnificent" were in the
height of their fame.   Sultan Solyman had the idea that the Turkish
Empire and the Mohammedan religion should become not only the
principal, but the only power and the only religion in the world.
He marshalled a very great army.   At that time two hundred and
fifty thousand men meant a much larger army than is to-day
represented by two millions.   He advanced right up to the walls of
Vienna, and there again the inhabitants of that "pleasure-loving"
capital for months and months were besieged, and eventually
succeeded by their own efforts in beating back the greatest
warrior of the time, and drove him back to Turkey, thus saving
not only Austria, but Germany, and perhaps the whole of Europe,
from the domination of the Turks, a domination which had
lasted many centuries in Asia.   This was in 1529.

In 1683 the same thing happened again.   Again a Turkish
Emperor, advised, I must say, by the Most Christian King of France,
Louis XIV., sent his Generals with an army still larger than the
previous one, and again laid siege to Vienna.   Not one finger was
raised for several months to succour the besieged Viennese.   Once
more the citizens of that pleasure-loving town succeeded almost alone
to hold the Turks at bay, until afterwards the Duke of Lothringen
and the King of Poland came to their rescue.   Thus, again, it was
Vienna which saved the whole country from the domination of
the Turks, and who is it who does not know what the domination of
the Turks in a Christian country means?   I have mentioned these
few examples only to show that the great reproach "that there is
not a spot on earth where Austria has done good" is not quite
correct.

In early times, at all events, in 1529 and 1683, Austria and the capital of Austria had certainly done Europe and the world a service which hardly any other town or any other nation has done for the continent of Europe. And yet it is unfortunately true that in some respects, especially as far as politics are concerned, Austria (I may not say is) has been very much backward in comparison with other nations. But other countries, other nations, have also had such periods—I will not say which countries. I will merely say that the development of political liberty, of all political rights, general suffrage and so forth, have also in other countries not always been the same, only that in Austria unfortunately the period of darkness has been much longer, and for the following reasons.

The House of Hapsburg had, in the sixteenth century particularly, a great many enemies, who not only fought against certain princes, but against the house, against the dynasty itself. Now, unfortunately, the reigning family at that time called in the help of a power which five hundred years ago had done very much to keep the people in spiritual bondage. They called in the help of the Jesuits, and to that order to the greatest extent is due the darkness which reigned during two hundred years and more in Austria.

The University of Vienna, which was founded in 1365, was at one time the greatest, or one of the greatest, of Universities, and quite on a level with the great Universities of Paris and Bologna. But since the sixteenth century, and especially since the Thirty Years' War, which did so much misfortune and harm to the centre of Europe, the University of Vienna, as well as all the lower educational establishments in Vienna and Austria, came under the sway of this order, and with them there was only one principle—blind obedience and no progress. The Vienna University at that time, instead of cultivating science and art, as it has done for more than two hundred years, became nothing else than a mere machine for turning out employés of the State, and this course it was which brought Austria so low, and which induced everybody else in Europe to speak of Austria as the China of Europe, the most backward State in Europe. This state of affairs lasted very long. Politics were entirely unknown. There was nothing but blind obedience to the commands of superiors. Freethought, investigation, all that was ruthlessly repressed by those who conducted the education of the country from the highest university to the lowest school in the Empire. But this state of affairs does not exist now, and that is the great error which people at the present time appear to be labouring under.

The history of old Austria closed entirely and completely so far as politics, culture, education, etc., is concerned, with the year 1848. There is no more comparison between Austria, prior to 1848 and the Austria of to-day, than there could be a comparison say between England under one of the Tudors, or even to come nearer to the present time, say during the reign of one of the Georges and the England of to-day. Indeed, I may say that the difference is even greater, because in England, after all, it was more a question of degree. In England certain liberties always did exist, but in Austria it was not so. Everything there had to commence. The history of Austria since 1848 is therefore the history of Modern Austria, and this history is certainly much more cheering and much more pleasant to speak about.

You doubtless all know that Austria, unlike most of the other European nations, cannot be considered a nation in itself, *i.e.* there is no Austrian, as you can say there is the Frenchman, the Italian, the Englishman. Austria is a political idea, and consists of a number of different peoples, a number of smaller or larger nations, which are collected together under the sceptre of the Imperial Family of the Hapsburgs, and they form the Austrian Empire. But it is a very great error, on the other hand, to suppose that because there is no such thing as an Austria in itself, that therefore the Austrian Monarchy as such cannot form a political union just as firm as, let us say, France or Great Britain. You all know that in this kingdom of Great Britain the people are not all of the same nation; they are not all of the same sect. We here have different component parts, but not to such a great degree as in Austria. There the foundation was formed on the creation of the archduchy of Austria, and they were Germans. Germans still form to a great degree the majority of the population of Austria, that is, when comparing each of its other nations separately. Austria and Germany have therefore always been in close accord, not only because the Hapsburgs were Emperors of the Holy Roman Empire, of German Nation, as it was called, but because the majority of the people in Austria are Germans, and because German culture, German science, were the same in both countries.

You are doubtless aware that in consequence of political events the Austrian Empire, which was created in 1806, was divided in 1867 into two parts—Austria Proper and Hungary. Of Hungary

I will not speak, only of Austria Proper, of the Austrian part of the Empire which is called Cis-Leithanian part of the Empire. Vienna, as you all know, is the capital of Austria, and a very pleasant and agreeable town Vienna is. As I said before, the reproach always was that the Viennese cared for nothing but their pleasures. But the inhabitants of Vienna showed in 1848 that they have within themselves the same fire, the same power to gain their liberties, as have been shown by other nations, say in 1688 in England, or in 1789 in France. One might say the whole system of Absolutism in Austria was overthrown by the Viennese themselves. In imitation of the Revolution in Paris, the citizens of Vienna rose in their wrath and said, "We will not longer be slaves." The saying itself would have helped very little, but they added the act to their word. Prince Metternich, the leading minister, and the mainspring of Absolutism, had to run away, and all owing solely to the deeds of a few thousand Viennese citizens, aided by the students of the University,

Vienna has not been much written about by Englishmen; but when they do write about Vienna, one finds the most marvellous errors stated. I have read this very day, for instance, a statement that nobody who has been in Vienna has ever been invited to dinner by a Viennese. Further, that the Viennese are the most immoral people. Indeed, it would be impossible for me to go into the details of the statements which the writer makes. But I can assure you that the people of Vienna are no more immoral than the people of most other towns. For one thing, they are not hypocrites, nor are they hypercritical. They show themselves just as they are, and do not say, "We are the most virtuous people, all the rest are immoral, etc." As an example, I will tell you what happened to myself the other evening. I had a gentleman friend visiting me from Vienna. We went to one of the leading theatres of London. We sat in the stalls, and just in front of us also in the stalls were seated a gentleman and two ladies. I do not know that I could, if I attempted, describe the dress, or rather the undress, worn by those ladies. My friend from Vienna, however, remarked to me, "What, are we really sitting in a theatre in virtuous London where they do not even permit a song or dancing in the Music Halls?" Well, my friend was actually ashamed. Yes, he really blushed. He, the hardened sinner from "immoral" Vienna, actually got red in the face. Now, the English writer says the Viennese are immoral people, and here I have given you an example how the most "immoral" people may be shocked when they come to London. It is, I will not say all, nonsense, but it is exaggeration to say that the people of Vienna are immoral. They have to work hard to make a living, and they do work hard; but when their work is done, they enjoy themselves thoroughly, they do not hide themselves away, they come into the open air and enjoy themselves to their heart's content. I wish you could see on a pleasant summer Sunday afternoon two or three hundred thousand of these "immoral" people enjoying themselves, like happy children, in the Prater. Vienna has the great advantage of possessing the finest surroundings of any large town in Europe. A half-hour's walk from the town on either side brings you to the country, where you could imagine yourself say in the Isle of Wight or in Devonshire, and on the opposite direction the scenery resembles that of the Highlands of Scotland. Thither the inhabitants go picnicing on Sundays and holidays. All the inhabitants enjoy themselves almost within sight of each other. How on earth, then, that high degree of immorality of which that English author speaks can take place, I, for one, cannot very well understand.

The Viennese are a good-natured people, and I have here a few books which were edited by that most unfortunate of men, the late Crown Prince of Austria. It has been said that the House of Hapsburg are the most cruel and despotic of tyrants, and so forth. But let me state what are the real facts. The Emperor of Austria lives in a house which there is no word in the English language to describe. It is like a passage, anybody and everybody can go through that house; in fact, it is the main communication between the inner town and the largest of the suburbs. Omnibuses and cabs, etc., pass through it. Twice a week the Emperor of Austria gives public audience to any one and every one. Those who have any petition to make, or any grievance to state, have only to send in their name in writing, and they are at once admitted. There are no policemen or guards to prevent any one going into the Emperor's house who wishes to have an audience with him. Now this Emperor had a son whose lamentable death you have doubtless all heard of. This son edited a book, in which you will see there are three sketches of typical Viennese—a Viennese cabman, a washerwoman, and a boy. If you will look carefully at these, you will appreciate more than you could from a hundred lectures what the inhabitants of Vienna are really like. Do that man's characteristics and type of feature give you the idea of a most awful person full of vice, etc.

Well, now, as I said before, the present Austro-Hungarian Monarchy consists of two parts. It would be very dry and uninteresting were I to tell you how many inhabitants each of these provinces has, and to no purpose. Allow me only to make a few remarks. The inhabitants of Austria number 39,100,000. You will see, therefore, that the Austro-Hungarian Empire is not "*une quantité négligeable,*" *i.e.*, not to be thrown entirely aside. It has more inhabitants than Great Britain and Ireland. The Austrian people are good natured, but they can give as good an account of themselves as any other people, more especially have they done so in the past when allied to English soldiers, which fortunately they almost always have been. There has been only a single case, in 1716, where Austrian and English soldiers were not standing shoulder to shoulder. And in the Austrian army and administration several of the very highest posts are filled by Englishmen, or let us say, by "subjects of Great Britain, because they happen to be Irishmen." The present Prime Minister of Austria, Count Taafe, is just as much an Irishman as, or much more I should say, than even Parnell himself. He comes from a very old Irish stock, and amongst the titles which he still writes after his name is one connected with the Castle of Bally "something." The Emperor's first aide-de-camp, O'Donnell, is also an Irishman. Lacey, one of the greatest Austrian generals, the same; and if I am not mistaken, several members of the Austrian Parliament are descendants of old Irish families. One of the best speeches, I think, I ever heard in the Austrian Parliament was by one named Skene, who was also of Irish descent. Therefore you will see that Austria and Great Britain have many sympathies in common, and I am sure nobody should say very much bad of Austria on that account.

I am afraid, what I have now to say will not be very amusing for most of my kind hearers. But the object of these lectures consists also in giving some information concerning the political institutions of different foreign countries; and, unfortunately, I know that politics are very seldom amusing, except for those to whom they are a stepping-stone to celebrity or wealth.

Austria, or rather that part of Austria with which I have to deal to-day, namely, the Cis-Leithanian part of the Austro-Hungarian Empire, is a constitutional country. Its constitution, or to speak more correctly, its constitutions, for there are several of them in existence, are all quite new, of very recent date. Until 1848 Austria was governed by the Emperor as Autocrat, or as Despot (in the old

Greek sense of this word). Though there had been diets in existence since the sixteenth century, they were mere shadows without the slightest influence or power. They languished as machines, without a will of their own, simply for the purpose of registering the decrees of the Emperor. Some of the Emperors governed despotically in the modern meaning of this term, while during the reign of some quite a patriarchal system of government was the order of the day. Poor Emperor Joseph, the son of Marie Theresa, nourished quite Liberal ideas, but the clerical and feudal opposition from the highest in the land was too strong even for him, and he died broken-hearted. Francis the Second was rather good-natured, and not at all cruel as long as nobody dared to oppose his absolute system of government, but even the least attempt to propagate Liberal ideas was crushed with terrible rigour. The people's duty was simply to obey and not to think for themselves. Public affairs were entirely "forbidden fruit" for the subjects; they might discuss the theatre, the opera, or the ballet; they might have given dinners to celebrate and to praise all the public virtues of a Barnum of that time; or the Press might have banqueted the great Pears of the period, and the greatest men in the land would have been proud to assist on those occasions, but politics were entirely tabooed. Notoriety hunters and self-advertising quacks among all the professions had it then all to themselves. But I am treading on delicate ground, and I will come back to poor benighted Austria before 1848, where such occurrences might have taken place.

The February revolution in Paris in 1848, the dethronement of Louis Philippe, excited the people of Vienna in the highest degree. Almost over night they also made a revolution, drove from power and country the all-mighty Metternich, and demanded a constitution, liberty of conscience, liberty of the Press, a Parliament, and all the rest of the institutions which existed in constitutional countries. The Emperor Ferdinand, a very weak, half-witted man, granted everything.

But it would take too much time to give you a history of the development of political life in Austria. You all know, perhaps, that the reaction carried on with a high hand from 1852 until 1860, when, after the Italian war, the Emperor again began to have recourse to constitutional means in a somewhat modest way. Only after the German war in 1866 the present constitutional and dualistic system of government commenced in the Empire of the Hapsburgs, in the Austro-Hungarian Monarchy.

Austria Proper (Cis-Leithanian) and Hungary form two separate parts of the Empire, united through the person of the Emperor, who is also King of Hungary, and further united by certain Parliamentary institutions, which both parts of the Empire have in common. Though each part of the Empire has a Parliament of its own, yet certain common affairs, viz. the army and navy, foreign and consular affairs, certain money matters, etc., are discussed and settled by the so-called " Delegations." These delegations are, so to say, committees of the two Parliaments, to whom the above-mentioned matters are referred. Each delegation meets and discusses separately the matters laid before it by the Cabinet ; they communicate with each other in writing ; and only when a matter cannot be agreed upon after three "opinions in writing " have been exchanged by the delegations, then both delegations meet together, and the question is discussed as well as voted upon by both delegations, who *ad hoc* constitute then *one* Parliamentary body.

The Hungarian as well as the Austrian Parliament possess all the well-known privileges, and do the same work as most other representatives of the people. There are two Houses of Parliament in Austria—the House of Lords and the House of Commons ; Cabinet Ministers have a right to sit and speak in both Houses, even if not members of the House. The ministers are responsible to Parliament. Both Houses have legislative powers, Bills can be brought in either by the Cabinet or by members. The multifarious business of the House of Commons in reference to matters of administration, etc., are dealt with in Austria by competent Government officers, and not by elected members of the House of Commons. The right of questioning the Government is much more limited than in England. In theory all this sounds very well, but in practice Austria cannot very well be called as yet a real Parliamentary country ; for, after all, in some departments, say, for instance, concerning foreign affairs and certain military questions, the Emperor, and not Parliament, is the supreme power, not *de jure*, but *de facto*. Austria possesses also besides its Parliament seventeen diets—Landtage. These small Parliaments legislate upon all matters which concern the interest of the province alone, and which do not touch general interests of the whole Cis-Leithanian part of the Empire. They are a kind of enlarged county councils, or, if you like to call them so, a species of Home Rule Parliaments for the different parts of the realm.

Concerning the religion of the Austrians, it may be interesting to know that out of the thirty-nine million population there are twenty-nine millions Roman Catholics. Next to them come Protestants, numbering 3,572,961. Orthodox Greeks (which means the same as the Russians are), 2,900,000 ; but, strange to say, in Austria alone are to be found Catholics who call themselves Greek Catholics, and among these there has always been the greatest trouble going on between Russia and Austria. This was one of the greatest and most serious difficulties between Austria and Russia. People think that politics are the worst difficulties between them. But the great question is whether the Greek Catholics should preponderate to Vienna or to St. Petersburg.

The great majority of the people of Austria live an agricultural life, and until 1848 the number of manufactures was indeed very insignificant compared, let us say, with England. But since 1848 very great progress has been made. Two-fifths of the population of the Empire are now employed in manufactures.

And now let me come to a point which is much more important, and that is education. After all, soldiering, wars, and such things do not occur, fortunately, very often, and especially do not interest many here. But the questions of education, how many children go to school in the country, that is perhaps for Englishmen the most important, the most interesting question. In Austria education is compulsory; that is to say, every child which is over six years old is compelled to go to school. But if I were speaking in Austria, people would laugh if I said a child is compelled to go to school. What, compel a child to go to school! Why, it is his great good fortune that he is allowed to go. On the contrary, it would be compelled not to go to school. Therefore it is not considered at all compulsory, but it is considered highly beneficent for the people that it is so. In Austria every child goes to school from the sixth to the thirteenth year of their age. From thirteen to fifteen they have Sunday schools in the afternoon for two hours. There are in Austria three million children of the age of six years who ought to go to school. Now, how many of these do not go to school? Only seventy. I should think you will agree with me, that is not a very bad record for such a benighted country as Austria. In Hungary, on the other hand, which is far superior to Austria as far as politics are concerned, it is quite different. In Hungary there are 1,312,371 children who ought to go to school, and there are actually attending school 1,304,000, so that actually 8000 do not go to school out of one million, so that the percentage is worse in that politically better developed country than in Austria. Now the question is this : Is it better for a nation that the children should go to school, or that every man over twenty-one years of age should once in five years be able to vote for a Member of Parliament? Permit me to say that the Austrians have the same right to vote for Members of Parliament, for there is also a Parliament for Austria. The number of Grammar Schools in Austria Proper is 131, and the number of teachers 2601. There are 11 Universities. In Vienna the University has 272 professors, teachers, and so forth, and 5606 students, not a very bad record for such a benighted town. Then, besides, there are special schools, technical, high schools, etc. In Vienna there is a High School for Agriculture alone. It has 31 professors and 340 students. There is also a School of Forestry, with 20 professors. So, you will see, the question of education is not lost there.

But the greatest claim of the Austrians, and of the Viennese especially, is that they are a music-loving people. You are, I daresay, all aware that Vienna claims to be, and that she has been and is, the seat of Music. I need only mention a few names to show that this claim of Vienna is not ill founded. Every one has heard the names of Mozart, of Schubert, and of Haydn. The operas of Mozart, the songs of Schubert, and the music of Haydn are certainly more or less known wherever civilised human beings meet ; and, I am sure, no one will deny that they give more enjoyment than the reading of all the Blue Books that have ever been published by Parliament. I, for one, take the liberty of saying that the country which has produced such men has given to the world more enjoyment and more of the blessings of real peace than any other.

The next proudest claim of Vienna to celebrity is her Medical Schools. It is well known in English professional circles that for twenty-five years and more that the Medical faculty in the University of Vienna was far above all others. The greatest English physicians have all been in Vienna and attended lectures there, which is not such a bad position for a country of which it has been said, "Show me a spot on earth where she has done any good."

Furthermore, the Austrians are the happy possessors of more good watering places than any other country in the world, such as Carlsbad, Gastein, etc. Even in this minor capacity Austria may be truly said to have been of much service to the sick and the aged, and therefore permit me to conclude my remarks by saying that, after all, Austria is not such a " poor benighted " country as it is alleged to be, and that a great many benefits have been conferred on the human race, not only by Austria, but by that " most immoral " city, Vienna itself.

III.

HUNGARY.

PROFESSOR AUGUSTUS PULSZKY.

ABOUT a century ago, when the sympathies of the people of Western Europe were first aroused in favour of wronged and struggling Poland, French writers often complimented the Poles on being "the French of the North," and this allusion to the similarity of character was invariably accepted as a flattering expression of appreciation. At the same period, and for many years afterwards, the denomination of "the England of the East" was sometimes claimed with fond complacency by Hungarians for their own country, desiring to impress foreigners with the marked difference between the people of Hungary and their unfortunate Northern neighbours. Of course, nobody dreamt of seriously comparing the culture, the development, the power, and the prosperity of the two nations, one of which, after centuries of freedom and enterprise, had risen to become the proud mistress of the seas, while the other had served as the bulwark of civilised Christendom against the attacks of Mohammedan Turkey, and bore resemblance rather to a shattered outlying bastion of a half-abandoned fortress than to the fields of the culture of the West. Still, as is generally the case with expressions that grow into stock phrases, there had been and there lingered yet a grain of truth in the analogy between Hungary and England. A certain similarity marked the origin of both—nor is it difficult to establish a parallel between the history, the institutions, nay, even between the very life and modes of thought of the world-renowned and splendid realm of liberty in the Western Isles, and of the comparatively obscure kingdom which had just but succeeded in maintaining its existence amidst the storms that had ravaged Eastern Europe, and which, after all, was the only state on the Continent that at the end of the last century had managed to uphold unimpaired its uninterrupted traditions of legal freedom. And to this very day, although the position and

C

the destinies of the two nations are as unequal as ever, a certain distant family likeness may still be detected between them. None of the other countries, except England and Hungary, are able to appeal to the unbroken continuity of ten centuries of constitutional development; none other have preserved a flexible constitution, capable of alteration by the regular methods of legislation, and not based upon any rigid written Charter; in none but these two did that mixed form of government continually prevail in which the distribution of the powers of the monarchy, and of the aristocratical and democratical elements, may have actually considerably changed in the course of time, without either of these having ever been entirely suppressed, or the balance of power irretrievably destroyed, even at the most critical juncture.

The secret of this resemblance of institutions and of the concomitant ideas and feelings is easily discovered in certain common features of the history of the two commonwealths. From the days of Queen Elizabeth, when England definitely adopted Protestant supremacy, the cause of national independence was always intimately allied to that of liberty. The political existence of the English nation, religious and civil freedom, were alike imperilled by the Spanish Armada. During the following century the more insidious but equally dangerous endeavours of Louis XIV. of France, though menacing more directly constitutional government, were none the less indirectly aimed against religious independence, and against the assertion of a separate national policy. Again, in the wars provoked by the aggressions of the French Revolution and the ambition of Napoleon, the defence of the existing constitution and the consolidation of the British Empire were indissolubly connected. The same holds good as to Hungary. From the day following the dire calamity of the lost battle of Mohacs, where the separate and independent development of the kingdom, together with King Louis II. himself, fell a victim to the victorious sword of Sultan Suleyman, throughout all the civil wars of the sixteenth and seventeenth centuries, throughout the political atrophy of the eighteenth, throughout the constitutional struggles in the nineteenth, the revolution of 1848-49 and the passive resistance offered to the attempts of Austrian centralization afterwards, down to the period of the definite arrangement with the dynasty and the so-called Cis-Leithanian hereditary kingdoms and provinces of the Emperor of Austria, the efforts for the re-establishment and support of a national state were at all times necessarily connected with the defence of constitutional freedom, with the vindication of religious tolerance and of the legal recognition of the different Churches, with the maintenance of the political rights of the people, with the gradual development of the liberty of the subject, and with the economical emancipation of the lower orders. The national aspirations, the full outcome of the traditions of the past, were never for one moment dissociated from the endeavours to realise any part of what constitutes moral and material progress. Elements which in other continental countries were continually clashing with each other, and, when fully revealed, showed themselves to be discordant and antagonistic beyond remedy, were in Hungary indissolubly fused into one single sentiment, leavened by law-abiding respect for formal rights, by reverence for institutions which formerly had been the expression of the national mind, and prompted in no lesser degree by yearnings for spiritual liberty and by the instinctive desire of acquiring prosperity. In connection with this prevailing feeling, the idea of attaining and ensuring the complete national polity of Hungary became endowed with a magnetic power that attracted into its sphere, and united in it all the motives, all the forces of the people, which otherwise might have impelled its different sections and classes in divergent directions.

Indeed, this all-pervading, deep-rooted feeling of the supremacy of the national interest is the keynote of the life and thought of the Hungarian people, and furnishes a clue to the explanation of the differences that strike the observer when comparing its characteristics with those of the inhabitants of the surrounding countries. For a citizen of the British Empire, which embraces the fairest portions of the globe, spreads over all the latitudes of the earth, and rules over countless races of mankind ; for a member of a commonwealth the population and wealth of which have long ago overflowed the boundaries of a merely national existence ; for an Englishman sure, as he may well be, of the language he speaks and thinks in, and of the civilisation in which he has been nurtured, and to the pale of which he belongs, of both his language and civilisation having struck root and flourishing in the most different parts of the world, and serving the needs and guiding the destinies of new nations which have grown equal to and are perhaps overshadowing the old ; for the scion of a people that can afford to be, nay, to a certain extent needs must be cosmopolitan, —it is scarcely possible to realise the intensity of the spirit of nationality, where all that makes life worth living, in a higher sense, where all bonds of community extending beyond immediate private ties and aims, where every nobler and more generous impulse that stirs the blood or fires the imagination is concentrated to a single object, and where, according to popular estimation, the virtue of patriotism, which elsewhere, too, ranks high, but is deemed to be equalled, and perhaps even overbalanced, by rival qualities, is accounted as paramount and incomparable to any other, because including and absorbing the attributes of all excellence proper to human nature. The consolidation of the German Empire, the unification of Italy, are examples of the magnitude of the immanent power set free by statesmen who were endowed with foresight and ability sufficient to arouse the long dormant sense of nationality. Still, the most striking illustration of the potency of the spell exercised by the consciousness of common and single national destinies is not afforded by the cases of these great agglomerations, to the perfecting of which innumerable other causes have contributed in no lesser degree, but rather by the persistent and unconquerable energy by virtue of which a people, comparatively weak in numbers, without racial affinity with its surroundings, isolated in its language, lacking natural means of communication, wealthy neither in intellectual traditions nor in acquired capital, continually menaced, on several occasions overrun, by enemies more numerous, more powerful, sometimes more cultivated than itself, has succeeded in holding its own during a thousand years, and in securing for the organism of its commonwealth the recognition of an adequate and firm position amongst the acknowledged civilised States of Europe.

The deep hold which the spirit of nationality has obtained over the citizens of Hungary, and the matchless importance it has acquired as regards all the interests of the community, the structure and the agency of the social fabric, comparable only with the supremacy of the questions of faith in England during the seventeenth century, is all the more interesting by the contrast it affords to the spectacle presented by the circumstances which led to the establishment of the national States of Germany and Italy. Nationality based upon a community of descent, language, thought, literature, and religious interest, was pre-existent in these latter cases; the aspiration towards unity, the violent irresistible craving for framing a single organisation out of provinces that had never been knit together, in the past, by an adequate tie, were only awakened after centuries of separate existence, were the realisation of an idea that had a long antecedent history. In

Hungary, as with the nations of Western Europe, it was the reverse process that took place. The Kingdom of Hungary had been established for countless generations, national and foreign dynasties had repeatedly alternated on its throne, before the full requirements and consequences of a truly national life were in their entirety apprehended, demanded, and enforced. Moreover, to this very day it is not the exclusiveness of pride in purity of race, it is not a supercilious contempt for aliens, or the separateness and aloofness engendered by religious prejudice, or intolerance of unaccustomed ways and expressions of thought, that form the backbone of national sentiment in Hungary. There is no place in the world where people belonging to more varied and distinct stocks live and mingle together, where on an area of equal extent more languages, so entirely unconnected, are spoken, where the allegiance of faith is divided amongst religions so numerous, and where true tolerance, in the sense of a ready admission of equal, or, at least, of proportionately assigned rights has, to such a degree, become absolutely necessary in the common relations of life. Speaking in round numbers, six and a-half millions of Magyars, two and a-half of Roumenes, two and one-third of Croato-Serbs, nearly two millions of Germans, only a few thousands fewer of Slovacks, three hundred and fifty thousand Ruthenes, and about a hundred thousand of diverse motley minor nationalities, such as Wends, Italians, Armenians, and Gipsies, live peaceably, side by side, in a population close to sixteen millions, all of them interspersed in the different sections of the territory of Hungary ; while the list of religions and creeds includes seven millions eight hundred and fifty thousand Roman, one million and a-half Greek, and three thousand Armenian-Catholics, over two million Calvinists, one million one hundred and thirty thousand Lutheran Protestants, fifty-five thousand Unitarians, two millions four hundred and forty thousand members of the Oriental Greek Churches, and six hundred and forty thousand Jews. Nor do the lines dividing different races and tongues coincide with those separating the religious denominations. Every nationality counts members belonging to different Church-establishments ; almost every creed includes adherents of several distinct nationalities ; besides, persons belonging to each are found in every class of society. All are equally citizens of Hungary ; still, the dominant sentiment of the country is, and cannot but be, the Magyar, not in virtue of any privilege in law, but simply because it is the Magyar element that has formed and upheld the Hungarian nation, because it has been the nucleus around which the other parts of the population have rallied, because the Magyars have known how to identify with their own the common interests of the rest, compared with which the separate aims of each were partly rendered compatible by a generous policy, and partly felt to be insignificant; because, to sum up the manifold reasons in a single expression, the Magyar State, culture, and law have unceasingly served as the sole possible condition of the development and liberty of every fraction of the people.

The causes that have concurred in producing these results may easily be seen written large in the course of history. It is exactly a thousand years ago, at the same period when the Northmen ravaged the shores of the West, settled in Northern France, and founded the houses of the rulers and the aristocracy of half of Europe, that the Magyars or Hungarians entered the country bounded by the Carpathians and by the flanking spurs of the eastern and southern Alps, which forms the great basin of the middle course of the Danube. They conquered it, settled in it, and for the first time in history established a united and stable realm in this part of Europe. Formerly only those portions lying near its boundaries had temporarily belonged to the sphere of civilised states; the great plains between and along the Danube and the Theiss had never formed the seat of a nation before the Hungarian immigration. A large part of the territory was at the time a scarcely inhabited waste; the mountainous and hilly districts, covered by forests, were sparsely occupied in the North and in the South by a Slavonic, and in the West by a German population. The number, however, of the conquering Magyars, though sufficient to ensure their victory and to render them terrible to their western and southern neighbours, was not large enough to fill the expanse of the provinces their valour had acquired and their determination was able to defend permanently. Hence foreign elements were introduced, first by compulsion, later on, as Christianity was adopted, by invitation and grants of royal privileges; and the policy ushered in by the great King Stephen, the Apostle-Saint of his people, and continued by his successors, consisted mainly in inducing immigrants from all parts to settle and gradually to infuse their life into that of the realm. The institutions of Western countries, the ideas embodied in the capitularies of Charlemagne and his successors, and in the laws of the Church, were adopted and adapted to the Magyar traditions, in which the germs of self-government and of the participation of the subjects in the sovereign power were deeply ingrained; constitutional government was gradually developed out of these rudiments in conjunction with the moral and legal conceptions, which formed the common heritage of mediæval semi-Latin civil-isation under the fostering care of the Roman Catholic Church. Thus in the twelfth and thirteenth century the annals of Hungary present an absolute parallel to those of the Western countries, all the more, because the pretensions of the Holy Roman Empire to over-lordship were successfully repulsed. It is therefore no mere freak of history that the Golden Bull of Andrew II., analo-gous both in its antecedents and contents to the Magna Charta of England, was granted to the nation within a few years of the success of the English barons at Runymede; nor is it a coincid-ence, occasioned by chance alone, that the demands of the Pope for feudal supremacy, and his attempts at foisting a sovereign of his choice on the nation, were equally resisted in Hungary as in England.

Still, the increase of the population was not able to keep pace with the advance of culture. The best blood of the foreign settlers was continually absorbed by the ruling Hungarian element, which was never chary of admitting into the pale of social and political rights all those who, unreservedly, took part in the tasks of the organisation and defence of the nation. As to the kingdom itself, it never recognised any aristocracy of race. Yet the continual drain occasioned by incessant wars—the strain upon the Magyars who had principally to sustain the military burdens—always rendered new immigrants welcome. Especially the great Mongolian invasion of 1241 decimated the country, and the Roumenian and Ruthenian populations were gradually settled in their present abodes, for the most part about the second half of the thirteenth century.

During the two hundred years that followed, from the four-teenth to the sixteenth centuries, Hungary, under the rule of the elective Kings belonging to the Neapolitan Anjou, the Bohemian Luxemburg, the Austrian Hapsburg, the native Corvine, and the Polish Jagellone dynasties, sought to establish itself as the centre of an empire, under the suzerainty of which Bosnia, Servia, Wallachia, and Moldavia were to occupy the position of feudatary provinces, and these efforts were to some degree crowned with success. The spirit of imperial destinies again attracted promin-ent members of every minor nationality to follow the instinct of the unity of the Hungarian State. At the same time, a continual tendency was manifested towards forming a stable union by the identity of the monarch in Hungary, and in one or the other of the great neighbouring kingdoms. This was attempted, as regards Poland, by Louis the Great, and by Sigismund with reference to the Holy Roman Empire. Later on, as the Turkish power loomed up, menacing from the South, the task of ensuring assistance in defence of Christendom against the encroachments of the growing Mohammedan power became more imminent, and both the House of Austria and Matthias Hunyadi rivalled each other in the attempt to join the hereditary eastern dominions of the Hapsburgs and Hungary permanently into a single system. The Jagellones at last actually succeeded in uniting the crowns of Hungary and of Bohemia on their heads. But in connection with these endeavours there necessarily arose in Hungary the conviction of danger to Hungarian independence and to constitutional liberty, from the Kings having under such circumstance an at least equal regard for the interests of another foreign country. Hence a certain tone of legal opposition was given to the national sentiment, which was destined to exercise a considerable influence over its further development—all the more because it was at this very juncture that the common law of the realm was systematically collected in the so-called Tripartite Institutes of the great jurist Verböczy; and that, in consequence, all the elements of the State became fully conscious of the precise extent and limits of their rights, and of the influence each in turn could claim in the shaping and determining the course of the nation's life.

Up to this period the tenor of the history of Hungary essentially coincides with the contemporary vicissitudes of other countries. But the simultaneous occurrence of three momentous changes, the Turkish conquest, the separation of Transylvania, and the Reformation, was to determine a novel and tragical turn in the fate of the realm. Its dynasty and power were shattered by the onslaught of the Turks, who subsequently for a hundred and fifty years occupied the central plains, and oppressed and devastated the homes of the richest and sturdiest part of the Hungarian people. The rest of the country was torn into two ; the western half raised to the throne and acknowledged the rule of the House of Hapsburg, which was thus able to unite in the person of the ruler the sovereignty of the Holy Roman Empire, of Bohemia and of Hungary, besides disposing of the strength of its

hereditary provinces, the hopes of assistance by which had constituted the principal reason for the election of the head of the
Austrian dynasty to Hungarian royalty. The eastern counties of
Hungary, not subject to the Turks, gathered around the principality of Transylvania, which, under elective native dynasties,
organised itself separately, with the firm intent, however, of
joining in the reconstitution of the realm so soon as this might be
feasible after the expulsion of the Ottoman invaders. The Protestant Reformation meanwhile rapidly spread over the whole
country; permeated all classes of the population; gave the people
a new interest in religion, in education, and in literature; supplied
a new opportunity for the development of self-government in its
ecclesiastical institutions; but it also inevitably entailed upon the
coming generations the secular dissensions and bitter struggles
which for the moment still further weakened the enfeebled nation,
although destined later on to elicit its full enthusiasm in the
defence of constitutional rights, and ultimately to lead to the
establishment of religious tolerance and of the liberty of conscience.

From 1526 to the end of the seventeenth century Hungary was
thus the scene of continual depredations, of wars, and of civil and
religious strifes; and in spite of the patriotism of great leaders on
both sides, of the Bathorys, of Bocskay, Bethlen, and Rákóczy, of
the Zrinyis, of Cardinal Pázmán, and of Eszterhazy,—in spite of the
brilliant successes achieved from time to time, which assisted in
keeping up the spirit of the people, and continually preserved the
consciousness of common interests and single national destinies,
the population, as well as the wealth of the country, was
diminishing fast; and although poetical and religious feelings
were aroused to a high pitch, although science was earnestly
cultivated, and thus the conviction of a happier future, and of the
assertion of the unity and independence of Hungary was maintained, yet the decrease in numbers, power, and influence became
undeniable, and the melancholy cast acquired by popular sentiment in those well-nigh hopeless days of darkness has ever since
remained a marked trait in the character of the people.

At last, in 1686, Buda, the ancient capital of Hungary, was
retaken, and by the end of the seventeenth century the territory
of the entire kingdom recovered from the domination of the
Turks. Not, however, by Magyar forces alone, but by the
imperial army, under Charles of Lorraine and Eugene of Savoy,
an army of which the Hungarian troops formed no small con-

tingent, but which otherwise was composed mainly of levies and volunteers from almost all the countries of Europe, and received considerable subsidies from Pope Innocent XI. The consequence was that attempts were made by the ministers of the Emperor and King Leopold I. to assimilate Hungary with the hereditary provinces of Austria, to suspend and abolish the constitution, to extirpate Protestantism, to germanise the Administration, to establish the absolutism of the Court of Vienna over a people that, it was supposed, would with the lapse of time forget the memories of its separate existence, and be content to merge into the mass of subjects, denuded of political rights, which constituted the bulk of the inhabitants of the inherited dominions of the Hapsburgs. But the Magyar population, although reduced in strength and pride, had preserved enough of vitality and energy to resist forcibly these endeavours of sanguinary proselytism and of despotical centralization; and it was only after long-undecided civil convulsions, coinciding with the War of the Spanish Succession, that peace was secured, the constitution of Hungary re-established, and the dynasty and the realm completely reconciled. But a great part of the territory had been laid waste, and was absolutely depopulated, and on this Serb, German, and Slovack immigrants were settled, " hewers of wood and drawers of water," who were a valuable addition to the resources of the country, but who required a long apprenticeship before growing ripe for political liberty, and being able to acknowledge as their own the inspirations of national life.

As the decades of the eighteenth century succeeded each other, without the internal peace of the country being disturbed, though there was no lack of foreign wars and of sacrifices for upholding the right of succession of the great Queen Maria Theresa, established by the acceptance of the Pragmatic Sanction, and for advancing the interests of the Austrian hereditary provinces, the community and mutuality of the defence of which, with that of Hungary, had been legally provided for—slowly and gradually the nation, and especially the upper and middle classes, composed almost entirely of landed proprietors, attained a considerable measure of material prosperity. Notwithstanding, a certain torpor, like the uneasy sleep of exhaustion after feverish excitement, crept over the minds of the people. Tied down to the feeble policy of the sinking Holy Roman Empire, removed from the great questions of European import, which were managed exclusively by the Viennese Chanceries, deprived of the healthy

stimulants of commerce and industry, which were monopolised by
the more advanced town-inhabitants and capitalists of Austria and
Bohemia, competition with whom was again excluded by an
elaborate fiscal system of duties along all the frontiers, and cut off
from immediate contact with the progress of Western Europe by
the system of absolutism which rendered the hereditary provinces
an almost impervious barrier to the entrance of novel ideas—
Hungary fell into a sort of fatalistic quietism, during which it
came perhaps nearer to losing its independence, its feeling of
proper personality and identity, even its very language, and thus
incurred a danger by far greater than had ever been the case
under the blows of its adverse fortunes. Its governing nobility,
apprehensive of the recurrence of events that might justify or, at
least, furnish pretexts for new schemes of subverting the constitution of the realm—already isolated on the Continent of Europe—
dreaded and warded off all legal change and reform, and became
attached to the doctrines and practices of extreme provincial
Conservatism. The technical Latin of mediæval documents quite
supplanted the Hungarian language in the business of legislation,
of administration, of the courts of law, and often even in the
common intercourse of private life. The watchword of liberty had
by a scarcely perceptible misuse degenerated into being synonymous with the expression of aristocratical privilege, and the
traditions of dearly acquired rights had been corrupted into
jealousy of their further extension. The masses were looked upon
as the "*misera plebs contribuens,*" a miserable populace of taxpayers; the few hundred thousands of the privileged classes
imagined themselves to be the totality of the nation, and in their
ignorant scorn were fond of repeating, "*Extra Hungariam non
est vita ; si est vita, non est ita*"—"Beyond Hungary there is no
life; if there is any, it does not come up to ours."

The turn of the tide, however, came yet in time to arouse the
nation. The well-meaning but impracticable bureaucratic innovations of the Emperor Joseph II., who refused to have himself
crowned King, being unwilling to burden his conscience with
oaths of upholding a constitution he wished to abolish, dispelled
the dreams cherished as to the security of the ancient institutions,
and evoked an active opposition to the denationalizing tendencies,
which had been carefully fostered, and now were openly avowed
by the court. The supreme importance of a national spirit in the
development of Hungary, if it meant to retain its individuality as
a State, the necessity of national ideals, of a broader and more

enlightened patriotism, even for the leading classes, flashed upon the minds of the whole people ; and the excitement occasioned by the democratical doctrines of the French Revolution, which had penetrated only so much as to merely touch the higher social layers, soon polished off the rust that had settled on their minds.

In the memorable Parliament of 1791-92 the principles of independence, of political, civil, and religious liberty were asserted anew, feelings of enthusiasm were kindled for the national language, and for the first time again, after a secular neglect, the interests of the masses began to be considered. The movement was arrested, and the realisation of the more high-minded proposals adjourned in consequence of the revolutionary and Napoleonic Wars and of the reactionary policy all over the Continent, of which the Viennese Government became the stronghold. For the first quarter of the present century even the manifestation of Liberal views was effectually suppressed ; and later on, all legal changes were hampered by the refusal of the Government to assent to them, and by the predominant influence of the Court in the House of Lords. But even though the actual institutions and the material conditions remained undeveloped, the progress of the ideas could not be stopped ; and thus eventually, as the times ripened, the changes could be effected in an easier and more even manner. Public opinion gradually grew too strong to be successfully opposed any longer. Great leaders of the nation arose. Count Széchenyi from amongst the members of the Aristocracy urged economical reforms in the first place, demanding laws for the establishment of credit, favouring industry, developing communication, instituting social and humanitarian clubs, and, above all, raising the cry for universal and equal taxation. Francis Deák, essentially the representative of the middle classes, but whose noble and enlightened patriotism, disinterestedness, moderation, wisdom, and eloquence were to render him the universally acknowledged spokesman and guide of his people, the arbiter of their destinies, was the presiding master-spirit of the party of reformers who prepared the ground for the achievements of 1848. Last, but not least, Louis Kossuth, rising from the ranks of journalism, communicated the fire of his extraordinary genius to the whole country, and decided the constitutional contest in favour of the emancipation and enfranchisement of the lower orders, and of the adoption of the system of responsible parliamentary government. The twenty years that elapsed between 1828 and 1848 were indeed the period of the

effervescence of the national spirit, which was manifested not only
in the brilliant debates of the Legislature, not only in the self-
governing activity of the counties, not only in the broad views of
generous religious tolerance adopted by the adherents of all
churches, nay, to a degree unprecedented in any other epoch or
country, by the clerical authorities themselves, but equally so in
poetry, especially by Vörösmarty and Petöfi, in literature, and in
all the walks and occupations of life. Nor was participation in
public concerns any longer confined to the formerly governing
classes. The necessity of a democratical remodelling of the
constitution was openly avowed. It was clearly seen that the
concurrent efforts of all elements of the nation were indispensable
to its being raised to the eminence from which it might proudly
claim a position equal to that of the peoples of other European
States.

The fruits of these struggles and labours were reaped in 1848.
The peasantry was relieved of the dues it had to pay to the landlords, in work and kind, for the use of its farms ; a considerable
part, nearly half of the land, was made over in fee simple to the
tenants, the compensation of the landed proprietors being assigned
to the fund of general taxation. Class privileges were abolished,
equality before the law was asserted, equal civil rights were
extended to the entire population, and political rights attached to
a comparatively low franchise. Ministerial responsibility was
introduced, Transylvania reincorporated into Hungary, and the
sovereign independence of the State not only theoretically re-
established, but practically given effect to in its several institutions.
The royal sanction was obtained to all these measures ; and the
general hope seemed to be well founded, that all obstacles to
peaceful progress had thus been overcome by lawful means,
without the reproach of a single deed of violence.

Once more, however, a cruel disappointment lay in store for the
country. The settlement of two questions had been neglected,
the attendant dangers underestimated, and the inexperience which
thus afforded the enemies of Hungary a handle for carrying out
their sinister plans was dearly paid for by the nation. Parallel
with the expansion of Magyar sentiment in Hungary, the ambitions
of the southern Slav population of Croats and Serbs had also
developed. In spite of the prophetic warnings of Count Széchenyi,
no account was taken of the symptoms of separatistic tendencies in
Croatia. Instead of offering to this province—the only part of
Hungary which was geographically and historically distinct from

the remainder, and which, while the rest of Hungary by its natural features is mapped out as an essential unity, seems to bear equally the evident marks of having been destined for a sort of Federal union—some degree of Home Rule, it was fused into the rest, nor was the equal use of the Croatian with the Magyar language in the Legislature conceded to its representatives. The feelings of dissension thus engendered, as well as the unreasoning hatred felt by portions of the Servian and Roumanian peasant populations, especially in the South and in Transylvania, against their former landlords, were still further inflamed by the intrigues of the reactionary party in Austria, and finally broke out in sanguinary insurrections. On the other hand, no contrivance had been effected by which the foreign and military policy, the common affairs of the Kingdom of Hungary and of the hereditary provinces of the Hapsburg dynasty, which constituted the Empire of Austria, properly so called, might be managed harmoniously and with common consent, especially since constitutional government had been introduced, not without the urgent insistance and assistance of the Hungarian Parliament, in Vienna, too. Besides, no arrangement had been made for Hungary's acknowledging and assuming any share of the burden of the public debt of Austria, incurred, partly at least, in the interest of the common policy of both countries. Hence misunderstandings and ill-will arose between the Governments and Parliaments of Vienna and Pest; and a pretence, wearing some semblance of justice, was thus furnished for meddling with the internal affairs of Hungary, which the Court, anxious to do away altogether with innovations and constitutional government alike, was not slow in making use of. Thus, first an armed civil struggle ensued in the South and in the East; then the Imperial Austrian Government, which, after quelling insurrectionary movements in Prague and Vienna, had practically restored Absolutism, supported the Croatian and Roumenian rebellions, and openly attacked Hungary. The war lasted for one year. The armed resistance of Hungary, strictly legal in the beginning, assumed a revolutionary hue when the abolition of the constitution and independence of the Realm became the avowed object of the Viennese statesmen. The Hungarian armies, victorious so long as they were opposed to the Croatian and Roumenian insurgents, and to the Austrian forces alone, were unable to cope with the superadded power of Russia, the intervention of which had taken place in the interests of despotism. By the end of the summer of 1849

Hungary was again prostrate at the feet of a relentless foe; her best blood was profusely shed on the scaffold, the flower of her citizens were cast into prison, or escaped as fugitives into foreign exile.

For twelve years the name of Hungary, as a State, was erased from the map of Europe. Bureaucratic Absolutism ruled supreme in Austria, and did its best to obliterate all Hungarian institutions. Germanisation was the order of the day, the German tongue being declared the exclusive language of official life as well as of the higher schools. Government was carried on by means of foreign, German, and Czech officials. No vestige was left, not only of the national independence, but either of Home Rule or of self-government of any sort; the country was divided into provinces without regard for historical traditions; in short, an attempt was made to wipe out every trace denoting the existence of a separate Hungary. All ranks and classes opposed a sullen passive resistance to these attacks against the existence of the nation; even the sections of the nationalities which had rebelled against the enactments of 1848, at the instigation of the reactionary Camarilla, were equally disaffected in consequence of the short-sighted policy of despotical centralisation; and it was at this critical phase of the national life that the diverse elements of the country were again welded into the unanimity of patriotic sentiment, that all minor differences were sunk in the passionate craving for the restoration of the realm and of its constitutional rights, and that the paramount importance of the national questions rendered the people definitely tolerant as to divergencies on all other issues.

Finally, after the collapse of the system of Absolutism in consequence of financial disasters and of the misfortunes of the Italian War of 1859, the Hungarian Parliament was again convoked; and after protracted negotiations, broken off and resumed again, the impracticability of a system of provincial Federalism having been proved in the meantime, and the defeat incurred in the Prussian War of 1866 having demonstrated the futility of any reconstruction of the Empire of Austria, in which the national aspirations of Hungary were not taken into due consideration—an arrangement was concluded under the auspices of Francis Deák, Count Andrássy, and Count Beust on the basis of the full acknowledgment of the separate national existence of Hungary, and of the continuity of its legal rights. The idea of a centralised Austrian Empire had to give way to the dual Austro-Hungarian

monarchy, which is in fact an indissoluble federation of two
equal States, under the common rule of a single sovereign, the
Emperor of Austria and King of Hungary, each of the States
having a constitution, government, and parliament of its own,
Hungary especially retaining, with slight modifications, its ancient
institutions remodelled in 1848. The administration of the
foreign policy, the management of the army, and the disbursement
of the expenditure necessary for these purposes, were settled upon
as common affairs of the entire monarchy, for the management
of which common ministers were instituted, responsible to the
two delegations, co-equal committees of the parliaments of
Hungary and of the Cisleithanian (Austrian) provinces. Elaborate provisions were framed for the smooth working of these
common institutions, for giving weight to the constitutional
influence, even in matters of common policy, of the separate
Cisleithanian and Hungarian ministries, and for rendering their
responsibility to the respective Parliaments an earnest and solid
reality. The financial questions pending in the two independent
and equal States were settled by a compromise ; measures were
taken for the equitable arrangement of all matters which might
arise in relation to interests touching both States, such as duties,
commerce, and indirect taxation, all legislation on these subjects
taking place by means of identical laws separately enacted by the
Parliament of each State. Every device human foresight and
political ingenuity, sharpened by long experience, could suggest
to ensure the requisites of both firmness and stability of the
entire monarchy, as well as the maintenance of the free and
independent national life of each of its realms, was adopted in
order to harmonise the conditions of imperial dominion with
those of the sovereignty of the separate constituent States.
Simultaneously with these arrangements the political differences
between Hungary and Croatia were compromised by granting
provincial Home Rule to the latter, an expedient which has not
quite done away with the difficulties that crop up from time to
time, but which still, on the whole, has diminished the chances
of direct collision, and, up to the present, has prevented the
occurrence of irreconcilable conflicts.

Thus the organisation of the Austro-Hungarian monarchy on
the basis of dualism, and the compromise entered into between
the two halves composing it, whilst uniting for the purposes of
defence the forces of two States of a moderate size and extent
into those of a great empire, able to cope with the exigencies of

an adequate position amongst the first-class Powers of Europe, restored also to Hungary its independence and its unfettered sovereignty in all internal matters. On this solid foundation it was rendered possible for the country to devote its attention chiefly to the reform of its institutions, and to the development of its resources, moral as well as material. The pressure, which for centuries had directed the efforts of the people mainly towards upholding constitutional rights, and had concentrated the national thought into opposition to absolutistic attempts in the service of foreign ideas, having been removed, new channels were opened out for the energies of the community in all those directions in which the modern life of civilised nations demands their activity. All the great human and social interests, scientific, educational, administrative, sanitary, and economical, which by the side of the paramount claims of the national cause upon the people, necessitating practically the sacrifice of all minor, though important, aims, had formerly received merely a partial, and rather theoretical than actual recognition, have thus obtained their due position in the public view, and are able to attract the amount of attention and devotion they deserve; indeed, the proper balance of national life in Hungary has been, in consequence, re-established.

A full picture of the life and thought of Hungary in the present would, therefore, merely repeat the well-known outlines of the social, industrial, mental, and moral features of other civilised communities in Europe. The Magyar has ceased to be a so-called "interesting nationality," Hungary has neither an eastern nor an antiquated character, but has simply resumed its position amongst the factors of Western culture. There are doubtless certain differences between its condition and that of other nations, but rather of degree than of kind, and manifesting themselves no longer in salient outward traits. Hungary is still far more of an agricultural than of a commercial, and perhaps more of a commercial than of an industrial country. Its acquired capital is not yet proportionate to its natural wealth, nor are its investments commensurate to the talent, skill, and industry of the nation. It is only by persevering efforts, with due patience for the accumulation of results in course of time, that essential and indubitable progress can be accomplished. There are, however, already certain social conditions as to which Hungary, even at this day, stands well nigh unrivalled. The bulk of the population in the plains and midlands is composed of a freehold peasantry, endowed with the franchise, accustomed to communal, and participating in county self-government, entirely independent in thought and bearing, who for public spirit, education, working power, and for their standards of life and comfort and wealth, may favourably compare with any other similar class on the face of the earth. The cities and towns, too, are rising fast, have become almost entirely Magyar in character, and are growing to be more and more centres of intellectual activity.

Political life, although happily no longer occupied by constitutional questions, has not lost its attraction for the people, and, as is natural in a free country, absorbs a great part of public attention. An enormous mass of political work has been done since 1867, and is still going on. Elementary education has been rendered universal and compulsory, and the institutions for higher and University courses have been taken charge of by the State, and rendered national. The system of railway communications has been perfected to a high degree, and the State has obtained direct control of almost all the lines. The franchise for the House of Commons, and the election of the members, has been regulated, and the House of Lords reformed, without, however, any elective element being introduced into it. Agricultural, industrial, and commercial laws have been passed in great numbers. The administration of justice has been assured by a system of an independent judiciary appointed for life, and removable only for cause, and even the great task of legal codification has been begun, and is in a fair way of being accomplished.

Of course, a considerable amount of the strength of the nation has been devoted to military armaments. Indeed, the sacrifices demanded by the circumstances of the Austro-Hungarian monarchy for keeping step in its military organisation with the immense and unprecedented development of the armed forces of the neighbouring empires, have proved a severe strain upon the finances, and have taxed to the uttermost the ingenuity of Hungarian statesmen, and the forbearance of the taxpayers, in order to be enabled to incur permanently the attendant expenses, without the utter ruin of the country. Compulsory universal military service for the men of all classes has been adopted, and besides the common imperial and royal army, the Hungarian Honvéd-army has been constituted and fully equipped. But though nothing has been spared to enhance the means of the defence of the monarchy, the even balance of receipts and expenditure in the Hungarian budget, which at first was endangered by the necessity of profuse state-investments and by the expenses for the army, has been re-established, and all political parties are unanimous in their determination of not allowing it to be disturbed.

As to social and political tendencies in general, the overwhelming majority of the Hungarian people is neither Conservative nor Radical, but adheres to tenets which in England would be termed the views of moderate Liberalism. The aristocracy has preserved a certain amount of prestige, and no one dreams of abolishing the House of Lords. The bulk of the political power is in the hands of the middle-class landed proprietors, whom the peasantry at this day, too, willingly accept as their political leaders. Democratical ideas have acquired a permanent hold over the minds, but not so far as to obliterate traditions, which in Hungary bear no tinge of reactionary associations, but rather point to devotion to the cause of national rights. There is no virulent sectarian feeling, nor any possibility of the success of ultramontane doctrines, Church matters being essentially regarded from the standpoint of broad tolerance. In consequence of all these circumstances, there is no strongly marked line of division between any sections of the people ; and although party feeling at times inevitably runs high, the implacable spirit of faction is seldom entertained, and then but by very few ; nor is there any important body of citizens advocating any doctrines other than those of steady and gradual progress in consonance with popular ideas.

Especially with regard to the foreign policy the whole nation is absolutely unanimous in favour of peace, not only for the moment, but on principle, so far as possible, for all times. Every one in Hungary knows that the country has nothing to gain, and much to risk, by any extension or conquest whatever. There can be no greater mistake than to suppose that the Hungarian people are eager for military glory, or desirous of revenge, because their ancestors have fought well on many a field, or because the last generation has given brilliant proofs of its valour in the wars of past decades. On the contrary, there is probably no nation in Europe in which any interference with foreign affairs is less popular. Even the occupation of Bosnia was accepted with reluctance, and only because it became evident that it was indispensable for the defence of the southern frontier, and as a counterpoise to eventual offensive plans of Russia. Naturally there is a resolute determination throughout the people to be ready for any sacrifice, in order to resist aggression, and to maintain the independence and the conditions of the free internal development of the nation. But war in any case would be regarded as the last measure of dire necessity. The consciousness that the strength of the realm is continually increasing in peace, that the welfare of the people requires all the combined efforts of the citizens of Hungary, is much too deeply ingrained by the lessons of the past to be lightly forgotten or set aside. It is universally felt that Hungary is, though quietly, on the road of progress; and in our days it is not the communities which know they are progressive that are likely to embark upon perilous adventures, or to jeopardise the benefits derived from the harmonious advance of the peaceful co-operation of mankind.

IV

GERMANY—POLITICS.

SIDNEY WHITMAN.

I FEAR it is only a sad repetition on my part if I begin by repeating what has been referred to each Sunday I have been present here, namely, our deplorable average ignorance of foreign countries in general. But I must even add to that, and mention our strange want of interest in other European countries.

Some years ago an excellent standard work on France, by an eminent German author, was translated into English and published by one of the leading London publishers. Now, although the book was published at a moderate price, although neither the author nor the translator received one penny for their work, the book at the end of an eight years' sale showed a loss of £28 on the bare costs of publication! Not a very encouraging speculation for author or publisher, you will admit.

One of the most ambitious of our monthly reviews lately treated a book on Germany by a person I am acquainted with to this nice little criticism: "A dull book on a dull subject." It is this arrogance which, inculcated by a certain section of our snobocracy, settles down in wider circles, and does us more harm than making us disliked; it keeps us in ignorance. Though, of course, this is an isolated flagrant case, still, if this same author had written a book in German on England, although many German reviewers might have called the book itself dull, I venture to say that in the whole of Germany it would be impossible to find one educated critic who could be such a self-satisfied Pharisee as to call the subject of England a dull one.

But it is only fair to state that we are by no means alone in our ignorance of our neighbours. I remember seeing the letter of a French prisoner during the war of 1870, who was interred in the city of Stuttgard, the capital, as you are doubtless aware, of a petty German kingdom nearly adjoining France. He wrote home, "I am a prisoner here in Stuttgard, on the frontier of Russia."

I have found very strange ideas prevailing in Russia with regard to us, and even with regard to Russia's immediate neighbours, the Germans. Even the Germans themselves, by far the best educated of Europeans, have some very strange notions about us, although, as I shall have occasion to notice later on, their acquaintance with other nations as a rule is extraordinary.

But it is not the ignorance of the untutored many that is so surprising as that of men in high and responsible positions. It is a well-known fact that the belief of Napoleon III., at the outbreak of the '70 war, that South Germany would join France, a belief shared by a great number of educated Frenchmen, could only have been the result of most culpable ignorance.

At that very time an exceedingly able Frenchman, Baron Stoffel, was military attaché at the French embassy in Berlin, and only too truly gauged the real state of affairs, but he was not listened to. Unhappily for France, the politicians of Paris did not want enlightenment; they preferred to follow the blind impulse of passion and hatred.

In our own country, the biographies and memoirs of political personages during this century again and again reveal an astonishing ignorance of the most simple facts regarding other countries—ignorance which, fortunately, has not involved us in any of the disastrous consequences above referred to, although more than once it has brought us very near to serious international complications.

Against the above, it is pleasing for us to know that the authors of the standard works on Germany's two greatest men of the last century were Englishmen. Carlyle wrote the *History of Frederick the Great*, and G. H. Lewes the best *History of Goethe.* These two works are each accepted in Germany as the standard ones in their respective subjects. That shows us what we are capable of doing when we set ourselves to familiarise our minds with the doings and thought of other countries.

It is indeed a start the Germans have over us that, firstly, through their superior general education, and, secondly, through the wonderful hunger for information and knowledge of all kinds that pervade that people, from the highest to the humblest, they possess an acquaintance with other countries that is perfectly unequalled.

This knowledge has assisted their leaders enormously in shaping their policy; it has assisted the mass of the nation in their unceasing efforts to rival other nations, and particularly us, in commerce and manufacture, as well as in science ; in fact, in every branch of national striving and activity.

The history of our time affords a very striking instance of this intimate knowledge the Germans possess of other countries.

During the Secession War in America we English, even leading politicians and the wealthy classes (I do not like the words upper and lower classes), were entirely at sea as to the aspects and prospects of that struggle. The masses of this country—to their honour be it said—sympathised with the North. The well-to-do classes not only sympathised with the South, but, a proof of great ignorance of the realities of the struggle, believed in the success of the South, and even invested their money in their belief.

In Germany there was perhaps less barren sympathy spent (the Germans, unlike us, are not in the habit of squandering that commodity broadcast) ; but every servant girl, every boots at an inn had his savings snugly invested in green-backs. Millions and millions of money were made in Germany by the population at large in this one instance, not to mention what larger capitalists made—a striking instance, I hold, of the usefulness of geographical and political information about other countries beside our own !

So much for the drawbacks of ignorance ! Now let me draw nearer to the subject of my lecture.

Of course, in the short time at my disposal, the limits of which I promise you not to exceed, it is quite impossible for me to tell you much about Germany ; anything, in fact, at all comprehensive. Nor can it be my sole aim to-day to point out to you by a series of parallels where the Germans are deficient or where they shine to advantage by comparison with us. The most I can do is to endeavour to give you some faint notion of the general political history that has gradually, after a lapse of over a thousand years, brought Germany to the position she occupies to-day.

All I can hope for is, that the subject may interest you sufficiently to warrant your pursuing it yourselves more fully to some purpose.

The Germans have reaped great benefits from studying us. It is high time we endeavoured to gain some more solid advantage by studying them and their institutions ; for we have reaped many advantages already by so doing. For instance, our wonderful progress in industrial art and manufacture, our technical schools that are springing up everywhere, not to mention our greatly improved educational status of late years, is almost solely owing to what we have learned of Germany.

But, believe me, there is still more to be learned from that source, particularly in the present day, than is dreamt of in our philosophy. I need only refer to the great problems of social progress which clamorously await solution with us. The study of Germany offers us valuable hints, believe me, in this important branch of politics.

With your kind permission, I should like to begin by dwelling for a few moments on the word politics itself, the one science everybody seems to think he understands without having learned it.

I presume the word itself is derived from the Greek—πολις : *polis* = a city. πολιτες : *polites* = a citizen.

Politics, then, in the original acceptation, might perhaps be termed the science that shall treat in a broad aggregate sense of the wellbeing and the prosperity and progress of the units of a nation—the citizens.

That must have been in remote ages when civilisation was simpler than it is to-day, and when the wellbeing of the citizen was, except for occasional interruption by war, famine, or flood, the whole concern of the rulers of a people. The greatest happiness of the greatest number is an ideal state of things.

In our time politics has come to mean in its full sense that vast and complex science which deals with the balance of power ; the supremacy of one people over the other ; the predominance of one race over another ; the dominion of one continent, or of one small island, over a great part of the inhabited globe.

That is what politics have come to in our time. Now, although it is a wise saying that you should not prophesy unless you know, I will venture to prophesy that we have reached an epoch in the history of civilisation when politics will have to go back to their primitive occupation and busy themselves more earnestly, devotedly, and unselfishly with the welfare of the unit—the citizen; the poor citizen ; the weak, who cannot fight the battle of life in a callous world rolling with wealth, and side by side with misery, poverty, and degradation.

And let me tell you, that the first step towards attacking—I do not say solving, that is still far distant—this most pressing political problem of our time was taken by the late Emperor William, assisted by his great minister Bismarck, in his proposals for the care of the aged, the sick, and the wounded in the grim battle of life—the life of the working man.

The science of politics, as I have endeavoured to point out to you, has mighty problems to solve, and yet we are daily in the habit of receiving and giving opinions on them with a very slender foundation of knowledge or experience.

What would the specialist think if we were to give a confident opinion, and back it by our vote, on an important point of a science which we have never specially studied? And yet we do this daily with regard to that most intricate of sciences—the science of politics.

Believe me, the question of home politics requires a close study, not only of our own social conditions of life ; in our time I think, I may safely say, it is also necessary to study and profit by the experience gained, through much individual effort and suffering, by other countries also.

But as for some of the broader questions of international politics, I make bold to say, it is unlikely for us to have three consecutive logical ideas on the subject, unless we are more or less familiar with the past history of other countries beside our own.

Now for a glance at the past history of Germany, in order the better to understand its product—the present.

The centre of Europe had been inhabited by a number of German tribes even before the time of Cæsar, nineteen hundred years ago, but it was not until the year 800 of our era that they were united into one great empire.

It was on Christmas Day of the year A.D. 800 that Charlemagne, the head of the Franks, was crowned at St. Peter's, in Rome, as Emperor of the Holy Roman Empire, King of Germany, and Arch Protector of the Christian Faith.

Thus over two hundred and fifty years before the battle of Hastings, from which our modern English history dates, we find Germany a great power—the central constituent of the greatest power in Europe.

I must pass over the history of centuries in leaps and bounds, merely mentioning that the dissensions of the sons of Charlemagne and their successors ultimately resulted in dividing the centre and west of Europe into three distinct monarchies :—

1. France, the least powerful, but the foundation of the France we all know.

2. The kingdom of Lorraine, a great part of which, together with Burgundy, is now merged in the France of to-day.

3. Finally, the kingdom of Germany, ruled by elective monarchs,

who at the same time were only crowned as Emperors of the
Holy Roman Empire, by this fact of being kings of Germany.

The time at my disposal does not allow me to do more than
refer to the splendour of the Empire of Germany during the
Middle Ages, when she was practically supreme over the whole
of Christianity, except independent little England. The dawn
of the Reformation found the German King or Roman Emperor
virtually ruler over a realm on which the sun never set.

We require an effort of the imagination even to recall that
there was a time when the ships of the Hansetowns brought over
unrivalled wealth to their harbours, and had a larger seaboard than
the whole of England, when Germany was the home of merchant
princes who helped their monarchs from their own private means,
when German architecture was most splendid, when German life
was most luxurious, and German manufacture the most renowned.

The greatness of Germany found its apogee in Charles V., and
began to decline immediately after his death.

Charles the Fifth lived 1520-55, and was cotemporary
with our Henry VIII., who, in fact, as well as Francis the First of
France, both competed for the German crown, which, as I have
already pointed out, was elective. Charles the Fifth practically
ruled over the whole of Central Europe, Spain, and those
parts of America which had been discovered by Spanish navigators and explorers.

France, who has within the memory of living men—though only
of the very aged—held sway over the whole of Europe, always
excepting England, was a comparatively small Power in these
days. But it was not to be very long before she should profit by
the most potent causes of decay of the German Empire—internal
rivalries, selfish family policy, and religious dissension—and rise
to power at its expense.

And this brings me to that part of the history of Germany—the
period of the Reformation, and one of its results, the terrible
Thirty Years' War, without knowing something of which, I think,
it is almost impossible to form a fair idea of the political aspirations of Germany of the present day.

We must bear in mind that it was Germany that bore the
brunt of the fierce struggle on the Continent against the
intellectual bondage of the Roman Catholic priesthood of those
days.

It was a German peasant's son, Martin Luther—whose birthday
it is this very day—who stood alone with the Bible in his hands,

before the Imperial Court at the Diet of Worms, and with the prospect of death before him, sooner than yield one inch of his convictions, held by these memorable words, "I cannot do otherwise. God help me. Amen!" When warned not to go to Worms, for fear of assassination, this mighty peasant's son replied, "And yet I will go to Worms if the house-tops were crowded with devils."

This battle cry of conviction, pitted against the power of Rome, backed, as was that power, by all the immense might of the Catholic Emperor, Charles V., found an echo far and wide among the best blood of the Fatherland. Thus began the dawn of a new era in Europe, the Reformation initiated in Germany by Martin Luther, although it took nearly seventy years to grow strong enough to pick up the gauntlet thrown down by Charles V.'s successors, backed as they were by the whole weight and power of Catholicism.

This led, in its consequences, to the Thirty Years' War, perhaps the most dreadful curse and calamity that ever befell a people. In that war the northern and central part of Germany fought for thirty long years, at times assisted by the Swedes, the French, and other foreigners, against the power of the Houses of Austria and Bavaria.

We in England also have our glorious pages of Protestant history connected with the Reformation. We need only recall Queen Elizabeth and the Spanish Armada. But with us its inception was more of a political and aristocratic character. In Germany the dawn of modern times sprang from the very heart of the best of the people, and they also it was who suffered most in its furtherance. We always had the advantage of being safe on this tight little island we love so much. Our country has never been invaded, and our population decimated, as was the case in Germany during the Thirty Years' War.

Before that war Germany had a population of over sixteen millions ; at its close less than five millions remained. Before that war broke out Germany was perhaps the wealthiest country in Europe ; at its close the population was on the verge of starvation.

To give you some faint idea of the horrors of the Thirty Years' War, reliable chronicles of the time inform us that towns which were only visited by it when it was half over lost seventy-five per cent. of their population.

For years hordes of robbers and thieves, disbanded troops, traversed the country from one end to the other, burning and stealing and murdering in broad daylight. Prosperous manufacturing towns with 10,000 inhabitants had a population of 500 left after the war. Hunger and famine led the people, in many instances, to tear the newly-buried from their graves and devour them. Disease carried off what the sword had spared.

When the Peace of 1648 put an end to the war, the country itself was one mass of waste, fields not tilled for a generation, whole towns swept away, burned or razed to the ground.

The Peace of Westphalia, as it is known in history, stripped Germany of the fruits of centuries of labour and effort, which even now she has only partially recovered.

It left the Protestant part of Germany impoverished, helpless, unable to defend itself, in the centre of Europe. France profited by a large extension of territory, and from that time onwards found it more and more easy to turn German soil into the battlefields of her ambitious rulers.

From that time down to our own, excepting the brief period of the French Revolution, when German sovereigns—not their people—endeavoured to coerce the French people, and paid dearly for it,—from that time the policy of France, the policy, in common fairness, it should be said, of French rulers and statesmen, not of the French people, has been the spoliation of Germany.

Any student of history can tell you that the whole of Germany is marked by mementoes of French battlefields and burnt ruined castles.

If I refer to Frederick the Great, it is to point out that with him rose in the last century a Protestant great Power in the north of Germany which in our time has crowned the long-longed-for edifice of National Unity.

He it was who, with a population of five millions—one quarter more than London to-day—held the determination to stake everything sooner than run the risk of falling back into the hideous political nightmare of the past.

In England we cannot understand the strength of this resolve ; we have practically never known a foreigner on our soil for eight hundred years ! But the Germans have hardly known anything else ! And I contend, not only that they are justified in holding on to the armaments ; but, I maintain, their whole history proves —even that of the last twenty years as well—that the Germans are a peaceful, non-aggressive people.

You may answer to this, that their government has lately

shown itself occasionally aggressive with regard to the African Colonies !

True, perhaps ; but what a paltry matter that is compared to the enormous annexations of territory we have accomplished during the last ten years !

And yet, even those small, but, I hold, perfectly justifiable, efforts to have colonies of their own, have met with great opposition from the German people. Believe me, the Germans do not aspire to rival us beyond the seas ; and if they did, they could not ! No more than, I honestly believe, they will ever beat us in the long run in commerce with all their cheapness.

But I do not say we should indulge in any sentimental feeling with regard to them. If Germany trespasses on our interests, let us defend them ; but do not let us cant over it. But England and Germany have every interest to remain at peace ; and thus, without any entangling alliance, they are both at one in the interests of peace as against all peace-breakers, and so will remain.

Further than this, I say we should try and inform ourselves as to the history and the qualities of a great nation, whose interests, whereas they nowhere seriously clash with our own, go hand in hand with them in many important matters.

We should try to look at such a nation, which is bound to play a great part socially, with judgment intellectually, as well as politically, unbiassed, without favour, but without prejudice, in order, if possible, to gain some benefit to ourselves, some experience in many important matters, social, intellectual, and political, by so doing.

How comes it that we find the united armies of Russia, Austria, and France, representing a population of over a hundred millions, at bay more or less for seven years ?

And when he passed away, it was not long before the greatest soldier of modern times, an avenging Attila in modern form, I mean Napoleon the First, appeared on the scene ; and profiting by the dissensions and incapacity, yea, even the want of character of German rulers, again turned Germany into the battlefield of Europe, and preyed on the vitals of the impoverished German people for nearly twenty years !

The history of the last two hundred years, and the sufferings the people of Germany underwent all through that long period, explains the readiness of Germans to-day to bear any taxation, to put up with any strain, even poverty if you will, and to stand and fall with their Emperor to retain the position they have bought with their blood.

If I have especially dwelt on the misery revealed in the history of the last two hundred years, it is because it affords an explanation of the central idea that governs the politics of Germany. If we find such difficulty, as we undoubtedly do, in appreciating that main principle, may it not be more or less in consequence of some such frame of mind as this :—If a nation prospers by different methods to our own, we do not regard them exactly so much with envy as with a certain diffident incredulous irritability that their prosperity must be " delusive," as it has not been secured by our own hallowed, patent process?

The success of Germany in our time can be distinctly traced to the initiative of great men. Our democratic age does not believe in great men ; it is rather inclined to sneer at them—at least at its own great men, who have yet to face the verdict of posterity. I would venture to say there is a time for great men ; everything in its proper time ; great men, majorities, and ballot boxes ; but nothing final, for all illnesses—like a patent medicine—in this great world of ours, in which nothing is final but change.

Our attention is drawn to the affairs of other nations. We know little of them. We have a hazy idea that they are somehow not so free as we are ; hence, we take our stand by the magic word " Liberty "—itself only a means to an end—and judge others by our standard of that magic quantity !

It is perhaps true that we do enjoy the greatest amount of political liberty of any country, consequently some of us think we are in a position to look down upon others and to pity them, their status and their aims, forthwith !

I am sorry to say that I am unable to endorse this view, much less to believe in its finality. And if I had not restricted the limits of my lecture to-day to the politics of Germany—after all, only one phase of a nation's life—I think I could easily prove to you that, as far as the comparative amount of happiness is concerned, that is to be found here and in Germany, we are by no means in the position to pity our neighbours or look down upon them.

I am sorry to say that the frame of mind which enables a man to call out, " I thank my stars that I am an Englishman," is one I cannot share. I hold that not only to be a reprehensible sentiment, savouring of the Pharisee of the New Testament, but one precluding any possible fair estimate of other countries. In this case it is doubly so, at least from my point of view, holding, as I do, that although we owe our first affections to the land of our birth, we do not owe it blind idolatry, which prevents the critic recognising where there is something beyond our seas to admire and to learn from.

I hope I cede to no man in my pride at what England and Englishmen have achieved and are achieving, but there my feelings stop; for if they did not, I should consider myself perfectly unfitted to address you on the subject before us. In fact, I might never have taken the trouble to study it!

But you may say, Yes, that is all very well, but you cannot deny that it is a sad state of things that, with all admitted prosperity and military success of Germany, there should be so little liberty there, that thousands and thousands of emigrants flee their native shores year by year in order to escape the hated conscription.

Well, I do deny the latter part of that contention. I even am of opinion that it is a libel on the manhood of Germany! I even believe that, without any conscription at all, emigration would be just as great, for it is the natural consequence of that mysterious law that seems to govern mankind since thousands of years to steer from east to west in search of fortune!

It is disproved by the thousands and thousands of Germans who hurried back to their native shores at the trumpet call of war in the memorable year 1870! It is indirectly disproved by analogy by the enormous emigration from Ireland! Is that caused by the law of compulsory military service?

Now, as regards individual political liberty, the contention must be admitted to be partially true. But what does it amount to? Everything gained on earth is the result, it would seem, of a compromise.

Must we not ourselves admit that, notwithstanding our boasted political liberty, we have a greater amount of social slavery, of drunkenness, of bigotry, of human misery to show than military-ridden Germany.

If you will not admit it, I pledge you my word of honour it is so, nevertheless.

The facts are simply these: The Germans had to accept national independence—the first condition of national life—whence and under what conditions it was possible. If they had waited until public opinion—I do not deny that public opinion was partially for it—a free press and the ballot-box had beaten off their enemies and cemented their hopeless internal differences, surrounded by enemies, as they always were, they might have waited in vain until the day of judgment !

Strong men had to come, but, mind, honest, fearless, self-sacrificing men ! And they came, and led, and conquered the right of a great nation to regulate its own affairs, without let or hindrance, from outside.

These advantages must remain ; their comparatively trivial drawbacks must yield gradually to the spirit of the time. You must remember in judging Germany that she has only just emerged from a life struggle for her very existence as an independent united nation !

What are twenty years in the life of a nation ? A day, a week in the life of a man !

Germany in some senses can only fairly be compared to England as it was centuries ago, and that comparison involves no disadvantage to her. She will soon be found in touch with, if not ahead of her time, believe me !

It is the policy of Germany to-day to retain the fruits of the sacrifices that have been brought. These fruits are necessary for her existence as a strong, independent, peace-loving Power in the centre of Europe ; she does not wish to add to these fruits from the mere lust of conquest.

At present, it must be admitted, there are many inconveniences to be met in Germany that jar on our unaccustomed nerves.

The officials are in many cases arbitrary, and inclined to think themselves the masters and the public their servants. These are disadvantages, I admit; but against these, and sundry others, believe me, there are many things to be met with in Germany for which we might well envy the Germans, police-ridden, military-ridden as they are !

If they enjoy less political liberty than we, they suffer less from heartless social tyranny, from ostracism of the poor, than we do. If their educated men frequent the churches less than ours do, on the other hand, when you enter a German church you will find the rich sitting beside the poor.

If their system of administration is somewhat cumbersome, irksome, and inquisitorial, on the other hand, the Government of Germany protects the poor from the unprincipled adulteration of articles of food, which is the curse of Italy, England, and America.

Imprisonment and enormous fines await the adulterators in the Fatherland ; here in the land of liberty an eminent statesman once told Englishmen that, according to these wondrous laws of supply and demand, adulteration is a mild form of competition! A nice creed for the working-man with £1 a week and a family to console himself with when he is half-poisoned with whiskey adulterated with sulphuric acid.

I will only add, for your information, that many of the stoutest planks of your Radical platform—a long way off practical application in this country—are already accomplished facts in poor Germany. For instance, local government, which exists all over Germany in excellent working order, side by side with, but subordinate to, the Imperial Parliament at Berlin.

I fancy I could tell you a deal more about Germany that would be new to you, but it is slightly outside the scope of my lecture of to-day.

With your permission, however, I should like to conclude with a word regarding the general acceptation of militarism and war—a subject we cannot overlook in dealing with political Germany.

We may like it or not, but the sad truth it is, nevertheless, that mankind is always at war.

The battle of life is one of the inexorable conditions of existence all the world over in the whole animal kingdom—mankind at its head included.

And, among mankind, let me tell you, there are few more persistent fighters than the entire Anglo-Saxon race.

In fact, we who now indulge in dreams of peace, we owe our very existence to our capacity for fighting and beating our enemies all over the world.

The Americans, our kinsmen, are at present silently at war with the North American Indians; we ourselves are at war with the Maoris in New Zealand, the aborigines in Australia, who, all in measurable distance of time from now, will as surely be cut off from the face of the earth, as the extinct bird, the dodo; as surely as if they were cut off by the sword in one single night.

The ordeal of battle is by no means the most terrible one humanity has to face, particularly if it has to be faced in an honourable cause by a whole nation in arms; the rich fighting in the ranks side by side with the poor; both equal, under the directing hand of genius. And the nation which shirks this ordeal when its honour and its existence are at stake is sure to go towards decay and ultimate obliteration.

Is that not war we see in our midst; the grim fight of the

dockers for a bare existence; the constant fight of the Sheffield grinders with death, which vanquishes them invariably before the prime of life; the struggle of the stokers on board the American liners, which finishes them in three to five years. Go into the slums of Salford and Manchester, and look at the population there, and come back and tell me whether you have not seen one of the most hideous struggles amidst dirt, improvidence, and poverty?

Let us endeavour to see things as they are, not as an over-excited, though kindly, imagination would picture them to us. We are told of the cruel wrong of taking men away from the blessed productive labour of peace! I cannot see much blessing or much happiness in a family during peace starving on ten shillings a week.

It is, doubtless, a grand achievement of our time that the *desire* to arbitrate should have arisen, even when only compara-tively trivial interests and imaginary honour are at stake; but, believe me, as surely as we owe our national and racial pre-dominance almost exclusively to successful fighting, so surely will it ever be in the future, that we must be prepared to back our arguments, in the last resort, by the sword.

The lessons of history teach us that it is imperative that a nation should be able to fight. Humanity teaches us to be merciful and just in the hour of victory.

To those who look at politics without illusions, and yet with a full belief in the onward progress of humanity, there can be few more cheering and consoling items in our time than the history of the great American Secession War of 1861-68, in which, although the passions were inflamed as much as ever in times gone by, yet in the moment of victory a new spirit of mercy and forgiveness came over the victors, that would not allow a drop of blood to be spilt, but sought to heal the wounds an unavoidable struggle had struck.

Why is America at peace now? Because she is humanitarian? No; because nobody dare touch her!

We hear of a war that throws a nation, and with it civilisation, fifty years back.

But this is not always the case. Even an unsuccessful war has before now been an admitted benefit, in some instances, to a nation, let alone a legitimate and successful one. Witness the case of Austria in 1866. That war acted on Austria like a storm that swept away the miasmas of stagnation. Austria since that period has become one of the most liberally constituted countries in Europe, if that is of any benefit to a nation.

Frederick the Great, on his return to Berlin after the Seven Years' War, could not restrain his tears when he heard the loyal cheers of the half-starved and beggared population that had suffered so much. And yet, who shall deny to-day that those sufferings of the Seven Years' War, as well as later those of the War of Liberation against the First Napoleon, steeled the nerves of the nation to do and die in our time?

And to-day, if you read the newspapers, you will find that everywhere the German Emperor goes he is received with enthusiasm. If you think that the poor enslaved Germans cheer their chains, you are very much mistaken. Whatever socialistic malcontents and opponents of every form of royalty may think, yet among the vast majority of the nation he is immensely popular, because he represents the national aspirations—if not all of them, at least the principal ones. When he said that eighteen army-corps would bite the dust before the ground which had been won by such sacrifices should be yielded, he gave vent to a sentiment which we Englishmen can only understand, if we imagine the eventuality of Ireland being threatened by a foreign Power!

To hear people tell about the peace of the world, the sympathy between peoples, etc., does credit to the illusions of those that propound these ideas, and credit to the heart of those that take them up and applaud them. But from the point of view of the student of politics, the hope of practical realisation of these sentiments has little basis in the history of the world!

I think it would be a little more natural to look for more sympathy between ourselves, as *man* to *man*, as *class* to *class*, before we go far afield in our desire to embrace the whole world in one bond of union and cheap sympathy.

We allow our politicians to make party capital out of the wrongs and sufferings of nations and races at the other end of Europe. I have never yet seen any benefit accrue to my countrymen from such doings!

Believe me, there is more real unhappiness, more hopeless misery to be met with within a mile of London Bridge than in the whole of Asiatic Turkey!

Let us drop our artificial sympathy with the sufferings of others. We cannot afford it. Let us strive to find out where there is something to admire in others; where they are ahead of us; where they are better off than we. And if we can gain some of the advantages others possess without their disadvantages, let us make up our minds that we will have them too, or know the reason why !

Before we indulge in dreams of cosmopolitan sympathy, our aristocracy, and particularly our middle classes that are led by the clergy, must get rid of the suspicion of looking upon poverty as next door to a crime.

Our democracy must get rid of that " envy and hatred " which it vents " sometimes " against those who do not share its views.

Listen to the tone of some of our democratic organs against the so-called military despotism of Europe.

What do they usually know of those countries, and their vital necessities ? Very often but little, I fear.

Then let us strive and add to our knowledge all round, so that we may be better able each of us to fulfil that little part in the battle of life unconsciously assigned to each of us, namely, *each* to contribute, according to his opportunities, his mite towards the solution of that great social political problem—to leave the world a little better than we found it !

V

GERMAN CULTURE.

SIDNEY WHITMAN.

IF I venture to submit a few words on German Culture for your consideration, it is that I was partly educated in that country, and have been lastingly impressed by much I saw and learnt whilst there.

I shall not be surprised if you even opine that my picture of German culture be rather a favourable one. If so, I can only say I am dealing with the *spirit* of things, and not with any preference for the nation as individuals.

There seems to be little doubt that a certain unpopularity of Germany has of late years made itself felt, not only in this country ; but history fails to show that temporary popularity, much less unpopularity, as distinct from the verdict of posterity, has much to do with the merits or demerits of a people. Every nation in its turn comes in for a gust of international dislike. The weaker a power, the less likely she is to earn foreign animosity; but that does not prove her to be any the better on that account.

About the year 1848, Lord Palmerston, our Foreign Secretary, was so disliked all over the Continent, that they used to sing a ditty in the streets of Vienna ending—

> "And if the devil has a son,
> He surely must be Palmerston."

Yet we are not told that this did Lord Palmerston any harm in his own country.

Now, as regards the partial unpopularity of Germany of to-day, all I can say is that, as a student of the German nation, I do not join in that feeling. Not that I deny there may be some cause for it ; but whatever it may be, I do not let it affect my judgment of the nation, which I respect, nor of its culture, which I greatly admire.

If the Germans try to beat us in politics, my common sense

6)

tells me that we, as a great power, are perfectly well able to stand up and defend our own interests if they are trespassed upon.

As for the poor German princes whom we think fit to call over to our shores, and endow with money and position, and who at our Radicals are constantly railing, my common sense again tells me that it is WE who are to blame for being so liberal, not *they* for accepting our bounty. I know of one or two impecunious English *noblemen* who pass through the bankruptcy court with amiable regularity, and who would only be too delighted to go and live in clover in Germany, if that country were so foolish as to pay them to do so. I also know of a few German princes who are almost as wealthy as our wealthiest peers, and who would not care to come over here and accept our favours.

As for German competition in the labour markets, there are undoubtedly pushing traders in Germany as there are here. Well, competitors in trade are never congenial acquaintances. But as for the Germans underselling us, and living on nothing in doing so, I do not believe these are the causes that need make us fear German competition. I believe there are as many poor Englishmen at the present time forced to live on starvation wages as any German. No, believe me, the main cause of German success in the labour markets is to be found in the superior culture and education of the masses !

I cannot hope to prove that to you to-day ; I can only ask you to accept it at present on trust, to be proved, perhaps, with your kind permission, on some future occasion. All I can do to-day is to draw your attention to some features of German culture which I think may interest you, and to be impartial in doing so.

In the first place, the very subject of my lecture, "Culture," almost precludes an exact division of light and shade, of advantages and drawbacks. These are to be found everywhere and in everything. We do not *all* believe in the Old Testament notion of the "chosen people." It smacks too much of privilege and favouritism for our taste. It seems more natural to believe that every people has its special failures and its compensating virtues. And if it happens to be my set task to-day to illustrate a bright side of the German people, that does not mean that you cannot find the same amount of envy and uncharitableness in Germany as we can show of cant and hypocrisy in England.

But we do not analyse shadows when we are dwelling on the characteristics of light. And those must be left to take care of themselves to-day, even at the risk of your fancying that I ignore their existence. It is well known that in Berlin and elsewhere the struggle of life is becoming as severe as with us. In Germany, as elsewhere, there are social problems to be solved which culture alone can neither solve nor put out of sight. But I believe firmly that there are hardly any political or social problems the solution of which will not be ultimately facilitated for any nation by widespread education and an exalted standard of thinking.

Culture, in its higher sense, has hitherto with us been the privilege of the few. I maintain that in the future many of its attainable features must become accessible to all. For when I speak of the *culture* of a nation, I do not mean an artificial refinement, nor do I refer to a privileged, cultured class. I refer to the thought and aspirations of many millions, including the best of all classes.

In this sense, I look upon "culture" as the very sun that brightens the daily life of a nation. And if on this point I am guilty of partisanship for Germany, it springs from the belief that I have sometimes seen more true dignity of life and enjoyment among the population *there* than *here*, strange as this statement may appear to you.

Only the other day I was talking to a friend, a hard-headed, matter-of-fact London solicitor. He said to me that he could not understand why I often seemed so favourably impressed by Germany. "Well," I replied, "you yourself have often been there. Tell me honestly, where has it struck you that there seems to be more happiness among the people—here or there?" His immediate reply was, "Undoubtedly in Germany." "Well, then," I answered, "that is my justification."

Let me take an incident at random from Christmas time in Germany as evidence of what I mean. The *Standard* contained a telegram the other day from Berlin stating that over 400,000 Christmas trees had been disposed of there. That means practically a Christmas tree in every family in the capital. That means a gathering of good-will and an exchange of presents, however trifling, in every family, down to the humblest working-man of the community.

Surely no insignificant sign that, notwithstanding blood-tax and heavy money taxation, there exists in Germany a universal feeling of culture in a family sense, and the means to gratify it in an almost unparalleled proportion. If I have admired the beauties of nature in Germany, the culture of the educated; if I have participated in the enjoyments of the wealthy, as well as in the simpler pastimes of the humble, my enjoyment has seldom been spoilt by the sight of the hard, cold, cheerless life of the many. And I adhere to this, notwithstanding the important fact that the masses in this country hardly pay any direct taxes at all, whereas they are almost always paying petty taxes in Germany.

These may seem strong statements to you, who mostly only hear of foreign countries as so much behind our own, and of their people as only deserving pity in their thraldom; but what is more, I am morally certain, that if you had lived in Germany or France, and knew these countries as I fancy I do, you would share my views. I have found plenty of travelled Englishmen who feel even stronger on this subject than I do.

And now I must ask your indulgence for the apparent egoism of these few preliminary personal remarks. But I judged them necessary, in order to enable you the better to understand the drift of my lecture. For it is really no easy matter to give you even a faint idea of German culture in the sixty minutes at my disposal.

To begin with, what is culture? Like most terms of far-reaching application, it is somewhat difficult to give a concise definition of it. The word itself would seem to mean simply the process of cultivation; something that is cultivated; a soil that has been ploughed, that is eager to produce. The Germans even use the very term *Kultur*, as applied equally to a high state of mental education and also to a tilled soil—*Culturboden*. And I think you will find the same wide application of the word in some English dictionaries.

And yet that will not give us a sufficient indication of the word's meaning. For the Americans, with all their excellent school training, are in some respects less cultured than the uneducated Italians. The French, again, although vastly inferior to the Germans in book knowledge, are, from some points of view, perhaps more cultured than the Germans.

The explanation of the above contradiction must be sought and will be found in the fuller explanation of the meaning of the term itself. Culture does not stand alone for the amount of exact knowledge or talents we possess, be they artistic, practical, or scientific. It includes in its significance the feeling for refinement, for the fitness of things in general. Thus a man who, with imperfect mental attainments, combines a refinement of feeling for the sufferings or the wants or susceptibilities of others —a fulness of true sympathy, as opposed to a false, hysterical, diseased sentiment—is in many respects more cultured than a walking encyclopædia of knowledge, combined with coarseness of manner and feeling.

Self-respect, in its best sense, is part of all true culture, even when possessed by the unlettered.   And this speciality of culture will be found most prevalent in those countries in which the dignity of labour is most generally recognised.   That rare quality, *tact of the heart*, which enables us to respect ourselves in showing a proper regard for the feelings of others, is a part of true culture that may be learnt by mixing with the world, but which is ever best exemplified when it is inborn.   I have seen it in *some* of very humble station, and found it wanting in *many* holding exalted position.

Again, a proper respect for women is a special feature of true culture, and one in which, I make bold to say, Englishmen are perhaps second only to our own race beyond the seas.

Another point of culture, in which the long stability of our political system has undoubtedly given us a striking pre-eminence, is the great respect we have in England for established law.   This feeling extends even towards the law's humblest representative. The moral ascendency of the English policeman I hold to be unparalleled in the world.

Another point, which I venture to think is not unconnected with our prosperous and great national history, is a certain generosity and breadth of mind we often meet with in England in judging others.   I may be biassed in this, but it has struck me in comparison with the rapidity and ease with which I have found slander and misrepresentation travel and propagate in some other countries.   Bigotry and intolerance, class pride and class selfishness, are incompatible with true culture, which itself is synonymous with a broad and generous cast of mind.

Again, the mere £ *s. d.* utilitarian, whose narrow mental horizon does not enable him to discern even the indirect money value of knowledge, let alone its power of adding to the dignity of our life, he will pooh-pooh our ideas of culture, and simply ask, " What is your bank balance ? "   " Very little."   " Well, then, you are a pauper, with all your culture."

Such was the frame of mind of an otherwise worthy citizen, to whom a friend of mine showed a complimentary letter he had been honoured with by Mr. Gladstone, whose birthday it is to-day. Now, I think you will agree with me, that whatever political party we may belong to, we may look upon a personal compliment from an intellectual giant such as Mr. Gladstone as a high honour. But our worthy citizen thought otherwise, and merely asked, " Is there a cheque in the letter ? " This man was slightly wanting in the sense of reverence—an important one in all culture.

It is true the apostles of culture do not often amass riches. The late Mr. Matthew Arnold died the other day little better than a pauper, from a banker's point of view. He did not write books that were read by the million. But the day may come when such books, though on a broader basis, will touch the minds of the million as Dickens' works now touch their heart; and then it will be plainly seen that the one goes hand in hand with the other—the heart with the mind—in educating us to feel the beauty and dignity of life on this earth. However, I will not tax your attention any farther by vague generalisations, but rather try and make my meaning clear by explanation as I go along.

To begin with, I think I can discern three distinct, broad lines of culture—that of the mind, that of the heart, and, thirdly, the culture of the body. Now, taking the last first, if we accept the splendid advertisements of "Pears' Soap," of "Sunlight Soap," of "Brooke's Soap" that "won't wash clothes," and many others, as any criterion to go by, we must either be dreadfully in want of soap, or we really ought to be bodily the cleanest nation on the face of the earth ; and if you believe it, no word of mine shall cast a doubt on your faith.

In that other important branch of body-culture—namely, our outdoor sports, and hygienic science in general—I think it is less open to doubt that the Anglo-Saxon race is really the first in the world. Indeed, the indomitable spirit of emulation and rivalry shown in the practice of athletics is not unconnected with our mighty history of colonisation and world-power. But as I do not believe in the uncompensated superiority of any people all round, so also I cannot help remarking that the prevalence of the spirit of gambling and betting is a direct outcome of some forms of sport, and goes far to moderate our complacency.

As for the culture of the heart, the splendid record of individual unselfish effort for the good of others that is stamped on every page in our national history, the charity of the wealthy, the devotion of the humble,—these show us what our race is capable of, and make me feel it unnecessary to stray at large under this heading in order to point a moral or adorn a tale.

Now, let us note what the great Russian novelist Turgenieff has to say on German culture. He expresses his views very unmistakably in a letter dated 18th August 1862 :—"When you leave muddy Poland and arrive on German soil, you find yourself, as it were, in a radiant land. The poor Slavonic race! We blame Hegel for having assigned to the Slavs a less illustrious mission than to the German family. Alas! every one can convince himself that Hegel was right. Civilisation is worked out, not by ideas, but by manners. Yes, here *es wird behaglich zu muthe* (a sense of comfort comes over me) ; this is mainly because my intellectual development is associated with Germany. Not to mention philosophy and poetry, even German humour is after my own heart. Alas! our Russian so-called education disposes us to imitate rather French morals, and the more is the pity. Moreover, what pleases us in French education are its bad sides—notably its licentiousness and its slipshod ways ; it is mostly these things that the Russian selects and assimilates. The German spirit, which is made up wholly of discipline, is not in harmony with our nature. What a pity that Russian tourists merely pass through Berlin, without entering into the spirit of the place! Only good schools can cure us of our superficiality."

It is to some aspects of the German spirit that I wish to draw attention, and particularly to one special feature thereof—the unconscious endeavour to make the everyday aspect of life less cold and cheerless, particularly to those who are not blessed with wealth and other worldly advantages. This special German feature seems to me to be a joint product of heart and mind, acting for generations past in rare unison, in a direction already marked out for us, although on somewhat different lines, by the ancient Greeks, the most cultured people of antiquity.

That truly great and good man, Abraham Lincoln—in my humble opinion one of the most cultured men we have seen in our time—had a jocular habit of illustrating his most important utterances by the following playful words : "Now, let me tell you a little story."

Among my memories of Germany, few have retained such a firm hold of my thoughts as a little woodcut taken out of an American illustrated paper. It represented an elderly German citizen in bed, reading by the light of an enormously long candle, stuck into a small shaky candlestick. The bedcover, one of those dreadful feather-bed counterpanes to be met with perhaps only in Germany, reached from his chin down to somewhere a little below his knees. Underneath this realistic sketch the following words were printed :

"The candle too long, the bedclothes too short; but what does it matter as long as you are happy?"

It seems to me there is a world of fact and of food for thought in that little sketch and in those accompanying words. In the first place, note the small, shaky candlestick. Could there be a more apt illustration of the one great drawback of much we might otherwise admire in Germany—namely, the want of practical ability in everyday matters?—one of the qualities the possession of which has long given the Anglo-Saxon people such a start in the race for wealth. I never remember seeing a properly-fitting candlestick in Germany, and it is only lately that German beds are anything like the practical coaxers to rest that we are accustomed to here. The political misery and the poverty of the past have undoubtedly had a deal to do with the neglect of this department of culture—namely, the culture of "comfort." But in this respect Germany has made great strides within the last twenty years.

Now, coming back to my woodcut, let me draw your attention to the fact that this man is in bed—at first sight a trivial circumstance, but in reality a most instructive one. He might be sitting up and drinking, or, worse still, be out at some music hall or public-house. Not that this German is a henpecked husband, who dare not go out and enjoy himself; or that he, like an English blue-ribbonite, never indulges in malt liquor. Far from it. He polishes off his mug of beer at his favourite beer-house, where the humblest, and some of the high and well-born too, mingle and behave themselves. He whiles away an hour there in the congenial company of the educated men of the town, for he is no psalm-singer, who denies himself the harmless enjoyments of life. But he keeps early hours, he goes to bed at a reasonable time—in fact, he is a moral man.

Oh, you may say, it is late, and the public-houses are closed; and there you would be sadly mistaken. In the first place, there are no public-houses in Germany. The culture of the German people would prevent their patronising such dens of adulteration and cold-blooded drink. In the second place, there are no Draconic early-closing laws in Germany. It is even a great question whether the politically down-trodden German would tamely submit to such tyranny, let alone local option or total prohibition. Only some years ago there was a riot, attended with bloodshed, merely because of an attempt to raise the price of beer. It would want a bold legislator indeed to dare to tell the humblest German to give up his harmless glass of beer, and turn out at the strike of the clock into the street like so many children. But as there is no coercion, so there is little drunkenness, although no teetotalism, and that notwithstanding the unlimited hours the beer-houses are allowed to remain open. The case of Germany goes to show, that it is self-respect, and not prohibition or enforced pledges of teetotalism, that will make a nation sober.

As I said before, the subject of my sketch is in bed, and even risking to set fire to the bed-clothes and to catch rheumatism in his lower extremities, in order to improve his mind before courting the slumbers of the just; for I feel convined that he is reading some instructive book—perhaps Darwin's *Origin of the Species.* Yes, it is this wonderful thirst for useful knowledge which distinguishes the whole German people, and mentally ennobles them. This is one of the most striking features of their wide-spread culture; for the Germans look upon intellectual know-ledge as something almost divine, something to be regarded with reverence, to be worshipped for its own sake.

It is this trait in the national character which explains the extraordinary influence the poet Goethe, as a man and as a thinker, has exercised over the minds of his countrymen. And here the Germans possess a great advantage over us, who unfortunately know next to nothing of the personality of our greatest countryman, *Shakespeare.* We can only judge what an immense loss this is to English culture, when we know what Goethe's personality has been to Germany.

Take away the poet Goethe, who, perhaps, of all moderns, has best rendered and revived the Grecian ideals of the beauty and dignity of life, and there remains the intellectual character of the man, to whom every fruit from the tree of knowledge and truth was a prize to live for, and the search of which was its own reward. "Oh," he once exclaimed, "that I could come again in a hundred years, if only to see and enjoy the sight of the progress mankind will have made in that time along the path of truth." And these words strike the key-note of the best culture of Germany—the love of scientific truth, of mankind, the unselfish interest in its progress and happiness.

No field of learning but what Goethe strove to work in it; not in a spirit of vanity, or with a feverish longing for worldly honour and the noisy recognition of the multitude; no, from pure love of truth itself, of which our own poet Keats so aptly says—

"Beauty is truth, truth beauty;
That is all ye know on earth, and all ye need to know."

Goethe, as is well known, foreshadowed the conclusions since drawn from Darwin's works, which in our time have revolutionised our conception of cosmogony. It was Goethe, the friend of princes, who, in the character of Faust, teaches the highest philosophy to all—namely, that happiness is only to be found in the fulfilment of duty, useful work done for the benefit of all. Faust, after passing through every stage of worldly power and enjoyment without obtaining rest, at last finds contentment as a tiller of the soil! But even where his efforts were incomplete or unproductive, his example has remained a constant spur to the intellect of Germany. Well might such a man exclaim, *without vanity*, on being created a noble: "The dignity of nobility has nothing surprising in store for me; I was not conscious of an addition to my standing." For him there could only exist the truly aristocratic distinctions of mind and character.

To Goethe is in great part owing the wonderful appreciation of Shakespeare, Walter Scott, Burns, and Byron we find all over Germany. Of Shakespeare he once said, "When I think of Shakspeare, I cannot understand how I can have the audacity to attempt anything." And yet Goethe knew that he, too, was destined to be immortal; but, like all true greatness, it is ever found hand in hand with the recognition of kindred genius. It is reserved for the Liliputian to cavil at those whose size makes him doubly conscious of his littleness.

I have travelled much in Germany, and I think you would be surprised if I could tell you of the widespread admiration and knowledge to be met with everywhere of our English literature, and of our English greatness of thought and action. The Germans stand first in their eager recognition of the best in foreign countries. We might well learn from them in this. A German schoolmaster once told me: "I always urge my pupils to read Sir Walter Scott. In the first place, he is a glorious novelist; and then the perusal of his works inculcates a nobility of aim and feeling that are only too rare nowadays in this money-making age."

Shakespeare is known to all in the Fatherland, and I might even say the same of Dickens—that great poet of the human heart, as an eminent German man of letters once styled him to me. The other day I read in the *Times* (Nov. 18, 1889) respecting German theatres: "The stage interpretation of Shakespeare is rapidly rising to a higher level in Germany even than in England." How neatly put, "even than in England"! I cannot understand these circumlocutions, when it is so easy to speak the truth. Why not state the plain truth—namely, that the stage interpretation of Shakespeare in Germany is not "rapidly rising," but rather that it has long been far above that, "even" in England? There are at least a dozen towns in Germany in which you may any day witness not only as good representations of Shakespeare as our best, but many masterpieces of Shakespeare that are never performed in England at all, because they don't pay. But they pay in poor, military-ridden Germany, because the Germans love Shakespeare. The mind of Shakespeare is one of the corner-stones of German culture. They have fairly gained a right to love the greatest Englishman that ever lived. They have won him for themselves by studying and reverencing his divine spirit—perhaps the proudest conquest in the field of intellect to be met with in the history of the world, this conquering love of a foreign nation of forty millions for a humble Englishman who lived three hundred years ago! If I wished to pay the spirit of German culture, in one sentence, the highest encomium I can think of, it would be that it is worthy of sharing the proudest boast of the Anglo-Saxon race—namely, the possession of Shakespeare.

The other day I was reading an account of the foundation of Cavendish College, Cambridge. I may add that its peculiar feature is to consist in its cheapness, and in the desire to help forward the industrious but poor student—a most praiseworthy intention, no doubt, and one which is hailed by a public organ with pleasure as a new endeavour to bring the universities and the people into closer communion. But it is somewhat strange to read such a mouthful about so little in the freest country in the world !

Why, in poor despotic Germany there are twenty-two universities, some of them far larger in number of students than any of our English ones. Talk of our tiny, new-fangled thread of communion between the universities and the people! Why, the German universities are almost identical with the German people ; the former are part of the latter, as the heart is part of the human frame. The youth of the German people, in their twenty-two universities, are not the representatives of the respectability of a class, but have long been the torchbearers of every national ideal striving towards independence and culture. The German nation did not want the threatening wave of democracy in order to open up the portals of instruction to the poor. Education has been gratuitously open to the poorest in Germany for generations.

If it be true, as a thinker has said, that "the elevation and expansion of the individual is the true aim of government," then I say, without fear of contradiction, that, as far as culture is concerned—the beautifying of our daily life, its dignity and its happiness—even the petty German governments of the past have in many ways more to show than we, with all our boasted machinery of ballot-boxes—which, by-the-by, the Germans have now got into the bargain, as well as universal suffrage.

It is but lately that it has been thought worth while to educate our people at all. The word education is not to be found in the gospel of the Manchester school of middle-class money-bags, with their ten commandments summed up into one, "Buy in the cheapest, and sell in the dearest market." Sell your soul to the devil, if necessary; but keep a bank balance, be respectable, and court popularity if you can. Germany has its unscrupulous devotees of the laws of supply and demand as well as we have. It has its greedy traders, who would adulterate every article of food if they dare—the only difference being *they dare not;* but they do not rule Germany, much less represent German culture.

We have certainly secured the almost unlimited political liberty of the subject. That is undoubtedly a great gain, though due as much to our favoured geographical position as to our matchless national virtues. But we have, up to the present, lived under an almost despotic social tyranny. We have hitherto neglected the mental and moral well-being of the helpless unit, and been content to leave him unfettered to fight the battle of "the devil take the hindermost" without much care of his mental status.

I do not deny that this hard struggle has done a great deal to foster that manliness and energy for which the English national character is noted throughout the world. I do not deny that our political freedom has given us, in some sense, the supremacy of the individual, as against a fussy bureaucracy. But I think well enough of my countrymen to believe that we might retain these qualities, and yet pour a little light on the lives of those whose fight in the battle of life is at best but sunless and dark.

Hitherto it is the strictly practical that has guided us most. I think it is time to mix a little ideality with the elixir of life. Fortunately, we are tending in that direction, but more through the initiative of private individuals than through the action of our responsible authorities. It is by means of such societies as that before whom I am lecturing, and of which so many have spontaneously sprung up in this country, that charitable individuals seek to make up and atone for a ruthless system of neglect.

We thought little of education as long as it only meant to us a higher perception of life to the people, a weapon to emancipate us from social and mental slavery. Not that I mean we are forcibly enslaved by others, but rather by *ourselves*, through our ignorance and want of true culture. Unlike some politically backward people, we are undoubtedly free in a political sense—the pity is that want of culture often prevents our using the freedom which the franchise has given us. For I contend, that being so favoured through our geographical position in our past political history, we ought to enjoy every advantage other nations possess, and a deal more besides which they have been unable to attain. In money we are the richest nation in the world; I see no reason why we should not be the happiest and the most cultured, *which, I maintain, we are not.*

We only adopted popular education when we adopted breech-loaders. When the German wars of 1866 and 1870 suddenly revealed to our surprise that education also helped to make a nation fight successfully; and when it had fought, to compete with us in commerce, and to send over its better-educated sons here, and take the bread out of the mouth of our neglected, untutored countrymen. And this may show you what I omitted to refer to at the beginning—namely, that superior education may also assist us to prosper in an £ s. d. sense.

Now, you may say this is all very well, but seeing is believing. Where are the tangible proofs and results of all this culture to be seen? How can you trace their connection with the well-being of the community?

Well, then, let us cast a glance at the outward aspects of the country. It is not so very long ago that the poet Coleridge referred to Cologne as the town of ugly wenches and nasty stenches. Now, I am not going to say that the physical beauty of the modern representatives of the mythical eleven thousand virgins—God bless them!—has improved since the days of Coleridge, nor do I say that sanitary science is as yet as far advanced in Germany as it is with us. This, as I said before, is a branch of culture in which we are still ahead of the Germans, though it may not be for long. For *there* at least we witness the honest and thorough application of old-fashioned principles by the corporations, whereas with us the best scientific systems are sometimes negligently and dishonestly applied by our parochial authorities.

F

However, I do say I only wish, in order to prove the truth of
a few of my contentions, that I could accompany some of you
on a fortnight's trip through the Germany of to-day.

It would be doubly instructive to you at the present time, when
we read daily of the dishonest extravagance of our hospitals ; the
jerrybuilding of our board schools, and its consequences of typhoid
fever and diphtheria ; the dirt of our metropolitan bakehouses,
swarming with vermin ; the dirt of our military barracks, of our
police-cells, and sundry other unsavoury little indications that
our institutions are not yet all that they might be.

I would only ask you to come in a fair frame of mind, not in
that of a lamented club friend of mine, whom I once met in one
of the most picturesque of the many lovely German watering-
places. "How do you like Kissingen?" I asked. "Why, they
haven't got a decent glass of brandy at the hotel, and I can't get
up a rubber of whist in the whole blessed place !"

I think I could show you dozens of towns in Germany with
finer and better-kept streets and public buildings than our own.
The town of Frankfort, for instance, one of the most beautiful
and most wealthy towns of Europe, has as low a death-rate as
even our most favoured seaside health resorts, and that notwithstanding a drainage system that does not come up to our
standard. Or, take a typical smaller town, such as Hildesheim, in
Hanover, a coloured print of which I have brought for your inspection. This is a town of about 20,000 inhabitants ; and if you look
at the print, you will see among its sights five different buildings
of public schools, every one of which is of interesting, if not of
commanding architecture.

Walk through the streets of any one of these German towns
on a Sunday. *You will find them as clean as a new pin.* You
will find the shops closed after mid-day, and the people enjoying
themselves in a sensible, healthy fashion. In larger towns,
where there are museums and picture-galleries, they are open
from early in the day. In the afternoon the population has
flocked out to the numberless coffee and beer gardens in the
suburbs, where they are sitting in family groups, all classes inter-
mingled, listening to the military bands. Suddenly the people
rise from their seats and take off their hats, but no one leaves
their places. It is only the king and queen taking an afternoon
walk with their children, and passing along the country road
adjoining the beer gardens. The king's family has reigned
over the country more than 800 years in one unbroken line.

He himself is acknowledged to be one of the best military leaders of the country. The people, although strongly democratic in feeling, have a great respect for their ruler and his family; but they don't rush after them and mob them. Their tact, their *self-respect*, prevent them doing so. Also, the royal family is to be seen almost daily walking among the people, and returning their respectful silent greetings. Towards evening many stroll back to town and crowd the theatres, where, on a Sunday, almost always some classical plays or high-class operas are given.

In few things is the CULTURE of Germany more apparent than in the sound character of their amusements, inviting all classes alike by their excellence and cheapness.

It is true you are reminded everywhere of the military characteristics of the nation. The whole nation is in arms; it is a sad fact, but at least it is not for conquest. But even here the effects of "culture" are strongly visible. Go back to the Franco-German war, and history — I believe even French history—will tell you that, during a six months' influx of nearly a million men in an enemy's country, flushed with the excitement of victory, there is not one single authenticated instance recorded of insult to a woman. If you want to know what that means, you can take the trouble to read up the detailed records of a few previous struggles in the history of this century.

I remember being present in Berlin at the triumphal entry of the troops, 45,000 men, in July 1871. The town was so crowded that I had to pay 15s. a-night for being allowed to lie down at night on the floor with several others in a fifth-rate hotel. I think I was on and off the pavement that day from five in the morning till nearly five the next morning, and I can assure you that I did not see one single drunken person.

But let us come back to our times. Look in on a German town on a week-day, and pass the public schools. You will be struck by the palatial buildings, situated on the finest sites, reserved for the education of all classes alike, at which instruction is given free to all alike. Come nearer, the windows are wide open, and you may just happen to witness the singing lesson, and hear the youthful voices sing one of those glorious choral songs of Martin Luther :—

> " God is a mighty citadel,
> A trusty shield and weapon."

Let us come away out for a stroll in the open country. You

may not see many mansions of the immensely wealthy nobility ; but what there is will not be walled round with bricks and ornamented with boards advising you that you will be prosecuted by the lord of the manor if you dare try to look at and trespass on the choicest bits of scenery of your country, the private property of a few. I say, it was want of culture of the heart that originally made landowners surround their property with brick walls, broken bottle glass, and iron fences. In Germany you can, as a rule, at all times walk, unhindered and unheeded, in the private grounds and gardens of the great. You can see and rejoice in all—gardens, orchards, and vineyards; and nobody will be there to watch you, and warn you that you are a trespasser. But also nobody would dream of robbing an orchard in Germany. A people is backward in culture, discipline, and self-respect that cannot be trusted to pass under a tree without pilfering its fruit. But the sight of fruit is no incentive to theft in Germany. A numerous peasant class exists. They are landowners and fruit-growers. In fact, throughout the greater part of Germany the public high roads are lined with fruit-trees, and passers by are kindly allowed to pick up whatever falls to the ground.

Walk on. You may come upon some big factory, nowhere a very picturesque sight ; but in Germany sometimes anything but an ugly one. You may even chance to come when work is stopped. The workmen are all marshalled in military fashion in a large courtyard, for they have all been soldiers, workmen, clerks, and employers alike, and as often as not the latter as privates in the ranks. You ask, What is the matter? It is the fifty years' jubilee of an old workman. There is going to be a little speech-making, and a concert afterwards by the band of the men. The head of the firm is going to hand a gold watch to the workman in question ; more important still, the reigning prince of the petty state has sent down one of his own ministers in *person* to deliver the gold medal for faithful service to the humble workman.

This may be a bit of the comedy of paternal government ; it may be mere sentiment. Then all I can say is, the world is the poorer for the lack of a little of such sentiment. Now, if you are not already tired of my company, then come back to the German town with me. It is already dark, but we are met by a vast surging concourse of people. A brilliant torchlight procession marches past, followed by a large crowd and a band playing— not one of those wretched German bands you see, and unfortun-ately hear too, in London, which do not hail from Germany at all, which are in fact forbidden there. No, it is a band composed of citizens, some of whom have fought in twenty pitched battles in defence of their country, and have the medal on their breast to testify to it. What is it all about? we ask. Oh, it is the twenty-five years' jubilee of a popular lady-teacher at one of the public schools, and the different trade-unions have turned out to do honour to her, and to bring her a serenade! Stand still a moment in the crowd, and let your thoughts wander. I fancy it would take a strong dose of insular prejudice to make you believe that you are standing in midst of the unhappy population of a down-trodden, despotic, military-ridden country!

Now, in conclusion, let me come back to the little woodcut I mentioned to you, and the words inscribed beneath it, "What does it then matter as long as you are happy?" There you have the key-note of my thoughts on the culture of Germany—the wish to point out a few items illustrative of the dignity, self-respect, and happiness of the greatest number; and I cannot but think that, notwithstanding the unavoidable blood-tax of a so-called, but wrongly so-called, despotic government, *in some respects the Germans are happier than we are, if not than we might be;* and if so, their culture, fostered by their government, has largely contributed to that result.

VI.

RUSSIA.

W. R. MORFILL, M.A.

M Y hearers may imagine that in the short space of an hour I should never be able to exhaust all that can be said about Russia—certainly one of the most interesting of European countries. All I can hope to do is to set before you on this occasion some of the most noteworthy points in the political, historical, and social life of this great people.

I have some fear that I shall not carry the sympathies of all my audience with me, and there will be some who will find my lecture dull, when I say frankly at the beginning that I have no stories of Socialists or Nihilists, no revelations of "underground Russia," as it is called, to communicate.

In the first place, we shall probably be best able to realise the importance of Russia as a factor in European politics if we consider the area of the country and the number of its population. The former exceeds 8,500,000 square miles, and, according to the valuable article contributed to the last edition of the *Encyclopædia Britannica*, the gross total of the inhabitants is one hundred and six millions. Of course in this aggregate a great number of races are included, the Slavs largely predominating. The Russians, if we add the Malo-Russians in the South, and the White Russians in the West, amount to more than sixty-three millions. These form the dominant race, and the dominant tongue is the Great Russian, which is now the only language allowed to be spoken at court, and has been so since the days of Nicholas. During last century and the early part of the present, French was in vogue— just as it was at the German court and in Sweden; but when a people have risen to self-consciousness, they don't care any longer to talk in the idiom of the foreigner. Such a habit argues a degraded condition in a nation, and it speaks well for the English that during last century, when the French language had such world-wide influence, our grandfathers and great grandfathers never tolerated anything else than their native Saxon. At the present time, no one can hold any office in Russia who is not acquainted with the national language in which all business is transacted.

After the Slavs come the Litu-Lettish, the Ural-Altaic, and Tatar races. These populations cannot be said to affect the solidarity of the Russian Empire. The first amount to about three millions. They are an ancient people, who have been driven, as it were, into remote corners by advancing races. They have been receding since the commencement of the historical period. They remained pagans longer than any other of the European populations. They were converted in a rather violent manner in the fourteenth century, but when Herberstein travelled among them at the beginning of the sixteenth, he found them in some places still worshipping lizards.

Russia, as early as the time of Peter the Great, had acquired a portion of Finland; the rest of the country was ceded by Sweden to Russia by the peace of Frederikshamm in 1809. Up to this time the Finns have been able to preserve their diet, and have enjoyed autonomy, but we have been hearing latterly that these valuable privileges are going to be taken away from them. Let us hope that the report will not prove true. Certainly the Finnish language has developed under Russian protection; under the Swedes it had been depressed, but now the professors in the University of Helsingfors deliver their lectures in it.

The Turco-Tatar races inhabiting Russia are numerous, amounting to 3,629,000. They are in a backward state, and offer little to our notice that is interesting. They do not exhibit any disloyalty to Russia, and indeed do not seem to have any powers of cohesion. During the last Turco-Russian war, as Leroy-Beaulieu has told us, prayers were offered up in all the mosques of the Caucasus for the success of the Russian arms. Perhaps it is true of Russia, as it is also true of us with regard to our own Mussulman subjects, that they would rise against us, if we showed any weakness; but this is the nature of subject-races, especially of the conceited and ignorant Mussulman, when he is under the dominion of the *giaour*, whom he is pleased to think his inferior. I remember reading years ago, in a book on the Indian mutiny, how changed the manner of the native servants became towards their masters, when they thought that the *raj* of the Europeans was coming to an end.

A few words must now be said about the Poles and Germans.

Of the former there are many in Russia, not only in the old kingdom of Poland, now divided into Russian governments, but also in the Ukraine and Lithuania, where they form the landed proprietors. They amount to nearly six millions. The feud between the Russians and Poles is of long standing. We have it as early as the time of the wars between Stephen Bathory and Ivan the Terrible, in the sixteenth century, and the occupation of Moscow by the Poles under Wladyslaw or Ladislaus the Second. The latter by force of arms caused himself to be elected Tsar, and held the supreme power for two years, owing to the exhausted state of the country, for it is impossible to conceive the Russians tolerating for any lengthened period a sovereign of the Latin faith. The iniquitous dismemberments of Poland which took place last century are well known. I shall say nothing to attempt to exonerate Russia in this matter, but we must remember that the blame is to be shared by the Prussians and Austrians. The spoliation was not begun by Russia, as must be acknowledged in all fairness. The plan was suggested to Catherine by Frederick the Great, through the agency of his brother Prince Henry, when he visited St. Petersburg. Austria has treated her Polish subjects well, but the same cannot be said of Prussia. A Polish gentleman once complained to me of the complete Germanisation of the province of Posen : the names of villages and small towns, some of which are of historical celebrity, are changed into Sedan, Weissenburg, and Bismarckdorf; the porters at the stations are Germans, and the apparent Germanisation of the country is complete, but you have only to step a few yards from the railway station and you will frequently find yourself in a country where hardly a word of German is understood. As I have said before, it is impossible on the present occasion to enter into a discussion about these melancholy events. I can only say that the Pole, in his relations with the Russian, is dealing with a brother Slav, who does not regard him as an inferior being, as the German affects to do. Some of my hearers will perhaps remember the sarcastic verses of Heine on the Poles, who, although by origin a Jew—a people who, we must confess with shame, have been grossly ill-treated and despised—still writes with the most aristocratic race-hatred when dealing with the Slavs; such is the inconsistency of human nature.

There is another powerful alien element in Russia—the German. Now we hear a great deal about the Germans in the Baltic provinces, and the Russian encroachments upon them.

The Germans nave plenty to say about the Muskovitischer, Byzantinismus, and other things of the kind; but, of course, the Germans dwelling in these provinces have no more to do in reality with the German Empire, than the inhabitants of the Channel Islands have to do with the French Republic. Prince Kropotkin, in his valuable article already alluded to, tells us that, in the Baltic provinces, the prevailing population is Esthonian, Curonian, or Lettish; the Germans (landlords in the country or tradesmen and artizans in the towns) in the three provinces, Riga included, hardly reach a total of 120,000 out of 1,800,000 inhabitants. The relations of the Esthonians and Letts to their landlords are anything but friendly.

I must here quote an anecdote which my friend, the late Yuri Samaun (one of the most eminent of Russian patriots), told me, which illustrates the spirit in which the Baltic Germans have but too often acted towards the native population. Some years ago an Esthonian Finn emigrated from one of these provinces to America and made a considerable fortune there. Being, I suppose, at length overcome by a sort of *nostalgie* or *mal de pays*, he resolved to return to his native country, and on coming back spent a part of his fortune in founding a handsome Finnish club. The German inhabitants, who had always considered the Finns a kind of prolétariat, were highly indignant; such a thing had never been known before. What right had a semi-civilised race to such social privileges? I merely quote this anecdote to show what has been the state of feeling there, and not to engender race-hatred, still less to speak disrespectfully of a race with which Englishmen are so closely connected, and which has furnished to the world so many eminent men.

The Semitic race is represented by three millions of Jews, chiefly in Poland, in west and south-west Russia, and the Caucasus. There is also the peculiar sect of the Jews called the Karaites in the Crimea; they are found in considerable numbers in the picturesque city of Baktshi-Serai, once the residence of the Khans. It is deeply to be regretted that in the last few years some obsolete laws to the prejudice of the Jews should have been revived in Russia. Some of them, however, have already been abrogated. I can only join with the eminent Frenchman Leroy-Beaulieu, who has written so well upon Russia, in his eloquent appeal to the Czar to grant complete religious freedom throughout his dominions—a policy especially necessary in a country which can show such varieties of belief among its inhabitants. Certainly the feudal maxim, "*Cujus est regio ejus est religio*," is long since obsolete. Whatever the policy of the government may be, the Russian peasant cannot be accused of intolerance. He is found living peaceably side by side with Mohammedans in many parts of Russia. If there is any antipathy felt towards the Jews by the peasant, it is because he thinks he is exploited by him. Careful observers of the matter all concur in this view. It is more the *Kahal*, or Jewish economic society, that the peasant fears than any dogma. In some periods of Russian history Judaism has actually made many converts.

Russia has not many populous cities. The list is headed by St. Petersburg with 929,090, but many of the so-called towns of Russia are in reality little better than villages. Catherine created several, which after her death fell into insignificance. The fact is, the Slav, where he is not mixed with other races, is a pure agriculturist, and has few trading tendencies. It was the want of an active middle class which threw all the trade of Poland into the hands of Germans and Jews, and was one of the main causes of the fall of the Republic. It has been truly remarked of that unhappy country that there was no sympathy between the nobility and peasantry, and therefore no national spirit. The Jews who busied themselves with commerce sold at the same time to the serfs and their masters, and thus prevented the two classes from coming in contact with each other. They carried on the economic functions of everyday life, and yet could not be considered a part of the nation.

I have but little time for anything more than a few general remarks on the physical geography of Russia, but something must be said, because it is only from realising this that we are able to explain some of the facts of the history of a nation.

Russia, as a whole, is a vast plain; high plateaus and mountains are only met with in the Asiatic parts of the Empire. These flat lands vary in their characteristics—sometimes they are dry deserts or low table-lands, or lake regions, or marshy plains. There is the splendid Caucasian range which separates Europe from Asia, and in the east of Siberia there are volcanoes. When in 1224 the Mongols invaded the country, the vast plains of Russia assisted them in their incursions. There were no mountain fastnesses in which an heroic people could make their stand; the cities were, for the most part, small and poorly fortified, and thus the country lay at the feet of these barbarians. Wordsworth has told us in a beautiful sonnet that liberty has two voices, that of the mountain and of the sea, but both mountain and sea were equally wanting to Russia. Of course, Russia has abundance of water power in lakes, huge rivers, and canals, and great diversities of climate.

When we consider the varieties of race in Russia—Slavs, Finns, Germans, Tatars, Georgians, Armenians, and many others—we can see that it must be no easy task to unite all these peoples, with their different religions and languages, under one government ; and perhaps this difficulty may furnish some slight excuse for the slow progress of Russia in constitutional development with the Aryan portion of her population. Her course is smooth enough, but it is difficult to imagine, at all events at present, a Parliament in which Chukches, Bashkirs, and Samoyedes would be members.

It does not come within the scope of my lecture to give any detailed account of Russian history ; too much of this would be merely of antiquarian and academic interest; but in order to understand a nation we must see what forces underlie it, what stages of experience it has gone through, and these I shall endeavour to trace.

No one can say anything with much certainty about the Slavs till the times of Procopius and Jordanes, in the sixth century A.D. The ancients knew nothing about them ; perhaps the Russians are to be found in the Budini and Neuri of Herodotus. There seems to be some continuity of the population there, because on the splendid electrum vase which was discovered in the tomb at Kertch, we find figures represented with the same expression of face and dressed in the same way, especially with their trousers tucked in their boots, as one may see any day among the peasants of Russia at the present time.

We have a lot of Sagas in the picturesque chronicle of Nestor, or that which is attributed to him. He was a monk of Kiev who lived in the eleventh century. It would be difficult to say how much of this has any historical value; certainly we meet with many replicas of his stories among the Norse legends. We hear of Scandinavian adventurers coming and making themselves masters of the Slavonic tribes. Novgorod and Kiev rise into importance, the former the great commercial city, and the latter the first to be Christianised. Round it gather the religious traditions of Russia. She receives her civilisation from Constantinople, and it is the Greek, not Latin, form of our common faith. We must thus recognise what some people are unable or unwilling to understand—how Russia to all the Eastern Christians is really the head of their Church. We owe her some gratitude for her protection of them. So great was the power of the Turks, and so apathetic were the Western sovereigns—as shown among other things, by allowing these barbarians to take Constantinople—that in a short time all South-Eastern Europe and the Christians of Asia, such as the Georgians, would have followed the example of the Bosnian Beys and gone over to Islam *en masse*. But Peter the Great turned the tide by showing the *rayahs*, groaning under the Turkish yoke, that they could look to Russia for protection. It is to her that the new nationality of Bulgaria, which gives such excellent promise, owes its existence   Granted that her conduct to the Bulgarians at the present time is ungenerous—and I am sorry to confess it—still no Bulgarian can forget that, had it not been for Russian blood and treasure, he would still be treated as a dog by a Mussulman master—still, withal, the smallest rights, politically and socially. We cannot, therefore, be surprised that the Christians of the East have felt grateful to Russia. Have we not played into her hands by refusing to recognise the young states rising upon the ruins of the decrepit and moribund Turkish Empire? We must reach out a hand to them unless we wish to lose our influence in the East.

In this early and half-legendary period of Russia, we have Vladimir of Kiev, the first Christian sovereign, the nine-hundredth anniversary of whose baptism was celebrated at Kiev in 1888. Yaroslav is the first legislator, and we have a specimen of his law-making in the *Russkaya Pravda*, which has come down to us in a manuscript of the chronicles of Novgorod. One of the great features of this early code is, that we see in it the Russians wholly unaffected by those Mongolian corruptions which afterwards vitiated them.

Russia was at that time a purely European country, and on a level with the other European nations. At this time the rural peasants were not bound to the soil; they were not in that condition till the sixteenth century. As yet Moscow has not arisen: the history of the country groups itself round Kiev and Novgorod. For nearly two hundred years after this, we have the most dreary period in the Russian annals. The country is divided among a lot of princelings. These little Slavonic principalities, like the small Saxon kingdoms of the heptarchy, are not destined at first to be united, although joined in brotherhood by a common language and common institutions. They have not the instinct of nationality, and at first the desire of private aggrandisement impedes unity. Thus they are ripe for the attacks of the

Mongols, who waste them with fire and sword. All Russia except Novgorod was under Mongol rule. During this gloomy period, there was little national life; but a great many monasteries were built, and in them the monks were cloistered, and busied themselves with the compilation of a series of chronicles.

The yoke of the Mongols was indeed humiliating, but it cannot be said to have had a great influence upon the country. They made no attempt to turn the people into Tatars. They were satisfied with the homage of the princes, with the poll-tax which was exacted, and the military contingents which were furnished. Intermarriages took place between the upper classes occasionally, and thus the Muscovite nobility received a certain Oriental admixture, although the amount of it has been greatly exaggerated. Napoleon is reported to have said: "Scratch a Russian and you will find a Tatar," but, like most epigrams, it is only half a truth. There is nothing of the Tatar in the tall, blonde men, with blue eyes, and frequently red or yellow hair, whom we see forming the bulk of the population of so many parts of Russia. They look more like Scandinavians than Tatars.

Many of the Russian customs—such as the seclusion of the women, and the dress, the long, loose, flowing caftan—now became Oriental, but this was altered by Peter the Great. People are apt to imagine that the Russian language contains a great many Tatar words, but in reality such is far from being the case. They are confined to a few expressions for clothing and names of material objects. To the Mongols is probably owing the introduction of the *knout*, the use of which is now illegal. The word, however, appears to be of Scandinavian origin, the same as our knot.

The little principality of Moscow during this gloomy period contains the germ of the future Russian Empire. It reminds one of the fine lines of Cowper on Yardley Oak. When speaking of the magnificent tree, he tells us there was a time when it was an acorn, and the thievish jay might have swallowed

> " All its close-woven latitude of boughs
> And all its embryo vastness at a gulp."

It is in 1147 that the city of Moscow first appears in the Russian chronicles, but for a hundred years after its foundation it remains an obscure dependency of the principality of Suzdal. Gradually the little state which has grown round it receives constant accessions of territory. During the Mongol invasion Russia lost much—Kiev, together with Volhynia, Podolia, and

Galicia ; and the last of these she had never regained. When
Ivan III. and his two vigorous successors are seen holding the
reins of power, and emerging from the chaos of the Middle Ages,
Russia has the powerful principality of Lithuania on the west—the
official language of which we must remember was White Russian—
stretching almost from the Baltic to the Black Sea, and by the
marriage of Jagiello, its prince, with Jadviga, the heiress to the
Polish throne, it has become united with that country. Thus
Russia comes into conflict with Poland ; the former symbolises
the Greek Church, the latter Catholicism. Their rivalries are to
last for two centuries ; nay, they are not terminated at the present
day. Russia is kept from the sea in the north by the Swedes, and
in the south by the Turks, in whom her old enemies the Mongols
are merged. She lies like a sluggish mass, cut off from communication with the outer world. When Ivan IV. wants artificers to
help him in his plans for civilising Russia, the Poles can block their
entrance into his dominions. Hence we shall not be surprised
at the welcome he gives to English seamanship, which brings
ambassadors to him by way of the White Sea. He has his idea of
getting an outlet into the Baltic, but it is too early. However, he
has some success in the south, and gets Astrakhan on the Caspian.
He also stretches his empire to Siberia. This cruel but far-sighted
man died in 1584.

The press had been introduced into Russia twenty years
previously. The country at this time swarmed with Englishmen,
who have left us some very amusing stories about Ivan. I only
wish I had time to tell some of them here.

The vigorous rule of the usurper Boris Godunov (1598-1605)
was on the whole beneficial to Russia. He also was a far-seeing
man, and had the courage to break with the exclusive traditions of
his country, for he sent some young Russians to England to be
educated. After his death Russia is again put back for nearly fifty
years by internal struggles and rival adventurers ; but Alexis, father
of Peter the Great, finally turns the tide ; the Western provinces,
including historical Kiev, are got back, and the transfer by the
Zoporoghian Cossacks of their allegiance from the Poles to Russia
brings her closer to the Black Sea. The country is full of useful
adventurers, including many Scotchmen.

Peter the Great comes before us as a titanic figure. Inheriting
all the traditions of autocracy, we must not feel surprised if, like
our own Edward I., he had no scruple about removing any
obstacles which appeared in his path. To the same cause must

be traced his lack of self-rule. He was descended, we must remember, from a long line of semi-Asiatic sovereigns; and if he had not been a man of powerful genius, would have been content as they were, with the idleness and luxury of a palace.

He was willing to abandon all these pleasures, so captivating to the ordinary mind, to put himself, as it were, to school; to endure privations and labour, in order to break with a system against which his intellect rebelled. At the beginning of his reign, Peter found Russia Asiatic, he left her European. He created a navy, and gave her an outlet in the Baltic; instead of the disorderly, badly-accoutred regiments of the Streltsi, he gave Russia an army, clothed and disciplined on the European model. He added many provinces to the Empire, constructed canals, developed industries, and caused useful books to be translated into Russian, so that his ignorant subjects might be instructed. By the way, it is a curious fact, and not generally known that the first Russian grammar was printed in 1696 at Oxford, while Peter the Great was in England. He gave Russia libraries and museums, galleries of painting and sculpture; and finally, from an obscure barbaric power, isolated from her European sister kingdom, he created a powerful Empire, able to make its voice heard in the councils of Europe.

The feeble reigns of Catherine I., Peter II., Anne, and Elizabeth effected little. A worthy successor to Peter did not appear till Catherine II. ascended the throne. Russia then advanced to the Black Sea, and gained the Crimea, and Odessa and Sevastopol were built.

There is no need of going through the well-known events which make her prominent in nineteenth century history—the great Napoleon War, the burning of Moscow, and the retreat of the French in 1812. Familiar to us are also the wars of Nicholas, especially our own conflicts with him, when the fields of the Crimea were soaked with our blood. With what sad feelings have I walked over the site of these fiercely-contested battles—

"How that red rain has made the harvest grow!"

The most noteworthy event of later times has been the great emancipation of the serfs in 1861. I have already said that the rural peasants were only fixed to the soil so late as the time of Boris Godunov, at the close of the sixteenth century. The *krestiane*, as they were called, had been personally free up to that date, and had the right of quitting their masters. This right was especially put in practice on St. George's Day, and the recol-

lection of it has survived among the peasantry till the present
time, in a solitary proverb, "*Vot tebe, babushka, yuriev dyen.*"
"Here's St. George's Day for you, old woman." After this time, we
find serfdom gradually developing. The first suggestion of their
emancipation belongs to Prince Golitsin, the favourite of the
Tsarevna Sophia, towards the close of the seventeenth century.
In his conversation with the Polish Ambassador Neuville, he
spoke to him of the necessity of putting Russia upon the same
footing as other more civilised nations, and he thought that the
first step towards this was the emancipation of the peasant, and
the transference to him of the land which he cultivated. Nothing,
however, at that time resulted from these intentions, and they did
not get their liberty till the time of Alexander II.

At the emancipation, twenty-three millions were set free. It
is now pretty generally known, that according to the system of
the Russian *Mir*, the land in a village is divided among the
peasants in proportion to the number of their families, and that
the re-distribution takes place at certain intervals, this and other
points concerning the *Mir* being settled by the village parliament,
at which not only men but women are allowed to vote.

My hearers will find all this clearly explained in the excellent work of Sir Mackenzie Wallace. Subsequent researches
on the subject have shown that this land system is of great
antiquity, and can be traced thoroughout Europe—to say nothing
of Asia. In India the English met with it as soon as they
had become well acquainted with the country, and were at first
puzzled by it. In Switzerland and Servia it is still found
flourishing, and there are traces of it in England and Scotland.
The subject is too vast to be treated here ; in fact, to do it justice,
I should require the time allowed me for the whole lecture.
Many persons have thought that in this institution the Russians
have the germ of self-government, but in other respects the
peasants and artisans show ideas of co-operation : thus the *artel*
or confederation of workmen, whereby they lodge and board
together, each contributing his quota, is very curious and interesting. People see in these things a certain power of cohesion
and independent action among the Russian lower classes ; and,
as Leroy-Beaulieu very truly remarks, the number of religious
sects among them, which suffered considerable persecution in
old time, and even now are put under disabilities, shows that in
matters of conscience the Russian will have his individual
opinion, and will not be dictated to.

I shall say something about these religious sects further on, but will now proceed to consider the condition of the serf in his newly enfranchised position. At the emancipation the commune (*Mir*) received the village land, and might either pay as before by so many days' personal labour from the inhabitants, or might elect to redeem the allotments by the help of the crown, and they then became free from all obligations to the landlord. The crown paid the landlord, and the peasants have to pay the crown for forty-nine years six per cent. interest on the money advanced, that is, nine to twelve roubles on allotment. Each village commune received 13½ acres (five desiatiue) for each male member.

For many interesting facts on the condition of the peasantry, I recommend my hearers to read the little work of Mr. Ling Roth, entitled, *Agriculture and Peasantry in Eastern Russia.*

As regards the government of Russia, which is a pure autocracy, I need say nothing ; it is well known to all of you. Concerning the Church, as I have said before, it follows the orthodox or Greek faith. An excellent book has been recently written on *Religion in Russia*, by M. Leroy-Beaulieu, which forms the third volume of his *opus magnum, L'Empire les Tsars et les Russes.* He does not consider the religion of the *muzhik* or peasant a mere system of fetish. Because it is overlaid with so many gross superstitions and ceremonies, it does not follow that there is no real piety or feeling underneath it. Tried by the same standard, the Italian and Spanish peasant, and, we might add, the Roman Catholic Irish, might be considered pagans. One of the most striking facts in the history of the Russian Church is the raskol (lit. cutting asunder, or splitting), the great religious schism which began when Nikon, the primate, corrected the errors which had crept into the religious books. This priest was a remarkable man ; some have not hesitated to call him the greatest man produced by Russia before the days of Peter. When summoned before the council, his answers exhibited remarkable boldness. Nikon was the Beckett of Russia, and might have carried the day with the superstitious Emperor Alexis, whose ecclesiastical proclivities have been noted for us in the quaint book of the physician, Samuel Collins, but the Boyars were too much for him. They talked the Tsar over, and Nikon lost his ecclesiastical dignities and ended as a simple monk. Thus came the *staroobriadtsi* or old believers into existence, and since that time sects have multiplied in Russia down to their latest development—that of the Stundists—a kind of offshoot of German Protestantism, who derive their name from the word *Stunde*. There are many striking parallels to these sects in America and England. When we see the *shakuni* or leapers, who make religious dances a great part of their ritual, and the *molokani*, or milk-drinkers, we are reminded of the Shakers and Quakers. Other sects recall the Plymouth Brethren and the Irvingites. M. Leroy-Beaulieu does not consider that the Tsar is as much the head of the Russian Church as Queen Victoria of the English. Neither Moscow nor St. Petersburg, he says, has ever seen an assembly of laymen like the English Parliament legislate in Church questions.

Much has been said about the ignorance of the Russian rural priest, but we must remember the laborious life he leads, the great extent of the parishes which are under his care, and the privations to which he is subject. Poor and half-educated as he frequently is, he is the consoler of the *mushik* in his troubles, and the partaker of his joys, as the Irish priest has been in the sister isle ; he is like the "soggarth aroon" of Banim's pathetic songs. We must all hope that Russia may advance gradually in the path of constitutional progress, but it is difficult to see how she can move in any other way than slowly and by degrees. The peasants are at the present time too illiterate and the middle class is too small, so that all power would necessarily fall into the hands of the nobility.

The late Emperor Alexander II. did a great deal for Russia ; his assassination was not merely a crime, but a blunder. I cannot do better than quote the words of Dr. George Brandes, the Dane, the author of *Moderne Geister,* and other works (p 129):—"Nothing has set Russia further backward than this last occurrence, which was pregnant with misfortune. It immediately prevented the formation of a sort of parliamentary constitution, which had just then been promised. It frightened the successor to the crown back from the paths his father had entered upon at the beginning of his reign, and it seemed to justify the rulers in reprisals and measures of persecution of every kind." With these words I turn from a part of my subject which suggests painful reflections, and gladly leave the heated atmosphere of politics to say a few words on Russian literature.

Russian authors are at the present time coming into fashion, and my audience may care to hear a few remarks upon them.

Beside their written literature the Russians have abundance of folk-song, legend, and folk-tale. The former are called *bilini,* which may be roughly translated, "tales of the olden time." They have been divided into various cycles, as, for instance, those of the older heroes, *starshie bogatiri*, those of Vladimir, the Prince of Kiev, of Novgorod and Moscow. The heroes of the first cycle are Titanic beings, who have the power of assuming various shapes. A great hero of the time of Vladimir is Ilya Muromets, an unwieldy giant, in whose history some writers have seen a symbolism of Russia herself. The cycle of Novgorod has stories to tell us about rich merchants, but perhaps the cycle of Moscow, with its legends about Ivan the Terrible, is most interesting.

An Englishman named Richard James, a graduate of Oxford, who for some reason was in Russia at the beginning of the seventeenth century, either copied out, or caused to be copied out, some curious contemporary *bilini*, or historical ballads. His pocket-book containing these pieces is preserved in the Bodleian Library. Beside the *bilini*, there are many collections of *skazki*, or prose tales, some of the most interesting of which were made known to the English public by my late friend Mr. Ralston.

As regards their written literature, the Russians have a series of chronicles, compiled by monks in their cloisters, and extending from that attributed to Nestor in the eleventh century to the time of Peter the Great, in the latter part of the seventeenth. In the earlier period of her history, in fact, down to the time of Peter the Great, the traditions of Russian literature were wholly Byzantine. We have sermons and lives of the saints in abundance, and perhaps there is more to please the antiquary and the philologist than the man of taste. There are a few exceptions, such as the prose-poem on the *Expedition of Prince Igor* in the twelfth century, and the *Zadontschina* of the fourteenth, which describes the great victory of Dmitri Donskoi over the Tatars. The fashion imitated was nearly always Byzantine, and that, it must be confessed, was not a noble school in which an infant literature could be formed. The Byzantine Greeks have been sarcastically called the European Chinese; their civilisation has been said to be the corpse of antiquity laid out in state, and all this is more or less true. Poetry was dead among them, unless we are to find it in the πολιτικοί στίχοι of Tzetzes, and history had degenerated in the veriest drybones of chronicles. But changes were coming, even before the time of Peter, when the Russians got back Kiev in 1686, which, although the cradle of their nationality, had for upwards of three hundred years been

in the possession of Lithuanian and Pole. Something of the
culture of the West was communicated to them by the Academy
which had been founded there, and Simeon Polotski, who came
to Moscow in 1665, and in 1672 was appointed tutor to the
children of Tsar Alexis. He began to write verses on the Latin
model and sacred dramas. With the reforms of Peter the Great
commences an entirely new period in the history of Russian
literature. From her Byzantine traditions, from legends of saints,
confused chronicles and orthodox hymnologies, Russia was to
pass, by one of the most violent changes ever witnessed in the
literature of any country, into epics moulded on the Henriade
and tedious odes in the style of Jean Baptiste Rousseau.

Then appeared Lamonosov, the son of a poor fisherman of
Archangel, who forms one of the curious band of peasant authors,
of very various merit, it must be confessed, who present such a
singular and unexpected phenomenon in Russian literature. The
life of this man, who died full of honours, exhibits the most
startling contrasts. The reign of Catherine II. (1762-1796) saw
the rise of a whole generation of court poets. The maxim,
" *Un Auguste peutaisement faire un Virgile,*" was seen in all its
absurdity in semi-barbarous Russia. These wits were supported
by the Empress and her immediate *entourage,* to whom their
florid productions were ordinarily addressed. Macaulay has
somewhere a homely but very vigorous simile to express the
relations in which a writer stands towards his public in countries
where education is little diffused. He says that the patron, if
he wants to have the odes of a poet, must support the poet—
just, he adds, as when you go to out-of-the-way countries, if
you want a mutton-chop, you must buy the whole sheep. In the
strict sense of the word, at that time there was no reading
public in Russia ; only in the dreary huts of the peasants, through
the long winter nights, the wandering rhapsodist kept up the
tradition of their popular legends. But the Gallicised courtiers
of the epoch of Catherine regarded these productions with
contempt, as the babble of savages. They were only to be
collected in the present century, when the great reaction against
the pseudo-classical school had set in.

The classicists, who numbered some prominent poets, Derz-
havin among them, lasted till some way on in the present century.
Then came the introduction of the romantic school by Zhukovski,
who survived to a good old age, dying in 1852. Alexander
Pushkin (1799-1857) symbolises this school at its height, with

strong influences of Byronism, in spite of which he has written poems national to the core, and was followed by Lermontov and others.

It was in Alexis Koltsov that the real voice of the Russian people first spoke, which up to that time had only been heard in the national songs. I will give some of the details of his life as it illustrates Russian society.

Lemonosov, Pushkin, and Zhukovski, were in one sense artificial poets, well acquainted with the literatures of Western Europe ; but in the new writer all Russia recognised a man of the people, who, like Burns, could tell their aspirations and griefs, and whose songs had been awakened by the influence of the popular lays of the country. It is in this sense that Koltsov is the most *national* of the Russian poets.

Alexis Koltsov was born at Voronezh, in the government of the same name, October 2nd (old style), 1809. His father traded in sheep, whose carcases were to be boiled down for the tallow factories. The family had been engaged in this calling for some generations, and were fairly substantial people of the burgher class. Still, educationally speaking, his condition was a low one. If Russian tradesmen show but little culture now, it was still more the case seventy or eighty years ago. Voronezh was once an active place, especially in the time of Peter the Great, but it is now dull and decayed. Koltsov grew up amid coarse and vulgar associations, and received a poor education. Till his death he used an ungrammatical style, and his orthography was capricious. Prosaic as some of the features of his life were, political accessories were not wholly absent. He was occasionally sent to tend his father's sheep on the steppe, and thus found himself in communion with Nature. The account given by his biographers reminds us very much of some of the details of the life of the Ettrick Shepherd, and the days he spent upon the solitary Scottish hills. It is of this steppe that the Russian poet is never weary of singing, and he has consecrated to it many of his most beautiful poems. His fancies were first stimulated by reading the works of Dmitriev, a poet of the classical school, who flourished in the interval between Lomonosov and the romantic revival under Zhukovski. Soon afterwards he was able to purchase some of the works of the Russian poets, but he did not make much progress in the art of composition till Kashkin, a good-natured bookseller, had given him a work on Russian parody.

There is a sad love episode in the life of the poet. His father, although a mere burgher, owned some serfs, and among them was a young girl who had grown up in the house, and had become half servant and half companion to Koltsov's sisters, and indeed there would not be much difference between them in matters of education. The girl appears to have been a beauty of the South Russian type. The poet fell in love with her, and his passion was reciprocated. His father, however, determined to put an end to such an attachment, which he thought little conducive to his son's interest. He accordingly took advantage of the absence of Alexis in the steppe, and sold Duniasha, as she was called, and her mother, to one of the landed proprietors dwelling in the district of the Don. The father of Koltsov appears in most of his actions to have been a hard, money-loving man ; but it is not easy to forgive him for this act of brutality. This sad instance of the abuse of parental authority occurred when the poet was twenty-two years of age. We are told that Duniasha soon fell into a consumption, and died through grief at parting.

In 1835 eighteen of the poems of Koltsov were published through the agency of his friend Stankevich, the son of a landed proprietor of Voronezh, and the book soon made its way. In 1836 Koltsov had occasion to visit St. Petersburg and Moscow, with a view to the settlement of some of his father's affairs. It was on this occasion that he was introduced to the chief literary lions of the two capitals, and the salons of the aristocracy were thrown open to him. The memoirs of Koltsov are full of painful details of the constant squabbles of the poet with his father, a coarse, selfish old man. After his return from Moscow in March 1841, Koltsov first began to show signs of that disease which was to carry him off in the following year. The disagreeable condition of his life is made only too apparent in his letters to the critic Bielinski. Fortunately, the poor poet fell into the hands of a kindly and sympathetic doctor. Life had, however, become distasteful to Koltsov ; he used to say to his medical man, "If my disease is inevitable, if you are only protracting life, I implore you not to do so. The sooner it is over the better, and I shall give you less trouble." On the advice of his medical attendant, Koltsov went to a friend in the country, so that he might bathe regularly in the Don, and for some time his health improved. "But this improvement," remarks Bielinski, "was only deferring death." For the re-establishment of his health rest was necessary, and that was denied him. As happened in the case of Burns, some of his friends, "flies of estate and sunshine," to use the words of George

Herbert, deserted him in his declining days.   The poet died on the 19th of October 1842.

The volume of verse which Koltsov has left us is not great in extent, but its contents are valuable.   He has all moods, but the melancholy one is predominant.   And we must remember that the sorrows of Koltsov were real ones, and his desponding utterances are not like the expressions of *Weltschmerz* of the poets of the Byronic school, who too often show their self-inflicted wounds to the world, as mendicants do for an alms.   We cannot say of him that he is

> "Sad as summer night for wantonness."

Another poet, whose life has great interest, and gives us a genuine picture of Russia, is Taras Shevchenko, the Cossack. He wrote a short autobiography, from which I shall borrow some incidents.

He was born on the 28th of March 1814, in the village of Mornitsa, in the Government of Kiev.   His parents were serfs on the estate of a certain landed proprietor named Engelhardt.   He has told us that he never knew any happiness after his ninth year. He appears to have been a dreamy child, full of strange impulses ; thus he was always gazing at the distant mountains, which he could see from his village, and thought that they must be iron pillars which supported the sky.   He accordingly wandered from the village to put his belief to the test, and would perhaps have been lost if he had not been brought back by some pedlars. In the year 1823 he lost his mother ; his father married again, and the new wife proved a severe stepmother to the children.   Taras, with his little sister Irene, who was his constant companion, used to go to the neighbouring Lebedinski monastery.   Here he saw an old monk who had been an eye-witness of the struggle between the Malo-Russians and the Poles in 1768.   This man had many a story to tell of the period, and gave the youth the material for his striking poem, *Haidamak*.   The father of Shevchenko sent him for instruction to a certain Hubski, but died soon afterwards. The stripling was then intrusted to a drunken priest named Buhorski, who treated him with brutal severity.   "This was the first despot I ever had to deal with," says Taras, in his auto-biography, "and he instilled in me for the rest of my life a loathing for every sort of oppression which one man can commit against another."   He also narrates his adventures with two other persons of this sort by whom he was instructed, and from whom he learned something of the art of painting, for they were employed in the preparation of *icons*, or sacred pictures. Thus, besides a genius for song, an inclination for art was developed in Taras.

But his fortunes were to undergo a change. In the year 1823 his old master, Engelhardt, died, and his son and heir took the youngster as his page. This new position, although at first it seemed to cripple his freedom, was, in the end, advantageous to him. His duty was to remain in an ante-chamber, to await the summons of his master. The poor youth, to wile away his time, was accustomed to copy the pictures hanging on the wall. This practice, however, on one occasion, brought him into trouble. He accompanied his master to Vilna on the occasion of a festival in honour of the Tsar. During the absence of M. Engelhardt and his family at a ball, given in honour of this fête, young Shevchenko set himself to copy the pictures which were hanging on the walls. While the rest of the household slept, the young artist secretly rose, lit a candle, and began drawing. He became so engrossed in the pursuit that he did not perceive when his master returned, and was rudely awakened from his artistic dreams by his ears being pulled by the angry nobleman, who terrified the young painter by telling him that by his sitting with a candle among the papers, he had not only nearly set on fire the house but the whole city. The unfortunate Shevchenko received a beating. A better time, however, was in store for him. M. Engelhardt resolved to send him to a house painter, with the idea of employing him on his estate. To a decorator of this sort he accordingly went, and luckily found a kind-hearted man.

In the year 1832, the master of the poet went to live permanently at St. Petersburg, and Taras followed with the rest of the servants. His talent for painting became more and more developed, and finally in 1838 some benevolent men raised 2500 roubles, the sum required to purchase him from his master, and set him free. Shevchenko now became a member of the Academy of Arts, and everything promised a successful career for him. In 1840 appeared his *Kobzar* containing a collection of lyrical pieces in the Malo-Russian language. But unfortunately, while staying at Kiev, he got mixed up with some secret societies, and was denounced to the Government. He was sentenced to serve as a soldier at Orenburg, on the Asiatic frontier of the empire, and remained in exile from 1847 to 1857. His fate was the more severe, because he was forbidden to amuse himself with painting.

He, however, contrived to secrete materials, even carrying a pencil in his shoe, and his proceedings were winked at, through the good nature of the officer in command.

The following story is told by the great novelist Turgueniev: —"One general, an out-and-out martinet, having heard that Shevchenko, in spite of the prohibition, had made two or three sketches, thought it his duty to report the matter to Perovski (the commander-in-chief of the district) on one of his days of reception; but the latter looking sternly on the over-jealous informer, said in a marked tone, 'General, I am deaf in this ear, be so good as to repeat to me on the other side what you have said.' The general took the hint, and going to the other side, told him something which in no way concerned Shevchenko."

The poor poet during his captivity lamented his fate in some sad poems. But a day of deliverance was at hand. In 1855 the Emperor Nicholas died, and soon afterwards Shevchenko, through the influence of his friends, was released. He returned to St. Petersburg in 1858; in the summer of the following year he paid a visit to the Ukraine, and saw his sister Irene in her native village. But he was so poor, that he was only able to give her a rouble; at that time all the rest of the family were serfs. Towards the middle of July he again made his appearance in St. Petersburg, and occupied apartments in the Academy buildings. A new edition of his *Kobzar* also appeared. He now became anxious to settle down in the Ukraine, but his health was breaking up. On the 26th of February 1861, the poet died suddenly in his studio. He had expressed a wish to be buried in the Ukraine—

> "When I die, one thing I crave,
>   Lay me by the Dnieper,
> That his broad and rushing wave
>   Lull in rest the sleeper."

His friends resolved that his wish should be carried out, and he was buried in a picturesque spot, in the presence of a great crowd of people. In imitation of the old Cossack tombs, a vast mound of earth was piled on the grave, which was surmounted by an iron cross. This tomb is an object of reverence among his countrymen, and a little while ago it was spoken of in one of the Polish journals as the Mecca of the South Russian revolutionists. I have unfortunately no time for a detailed criticism of the writings of Shevchenko. He loves to describe the wild exploits of the Cossacks in their independent days. He has in a clever manner interwoven with his poems the popular superstitions and customs of his countrymen, hence his pieces are full of national colouring and racy of the soil.

The Russians began early to write historical novels, under the influence of Scott—that wizard whose genius pervaded Europe. But it is in the realistic novels of modern life that they have been destined to achieve their greatest success. We might perhaps say that Nihilism, the exiles in Siberia, the supposed progress of the Russians towards India, and the Russian novel are the only Russian subjects about which the ordinary Englishman feels any curiosity. In the stream of realistic fiction the Russian mind has flowed ; and this is only what we must expect, when we reflect that in the nineteenth century the epic and the drama, as forms of fresh creative literature, are dead throughout Europe. The novel of everyday life, in its higher development, giving scope for fine psychological analysis, is everywhere triumphant. It was introduced to the Russians by Nicholas Gogol (1809-1852), a writer of striking talents. As he was a native of Malo-Russia, the colouring of his tales is taken from that picturesque part of the empire. But even he, great as were his merits, hardly during his lifetime succeeded in making himself known beyond the boundaries of his native country. This was done by Ivan Turgueniev, who died in 1883. Much has been written by way of criticism upon the writings of Turgueniev, but of his biography little is yet known, especially in this country. In the latter part of the year 1884, there appeared in the pages of the Russian Review, *Viestnik Yevropi*, some interesting papers by a Madame Zhitov, who had been adopted by Turgueniev's mother during her long widowhood. We get from them a curious view of Russian domestic life in the earlier part of the century, and the sketch forms a fitting pendant to the biographies of Koltsov and Shevchenko.

The mother of the novelist, Barbara Lituvinova, was descended from an old and wealthy family. Unfortunately, her mother, who became a widow at an early age, married again ; and both she and her second husband ill-treated the daughter, for whom she never seems to have felt any affection. The poor girl, persecuted by her family, at last took refuge with a rich uncle, who treated her well in the main, although he seems to have been a man of harsh character. With him Barbara remained till his death, at which time she was nearly thirty years of age. He left her all his property, which was considerable. She soon afterwards married Sergius Turgueniev, a man of noble family and handsome appearance, according to tradition. By him she had two sons, Ivan and Nicholas. Her husband died early, and Madame Turgueniev appears for the rest of her life to have vented her spleen and melancholy upon the unfortunate serfs in her power. It was from what he saw on his mother's estate that Turgueniev drew the vigorous pictures of serfdom to be found in his works, especially that which was the earliest to become celebrated, *Zapiski Okhov-nika—The Memoirs of a Sportsman.* In his mother's house occurred the pathetic incident of the dumb porter—a man whom Madame Turgueniev had chosen for the post on account of his gigantic stature, and who consoled himself in his desolation by the companionship of a dog. His cruel mistress had the animal removed, because he occasionally made a noise. Ivan, the future novelist, was continually devising means whereby the cruelty of his mother to the serfs could be baffled. Thus, when she ordered the child of one of her female serfs, whom she employed in attendance upon herself, to be sent to another estate, because it diverted the attention of the mother from her mistress, Ivan, to spare the poor woman's agonies, caused the child to be secretly brought up on a part of the estate where the mother could visit it, and Madame Turgueniev never discovered the trick which had been played upon her.

She had educated one of her serfs as a medical man. He had acquired such skill that his services were in great request in the families of the district, when Madame Turgueniev was willing to lend them. The serf-doctor was employed to attend the young protegée of his mistress (Madame Zhitov); but as the little girl got no better, Madame made up her mind to send to some doctors in the neighbouring town. But the serf, whose name was Porphyry, would not agree to this. The rest shall be told in the words of Madame Zhitov :—

"With his air of imperturbable quiet and heavy step he entered the room of his mistress, at the very moment when she was writing a letter to invite the physician to attend.

"'Do not trouble yourself, madam, to write to any one. I am attending the young lady, and I will cure her.'

"Madame Turgueniev cast her eyes upon him, put her letter aside, looked closely at the audacious speaker, and said, 'Remember, if you don't cure her, a journey to Siberia awaits you' —whither in old times rebellious serfs were sent as a punishment.

"But this did not trouble our good doctor. He went out of the room as slowly and quietly as he came, sat behind my bed, and never left me day or night till the disease had taken a favourable turn. Then, in the same phlegmatic manner, expressing neither triumph nor joy (although he was very fond of me), he went into the room where he had been threatened with Siberia, and said, 'The young lady is now alive and safe, only it will be some time before she is convalescent.'"

With Turgueniev, Count Leo Tolstoi and Dostoievski (who died in 1881) divide the honours at the present day. Tolstoi allures his readers by his vigorous portraiture and the strange undercurrent of socialism which runs through all his writings. Dostoievski has an overpowering realism. This realism in art, which is so great a characteristic of the Russian mind, besides appearing in the novelists, is conspicuous in the paintings of Verestchagin, and also in the poetry of Nekrasov, who died a short time ago. Count Melchior de Voguë, who has written a powerful book on the Russian novel, says very truly the Russian thinker goes with a bound to the depths of things. He sees the contradictions, the vanity, the great nullity of life; and if his artistic temperament urges him to reproduce it, he does it with a disdainful impartiality, at times with a frigid despair, most often with the fatalism which is inherent in the Oriental parts of his soul. It is this fatalism which makes the Russian accept with such apathy and even with apparent cheerfulness whatever misfortunes he finds himself compelled to undergo. Thus in spite of his exile and the many physical and mental sufferings which he underwent, Dostoievski returned from Siberia with an unbroken and loyal faith in the political and religious institutions of his country. Aksakov has told us that once Dostoievski, together with Mackenzie Wallace and others, were spending the evening with him, when in the course of a conversation on the Emperor Nicholas, the novelist warmly eulogised him. After his departure the Englishman came up to Aksakov and asked,

"Did you not tell me that was Dostoievski?'

"Yes."

"The author of *Memorials of the House of Death*"?

"The same."

"But it cannot be he who was exiled to the mines?"

"No other; and pray why not?"

"Why, how could he eulogise the very man who sent him to the galley?"

"You, as a foreigner," replied Aksakov, "may find it difficult to understand, but to *us* it is intelligible, and is thoroughly Russian."[1]

A few words are due about the Russian press. Many of the newspapers are known in England by name, but little more. Thus there is the *Novoye Viemya*, the proprietor of which is Suvorin, the publisher. At Moscow is published the *Russkia Viedomosti*, probably the most widely circulated paper in Russia, edited by Sobolevski, formerly a professor, and the *Moskovskia Viedomosti*, which used to be the organ of the celebrated *Katkov*. There is also the *Grazhdaniu*. The *Golos* has, we believe, come to an end.

Of the Reviews, the most noteworthy are the *Viestnik Yevropi*, edited by Stasiulevich, in which some of the novels of Turgueniev first made their appearance. There is also the Moscow periodical, *Russkaya Misl*, Russian Thought, and to these may be added the *Russkaya Starina*, Russian Antiquary, and *Istoricheski* and *Viestnik*, both of which are published at St. Petersburg. The former is an invaluable magazine to all who study Russian history, containing, as it does, articles relating solely to the life and thought of that country in previous times. It is edited by Semevski. The *Istoricheski Viestnik* has a wider range, inasmuch as it includes also the histories of other countries besides Russia. The articles are of a very substantial character. It is edited by Shubiaski, the author of some very interesting historical monographs.

So vast a subject as Russia it would be impossible to fully treat of in a single lecture. All I have attempted to do is to put before you some of the landmarks of the history and literature of this strange country, which has only lately been studied among us.

Let us hope, as I have previously said, that Russia may advance slowly and safely in the path of constitutional progress, and play the great part which she seems destined to do in the history of the nations. Nor need any of my hearers be terrified by the bugbear of Panslavism, which is so often brandished before us like a red rag. There seems to be an idea that Panslavism was invented by the Russians, but as every one properly informed on the subject knows, such is far from being the case. The first person to start the idea was a certain Yuri Krizhanich, a Serb, who was in Russia for some time during the reign of Alexis, the father of Peter the Great, but from unknown causes was banished to Siberia, and is supposed to have ended his days at Tobolsk. His works are full

[1] Turner's *Modern Novelists of Russia.*

of interest, and show great acuteness; he carried his enthusiasm so far that he believed in the possibility of a common Slavonic language.

It seems to me impossible that a political union of the Slavonic races should ever be formed. That there should be a certain amount of sympathy among them is not to be wondered at, but language and religion alone will prevent their complete fusion. The Eastern Slavs are members of the Orthodox or Greek Church, the Western of the Latin; and each clings to his special alphabet, in one case leading to the almost ludicrous result that the Serbs and Croats, practically the same people, are divided into two families, one of which uses the Latin and the other the Cyrillic letters. Nay, we may actually see literary journals, one column of which is in Cyrillic, and the other in the Latin alphabet. Moreover, although the various Slavonic languages have roots, and forms in common—as must necessarily be the case from their belonging to the same family—yet the people who use different languages are not mutually intelligible. In the same way, show an Englishman a page of Dutch or Swedish, and he will immediately point out a great many words, obviously the same as English, with slight modifications, but we hardly expect to hear an Englishman engaged in easy conversation with a Swede or a Dutchman, unless he has learned their languages. And just as this Panslavistic idea is a mere "scare," so the result of all my reading has been to find that the will of Peter the Great "is a fond thing vainly invented;" but I have no time to go into a discussion upon it here. The subject is far too lengthy.

In conclusion, I can only say of Russia, in the words of one of her own poets, which I have attempted to versify, who is listening to the peasant as he sings:—

> "More boldly those songs of half-sadness are flowing.
>   And full of a strength that is young;
> They tell of a soul that triumphant is growing,
>   Tho' for years it was tortured and wrung.

> "Maybe, thou hast bowed, native land, 'neath thy sorrow,
>   And harsh was thy fortune to bide,—
> But nay—I'll believe not that freedom's glad morrow
>   And her songs to these fields are denied."

VII

POLAND.

ADAM GIELGUD.

IT was, I think, a happy inspiration which prompted the Committee of this Institute to include Poland in the series of lectures on the European nations now being delivered to you. There is certainly no country that has played an important part in European history of which so little is known among the present generation of Englishmen as Poland. I have often heard people, fairly educated people too, ask whether such a nation as Poland still exists, and whether the Poles are not the same as the Russians. Nor, indeed, is this very surprising. It is now a hundred years since, by an act of spoliation unexampled in history, Poland was divided among three great powers—Russia, Austria, and Prussia—which have exercised every means of persuasion and violence to wipe out the Polish national spirit, and to assimilate their Polish to their other subjects. A hundred years is a long time even in the life of a nation, and only a very sturdy and patriotic one could have survived this disintegrating process, carried out with steady persistence by some of the greatest statesmen of Europe, with vast armies, ample funds, and all the resources of civilisation at their command. No wonder that people conclude that Poland must be dead, and that the Poles have accepted their fate and made friends with their rulers, as, looking at the matter from a purely material point of view, it was obviously their interest to do.

It is, perhaps, a little singular that a nation which inspired English poets, historians, and orators—whose cause was supported, within the memory of many now living, by splendid entertainments, in which the chief members of the English aristocracy, with the Duke of Sussex, the Queen's uncle, at their head, took a leading part, and by public meetings of Conservatives, Liberals, and Radicals, addressed by such representative men as Edmund Beales and Lord Dudley Stuart, who may be said to have lived

H

and died for Poland—that a nation whose valour and misfortunes
have been the subject of endless debates in Parliament, and
nearly caused a war between this country and Russia in 1864—
should now be almost entirely forgotten. Possibly this may be
explained by the advance of what is called materialism. These are
not times when men's pulses are stirred by such names as Kosciuszko, Garibaldi, and Kossuth. We are a more practical age ; our
admiration and sympathy are for success, not for misfortune ;
and Bismarck and Moltke have eclipsed the heroes of our youth.

The unfortunate, like the absent, are always in the wrong, and
it has become the fashion to say that Poland fell because she did
not deserve to live, and that the Poles are a turbulent, impracticable race who will never be capable of self-government. Such
wholesale accusations against a nation are very unphilosophical,
and are generally falsified by events. It is not very long ago that
the general notion in England about the Germans was that they
were a nation of dreamers; about the Italians, that they were either
mere *dilettanti* or visionary conspirators ; about the Roumanians,
that they were sunk in luxury and corruption ; and about the
Bulgarians, that they were ignorant boors with not enough spirit
to turn out their Turkish oppressors. Yet we now know that
the Germans and Italians are among the most practical politicians
in the world, and that Roumania and Bulgaria have not only
obtained their independence, but successfully resist even the
bullying of a great power like Russia. The fall of Poland, we
are told, was to a great extent brought about by her internal
dissensions. This is undoubtedly true. Internal dissension is
a bad thing for a country, especially when it is surrounded by
three great powers who are eagerly waiting for an opportunity
of pouncing upon her and seizing her territory; but people who
look for a reason for the fall of Poland, are too apt to forget that
countries which are now the greatest and most flourishing in
the world, have been the scene of internal dissensions as bad as
those of Poland, though, owing to their more favourable geographical position, they have not been punished for them as she
has been. This has, indeed, for centuries been the chronic
disease of all Europe. Look at England : from Wat Tyler's revolt
and the persecution of the Lollards to the wars of the Roses,
from the wars of the Roses to the blood-stained annals of the
Tudors and the dynastic civil wars of the Stuarts and the Georges,
her history has been an almost unbroken succession of internal
struggles; and even now, though Englishmen have ceased to

settle their differences by the sword, we all know that political adversaries in this country attack each other as bitterly in Parliament, at public meetings, in the press, and even in the law courts, as they ever did on the battlefield. In French history we see the risings of the peasants and traders against the nobles in the fourteenth century, the civil war between North and South in the fifteenth, the thirty years' war between the Huguenots and Catholics in the sixteenth, the wars of the Fronde in the seventeenth, and the horrors of the Great Revolution in the eighteenth; Germany had the Hussite war in the fifteenth century, the nobles' war in the sixteenth, the thirty years' war in the seventeenth; and the Italians, after the hundred years' war between the Guelphs and the Ghibellines, continued to fight each other almost incessantly until Italian unity was finally established in 1871.

Now no one would be so foolish as to say that the English are a turbulent nation incapable of governing themselves, because during some three centuries of their history they were chiefly occupied in cutting each other's throats. Why, then, should this be said of the Poles—unless, indeed, it be that having failed to help them, we try to console ourselves for the failure by saying that they did not deserve to be helped? The radical error of this view of Polish history is, that it passes a sweeping condemnation on the Poles for faults which were not specially Polish, but were those of Europe generally before the great French Revolution. It is all very well for us in England, at the end of the nineteenth century, to hold up our hands in horror on reading of the anarchy which prevailed in Poland a hundred and fifty years ago. There was plenty of anarchy at that time in the other countries of Europe. The condition of Germany, for instance, is thus described by one of the most recent of our radical historians, Mr. Fyffe, author of the *History of Europe:*—"A system of small States, which in the past of Greece and Italy had produced the finest types of energy and genius, had in Germany resulted in the extinction of all vigorous life, and in the ascendancy of all that was stagnant, little, and corrupt. If political disorganisation, the decay of public spirit, and the absence of a national idea, are the signs of impending downfall, Germany was ripe for foreign conquest." Germany, France, Italy, Holland, escaped the fate of Poland, not because they were more orderly and peaceful, but because they were not, as Poland was, surrounded by despotic powers, each with far greater resources than herself, which not only coveted her fertile plains, but hoped in crushing Poland to stem the rising flood of liberty on the Continent. The truth is, as the poet Campbell indicated in his famous lines, that Poland was the victim of her love of freedom; in signing the Constitution of the 3rd of May 1791—that Constitution at whose promulgation Burke said that "humanity must rejoice and glory"—she signed her death-warrant. That this was the case, is proved out of the mouth of Frederick William himself, who, after complimenting the Poles through his ambassador on their Constitution, sent an army into their country, and justified himself before the other powers by asserting that "the principles of Jacobinism were gaining ground in the country, and the spirit of the French democracy was taking deep root among the Poles." Catherine, less Jesuitical, simply protested against the Constitution, and backed up her protest with an army of 100,000 men. I will not here give any more details of the sad and well-known story of the intrigues of the Fredericks and Catherine; it will suffice to quote the words of our last and greatest historian on the subject, Mr. Lecky, who, in his *History of England in the Eighteenth Century*, says :—

"It was the deliberate and systematic policy of Russia and Prussia to maintain anarchy in Poland in order that it might never rise to prosperity or power or independence. The policy of Russia towards Poland was one of cynical, undisguised rapacity; while the King of Prussia not only broke his word and betrayed his trust, but took an active part in the partition of the defenceless country which he had bound himself in honour to protect." I know that Carlyle takes a different view; but hero-worship was one of the defects of that great and rugged genius, and he chose his heroes from among the mighty ones of the earth, who are not always the noblest or the most generous.

What I would specially call your attention to is, that Poland has from the beginning of her history been the land of liberty, and that it was because she was the land of liberty that the despotic governments which surrounded her have always been her enemies, and have always striven to compass her destruction. It is the fashion to blacken the idols and to glorify the villains of our forefathers; and that clever apologist of Russian despotism, Madame Novikoff, has probably persuaded many people that Poland was not a free country after all, but was ruled by a turbulent aristocracy who, when they were not fighting among themselves or with the neighbouring States, were chiefly occupied in oppressing the peasants. The latest disciple of this ingenious lady is, I see, a writer in the current number of the *Quarterly Review*, who affords a good illustration of the ignorance which prevails, even among writers in reviews, with regard to Poland. With a complacent dogmatism, which is the usual accompaniment of imperfect knowledge, he boldly asserts that Poland will never again be an independent nation; that the Poles were politically imbecile, because in 1811 they hesitated to join their old enemy Russia against France, in whose army there were whole regiments composed of their countrymen; that one of the causes of the fall of Poland was the "lowness of the suffrage" (a bad look-out for England); and that the Polish nobles were slaveholders. In support of the latter assertion, which, as I shall show presently, has no foundation in fact, he produces a bit of philology which will make those who know the Polish language and people stare. "The common appellation for the peasant," he says, "in the language of the upper classes (chlop), is equivalent to 'the dirt of the earth.'" Now the word "chlop," as any one who has resided in Poland will tell him, is the appellation for the peasant used not only by what are called the upper classes, but by the peasants themselves. Its precise origin is unknown, but it was certainly never equivalent to "the dirt of the earth," except in the sense in which bad landlords everywhere treat the peasants as the dirt of the earth. The word is, indeed, usually derived by philologists from "leb," head, and it originally meant the head of the family, the kindred word "chlopiec" meaning "boy" to this day.

But to resume our subject: According to Madame Novikoff, the partition of Poland was not a crime, but a good deed, as it put an end to the tyranny of the minority over the majority—an assertion which sounds somewhat strangely in the mouth of the principal advocate of a system of government under which all power is concentrated in the sovereign, whose mere word is sufficient to consign any one of his subjects—whether innocent or guilty, whether a murderer or a political writer—to those horrors of exile in Siberia of which we are now again hearing so much, and which Mr. Kennan has so graphically described in the *Century* magazine. Now let us look into this charge a little more closely. There is a certain air of plausibility about it, for it is unquestionable that political power in Poland was, until the passing of the Constitution of 1791, entirely vested in the hands of the nobles. But here we see the danger of employing words which bear a different signification according to the country in which they are used. In England a nobleman belongs to a small class of persons with "handles to their names," whose town and country residences and ancestry are recorded in Burke and Debrett; in Poland there were no titles of nobility; and when a man became a noble, he simply acquired the right of bearing arms, together with certain political privileges, of which the most important was the right of voting at elections. Among the nobles were lawyers, doctors, and merchants; and a Polish proverb said that "a noble on his field is equal to a lord in his castle."

In the eighteenth century the number of "nobles" in Poland was so great that it constituted a fifth of the whole population, which is a much larger proportion than that of the people who enjoyed the franchise in England after the first Reform Bill. And this Polish patent of nobility—the right to take part in the government of the country—was not, as with us, given indiscriminately to all who were above a certain standard of material prosperity; it was the reward of the peasant for services, civil or military, rendered to the State; in a word, for noble actions. It is absurd, therefore, to talk of Poland having been ruled by an aristocracy in our sense of the term. The poorest noble, that is to say, the poorest voter, had precisely the same amount of political rights as the richest; and to the exaggerated development of political individualism, which made every voter an active politician, was partly due the anarchy from which Poland suffered.

I have already stated that the main cause of the partition of Poland was that she enjoyed free institutions such as at that time were not possessed by any other continental nation. Towards the end of the eighteenth century revolution was in the air, and the despotic sovereigns of Europe were trembling on their thrones. In the midst of them was a country as large as France, with a people brought up in the principles of freedom, having the widest powers of self-government, and under a king whose power was even more strictly limited than those of the present sovereign of England. What wonder that the despotic rulers of Russia, Prussia, and Austria should have feared that the "canker of liberty," as a Russian writer has called it, might spread to their own down-trodden subjects? No doubt they were influenced to a great degree by the greed of territory; but they were much more influenced by the instinct of self-preservation; and Campbell and the English statesmen of the time rightly judged that the fall of Poland was a deadly blow to the cause of freedom all over the world.

We now come to the second count of the indictment—the

oppression of the peasants. But where were the peasantry not oppressed in the eighteenth century? All modern civilised nations have gone through the same phases of equalisation of the rights of the various classes in the State. First, all political power and privilege is concentrated in the sovereign; then some of it passes down to the great feudal lords or barons; then it is extended to the professional and mercantile classes; and, finally, it descends, in a very attenuated form, it is true, to the artisans and peasants. In the eighteenth century this process was barely in its initial stage in every great country of Europe, except England and Poland. In Russia all power was, as it is still, in the hands of the sovereign, and the peasant was nothing but a slave, as he could be sold like a dog, separated from his family, and moved about from one estate to another. In Germany and Austria the monarch was also practically absolute; while the peasants, under the system known as "Leibeigenschaft," were serfs attached to the land and forced to work for the landowners. In Poland, much the same system prevailed as in Germany; the Polish peasant was entirely maintained by his master, who had considerable powers over him, which were, however, to some extent restricted by law and custom; he had no political privileges, but was frequently rewarded by the diets for services to the State by being made a noble; he was obliged to work for his master during a certain number of days in the week, and he could not, as in Russia, be moved from the estate to which he belonged. That the Polish landowners, like those of other countries, often terribly abused their power over the peasants is unquestionable. But landlords were no better in other parts of Europe, as we know from the statements of French and German writers—which may be mythical exaggerations, but must have been based on a substratum of fact—about such monstrous practices as that of the *droit du seigneur*, and the still more atrocious one of the *bauchrecht*, *i.e.*, the right of the master to warm himself, when hunting on a cold day, by stabbing his serf in the stomach and placing his hands in the wound. In Poland, at least, the more enlightened people publicly denounced landowners who ill-treated their peasants; and with the general advance of humanity and civilisation, the peasants of Poland have long since shared in the improvement which has taken place all over Europe in the relations between the various classes of the agricultural population. In 1760 Count Zamoyski and several other wealthy Polish landowners substituted the payment of a money rent for the old system of forced labour; and the Constitution of the 3rd of May 1791 made the peasants equal to all other citizens in the eyes of the law. The relations of the peasant to his master then became those of landlord and tenant; and this system worked so well that, according to M. de Lavergne, the eminent French economist, one-fourth of the property of the country passed into the hands of persons not of the noble class, and the value of land trebled. Many of the Polish landowners in Lithuania, which was then under the Russian government, proposed that their peasants should be made proprietors of their holdings; but the Emperor Nicholas steadfastly rejected these proposals, though they were made to him by some of the most eminent personages in the country. Then came Alexander II., who, after introducing peasant proprietorship in Russia, could hardly persist in the refusal of his predecessor to grant it to Poland. But an ingenious method was adopted by which the grant of compensation to the landlords was arranged without any expense to the Imperial Treasury. The compensation allowed them was fair enough; but, at the same time, they were ordered to pay a special tax, the amount of which rather more than covered the sum due to them as compensation. They were compensated as landlords but taxed as Poles. What would our Irish landlords say to such a scheme? It would be a very convenient way, no doubt, of settling the thorny question of land purchase in Ireland, for it would absolutely save the English taxpayer; but the Irish landowner would certainly not bear as tamely as his Polish colleague had to do, what in England would be called sheer robbery, though in Russia it bears the more euphonious appellation of "an administrative measure."

But to return to the Polish peasants. In Prussia the peasants remained serfs until 1809; in Austria until 1811; in Russia until 1861; while in Poland they were placed on the same legal footing as the landowners in 1794. There could not, therefore, have been any reason for political antagonism between the Polish nobles and peasants, and as a matter of fact they have always acted together in the great national movements which have taken place since the first partition. The notion industriously propagated by the enemies of Poland that the nobles are a class apart from the rest of the population, that they alone wish for the restoration of Poland, as it would restore to them the privilege of oppressing the peasants, and that the other classes are content under Russian and Prussian rule, is a silly fable which will not stand a moment's examination. Is it credible, I would ask not only the student of history, but any man who knows human nature, that the tens of thousands who, from the insurrection of Kosciuszko in 1794 to the last disastrous rising of 1863, escaping the vigilance of the Russian police, went out at night into the woods to fight for their country armed only with a scythe or a knife and stick, and kept the whole Russian army at bay for months, belonged to the aristocratic class? No, gentlemen, these unknown heroes who silently died a soldier's death against the enemy, or disappeared from among their relations and friends to linger in the nameless tortures of Siberian exile, were for the most part what we would call working men, that is, artisans and peasants. Kosciuszko, himself a noble, was followed in the memorable rising of 1794 by 4000 peasants armed with scythes ; and his first achievement with this little band was to attack 12,000 Russians near Cracow, who, after a battle of five hours, in which the Polish peasants captured the Russian artillery and turned it against the enemy, were beaten with a loss of 3000 killed and many prisoners. The insurrection which broke out shortly after at Warsaw was headed by a banker, Kapostas ; a shoemaker, Kilinski ; and a butcher, Sierakovski. The revolution of 1830 was begun by the non-commissioned officers and privates of the Polish army ; that of 1863 by the artisans of Warsaw. The fact is that in Poland, as everywhere else, revolutions were made by the middle and poorer classes, and not by the aristocracy, who knew too well the fearful odds to take the responsibility of leading the nation to almost certain destruction, though when the people had once risen, they cheerfully sacrificed their lives and their properties for the cause of their country. The working men had only their lives to give, and had not even the prospect of leaving to their children a glorious name ; but they emulated none the less their more fortunate countrymen in the brilliancy of their courage and the purity of their self-devotion. Thus we had the noble spectacle of a whole nation struggling with its oppressors, never knowing when it was beaten, but rising again and again to resume the unequal conflict.

Nor is it only in insurrections that the peasantry of Poland have acted in unison with the other classes of the nation. In the Polish parliament of the Austrian province of Galicia, peasants sit and speak side by side with landowners, lawyers, and merchants—a consummation at which we have not yet arrived even in our Parliament at Westminster, since Mr. Arch sat in the House as the representative of the agricultural labourer. In

Prussian Poland, too, the most sturdy opponents of Germaniz-
ation are the peasants, who at large meetings in the country
districts have made eloquent speeches protesting against the efforts
of the Prussian government to suppress the Polish language, and to
swamp the Polish population by German settlers.

The result of the elections which have just taken place in Germany, and which are carried on under a system of universal
suffrage, shows that the number of Polish deputies in the
Reichstag has been increased to 16; and although (Prussian
Poland being an agricultural country) the great majority of the
voters must have been peasants, the whole of the sixteen deputies
whom they have elected belong to the class of so-called nobles,
and one of them is a member of the aristocratic family of the Czar-
toryskis. The unity shown by these Polish voters, all going like
one man to the poll to vote for their candidate, is held up by the
German press as an example to the German voters, who are split
up into numerous parties, each with its own candidate, and
whose votes consequently often neutralise each other.

I may add, to show the growth of the Polish nationality in
Prussia, that while in 1881 the number of Polish voters voting for
Polish candidates was 194,894, in 1890, it was 245,852—an
increase of nearly thirty per cent.

Undoubtedly the political system of Poland was very defective.
The Poles had the faults of a warlike and high spirited race; they
were impatient of restraint, fond of luxury, and demoralised by
the dissolute manners introduced by their Saxon kings; and the
result was a laxity in the machinery of government which in
the eighteenth century almost stopped it altogether. That this
did not arise from the incapacity of the Poles for self-government (they had governed themselves for 800 years) was
proved by the constitution of 1791, which was admitted by the
greatest statesmen of the time to be the most masterly measure
of the kind which had yet been devised, and which, if Russia and
Prussia had not crushed it in the bud, would certainly have
proved an effectual remedy for the anarchy from which Poland
suffered. I have shown that in this respect, and in the oppression
of the peasants, there was at that time no great country on the
Continent which could have cast at her the first stone. But,
it might be said, a mere negative admission of this kind is
hardly a sufficient justification for a country's claim to exist.
England, the first home of liberty, "the mother of parliaments,"
the saviour of Europe from the tyranny of Napoleon, the

propagator of civilisation in three Continents; France, the apostle of ideas and literary culture; Germany, the school of philosophers; Italy, the nursery of the Arts,—all these countries have established a right to the gratitude of humanity, and we should all be losers by their extinction. What has Poland done for the good of the world?

We have all heard that Sobieski saved Vienna from the Turks, but it is not so generally known that this event was only one of a series of similar ones. Poland had for centuries been the vanguard of European civilisation against the incursions of barbarous invaders from the East; and to her it was mainly due that our modern Europe was preserved from the withering scourge of an Attila or a Brennus. While Russia was groaning under the yoke of the Mongols, who utterly defeated her in the middle of the thirteenth century, and ruled her with a rod of iron for two hundred years, Poland was an insuperable barrier to their advance southward, thereby rendering, at the price of her blood and of some of her richest towns, which were repeatedly destroyed by the Tartar hordes, a service to Europe which can hardly be over-estimated. Yet though warlike, the Poles were not aggressive. In the earlier part of their history, when they had to build up the Polish State, they did it by conquest, as such things are always done. But from 1333 to 1587, when Poland was at the highest point of her prosperity and greatness, she did not add a single inch to her territory; not once did she make an aggressive war, and though there was a great deal of fighting, it was only to repel the attacks of the Germans, the Russians, and the Tartars. "Defence, not Defiance," was her motto, like that of our Volunteers. And she was not only the defender, but the propagator of civilisation. As early as the fourteenth century the Poles were celebrated in all Europe for their learning and literary culture. Latin was the language, not only of the universities and of diplomacy, but of good society, and in the Polish Parliament the debates consisted of Latin orations worthy of the best period of ancient Rome. The University of Cracow, founded in 1364, was attended by about 15,000 students yearly from all parts of Europe. It was here that one of the first printing-presses was established, and the original wood blocks of a very early edition of the Bible are still preserved there. Copernicus, the great astronomer, and Veit Stoss, the famous sculptor of Nüremberg, were both Poles, and did most of their work at Cracow; the best Latin poets of the Middle Ages were a Scotchman, Buchanan, and a Pole, Sarbievius.

I have said that Poland was the land of liberty. The great

principle of our Habeas Corpus Act, that no man should be imprisoned without trial, was the law in Poland so early as the fourteenth century. Feudalism did not exist among the Poles; there was no vassalage nor holding of the land subject to the lord. Personal liberty and the independence of every citizen in the State was the leading principle of the social organisation, and even prisoners of war became proprietors of the land on which they were placed after they had cultivated it. Among the freemen, or nobles, as they were called, the feudal idea of personal service was unknown; no man was another man's servant, he was only the servant of the State. The result of this principle was naturally to give the people a predominating share in the government from the earliest ages. The first Polish Parliament, composed of the bishops, the high state dignitaries, and the freemen of the lower class, met as early as 1331, and for two hundred years before that date no decision of any Polish King was held to be valid without the consent of his council, composed of the leading men in the country. A Prussian once said to a Pole, in astonishment at the limited power of the Polish sovereigns, "Why, you have no king!" to which the Pole answered, "Yes, we have, but your king has you." The drift of public opinion on any question of the day was ascertained at *conventus* or public meetings, at which all men freely expressed their opinions, and the parliamentary representatives learnt the views of their constituents. There were three estates of the realm—the King, the Senate, and the House of Representatives, or, as we should say in England, King, Lords, and Commons; but all real power was in the hands of the House of Representatives. There was not a single case of a Polish king rejecting a proposal made by his Parliament, or acting in opposition to its wishes. On the contrary, the Polish kings often had to listen to some very plain language in the House of Representatives, where they were obliged to be present during the debates. In 1459 King Casimir II., after opening Parliament, was thus addressed by one of the deputies:—

"Sire, our calamities are notorious, and you are the author of them. If the nation had not been protected by Providence, it would have perished. We have been obliged to demand the convocation of the present assembly in order to ask for reform; we are your subjects and your sincere friends, but we deplore your hostility to our country, and we are not afraid of saying so, in spite of the army you have brought to coerce us. We demand your protection for those who claim justice; we ask you to cast

off your indolence, to show that you are a man, and are ready
and willing to defend the country against its enemies. If
you do this, you may reckon on our fidelity, we will hasten to
obey your orders, we will sacrifice our fortunes for you and the
State, and we will watch over your happiness; if not, you may
rely upon it that we will not give the smallest part of our wealth
to assist you." This threat to refuse supplies soon brought the
king to his senses, as similar threats have done in English history.
Even the great Sobieski, during a debate in which he was accused
of intriguing to appropriate to himself property belonging to the
State, was addressed by one of the deputies in these bold words,
"Sire, either reign justly, or cease to reign." What a contrast
between this free country, where any man could speak his opinion
of the government and criticise the sovereign to his face, and its
neighbour Russia, even in this nineteenth century! After the
speeches I have just quoted, it is curious to read the account
given in the *Times* last December of the late General Trepoff by
an Englishman who lived at St. Petersburg when the General was
chief of the police there. "He was a typical specimen," says the
writer in the *Times*, "of the Russian military despot, and the
policemasters of other Russian towns set themselves to imitate his
example. When he walked along the streets, the cabmen took off
their hats and crouched before him with fear. . . . When the Czar
returned to his capital after a long absence, Trepoff drove at a
gallop in front of his Majesty through the crowded streets, standing erect in his open carriage, glaring round with knitted brows,
and commanding the people to cheer."

Such a scene would be impossible in any other European
country except as an incident in a burlesque, yet it is not uncommon in Russia, where you constantly hear people of the most
unblemished reputation speak with bated breath of the power of
the police; and one can only account for the submission with
which the Russians bear so outrageous a state of things, by the
assumption that they must have had the spirit of independence
and self-respect, which is the natural birthright of every man,
knocked out of them by seven centuries of barbarous and
tyrannical government. I have not a word to say against the
Russian people—they are kind-hearted, intelligent, and intensely
patriotic; they have a fine literature, and they have shown wonderful
enterprise and determination as soldiers and administrators; but
they are to be pitied for having a detestable government, and
for not having the spirit to shake it off.

To return to our subject—There were two other points in which Poland was in the fourteenth and fifteenth centuries far ahead of any other country in the world. These were religious freedom and freedom of trade. While the Huguenots were being massacred in the streets of Paris; while in England, France, Spain, men were being dragged by hundreds to the stake and the scaffold for their religious opinions; while the Jews were being hounded out of nearly every country in Europe, Poland, though the great majority of her people have always been devotedly attached to the Roman Catholic Church, opened her gates to the persecuted of all creeds.

"The people of Poland," wrote an Italian traveller in the fifteenth century, "have among them a multitude of Jews who are not, like in most countries, reduced to a life of misery as usurers or menials. Several have fields and offices of their own, in which they transact business as merchants; others adopt literary and scientific pursuits, chiefly astronomy and medicine. The Jews in Poland often become rich and celebrated, and are treated on the footing of freemen; there is no distinction made between them and Christians; in fact, they are in all respects on a footing of equality with the other inhabitants of the kingdom."

The Protestants, after the Jesuits had obtained a footing in Poland, were under certain disabilities, like the Roman Catholics in England up to the passing of the Catholic Emancipation Bill in 1829, but they were never persecuted as the Protestants were in France, Germany, and Austria, and they were admitted to the franchise like all other freemen, which was not the case with the Catholics in England before the Emancipation.

One of the chief articles of the *pacta conventa*, or contracts made by the Poles with their kings on their election, was, that no person should be oppressed on account of his religious opinions, and that full liberty should be accorded to every man in Poland to practise the rites of his religion. It was on account of this stipulation that Henry of Valois, Duke of Anjou, when the Poles sent a delegation to Paris to offer him the Polish crown, hesitated to accept it, as he had just been fighting the Huguenots. But the Polish delegates declared that if he did not agree to the stipulation he would not be their king; and it was only when he thus became convinced that he could only get the Polish crown by binding himself to give equal rights to the members of all religions that he gave way. Lutherans, Calvinists, Greek sectarians, Mahomedans, Armenians, and Jews flocked into Poland, where alone they could not be molested on account of their creed ; and you can now see in the Tudor Exhibition in Regent Street the portrait of the Duchess of Suffolk, who, being a Protestant, fled from the persecution of our Catholic Queen Mary, and was received with the utmost kindness by the Catholic King of Poland, who gave her an estate, where she lived until the accession of Queen Elizabeth enabled her to return to England.

As regards freedom of commerce, it was England that chiefly profited by the free admission of foreign goods into Poland. A treaty of commerce was concluded between England and Poland so early as 1386, under the reign of Richard II. In the fifteenth century great numbers of English and Scotch merchants settled in Poland, and established their offices there. In 1579, under the reign of Queen Elizabeth, a British Eastern Company was founded for the purpose of trading with the ports on the Baltic ; and a letter from the Queen to King Sigismund of Poland, dated Greenwich, 16th January 1589, is still extant, in which she begs the king to extend his protection to British trade in his dominions. So friendly, indeed, were the relations between England and Poland, that in 1650 the Polish Parliament decided specially to relieve all English merchants in Poland from the payment of taxes, in order to enable them to pay a contribution of 10 per cent. on their incomes which had been imposed by the Government of Great Britain, and which was duly handed over to the British Minister at Warsaw by the Polish tax-collectors for transmission to London. Another treaty was concluded by Queen Anne in 1707, for the purpose of acquiring very advantageous commercial privileges for English trade with the Polish harbour of Dantzig ; and this treaty was fully confirmed by Article 13 of the Treaty of Utrecht in 1713. The Poles were, however, always opposed to monopolies, even when they would have been highly advantageous to the Polish Treasury. Thus Philip II., King of Spain, offered to pay a very large sum for the exclusive right of buying corn and wood from Poland, but his offer was rejected. The rule was to treat all foreign states alike as regards commercial privileges, and England was the only exception to that rule. The consequence was, that in the eighteenth century the trade of England with Poland was greater than it was with France. From 1697 to 1773 the trade of England with Poland amounted to £22,651,901, while that of England with France was £19,013,818. Burnett, in his *View of the Present State of Poland*, 1807, says—" England is the best customer of Poland. . . . Almost every article of manufacture imported is either really or nominally English. Having occasion to buy a hat at Lemberg, I found the name and ticket of a well-known London hatter, on it, though I perceived plainly that it was of foreign manufacture."

After the partition, owing to the obstacles imposed by Russia and Prussia on Polish trade, all commercial relations between England and Poland ceased; when part of Poland gained a sort of autonomy after the Congress of Vienna, they revived; and when her liberties were finally extinguished by the Emperor Nicholas, her trade with England also disappeared. Indeed, this sympathy between England and Poland, for centuries the only two great nations in Europe that were free, is of very old date, and it was a common practice with the wealthy families of Poland to send their sons to complete their education in England, where they studied constitutional law at Oxford, and witnessed some of the most memorable debates in English parliamentary history at St. Stephen's.

I have, I think, now shown what Poland has done for mankind. She protected Europe from Tartar invasions; she alone for many centuries held high the banner of freedom amid the despotic States of the Continent; she was the patron of learning and the arts; she was the refuge of all who were oppressed on account of their religious opinions; she was the first State that practised free trade, a system which, though in some countries it may be inapplicable, has undoubtedly been of great advantage to the world at large. I have shown you what Poland was; I will now endeavour to show you what she is. Among the historical fables which, though they have been amply proved to be untrue, are still generally believed, is the saying "*Finis Poloniæ!*"—Poland is no more—which was put into the mouth of Kosciuszko at the time when, himself wounded by the Russians, he saw his faithful followers being cut down by the conquering enemy. I do not know whether the similar saying attributed to Lord Chesterfield after the capitulation of the Duke of Cumberland's army to the French in 1757—"We are no longer a nation"—was as fictitious as that alleged to have been uttered by the Polish hero. But of one thing I am quite certain, from my personal knowledge of the country—that Poland is still living; is indeed very much alive. Her population has nearly doubled since the partition a hundred years ago; it is now 31½ millions. The number of Polish newspapers and other periodicals published in Poland is nearly 300; of Polish books, 1500 a year. The Poles have a very varied and extensive literature, but it is almost entirely occupied with national subjects, and is therefore not of much interest to people of other nations. Their greatest writers, however—Mickiewicz and Krasinski among the poets, and the contemporary novelist Sienkievicz—have been translated into all the European languages. Two of their painters, Mateyko and Siemiradzki, stand in the front rank among artists of the Continental schools; and among the chief singers at the opera in London within the last few years have been the two Reszkes, Mierzwinski, and Madame Sembrich, all Poles devoted to their country. Notwithstanding the obstacles imposed by the Russian frontier authorities on importation and exportation, there has in Poland been a considerable development of trade and industry. The chief articles of export are wood, meat, skins, and eggs. The country is mainly agricultural, but the exports of wheat have much diminished, owing to the competition of the United States and other non-European countries. There is, however, a large manufacturing industry; the number of workmen employed in manufacturing establishments, in coal mines, and on the petroleum oil wells in Galicia, is about 200,000. The chief articles of manufacture are textile fabrics, employing 45,000 workmen; machinery; beer; spirits; and sugar; and the total value of the manufactures of Poland is about £35,000,000 a year, not an inconsiderable sum for a country whose industry on the greater part of its territory is impeded at every step by a Government whose object is to crush the Polish nationality at any price.

The tyranny of the Russian government is indeed a byword; and when Mr. Chamberlain in 1885, and Mr. Gladstone in 1888, compared the conduct of the government in Ireland to that of the Russian Government in Poland, they doubtless considered that no comparison could be more opprobrious. I am not going to say one word about the Irish question; this is not a political meeting, and party politics would be out of place in a lecture which deals mainly with facts and not with arguments. But I would point out that any comparison between the system of rule in Ireland and that in Poland must be fallacious, because the circumstances are entirely different. Poland lost her independence at the end of the eighteenth century, when she was a civilised State and one of the great powers of Europe; Ireland was conquered in the twelfth century, when all the countries of Europe were more or less barbarous, and Ireland not the least. Poland has a language and a literature of her own, not inferior to those of the most cultivated nations ; the Irish language has practically disappeared, and the language of all educated Irishmen is English. In the Polish province of Lithuania, the Poles are fined for speaking Polish, and any person teaching the Polish language is subject to a fine of 300 roubles (£30) or two months' imprisonment ; if Irishmen paid a fine each time they spoke or taught English, what a handsome source of revenue it would be for the Treasury ! In Russian Poland a Pole is not allowed to buy land. In Ireland the government assists the Irish tenants to become proprietors by purchase of their holdings. In Russian Poland a man suspected of conspiracy against the government is seized in his own house in the middle of the night and dragged away without trial of any kind to Siberia, where he may linger for years without his family knowing what has become of him. In Ireland there is at least no secrecy ; the man is openly tried by a magistrate, and we have long ceased to transport our criminals, political or other, to distant parts of the Empire. Again, in Russian Poland whole villages of peasants have, by a liberal use of bribes, and failing these, by shooting down all objectors, been converted, as it was called, *en masse* to the Russian Church, and members of other religions are impeded in every way in their business and family relations, so that many Jews have found it worth their while to pay fifty roubles to a priest to make them orthodox Russians. I need hardly say there is nothing of the kind in Ireland. Finally, in Russian Poland not a word can be printed in any newspaper or book without the permission of the government, and English newspapers often arrive with whole columns ruthlessly obliterated with printer's ink when they contain any remarks likely to be disagreeable to the Czar or his officials ; while in Ireland, as you know, the most violent fulminations against the government in the *Pall Mall Gazette* or the *Star* are admitted without even a pencil remonstrance in the margin.

In a word, there is not a single point in which what is most characteristic of Russian rule in Poland exists in Ireland. Whether the government in Ireland is bad or good is quite another question ; all I say is that that government is utterly different from the government of Russia in Poland, and that the two things cannot be compared. We are, happily, a free country (though we don't seem to appreciate the blessing as much as we used to do), and it would be absolutely impossible for any English Government, however bad, to do in Ireland what the Russian Government is doing in Poland.

The oppression of the Poles in the German part of Poland is, of course, not so barbarous; but it is far more insidious. There is a show of constitutional government, as Polish deputies sit in the Prussian and German parliaments; but they are naturally, as the representatives of three-and-a-half millions of people out of the fifty millions that constitute the German Empire, in a small minority; and the German majority have cheerfully voted, under the inspiration of the wily Bismarck, laws for the exclusion of the Polish language from courts of law and schools in Prussian Poland, and large sums of money for colonising with Germans estates vacated by Polish proprietors. These ingenious schemes, however, are not so successful as was hoped by their promoters. Not being allowed to have their children taught Polish in the schools, the Poles in Prussia have them taught at home; and every number of every Polish newspaper published in Prussia contains in large capitals an exhortation to its contributors to teach their children Polish. The attempts of the Prussian Government to settle Germans on Polish land, too, are counteracted by a bank, founded by Poles from all parts of Poland, which helps landowners when they are in financial difficulties, and bids for Polish estates that are in the market so as to prevent their getting into German hands.

One of the strongest witnesses to the vitality of the Polish nation is the great Bismarck himself, who, in a speech which he made in the German Parliament, declared that the three-and-a-half millions of Poles in Prussia constitute a danger, by their indomitable patriotism, to the vast German Empire; that they are much more prolific than the Germans; and that, when a German marries a Polish woman, he almost always becomes a Pole himself—not a very cheering prospect, one would think, for the promoters of German colonisation among the Poles. His statement is, how-ever, perfectly true. Like France, England, and other vigorous European nations, Poland has a force of assimilation which draws to itself the members of other nationalities living on its soil; and experience shows that Ruthenians, Lithenanians, Germans, and Jews, residing on Polish territory, become Poles not only in language, but in national feeling. Poland, like England, is made up of many races; but it is one nation, with the same history, the same literary language, the same literature, and the same political traditions.

I have mentioned above that the greater part of Poland is still under governments which use all the immense power at their command to crush out the Polish nationality. There is a small part of Poland—the Austrian province of Galicia—where a more humane and enlightened policy is pursued. This province is not small in itself, for its area is 29,937 square miles, and its population six millions, but it is small compared with the whole of Poland, whose area is 300,000 square miles, somewhat larger than that of France, and whose population is thirty-one and a half millions. Now Galicia, though relatively not so rich in industrial establishments as Russian Poland, is a very fair illustration of what Poland would be if it were independent. Since Austria lay at the feet of Prussia after the disastrous war of 1866, the western half of the empire has been organised on the federative principle, and Galicia practically governs herself, subject to the central authority at Vienna, where she has a minister and delegates of her own. It is interesting to see how this Poland in miniature is governing herself. She has a council of administration and a parliament, with Polish officials, a Polish university, and other local institutions which are just the same as if she were an independent State. To judge by the statements of the enemies of Poland, who represent the Poles as irredeemable revolutionists and anarchists, one would suppose that Galicia is a sort of cockpit of political factions all fighting together, oppressing the peasants, and without the slightest regard either for law or order. But what are the facts? The Galician Parliament, or diet, is composed of men of all nationalities, classes, and religions. Jews, Ruthenians, united Greeks, peasants, sit side by side with Roman Catholics, Poles, great landowners, and professors.

Yet the debates in the Polish Parliament, though they are often very animated and show plenty of party spirit, are conducted with an order and regularity which might serve as a model for several representative assemblies nearer home. Poles and Ruthenians quarrel a good deal—there was even a duel between a Polish and a Ruthenian member the other day, on account of a speech made by the former in the House—but there is no obstruction, no "talking against time," no disturbance of the order of debate by frivolous motions whose only object is to wear out one's opponents. And as to respect for the law, there is no nationality in the Austrian Empire which is so law-abiding as the Poles. Crime is rare, and the streets of Cracow and Lemberg are much safer than those of Vienna or Prague. Owing to the poverty of the country, exhausted by incessant wars and the oppression of former Austrian Governments, trade is not very flourishing, but the petroleum industry is gradually developing itself, and it would become a mine of wealth to any foreign capitalists investing in it. The want of capital is, indeed, the chief obstacle to the development of Galicia, which is very rich in natural resources, and the construction of railways, of mills, of dyeing establishments, and of manufacturers of textile fabrics on a large scale would be very profitable.

And finally, as to the political capacity of the Poles, who have never been wanting in statesmen, I need only mention the foremost, next to the Prime Minister, of the members of the Austro-Hungarian Cabinet, M. Dunajevski, the Minister of Finance, who is universally acknowledged as a man of extraordinary ability, endowed with the highest qualities of statesmanship, and by his skilful management of the Austrian finances has now for the first time for many years produced a budget with a surplus.

We have now seen the past and the present of Poland. What of her future? To prophesy in politics is foolish and dangerous, but the field of speculation is wide, and stranger things have happened than even the restoration of Poland, the only great historical country (now that Hungary, Italy, and Greece are free) which still lies in bondage. What a blessing it would be to humanity if "the canker of liberty" could be made to revive in Northern Europe, and by eating away the accumulated slough of centuries of despotic rule, leave the great Russian and German nations free to pursue their natural development—if a nation like Poland, independent, high spirited, not aggressive, but with the highest qualifications for self defence, and nurtured in traditions of freedom from its infancy, could show the Russians that servility, with her handmaid corruption, is a curse, and the Germans that there are higher things to strive for than mere empire—if there would then be an end of the Russian greed of conquest, carefully fostered by the Russian officials in order to divert the minds of the people from the scandalous abuses and oppression of their government at home; and if the nations of Europe, relieved of the incubus of Russian aggressiveness, were enabled to reduce those enormous armaments which are among the most crying evils of our time! You will say that this is a dream; but the dreams of nations sometimes come true, and the friend of liberty will never despair of Poland; for if the world's progress is not a mere phrase, Time and Education, the great levellers, must gradually undermine the great absolutisms of the Continent, and Poland will surely then be called to resume her place and her beneficent mission among the fraternity of European nations.

VIII.

ITALY.

J. STEPHEN JEANS.

IT is not too much to say that no nation of either ancient or modern times has played so distinguished a part on the stage of history, has had a more varied and chequered career, has contributed more to the advancement of laws and learning, arts and sciences, commerce and colonisation, than Italy. There is not an inch of her soil that is not classic; there is not a hamlet, village, or town in her whole extent that has not its story of pillage and slaughter, resistance to oppression, feudal customs, priestly tyranny, high purposes, and noble achievements. "The rude forefathers of the hamlet" have often, in Italian history, lit beacon fires of freedom that have been reflected throughout the world. Italian art remains the envy and the despair of the art of all other nations and of all other times. Italian jurisprudence, whether in the form of Roman law, or in the later phases of mediæval codes adapted to altered conditions, has been the foundation on which most of our legal precedents rest even to the present day. Italian navigators, Columbus, Marco Polo and his brother, and their antetypes, have been the pioneers of travel and commerce all the world over. Italian liberty, as enjoyed by the Free States of Venice, Florence, Genoa, and Lucca, has been the basis of later political systems that recognise equality before the law as the first principle of just government, and have upon that foundation reared a superstructure that is indestructible. Education and literature have been equally under obligation to Italian minds. The Universities which were founded at Bologna, Naples, Padua, and other Italian cities were the forerunners, and in many cases the types of those that have since been able to achieve perhaps a more illustrious name in other lands. The great libraries of the Vatican and of the Florentine Republic preceded by many years the establishment of most of the other libraries of

Europe. Municipal Institutions are equally indebted to this remarkable country. Buried for generations in the grossest of superstitions, and under the most galling tyranny, municipal freedom every now and again, even while the unbridled license of personal rule seemed to be the only alternative available for the whole of Europe, assumed a certain definite form which at least kept it alive, and interposed some sort of check, however feeble and ineffectual in the main, to the autocracy of the Popes, the dukes, and the other powers of the period. Eager in the pursuit of commerce, and adventurous beyond nearly every other nation, the citizens of Florence, followed by those of Venice and Genoa, established some of the first trading companies and guilds for mutual protection and the advancement of material interests. In an age when railways were not, before the principles of road-making were understood as they now are, and when engineering was almost entirely neglected elsewhere, the Italians not only provided themselves with excellent roads, but with navigable waterways as well, of which the Canal between Milan and the Ticino is one of the most striking examples. The Roman aqueducts, whereby water supplies were conveyed to the towns and villages from the adjoining hills or mountains, are masterpieces of art and of engineering skill, and many of them are in constant use even at the present day. The architectural skill and taste of the early Italians is attested by many examples, alike in churches, palaces, and other buildings, scattered up and down the face of the country, and making the Italy of to-day perhaps the most interesting land to visit that the world can show. These are but a few of the considerations that throw a halo of romance around the name of Italy, and compel the admiration, if not the adoration, of all time.

In undertaking to speak of such a country, the difficulty is, of course, to know how and where to begin. But as we must begin somewhere, and as it is necessary to a correct appreciation of the subjects to be afterwards dealt with that we should have the position and form of the country clearly in our minds, I may at once proceed to say that Italy is mainly a peninsula, to which is added the large islands of Sicily and Sardinia, the island of Elba, and about sixty-six minor islands. It has a total area of nearly 111,000 square miles, or about 12,000 square miles less than the United Kingdom, while its population at the last census amounted to about thirty millions, being about eight millions less than that of our own country.

One of the most striking physical features of the country is its immense length in proportion to its breadth. The total length of the Peninsula is about 700 miles, but its breadth in some places does not much exceed 20 miles. This, of course, involves another remarkable physical characteristic — namely, the exceptional extent of coast line, which in Europe is only equalled by that of our own country, and amounts for the mainland to about 2000 miles, and for the islands to nearly 2000 miles more. Another prominent feature of the country is that it is traversed throughout the greater part of its length by the chain of the Apennines; and as its northern limits are formed by the chain of the Alps, which separate it from France, it is obvious that the country must have a considerable extent of mountainous territory. This is not only the case, but it is the case to so considerable an extent, that less than one-half of the total area is under cultivation, so that relatively to her size, Italy can hardly be regarded as a productive country in the same sense as that term may be applied to the much more prolific and densely-populated countries of Belgium and Holland.

In a country extending from north to south through ten degrees of latitude, there must be a great difference of climate due to position alone; but besides that, the climate of Italy is influenced by the proximity of the lofty mountain ranges referred to in some of its divisions, and by the influence of the air from the sea, which almost surrounds the other parts. If we follow the classification of Saussure, we may divide the climate of Italy into four regions. The first extends from latitude 46.28 to 43.30, and thus comprehends the whole of the Austrian and Sardinian dominions, and the other territories to the north of the Apennines, with Bologna, Ferrara, and Romagna. In this region the quicksilver in Reaumur's thermometer descends to ten degrees below zero; the lagunes at the mouths of the rivers are frozen; and sometimes in January and February the snow remains from ten to fourteen days on the ground. Delicate plants do not grow except in sheltered situations; but the mulberry trees flourish, and rice is grown. The slight night-frosts appear in November, and some years as late as April. Even in summer a benumbing cold is brought down from the Alps by a violent storm of northerly wind. The second region extends from 43.30 to 41.30, comprehending Tuscany, Lucca, the Papal States, the Abbruzzis, and the whole of the western shore to the south of the Apennines, though some part of the latter does extend as far north as 44, but, from being sheltered by the moun-

tains, has a climate similar to the southern part. This is the
appropriate climate for the growth of the orange, the lemon, and
the olive; but even in this region the snow is occasionally to be
seen on the fields. The third region extends from 41.30 to 39,
and comprehends the greater part of the continental dominions
of the former kingdom of Naples. Here snow is rarely seen,
and never remains; the quicksilver seldom falls below three
degrees, and all plants of the agrumenous tribe flourish in the
open air. The fourth region extends from 39 to 35.50, and
comprehends the southern part of Calabria and the island of
Sicily. The quicksilver rarely falls below zero, and snow and
ice are unknown except on the summits of the mountains. The
tropical fruits come to perfection in the open air, the sugar-cane
flourishes, the cotton plant ripens, the date trees are seen in the
gardens, and the enclosures of the fields are formed by aloes. It
will be obvious that this classification cannot be universally
applied, and principally attaches to the flat land of Italy.

Thus the positions on the sides of high mountains, the vicinity
of the sea, and the volcanic nature of the soil, all have an
influence which must cause many local variations in any classifica-
tions, and form exceptions to what is generally correct. The
tops of the Alps in Savoy and Piedmont are covered with perpetual
snow.

The Apennines are also commonly clothed with snow from the
middle of October till the beginning of April; and on the highest
mountains of Abbruzzo, the Majella, and the Velino it remains
from September till May.

The northern part of Italy, including Tuscany and the Papal
States, does not generally present that charming aspect which
people from the North picture to themselves of the garden
of Europe; and they are only introduced into that region on
proceeding to the east from Manfredonia, or to the west
from Terracina. There the winter is scarcely colder than our
September; vegetation proceeds without interruption; and the
air is filled with the most aromatic odours.

There are many ways of writing history. If I were called upon
to give you, in an hour's lecture, a historical sketch of the
development of Italy, I should probably be expected to occupy at
least one-half of that time with references to the rulers who had
at one time or another misled, oppressed, and deteriorated the
people. But I do not so read the functions of history. The
nations of the world are no doubt very much what their rulers

make them, but they are also largely responsible for the making of their rulers. In my view, the ruler of a nation is the embodiment for the time being of the acts, aspirations, and characteristics of the people over whom he wields authority. That is no doubt the case to a much larger extent now than it was in former days. It is due to the electric telegraph, the newspaper press, the railway, and other modern institutions, that a national sentiment can be diffused and acted upon much more quickly than formerly. One-man power is now only wielded so long as it is permitted. The will of the people is the potent and sovereign factor; not the will of the ruler, who is only their temporary mouthpiece and agent.

The real circumstances of a country are, therefore, to be sought for not in the pomp and pageantry of courts, nor the tread of armed men, nor the incidents of a campaign, nor the personal relations of different sovereigns; but in the typical features of race, climate, social condition, physical powers and attainments, degree of well-being, stability, endurance, and growth of the means that make for civilisation and improvement. Of all these, so far as ancient Italy is concerned, and, to a large extent, as regards modern Italy as well, there is less absolute and complete knowledge than we could wish for. An occasional ray of light is projected across the dark surface of mediæval times, but the glimmer is short, un-certain, insufficient. We know much of the rulers and their ways; of the habits, feelings, hopes, and condition of the people, only very little. But we can imagine more than we actually know. For hundreds of years Italy was not the cockpit perhaps, but certainly the chief battlefield of Europe. The opening of the Christian era found Italy the centre of Roman power, with wars and revolutions on hand in almost every quarter of the then known world. A hundred years later, and it was still the same. Rome was at war with Parthia, Media, Armenia, and other States; the Christians were undergoing their third persecution; the philoso-phers were being expelled from the Imperial City; and con-spiracies, heresies, and schisms were rampant on every hand. It was the same old story, with an infinite variety of detail, both of scene and circumstance, until in 476 an end was put to the Western Empire of Rome by the deposition of Augustus. There-upon began the long night of the Middle Ages. Italy was delivered over to the rule of a Scythian chieftain; Odoacer was placed in supreme power by a revolt; and for a long time the country was controlled by bands of foreign and licentious mercenaries.

In speaking of the history of Italy, we do not, of course, mean to refer at any length to the history of ancient Rome, which has, for our present purpose, a very limited interest. It has been well observed that the history of Rome and the history of modern Italy are no more related to each other than a tragedy is to the after-piece. Not only the nations and their language, not only manners and morals, laws and gods, have given place to others; not only the monuments of men have been swept from the face of the land, but the land itself, its general aspect, and its very climate are changed.

The history of Italy since the old Roman Empire perished by inanition, and was overrun by the hordes of northern barbarians, may be divided into six distinct eras or epochs, which I shall briefly summarise.

I. The period of the Middle Ages, A.D. 568 to 1183, the age of the fathers of the Church, of the monkish chroniclers of the Middle Ages, of the theological and philosophical universities founded by Charlemagne and his successors, of the sources of modern institutions, manners, and feelings, arising from the contact of the rude but active temper of the northern conquerors, with the more enlightened manners of the conquered, and of the new religion of Christianity, which, displacing the Paganism of the ancient Romans, and the idolatrous worship of the Goths and Greeks, levelled the distinctions of caste and race, and provided the germs of a new morality.

II. In the second epoch the Italian republics were in the full plenitude of their power and greatness, controlling and administering the commerce of the world, and establishing principles of freedom and independence which tended to promote arts and letters, to excite energy and enthusiasm, and to get rid of tyranny and feudalism. In this age Genoa, Pisa, and Venice shared between them the empire of the seas; Milan and Florence were the workshops of the then known world. This was the epoch of Leonardo da Vinci and Michael Angelo; of Colonna, Strozzi, and Dandolo; of the Cabots, Amerigo, and Columbus; of Dante, Varchi, and Macchiavelli.

III. and IV. The third period, which extended from 1434 to 1748, has been described as that of Italian principalities, of domestic tyranny; when the noble families of Este and Medici achieved a splendour and maintained a state that contrasts sharply with the simplicity of the republics which they superseded; while the fourth period, which, to a large extent, overlaps the third, and extended from 1530 to 1789, has been described as that of foreign dominion or the age of decline; an age during which the French, the Spaniards, the Austrians, and the Swiss were by turns invited and expelled by the Italians themselves; an age that witnessed the long struggles of Venice against the Ottoman powers, the wars of the House of Savoy against France and Austria, and frequent revolts against inquisition and despotism. During this period literature was all but dead; it was a literature of Inquisitors and Jesuits, of fetters and fagots.

The fifth period of modern Italian history brings us down to the year 1848, and embraced the stirring times of the French Revolution. This period was distinguished by a long peace under the tardy and sleepy rule of the Austrians, during which the rigours of the Inquisition were entirely got rid of, and many political and religious reforms were introduced, not, however, without much pressure, as evidenced by the revolutions of Naples and Turin in 1820, and the insurrections of Modena, Parma, and Romagna in 1831.

Finally, we come to the era of unification and regeneration, of which we shall speak later on—the period of valour, trial, and triumph, with which we associate the names of Victor Emmanuel, Garibaldi, and Cavour.

Hitherto we have said but little of the Italians themselves. We must now endeavour to see what sort of people they are and were.

Most prominent among the sons of Italy are the Lombards, who have for many centuries inhabited that vast tract of country which lies between the Alps and the Apennines, down to the Adriatic Sea—the richest part of the Peninsula, with a fertile soil and a healthy climate. The Lombards, unlike the Southern Italians, are distinguished by fair hair and complexion, comparatively large stature, a sanguine temper, and an enterprising and active habit of mind. They have always been the most prosperous among the races of Italy, and have been conspicuously successful in agriculture, commerce, and industry.

The Genoese are the descendants of the fierce Ligurians, and, until recently, at all events, had to a great extent escaped foreign admixture. They are a hardy and thrifty race, and have for generations enjoyed the reputation of being the best sailors on the Mediterranean. This characteristic has naturally produced a race of rovers and adventurers, who have navigated and, to a large extent, settled in the four quarters of the globe.

Very different to the Genoese are the inhabitants of Tuscany—a soft, gentle, and highly refined people, of elegant but effeminate features, and slender frames, who have made Florence for many centuries the ruler of arts and letters, and have produced a greater number of eminent men than all the rest of Italy put together.

The island of Sicily, and the southern parts of the Peninsula, were early settled by Dorian colonists, who imparted to the inhabitants of the seaboard a more or less Grecian character, with schools, games, poets, and philosophers, which rivalled those of the Fatherland. Both claim that the character of the Neapolitans is essentially Greek, although the calamities of the feudal system, of the Provençal, Spanish, and Austrian yokes, and of the tyranny and troubles that they have endured from other sources, have tended to sadden them, and modify their Grecian levity and play-fulness, their taste for sophisms and specious arguments, their delight in national dances and festivals.

The inhabitants of Calabria, on the other hand, are a mixed race, very different from those of Tuscany and Piedmont. Traces of Greek, Norman, German, French, and Spanish blood may be found among them, and they have little in common with their neighbours, whether as regards their race, their character, their history, or their national aspirations.

When we remember that all these various elements of race and blood had been for centuries warring against each other ; that Milan and Pavia, Pisa and Florence, Naples and Palermo, Venice and Verona, had been rival cities, with different rulers and systems of government, with opposite and opposing interests, with few traditions or memories in common, with bloody grudges and long-cherished antipathies, the work of Italian unity, which was commenced less than half a century ago, and is now an accomplished fact, would seem, on the first blush, to be the merest chimera.

External circumstances were apparently leagued against the consummation of this ideal to a still more serious extent. Italy had a powerful and jealous neighbour in France, who, whatever her professions may have been, could hardly be expected to favour the rise of a great and independent Italian kingdom, which should assume its due place in the councils of Europe, and be a for-midable rival in those waters which France desired for herself.

Another very near neighbour, the kingdom of Austria, held Venetia by the title of treaty and the possession of nearly seventy years, and there could be no united Italy without Venice. The creed of the great mass of the Italians was that without Rome there could be no Italy; but Rome was held by the Papal troops, aided and abetted for a time by the legions of France, and the Pope had, besides, at his back, the prescriptive authority of centuries and the countenance of Christendom. Although subjected to the galling yoke of an infamous tyrant, Naples looked coldly on the project of Italian unity, and did but little to advance it, while the King himself bid defiance to those who sought his deposition. Garibaldi, eager, daring, and impetuous, was likely to precipitate a crisis by engaging in a war with Austria for the liberation of Venetia, which could hardly have been regarded with favour by the rest of Europe. On the other hand, there was the possibility that if the King appeared backward in the cause of Italian unity, Garibaldi would join with Mazzini, and set up a Republic at Naples. Finally, there was the jealousy of all the other states and provinces of Italy at the ascendency of the star of Victor Emmanuel and Sardinia.

When, therefore, the captivating cry of "Italy for the Italians" was raised, its realisation appeared to be unattainable in the face of the difficulties to which allusion has been made. That it should be realised through the House of Savoy and the kingdom of Sardinia was wildly improbable. That State had an area of only 29,500 square miles, or about one-fourth of that of Italy as a whole; while its population was very little above four millions, being only one-fifth of that of the consolidated kingdom proposed to be established. Victor Emmanuel, however, knew what he was about. He engaged with the Western Powers in the struggle against Russia in the Crimea, without any imaginable cause of war, and thus forced his kingdom and his personality into prominence. The times were, moreover, ripe for a change. From the kingdom of Naples, with its area of 43,000 square miles and its population of 7,500,000, down to the little republic of San Marino, with its area of forty-four square miles, and its population of only 8400, the governments that ruled in Italy were unsatisfactory, and their tenure of power was unstable. The question was, What should supply their place? It was all very well to speak of Italy for the Italians; but it was well said that "since the time of the Roman Empire there had never been a time when Italy could be called a nation, any more than a stack of timber could be called a ship." Besides, even if it had been otherwise, the problem arose, "Who was to bell the cat?" To realise the fruition of the aspiration, there must be insurrection against established Italian governments, or the overthrow of Italian dynasties. In other words, it appeared to be inevitable that one independent state, as then constituted, should foment insurrection in the dominions of another. A parallel case would be the invasion of Saxony or Bavaria by Prussia, under the pretext of securing "Germany for the Germans."

Such was the position of affairs when, in November 1859, by the Treaty of Villafranca, Lombardy was, under one instrument, ceded to France, and by another was ceded by France to Sardinia. The area of Lombardy, then held by Austria, was 18,450 square miles, and its population was 4,279,000, Milan being the capital. Insurrection in the island of Sicily in the following year led to the deposition of the king; and, a few weeks later, Garibaldi assumed the dictatorship of the island in the name of Victor Emmanuel. This secured for the House of Savoy the control of three-fourths of Italy. The conflict with the Papal States and the termination of the temporal government of the Pope followed. Italy had practically become *Italia Irredenta* when, in 1870, the capital was transferred to Rome, the Eternal City, upon which, as Cavour expressed it, "five-and-twenty centuries have accumulated allglorious memories, as destined to become the splendid capital of our Italian kingdom."

I have spoken of a body who are known as the Irredentists. This is the name given to a political organisation formed in 1878, with the avowed object of freeing all Italians from foreign rule, and of reuniting to the Italian kingdom all those portions of the Italy of old which have passed under foreign dominion. The operations of the "Italia Irredenta" party are chiefly carried on against Austria, in consequence of the retention by that Empire of Trieste and the Southern Tyrol. Until these territories have been relinquished, Italy, or at least a certain part of it, will remain unsatisfied. Whether this may, in the near future, precipitate an Austro-Italian war is, of course, a moot point; but in the meantime, at all events, Italy and Austria are good friends, and lie down together under the sheltering wing of Prince Bismarck.

It would hardly be proper to pass from the consideration of Italian history without making some reference, however incidental, to the part which has been taken in the record by the Papacy. I do not hesitate to say that, in my view, that part has made wholly for evil. I say this alike of the system and its professors. You cannot, indeed, separate the two. If we go back to the earlier centuries of the Christian era, we find that the Papacy was distinguished chiefly for its grasping covetousness and assumption, under the guise of religion, of powers and prerogatives to which it had no claim. In a stand-up fight between any two interests or systems, as between any two persons, a fair-minded man would naturally desire that there should be an entire absence of "fear, favour, or affection," and that both sides should have a fair chance. But the Papacy never did, and, in the very nature of the case, never could give its opponents a fair chance. It has an armoury of spiritual weapons to which they cannot possibly resort, after its temporal means of defence or defiance have been exhausted. It works upon men's hopes and fears with regard to the future. It has encouraged and profited by superstition, and has made full use of that fearful engine of oppression—the holy Inquisition— through whom it has martyred countless thousands in every nation in Europe. Its sacerdotal pretensions have not been more absurd and offensive than their application has been iniquitous. All this, however, might have been borne if the character of the popes and the priesthood had been above reproach. A bad system may, indeed, have good and righteous apostles, and the most holy zeal may be enkindled and applied on behalf of a lie. But in the case of the Papacy there has been grave fault to find with the personal character of its leaders. Many of the popes have been notorious for their depravity. Where their authority has been divided, as it was on several occasions during the Middle Ages, they have proved their human frailty by abusing one another like so many Kilkenny cats. One Pope even stooped so low as to earn part of his income by the licensing of brothels. They have often cast in their lot and influence with tyranny and wrong where the course of right and charity lay clearly marked out before them. They have placed under a ban many of the most potent agencies of modern civilisa- tion, including the printing press and the railway system. They have claimed an authority over the consciences of men which nothing could possibly justify. And, finally, when their temporal authority was assailed, they have ranted like the fishwife whom Dr. Johnson spoke of as an individual. Pray do not let me be mis- understood. I am far from seeking to make an attack upon the Roman Catholic Church as such. That Church has, perhaps, as much cause to be satisfied with itself and its work as any other. On that I express no opinion. But I do unhesitatingly say that the influence of the Papacy upon Italy from first to last has not been salutary; and but for that influence, Italy would probably have become a united and homogeneous kingdom much sooner than it did. At the same time, we would be ungrateful did we not remember that some of the popes have been equally distinguished for piety and learning, and have done good work alike for art and for literature.

We have seen that the task which Italian statesmen have successfully accomplished has been that of uniting the many conflicting interests of the different States and Duchies already named, with their divided authorities and unconformable financial arrangements, into one compact, united, and consistent whole, subject to the same supreme temporal head, with identical political laws and institutions, and with a prestige and strength sufficient to place it in the fifth or sixth place among the great powers of Europe. All this has been accomplished in the face of the most determined opposition, alike of temporal and spiritual powers, with slender financial resources, with lukewarmness on the part of a large section of the population, and with very limited co-operation on the part of other states. The heroes of the achievement have been Garibaldi, Cavour, and Victor Emmanuel. Their labours have borne fruits that could hardly have been anticipated, and England rejoices at the result. The vow which Victor Emmanuel took after the crushing defeat of Novara in 1849, *Per dio l'Italia Sarà* ("Italy shall be"), has been fulfilled. Something, however, remains to be done. "Italy is made, but who will now make the Italians?" This question, originally propounded by Massimo d'Azeglio (who was Prime Minister of Sardinia before Cavour commenced his great work of Italian unification), has not yet been satisfactorily answered. Italy is poor ; she is burdened with an enormous debt ; her armaments are large and costly ; her people for the most part are imperfectly educated ; her death-rate, notwithstanding that she has the finest climate in Europe, is exceptionally high ; her commerce is of limited dimensions ; her industries are few in number, and fail in the majority of cases to compete with those of more Western nations. All this is only what might be expected under the circumstances. A kingdom is little more than a geographical expression, which may be called into existence to-day, and blotted out to-morrow. A people are what their circumstances make them; and if, as in the case of Italy, those circumstances have been inauspicious throughout a long course of years, the processes of elevation and amelioration are likely to be slow, and perhaps tedious.

One of the most unpromising features of the recent history of

Italy has been the great increase of her national debt. Between
1858 and 1868 the national expenditure of Italy rose from 20½
to 47¾ millions; and in 1872, two years after the final touch
had been given to the consolidation of the kingdom by the occupation of Rome, the expenditure had increased to 54¾ millions.
The present annual expenditure may be put at about 70 millions,
which is only 10 to 15 millions under the expenditure of a rich and
prosperous country like the United Kingdom. Much of this
expenditure has perhaps been wasteful, and a great deal may have
been unnecessary. A state like Italy, which has been consolidated by frequent appeals to the sword, and as the ultimate result
of force, cannot halt by the way to consider cheeseparing econo-
mies, nor can it easily restore the balance between revenue and
expenditure. That balance, in the case of Italy, was for many
years on the wrong side. The task of adjusting the two sides of
the account, difficult even in a rich country under ordinary circumstances, demanded, in the exceptional circumstances of Italy,
that expedients should be adopted that pressed with severity upon
the people. The duties on salt and tobacco had to be increased.
Additional taxation was imposed on postage, on petroleum, on
corn, and on colonial goods generally. State lands were sold,
and fresh Treasury bonds were issued. The usually oppressive
grist tax had to be increased. Lotteries, at all times an unsatisfactory source of national revenue, had to be resorted to again
and again, and in some years produced close on 4 millions
sterling. All incomes were made liable to taxation, those derived
from manual labour as well as those from capital and *rentes*.
Manifestly, therefore, Italian emancipation has not been purchased
without entailing grave inconvenience, much suffering, and not a
little permanent hardship and sacrifice on the part of the people
generally. But there is no evidence that the sacrifice has been
unwillingly borne. On the contrary, as all the world knows, it is
the ambition, and apparently the fixed determination, of Italy to
become and to remain one of the great powers of Europe, able to
hold her own in the councils of the nations, whether in war or in
peace. With this end in view she maintains a vast army and a
powerful navy, which would be likely to give a good account of
themselves in any issue that could possibly arise to demand the
arbitrament of the sword. It is questioned whether this force is
needed to secure Italy from external attack and preserve internal
peace. But Italian statesmen appear to deem it indispensable
that their country should be equal to meeting any force likely to

come against her, whether by land or by sea. Nor must it be forgotten that Italy has some reason to regard her powerful neighbours with distrust and suspicion. Nations have long memories. Austria is not likely to forget the humiliating circumstances under which she was compelled to cede the greater part of Lombardy in 1859, and Venice in 1866. Recent events in Africa demonstrated the constant liability to misunderstanding and rupture with France. The opening of the St. Gothard Railway places Italy at a greater peril of invasion from Germany. The relations of the Italian Government and the Pope are not yet so satisfactory as could be desired, and there is even now a question of wounded *amour propre*, which increases the strain. All these considerations appear to justify the Italians in their demands for a strong army and navy; but these can only be purchased at the price of considerable sacrifices on the part of the people generally; and so long as this policy is adopted as expedient or necessary, so long will the material prosperity of the country be retarded.

Indeed, the ordinary taxpayer in this country can hardly form any idea of the crushing character of the burden of taxation which the Italian peasant and mechanic are required to bear. Taking the national and the local taxation of Italy together, the revenue that has to be raised annually amounts, as I have just stated, to about £70,000,000, or, roughly, 50s. per inhabitant. This sum is not nearly so large as that which has to be provided in the United Kingdom and in France. But then the national income of Italy is incomparably less than that of either of these two countries; and when we come to apply the test of income, or ability to support taxation, it comes out that in Italy the taxes represent 20 to 25 per cent. of the national income, as compared with only 10 per cent. in the United Kingdom, and 14 to 15 per cent. in France. Not only so, but in the United Kingdom, and to a less extent in France, the incidence of taxation is so contrived as to press with but little severity on the great mass of the population, whereas in Italy taxation is levied largely upon the necessaries of life and the incomes of the poor, so that the most abject destitution cannot purchase exemption from its baleful demands.

In considering the important and pressing problem of how the effects of this crushing taxation can be mitigated, one question that will naturally be uppermost in the minds of Italian economists is that of whether more can be made than is made at present of the produce of the soil. The great point to be determined is whether the country is adapted to growing with advantage crops that will return a better ultimate result than those that are generally cultivated at present. The time has gone by when a nation required to be self-contained in all the essentials of existence. Independence of outside supplies of food is no longer the shibboleth of political and fiscal reformers. In all the other countries of Europe, as in Athens of old, external sources of supply are now called in. It has been demonstrated that in most of those countries the cultivation of wheat and some other cereals cannot be followed with advantage, in the face of the severe competition of the United States, India, and one or two other countries. Italy is among the countries which do not grow sufficient wheat for their own wants. She is also, despite the remarkable climate with which Nature has endowed her, among the nations that have, relatively to population, a low income from the soil. The agricultural product of Italy per head of the rural population is calculated at less than £11, or only about one-half of that of our own country. This is due to a variety of causes, some of them remediable, others the reverse. The cultivable area of Italy is relatively less than that of most other European countries. This defect of sterility of soil is one that cannot be cured. The average yield of the corn and other crops of Italy is also exceptionally low. The difficulty of providing for adequate rotation of crops, fertilising the soil, and applying scientific husbandry, is probably the chief among the preventable causes. The system under which the metayer holds and cultivates his farm is one that has a tendency to leave much to be desired in this respect. He is not, like the French peasant, the proprietor of his little farm, but holds it on a lease from a large landowner, to whom in too many cases he is under heavy pecuniary obligations, and with whom he divides his produce in varying proportions. Hence the frequent origin of difficulties of which we have had recent experience in our own country in the agrarian troubles of Ireland and the Crofter's agitation in the north of Scotland.

The part which Italy has played over the occupation of Massowah may be regarded as a pledge that she means to continue in fact, as well as in name, one of the great powers of Europe. It will be remembered that when Egypt evacuated the Soudan, Massowah, which was a portion of Egyptian territory, fell into the possession of Italy by force of arms, although the town was claimed by the Abyssinians as the natural port of their country.

England has concurred in the Italian occupation, presumably because we did not desire that the natives should be in possession. Neither Turkey nor the other great powers have, however, recognised the part taken by Italy in this matter, and it is held by eminent jurists that the claims of Italy cannot be maintained in international law. France has actively intervened against the Italian occupation, and at one time it looked as if this intervention would lead to an open rupture. France, however, not having any real interest in Massowah, has not proved her objections so far as the point of the sword, feeling assured, no doubt, that if she did, Germany, which has countenanced the action of Italy, would have supported that power. In such a case, of course, France would have been embroiled in a war with Germany and Italy, and could hardly have hoped for victory.

The fear now is, that having been so successful both in their arms and in their diplomacy, the Italians may deem themselves invincible, and rush upon a conflict that will reduce them to a much lower rank among the great powers than that which they now occupy. The Massowah matter appeared to indicate that Italy would not be averse to trying conclusions with France, hoping thereby, no doubt, to secure a firmer footing on the Red Sea and in the East, as well as to come abreast of that power in the European family. A country that has, like Italy, a great and unsatisfied ambition, is usually liable to attempt more than its strength will justify. Behind Germany, Italy could, no doubt, make a good fight, but single-handed her chance of success in a war with France is not very bright. Her political and diplomatic prospects are at present, however, tolerably reassuring. She is a member of the Austro-German alliance, and may count upon the co-operation of these two empires in the event of her prestige being assailed.

It will be perfectly evident from the short sketch I have attemped of her history, that during the last half century Italy has been the most fortunate of European powers. She has advanced from the position of a congeries of petty states, with no cohesion, unity, or real strength, to a power of the first rank, with interests in the East, and a voice in the settlement of international affairs. She has fished in troubled waters, and has succeeded in obtaining many concessions and advantages where she might just as readily have met with resistance and annihilation. She engaged in the Crimean War, and thereby laid the foundations of an alliance with France, which, however much she may now affect to disregard its results, has in reality been of great use to her, seeing that it secured Lombardy and the Duchies for Victor Emmanuel, and a little later, Naples and the Papal States. By the war of 1866 she added Venetia, and by the war of 1870 she secured possession of Rome.

Italy has shown within recent years that her rulers fully appreciate the great importance of the development of her material resources by the construction and efficient maintenance of public works. The part which Italy has taken in the construction of the St. Gothard tunnel, and in thereby improving her intercourse with the rest of Europe, is sufficiently well known. The railway system of the kingdom has also been advanced with remarkable strides for a kingdom that has so limited a store of wealth and so comparatively small a traffic. The ports and harbours of Genoa, Venice, Naples, and other leading towns have been put into a creditable condition of repair; and it is now proposed to increase the maritime resources of the country by canalising the classic Tiber, and by constructing a canal right across the Peninsula for a distance of 180 miles, with a view to avoiding the long journey round Cape Lucca. The latter enterprise, if it is ever carried out, is estimated to involve an expenditure of some twenty millions sterling, and it would also involve the draining of two large lakes—those of Bolsena and Thrasimene.

Italy, as we all know, has been justly celebrated for the liberal and enlightened part which she has always taken in advancing academic and scientific institutions. Many of the sciences were greatly developed there before they had obtained even a foothold elsewhere. And it is not without interest to recall the fact that although many of our schools and universities are even still hesitating whether they should admit ladies to degrees and professorships, and while women are still excluded from seats in the Commons House of Parliament, the Academy of Sciences in Bologna, as far back as 1712, not only admitted ladies as members, but gave them professors' chairs. In that famous school of learning it is still remembered with pride that nearly two hundred years ago Anna Manzolini was professor of anatomy, and Laura Bassi was celebrated for her knowledge of the abstruse sciences. As there were at that time some 550 academical institutions of the kind in Italy, the country may fairly be reckoned the nursery, as well as the depositary, of many of the arts and sciences that have since blossomed into the noonday effulgence of nineteenth century practice.

The Italy of modern times has been a strange compound of ignorance and superstition, of coarseness and refinement, of religion and impiety, of liberty and the most galling yokes, of toleration and intolerance. The same Italy that was founding the academy of sciences at Bologna, originating the modern school of xylography, drawing up the statutes of the Cosmographical Academy at Venice, advancing by the establishment of several learned institutions the cause of economic science, and enfranchising the serfs in Savoy, was, through the Pope, denouncing Freemasonry, expelling the Jesuits, and confiscating their property, and practising the terrors of the Inquisition. But the lamp of science, although it often burnt dimly, was never wholly extinguished. While Genoa was being besieged by the Imperialists, Beccaria was making those electrical experiments which tended to lay the foundations of the modern science of electrical engineering. While the people were sunk in the direst misery from the ravages of a prolonged war, the first chair of political economy was being established at Naples, and a new code of laws was being issued by Charles. While the finances of the country were in a frightful state of disorganisation, and the great bank of Genoa was being declared bankrupt, Herculaneum was being disinterred from the ashes which had overlain her temples for nearly one thousand seven hundred years, and a meridian arc was being measured by Boscovich and Le Maire from Rome to Rimini. Truly these Italians were a versatile people, and such as they were, such *mutatis mutandis* they are in our own day.

If we were asked to furnish a notable example of the truth of this latter statement, we should point to the crushing load of taxation which the people appear to bear without a murmur in order that their country may take the place to which they aspire in the family of nations; to the existence of the galling system of conscription, which requires every male to serve in the army, unless subject to physical disqualification; and to the risks that they appear prepared to undertake in order to maintain their national prestige. Italy has really little interest in any part of the world outside of her own borders; and if she limited herself to these, it is exceedingly probable, now that her relations with the Papacy are more cordial, that she would escape molestation from any outside quarter. But, as we have seen, she is prepared to run the most fearful risks—even that of being utterly annihilated and wiped out—for the sake of so trivial a mess of pottage as the colonisation of the dreary desert port of Massowah, at the same time that she is building up a solid and substantial basis of prosperity and permanence at home. To my mind, Italy seems to have just as much business with Massowah as Tenterden Steeple has with Goodwin Sands, and her chances of profiting thereby are about equally remote. It is a well-known principle in human affairs that the less a man has to lose, the more ready he is to lose it. Italy has not so much to lose as some other European powers ; but that which she does possess has been purchased at the cost, and by virtue of, many sacrifices, great endurance, patience, and heroism, unlimited loyalty and devotion to the present dynasty. She now acts as if she were ready to throw all these, and much besides, upon a reckless cast, and stand the hazard of the die.

The condition of the people of Italy is still unhappily far from prosperous, although it is much more satisfactory than formerly. Less than half a century ago, a writer who knew something about the country, described the circumstances of the inhabitants in the following terms :—

" The greater part of the population of Italy is to be seen in the country devoted to the pursuits of agriculture. A few, a very few, of them are in circumstances of moderate affluence ; a few more may be represented as in a state of comparative ease, enjoying a bare sufficiency to support life ; but the great body, to whom all others bear a slight proportion, are in the most wretched condition. They are the occupiers of small portions of land, some of them not exceeding an acre in extent, and most of them less than four acres, where, in miserable hovels, barely sheltered, they labour in the fields, and subsist, themselves and their families, on half the produce of the land, the other half being delivered to the proprietor at the time of harvest as his rent. Their food, simple as it is, is far from being sufficient to keep them in a healthy state. They taste neither bread nor animal food. Their chief subsistence is called *polenta*, made from Indian corn, which is merely pounded and then boiled, no expense on account of the miller or the baker being incurred. This kind of meal, made to the consistence of hasty pudding, would certainly be an aliment sufficient to support life when the quantity could be adequately supplied ; but, with the utmost parsimony during the whole year, the termination of it, as the next harvest approaches, often finds them utterly destitute, and with no other resource but beggary or starvation. This is the condition of the larger class of human beings in the north and middle of Italy; whilst in the south the lazzaroni of Naples are living proofs of the wretched condition of great numbers in that more fertile soil and more temperate climate."

I have left myself but little time to speak of the political institutions and systems of government which obtain in Italy, although I can hardly altogether leave these unnoticed.

The legislative authority of Italy rests with the King and two Chambers—the Senate and Chamber of Deputies. The former (unlimited in number) is composed of princes of the royal house after attaining their majority, and of members nominated for life by the King. The Chamber of Deputies is elected by *seratin de liste*, by conditional universal suffrage for periods of five years, and contains 508 members, or one to every 57,000 of the population. For electoral purposes, Italy is divided into 135 districts, which again are sub-divided; one-eighth of the inscribed electors must vote to render an election valid. The present Chamber of Deputies was elected on May 23rd, 1886, a dissolution having been decreed by the King on April 27th.

The division of parties in the Italian Chamber is unusual. The majority, and the bulk of the minority alike, profess Liberal principles; the one being known as the Ministerial left, and the other as the Opposition left or Pentarchists. There is, besides, but little difference in their political programmes. The Opposition includes some minor groups of varying tendencies, a knot of advanced Republicans or Socialists, and the so-called Moderates. There is little or no union in the Opposition; and it is this that has constituted the chief strength of the Ministerial left, which after successfully surviving some nine or ten Ministerial crises, has been uninterruptedly in power for twelve years, a result in a large measure due to the skilful leadership of the late Signor Depretis. On the death of the latter on July 29th, 1887, the ministry underwent no change; as a matter of form, its resignation was tendered, but was withdrawn at the request of the King, Signor Crispi taking over the Presidency of the Council in addition to the Portfolios of the Interior and of Foreign Affairs. Since his advent to power, Signor Crispi, although an old Garibaldian, a Republican, and a professed friend of France, has been the loyal and devoted servant of the monarchy; and so far from disturbing Italy's relations with Austria and Germany, as the Irredentists fondly hoped, it has remained for him to definitely cement the alliance of the Central European Powers. In spite of Parliamentary differences, however, on one point Opposition and Ministerialists are alike united— namely, in the desire to maintain the present Savoy dynasty, which they regard as the keystone of Italian unity. So far as present appearances go, that dynasty has a great future before it. We must all hope that nothing may occur to mar the fortunes of so august a house, or of so spirited, capable, self denying, and patriotic a people as that over which it presides.

IX.

SPAIN.

PROFONGO ALGO Y CONCLUYO NADA.

MRS. CUNNINGHAME GRAHAM.

THE Portuguese have a word called "saudade," which means a longing after, a desire to see some long unvisited place, some long unseen face. It seems, if the following story is true, that one feels these "saudades" even in heaven itself.

Adam got weary of Paradise, and asked leave, if only for a few hours, to revisit the earth. He was told that he would find all changed.

No use!

He must go!

England, he found one workshop. Even the face of Nature was altered. Nothing as he left it! France, Italy, Germany, failed to evoke any remembrance. All was changed. So, southward, like the swallows, to Spain!

As he felt the hot sun bite his cheek, and his eye swept over the fertile vegas of Murcia and Valencia; as he observed the uncultivated country, desolate and unpopulated, he exclaimed with rapture: "This, indeed, is the earth I knew. Under that olive tree could I sit me down and rest, and begin once more to name the animals, male and female, after their kind."

A foreigner happened to relate the foregoing story in a tertulia or conversazione of Madrid. A distinguished Spaniard, who was present, remarked, and he expressed the opinion of all present: "Si, Señor, y tenia razon, La España es Paraiso." "Yes, Sir, and Adam was right, for Spain is Paradise."

These two anecdotes, which are to be met with in almost any handbook of Spain, and which, if not true, might well be so, completely synthetise her present position, and the view which every Spaniard, born and bred, is supposed to take, or ought to take, of his country.

157

The modern influences of the nineteenth century have not worked much change on Spain. The railroad here assumes a certain listlessness, foreign to all idea of hurry and rush; one can almost watch the grass as it grows between the rails; we might still fall asleep and dream that Philip II. still reigns, and the Inquisition also, as we wander through the sombre mediæval streets of the decayed cities of Castille. There is nothing to destroy the illusion, except the ugly clothes which we have donned as the world has grown uglier.

Away from the narrow converging lines of railway (an admirable lesson in perspective; I wish for ever they had remained in prospective) there indeed the illusion grows so strong that it wants little of reality.

Let us conjure up a traveller, and send him by sea to Spain. Let us follow him as he arrives fresh from the Northern greyness into the pellucid atmosphere of the South. Let us watch how his first impression of a new country, vivid as a flash of lightning, almost bewildering in its suddenness and strangeness, affects him. Let us suppose that it is night before the ship anchors in the smooth waters of a Spanish seaport. Let us take Vigo, for instance, with its incomparable bay and magnificent scenery. In the calm bosom of the gently heaving water, shut in on all sides by dark and mysterious shadows, are mirrored thousands of twinkling lights. They are the lights of the town in front of him, which climb up and cling to the dark mass of an eminence whose vague and rocky outlines he can feel rather than see. The feeble lights which twinkle redly from the houses alone illumine the mystery of an unknown town. The long quavering notes of the bugle, sounding the "Retirada," are. wafted over the water. In the early morning he hastes to seek the solution of the problem of the unknown.

Against a broken mountainous background, which rises against a sky which every successive moment thrills with fresh pulses of colour, translucent, cold, and serene, like that we see framed by the dark shadow of a door or window in old German pictures; the serried lines of houses which form the town glimmer whitely in that cold light which precedes sunrise. Hither and thither, above the irregular outlines of their roofs, rises the grey cupola of a bell tower, in which, even as he watches, the bells begin to move, and with grave and sombre sound wake the sleepers to life and prayer.

He lands enthusiastic. He has only seen such scenes before

painted by Hawes Craven, when he has been to see Irving at the
Lyceum Theatre. An hour spent on the quay, in company with
a sleeping cur, waiting for the Custom-house officer who never
comes, somewhat damps his enthusiasm. The lazy curiosity and
remark, excited always in Spain by the appearance of a stranger,
and especially if that stranger be a foreigner, of the loungers and
unemployed boatmen (unemployed, you must understand, not so
much for want of work as will) who lean over the railing at the
landing-place, and while away the morning hours over a cigarette,
irritate him. He resents the suspicious attitude of the green-
gloved Carabiniers, who lean on their muskets, roll cigarettes,
and watch him grimly. The sun begins to bite his unaccustomed
cheek shrewdly. He savagely meditates a letter to the *Times* on
the barbarism of Spanish institutions and officials. He curses
the hour that brought him to Spain ! A Spaniard, accustomed
all his life to patience and longsuffering, to whom time is no
object, and discomfort cannot exist, is calmly indifferent, offers
his cigarettes freely to all around, and "takes the sun," which
is gilding the world around him. But our Englishman fumes.

At last he finds himself in what we will courteously allow to
be an hotel (for such it calls itself), which is very little removed
from the Arab caravanserai, or Fondak. Indeed, the word
" Fonda" shows that its origin sprang from the East. His room
has no curtains, no carpet, an iron bed and a straw chair are all
the furniture. Depressed by the comfortless interior, he stands
gazing vaguely out on to the sunlit patch of grass, which stretches
in front of the hotel to the mole. He follows the movements of
a horse feeding, the play of two yellow curs, a woman cutting
grass with an antediluvian sickle. As she cuts, she intones one of
those nasal, melancholy songs peculiar to this Scotland of Spain.
He will find, too, that the sun has its melancholy, a calmer and
serener melancholy than that of the long grey days of a northern
climate, but a melancholy all the same. The senses seem to be
steeped in an unknown sadness, a sadness which is reflected in
the rich, fertile, beautiful, but most melancholy landscape of
Galicia, in the wild undefinable burden of the song of the
labourer, and the women washing at the stream.

After breakfast, when he saunters up the hill into the town, he
will find himself in the midst of an arcaded plaza or square. It
is surrounded by great stern old granite palaces, which were the
town houses of the powerful families who owned land in the
vicinity of Vigo. Coats of arms project from their angles, and

hang threateningly over the sombre gateways; and yet, one of the contrasts of Spain, alongside of them, nay, in their very ground floors, little shops and booths, open to the street, flaunt their gaudy wares to entrap the innocent countryman.   He passes before the prison, where murderers, smugglers, men and women are confined pell-mell.   A basket dangles from the grated window, tied to a cord of esparto grass, in which the relations deposit food; the charitable, as they pass, a copper.   The Spanish Government, no pamperer of men, contents itself with securing, not nourishing, the persons of its prisoners.   Here rank is taken from the nature of the crime.   The greatest ruffian smokes calmly at the window, the observed of all.   The idlers step aside respectfully as his wife comes up, bearing tobacco and provisions. Her cry of "Gentlemen, my husband is the murderer!" at once commands respect.

What is it that he misses?   At first he does not analyse, but presently, like a flash of lightning, the thought strikes him, that there is no sound of wheels!

Let us go with him as he passes out of the brilliant sunshine of the plaza into the narrow, precipitous streets, full of cool shadows, where the sunlight is blotted out by the almost meeting eaves of the roofs on either side.

The street is badly paved, uneven, tortuous.   If any sound there is, it is of the echoing ring of a donkey's hoofs pattering over the cobble stones, the low murmur of voices from an open doorway.   A closely veiled figure returning from early mass glides past him with prayer book and rosary.   He almost stumbles over a little pig, which runs squeaking between his legs.

The street brings us out on to the Alameda, the public garden, which looks down upon the sea, which lies spread out beneath it, an inland lake shut in by mountains, studded with the white sails of fisher-boats coming in from the open sea.   It is hot; the atmosphere balsamic with the scent of pine woods and the fresh salt smell of the sea.   He begins to feel the soporific influences around him, a conquering laziness, an apathetic indifference. Care seems to have been left behind in duller climes.   He stretches himself on a bench, twists a cigarette lazily, and complacently watches a blind beggar sitting in the sun, a mass of rags, merry, and jesting with all who pass.   Silent and dignified, he utters no words but, "Your grace, for the love of God!" Curious, is it not, hardly to be conceived, that this being, so deformed and hideous as to be terrible to look upon, maintains a certain dignity? Yet, is he not a Spaniard, a Christian—a gentleman? Give him of your copper largesse. He desires, courteously, that "your grace may go with God." If you refuse it, he will not implore curses on your head, but gravely regret that "your grace's heart is not open to the cry of poverty." His condition implies no disgrace. It is his trade, just as another man happens to be a carpenter or blacksmith.

The priest sweeps by in long black robes, which leave a trail on the dusty road. The black-gaitered "pareja," the pair of Guardia civiles; the successors of the Hermandades of Isabella the Catholic, with muskets shouldered, their tricornes glittering in the sun, step briskly past into the country, to patrol the King's highways.

It is night before our traveller returns to his hotel. His footstep reverberates as he passes down the empty street, full of deep blotches of shadow. A narrow strip of starlit sky, alone, is visible between the spectral forms of the houses. Under a dark archway where an oil lamp flickers feebly before a blackened oil painting of our Lady of Grief, he is startled by the apparition of two dark-cloaked figures bearing pikes and lanterns. They are the *serenos*, the watchmen, the guardians of the peace of the sleeping town. They light him home to his hotel, and wield the iron knocker on the gates until the street resounds with answering echoes. His mind reverts involuntarily to a sixteenth-century street in an English country town. Ah! my friend! never more in Messina (read Stratford-on-Avon) shall Dogberry and Verges sleep without offence at the church gates!

Oblivious of England and Spain alike in the mysterious country of sleep, the traveller's dream is broken by the cry of the watchman (ever an old man and creaky), who in slow and guttural accent cries the midnight hour and the state of the night.

And as days go by and the charm overpowers him, he remodels his manners, throws off his British prejudices and *mauvaise honte* and reserve, learns to treat those who serve him, the same people that in England he would call the "lower classes," with a familiar courtesy, that the humblest Spaniard never imposes on.

Not until he succeeds in doing this—not until his Anglo-Saxon blood assimilates some of the Gotho-Spanish ceremonial and formality of manner—does Señor Don Juan Bull, honest John Bull in England, become, as the Spaniards say, "an hombre muy formal," a man of weight and gravity—the quality ever prized

most highly by the Spaniard.   Not until then does he receive the
signs of goodwill and affection at the hands of the most unaffectedly good-natured and warm-hearted people on the face of
the earth.

Well, let us leave our stranger in Galicia, for my subject bears
me away from it, although it gives me a pang to turn my back on
the deep stony roads, water-courses in winter; in summer
shadowy and fragrant with aromatic essences of furze and pine,
made musical with the slow creaking of ox carts;—to leave its
old grey battlemented houses, with their square "towers of homage," where the lords of the domain in days long gone by, swore
fealty to the king, which gleam white against the shadowy forest
of dark pines on the hillside.

I am going to speak of Spain as she is, and always has been.
With the Spain of *opéra comique* I have nothing to do.   Spain,
brown, arid, wind-swept, desolate ; the Spain that centuries of war
have made her ; of its people, quiet, dignified, oriental, self-
possessed ; wrapped in brown cloaks, laborious yet indolent ;
pitched within and without with that strange subtle melancholy,
which separates them from all other nations.

The Spain of French opera, the French illustrated papers have
made familiar to the world.   The sun, the fleas, the bull-fight,
the smuggler, the lean hidalgo, the fat peasant, the black eye
peeping from a lace mantilla, the castañet, the gipsy dance,—are
not all these depicted in chalky water-colours on the fan and tambourine, which you may buy for a few pence at Biarritz or
Arcachon ?

This Spain, if indeed it ever existed except on the aforesaid
fan and tambourine, is but a reflection, a distorted tradition of
the Calderonian drama, of that specifically styled of "cloak and
sword," of the merry rascals of the Picaresque novels, of the
corrupt society of the Bourbon kings.

The sun, yes ! remains unchanged ; bull-fighters and gipsies are
not quite extinct ; guitars still tinkle on the starry night ; thieves
exist, but do more damage to the unwary traveller in the nice
presentation of the hotel bill than with blunderbuss and slugs
upon the highway !

No ! the Spainards are not a nation of fiddlers and dancers,
nor yet of bull-fighters and smugglers.   They do not live exclusively on cigarettes and garlic ; their lives are not entirely
devoted to dancing the *seguidilla*.

These things, these types, have added their quota to the composition of the national character; other and far different elements have made it what it is.

An old English writer says, "A Frenchman on arriving at your house asks at once for food; a Spaniard would rather die than do so." The witty Voltaire makes no man a hero to his valet. The ingenious Cervantes makes Sancho perceive that his master is a madman, but, whilst perceiving, still respect and love his noble nature.

Neither am I going to laugh over the foibles and failings of the people I love. No! I will leave that unenviable task to others. It is very amusing, very easy, to give a grotesque idea of the Spanish character by a little judicious exaggeration and elaboration. (Ford, and no stranger knew it better, erred a little on this side.) I, for my part, see more to respect, to love, to admire in the proud, self-respecting dignity, the simple sober habits, the native good manners and kindness, which are the characteristics of all classes of the nation.

As I have said, modern ideas of progress (mind, I, for my part, neither call nor think it progress) have fleeted over the surface of Spain without taking root there. Foreign companies, Belgians and English, anxious to pocket her money, have made her railways, and work her mines. The Spaniard, with his hands in his pocket, has stood by, indifferent that the rest of Europe was being propelled in carriages by steam; the modes of travelling used by his forefathers were good enough for him. He has clung, and still clings, to his "coche de colleras," the old ramshackle, lumbering, wooden coach, drawn by eight or sixteen mules, which everywhere else has become a dim tradition. In the remoter districts, inaccessible even by diligence, he travels on "caballeria." A "caballeria" may mean anything equine, from the meek donkey buried under the straw-stuffed "albarda," the saddle left by the Moors, and which you may see unaltered and exactly the same in Morocco at this day, to the small springy Castilian horse. With saddle-bags strapped on behind,—the classical "alforjas" in which Sancho bore his brown bread and garlic when he followed his master in search of adventures of knight errantry,—and the "bota" or pig-skin bottle full of wine, and a rusty blunderbuss slung on in front (both equally potent as weapons in disarming ill-will, and the former especially a royal road to good fellowship), the Spaniard, muffled to the teeth, starts on his journey two or three hours before dawn, to get under shelter before the heat of the mid-day sun overtakes him; the same scenes, the same people, congregate before the door of the wayside inn as before that at which Don Quixote arrived, at the end of his first journey over the ancient and well-known plain of Montiel.

The traveller, before dismounting, calls loudly from the road for the lady hostess : " Peace be to this house ! " says he. " Is no one there ? "

The hostess appears. The larder is well provided. There is of everything—rabbits, partridges, chickens, geese, goats' flesh, and pigs' feet ; but the rabbit is still to be caught, the partridge to be shot, and so on with the rest. They are, indeed, there, but making the most of a short existence in the courtyard within. At least there is provender for the animals—hay, chopped straw, and barley, and sour wine—what heart of man can be so unreasonable as to wish for more on a journey ?

Much of the travelling in Spain is still done on caballerias, donkey-back or mule-back, and may it be so for the rest of my life ! It is in these remote hamlets, in the long days spent on the by-ways of Spain with muleteers, ferrymen, at the " ventas " or country inns, where the wants of man become subservient to those of the beast he bestrides ; where rough herdsmen, and shepherds from the mountains, congregate ; in the peasants' huts ; in the houses of the simple and credulous country priests, where in these remote districts it is often necessary to take shelter for the night and hospitality, that we find the national manners and customs unchanged since the Middle Ages, virtually unaltered to what they were when the Moors and the Spaniards lived side by side together in the heart of the Peninsula.

Until 1830, it must be remembered that the high roads of Spain were all but impracticable. The road, for instance, from Madrid to Avila could only be traversed by mules or donkeys, dwindling into narrow paths, through rough wild pasture land, winding along the edges of steep precipices, or forming a narrow zigzag line along the slopes of mountains. The traveller, overtaken by a fall of snow or a fierce mountain storm on this wild exposed road, in the midst of unpeopled solitudes, where not even the shelter of a " venta " could be hoped for, went in danger of his life.

The road from Avila to Talavera (I am confining myself to the roads of a particular district, which I have myself explored), traversing the lofty sierras between the provinces of Avila and Estremadura, was a thousand times worse. Difficult for carts, impossible for coaches, a Spaniard, before he travelled, made his

will; I believe he does so still. Not alone was there risk of
falling in with "mala gente," robbers, smugglers, and others of
the same caste, and of being robbed and murdered; there was
that not only of coaches and strings of mules, but of the traveller
on horseback getting stuck inextricably in the bogs, or of being
drowned in the rivers, across which they were borne by "ford-
ders" in the absence of bridges, that is, men who swam across
bearing passengers, coach, and all, or the mounted equestrian,
from one bank to the other. In the winter the journey must
either be renounced altogether or an enormous circuit made to
avoid the obstacles.

We have touched briefly on the traveller. Let us see how the
Spaniard fares at home. The outside of his house is grim and
gloomy. The windows are protected by wrought-iron balconies
and sombre gratings. Across the principal balcony is a branch
of blessed palm, blessed by the priest on Easter Sunday, which
drives away all spirits and influences of evil. His house, the
great granite staircase, everything about it grand and vast and
magnificent, would be a monument in any other country. You
wish to enter; you wield the heavy iron knocker until you wake
hollow echoes in the great empty gateway and desolate staircase.
An eye of an invisible person surveys you for a moment through
the narrow grating. "Quien es?" "Who is it?" cries a voice.
"Gente de paz," you answer, "People of peace." Or the salu-
tation takes the form of an Ave Mary, and you answer gravely,
"Conceived without sin." This is the indispensable ceremonial
before entering a Spanish house. It takes one back to the
comedies of Calderon, to the days of intrigue, rapiers, and
gallants muffled to the eyes. It is a relic of more troublous
times, when every man's house was his castle, in which he stood
on his defensive.

You enter, and traverse the vast stone passages, which lead to
the great room of reception. You are led with state to the seat
which stands at the head of the vast and empty room. It is the
seat of honour, the "estrada," the dais of the Middle Ages. There
are neither carpets nor curtains. A woven grass mat covers the
brick or stone floor, which strikes cold to the feet. (I am speaking, be it remembered, of the Spaniard of the provinces, the
Espanol rancio, of the Spaniard who clings to the ways and
manners of his fathers. To whom to speak in Christian means
to understand Castilian.) On the other hand, the window
shutters, the doors, are heavily and quaintly carved and gilt.

They are *renaissance* and works of art. But you notice that neither window nor door fulfil the office they were meant for. They shut badly, and neither exclude the sunlight nor the cold draughts of air. When the rooms are to be darkened the shutters are closed, and that is all.

A few dusky oil-paintings hang on the whitewashed stone walls. A carved wooden image of a saint stands in its niche, and a holy-water "stoup" hangs by the door. You notice that there are no fireplaces. The huge chimneys before which his ancestors crouched on the winter nights before the blazing logs, have been done away with, bricked up to exclude the wind which rushed down them. Yes; there is one in the dark, damp, dungeon-like kitchen, a slab raised about four feet from the ground, from which the thin smoke of a little charcoal fire meanders up the vast bell-shaped Moorish chimney. Roasting, therefore, is an art unknown in the Spanish cuisine. The earthenware pipkins which stand on tripods over the smouldering charcoal contain his favourite and frugal dishes; his "puchero;" his "estofado," his stew; his bread crumbs fried in oil; his chocolate.

In such a house it is needless to look for mechanical or snug bourgeois comfort. The Spaniard's house reveals his Eastern origin. To a race half African, half Hebrew, wholly Eastern, a house serves rather to bivouac than to live in, and contradicts every modern notion of life. A true Castilian knows and needs no other fire but the genial glow of the sun—the sun which is his God. Whatever the agony he suffers as he crouches in his vast, bare, cold house over the ashes of a brazier, wrapped in his cloak, he forgets it all if he can but "take the sun." He takes it as we take food or medicine, or something necessary to our existence. "Cuando Dios amanece," when God rises, is his usual expression for daybreak. Like the Arab or the Moor, his life is spent in the field or the street. In his house, indeed, he eats and sleeps, but it is in the street that he lives; in the street that he meets his friends, transacts his business. The street oftener than not is his counting house.

What about his women? He leaves them shut up in the gloomy house he flees from in a seclusion as complete as that of a Moorish harem or a Christian convent. On high festivals and Sundays alone they may be seen abroad in the public walks and streets; the mother swathed like an Arab in folds of thin black cashmere, which very often covers a religious habit, a dignified, sad-faced figure, which impresses us sadly with the vague idea it

implies of resignation, self-sacrifice, and female nullity. The
daughters wear the classical mantilla.

Let us follow him to the country, where his antique methods of
agriculture transport us back to the idyllic days of Theocritus.
The plough made of two forked sticks drawn by a donkey or an
ox—the same as that depicted in the Egyptian hieroglyphics
—exactly what we may see to-day, as we wander through the
British Museum, painted on the sides of a mummy case. His
whole country life he has inherited from the Moors; the terms he
uses for his rural implements, his trees, his plants, are purely
Moorish; so are the names of his weights and measures for corn
and wine and oil. His garden is the Moorish *huerta*, a place of
shade and running water, fragrant with the scent of orange flowers
or fruit; where vegetables, fruit trees, and flowers, corn, maize,
and grass are alike cultivated. A few clumps of trailing odori-
ferous flowers, and sweet-smelling shrubs, roses and red sage,
sweet basil, violets, the tall spikes of lillies,—alone serve to
connect it with the conventional idea of a flower garden. The
shallow channels which intersect the whole of the ground in
every direction, in the morning and evening flushed with water,
become rivulets, whose crystalline murmur soothes the ear with a
refreshing sense of rest. This method of irrigation, the best in
the world, was also introduced by the Moors. The Spaniard's
country house is patriarchally simple, a long, low, rambling, sunlit
grange. If he is an hidalgo, there is the grey "tower of homage,"
and on the great stone stair which leads to the living rooms a
heavy slab covers the well, which, in times long gone by, was left
open at night, so that thieves and untoward visitors, coming up
the stairs, might fall into its depths. The interior, old, falling to
pieces, never repaired, spotlessly clean, smells of lavender and
rusticity. A heap of maize in the corner of the sitting-room, a
greyhound asleep in the sunlit gallery, an old gun and game-bags,
testify to the rural occupations of its owner.

Through the chinks of the floor rises up the strange, penetrating odour, not unpleasant, of the cattle and horses stabled
beneath, and which you can hear as they slowly ruminate, or pull
at the chains of their halters; the scent of the breath of oxen, the
sweet smell of dried grass and clover.

My time will not allow me to do more than touch on the quaint
and original aspect of a Spanish town; on its arcaded market
places, round which are deep and sombre warehouses, their low-
browed gateways forming deep blotches of shadow within the

arches, once, in Charles V.'s and Philip II.'s time, filled with bales of merchandise. Botas, pig-skins full of wine, lie piled before some of them; the public weights hang up in the most conspicuous corner for the use of all comers; little booths fill up the spaces between the arches, where country men and vendors bargain and chatter.

Nor must I forget the ragged donkeys, that intimate part of the life of Castilian man, groups of them patiently nodding in the centre of the market-place, waiting for their masters, or laden with red earthenware jars, the fashion of which involuntarily takes us back to the East, whence they originated; nor the market-place itself, paved with pebbles, uneven as the waves of the sea, where the sun sleeps, and long trains of mules stand motionless in the heat; filled with a busy, merry, vociferous crowd, engaged on nothing; the strident voices of market women; the strange wild strain chanted in guttural accents by a muleteer; the pilgrim bound to Santiago, who shoves his way through the throng, bearing the classic staff and gourd, with cockleshell sewed on his breast, and begs for a copper to lighten his journey.

You will find such things, such contrasts, nowhere else in modern Europe, and this, to my mind, constitutes the intimate charm of Spain; her inability to absorb the thoughts and habits of any other nation, her want of receptivity of all modern influences, the difficulty of reducing her to the ordinary insipidity and tameness which makes all modern life the same, be it Berlin or Bucharest.

Let us stop to inquire a moment into the causes which make the Spanish nation so obtuse to all modern influences. The first arises from the most prominent attribute of the Spanish national character—its entirety. A Spaniard prides himself on being " muy entero " (very entire), which means that he sticks doggedly to opinions once formed. Well, the Spaniards formed their opinions in the reign of Philip II., and have stuck to them ever since.

Let me illustrate this trait of the Spanish character by a historic fact, which I will try to make as little dull as possible.

The vulgar idea of Spain is that she was a country which hung breathlessly on the decrees of Rome. Not so. We shall find that Ferdinand and Isabella, pre-eminently the Catholic Kings—such the title awarded to them by the Pope of the day—neither understood nor brooked the exercise of Papal authority within their dominions. The Pope might be Prince of Rome, but they were

Kings of Spain. They reserved to themselves the right of nomination to all ecclesiastical dignities; the Pope's bulls were submitted to a rigorous examination by the Supreme Council of the State before they were allowed to be circulated, and were suppressed at pleasure, if thought well to do so. The grim Sphinx of the Escorial—the tetrical, strange, weird Philip II., still a riddle to historians unable to solve whether he was saint or devil —inherited from his father, Charles V., and carried on to the full the traditions of his grandfathers. The Pontifical decrees were still placed under the strictest and most rigorous examination as to whether they contained anything contrary to the prerogatives of king and kingdom, and if so, their circulation was suspended until appeal was made to the Pope either to withdraw or modify them or to dictate fresh ones.

And here comes in the Spanish character. The retention was qualified under the form of a suspension, and an appeal from the Pope misguided to the Pope better informed — from "Philip drunk to Philip sober." This humble and submissive form was but a hypocritical manœuvre. If another decree to the same purpose arrived from Rome, it was again withdrawn under the supposition that the Pope continued in his ignorance. If the Pope excommunicated the authors of this obstinate conduct, his anathema was invalidated and worthless. A third order to the same effect as before would have revealed, according to Spanish ideas, a tenacity against all propriety and order, and, viewed in this light, inconceivable; and so the Spanish juris-consults declared this proceeding (indeed unheard of) as contumacious.

There is a second cause to which we owe the survival of the genuine, distinct, and most curious national life of Spain.

And that is in the Inquisition. The very name makes one shudder! But, putting religious prejudices aside (for the religious history of Protestantism and Catholicism can only be written with impartiality in the century to come, and we shall never live to see it), the cold machinery of the Inquisition, which mangled men's bodies and put fetters on their minds, was in its worst days as much, nay, more a political than a religious instrument. She gave religious unity, and, under the wing of that unity, perpetuated the national life of Spain. Sects, Sectarians, Anabaptists, Shakers, Quakers, Anglican clergymen—broad, high, and evangelical—have never reigned rampant over Spain. The loud-voiced freethinker of the towns still sneaks furtively to mass as if about to commit a felony. The churches are thronged on the solemn feast days;

here in the great and shadowy cathedral, inarticulate with awe, the rude herdsman contemplates the famous Christ, which his father, his grandfather, and their forefathers, back to the time of the Catholic kings, have venerated also.

And now I must briefly touch on the peasantry, the secret of Spain's greatness in the past—perhaps, who knows, of her greatness in the future. No other like it exists in Europe for its freedom, independence, endurance, and native nobility. Hallam, who has noticed it, as have all who have written of Spain, suggests that because, unlike England or the other European countries of the Middle Ages, villainage was never known in Castille. All its men were soldiers ; each man who bore arms against the Moors was ennobled,—ennobled not only by the use of arms, but the grand ideal he had before him of fighting for his country's freedom. Whole provinces of Spain are still ennobled. In Castille every man is an hidalgo, and looks it, down to the roughest, uncouthest savage herding sheep in the pasture land which surrounds some country hamlet, whose stalwart bearing is full of resolution, fearlessness, robust and self-respecting dignity. The essentially democratic spirit of the nation which these causes fostered was never more conspicuous than during the dark days of the Inquisition and Philip II. The nobles had little weight or influence in the National Councils. Spain swarmed with gentlemen and adventurers—between whom the line was not always easy to draw,—it was hard to find where the gentleman ended and the adventurer began. There was neither great wealth nor poverty; of poor gentlemen no end. To-day this principle is the pervading and remarkable characteristic of Spanish society, where a Duchess thinks it no lessening of her dignity to shake hands with the shopman who sells her ribands, and to chat with him as he smokes a cigarette behind the counter.

Whether such a democratic feeling is the cause or effect of the greater racial refinement of the Spaniard, which is especially conspicuous in the peasantry; whether climate, the happy influences of sun and light and warmth, under which the carking cares of life can never weigh so heavily, have developed a superior mental and physical susceptibility of the Latin and southern races to all refining influences; or whether it is the greater leisure given to body and mind by the greater opportunities for enjoyment afforded by the great number of feast days and Church holidays, which constitute a good half of the year; or whether it arises from the superior æsthetic influences, brought to bear upon him

from his earliest youth, in the splendid ceremonies—the worship
full of ceremonial and symbol of his Church; the great and
solemn processions wending through dim and shadowy aisles of
vast cathedrals; the plain song, sombre and grave, which echoes
through the rafters of the roof; the sweet perfumes which arise
from swinging censers, like a cloud of vapour; the flush of sensu-
ous colour, light, and sound; the organ which interprets to earthly
ears the Te Deums of angelic choirs; the images, pathetic, sad,
benignant, bland, and merciful, the advocates of his humble
prayers,—I will not attempt to decide.

Certainly, in Spain the peasantry cannot be called the lower
classes. We might seek in vain for anything dimly approaching
the degradation, the drunkenness, the inhuman horror, the
debased and squalid humanity, which form the bulk of the population of London, Glasgow, and the industrial towns of England.
The Spanish peasant or artisan—the artisan is here called an
artist, a master, as in the Trades Guilds of the Middle Ages—
rarely drinks; he loves fine clothes and clean shirts; he cultivates
a pretty taste for gambling, whether in the State Lottery or at
cards. His amusements are of a nature which we find in England almost exclusively confined to what convention calls the
"better classes." To see the people in those happy moments
when they escape from workshop or field; as they twang the
guitar, and dance before the wine-shop door in some country
hamlet; or wend their way on some "romeria" or merry pilgrimage to a local shrine, following the custom of remote generations
of their fathers, is a picture in which the artist may find infinite
grace, infinite colour, infinite beauty! (Happy if he can render it!)

Political economists have decried the feast days and holidays
—they have gone so far as to attribute to them the decadence of
Spain. Even old Feyjóo, the wise old Galician Benedictine
monk, who from his cell in the monastery of his order at Oviedo
(which it has been reserved for a succeeding generation to turn
into a public office, where a lying official cheats people and
Government alike) wrote those wonderful treatises on the errors
and prejudices of his age, incurring thereby obloquy and fame,
alike the immediate reward of those great minds which go before
and pave the road of progress; who spoke of the position and
education of women, in a way that I doubt whether any Spaniard
of the middle or upper classes would assent to now (oh! the
mental ignorance of your *bourgeois* and foolish noble);—even he
professed to find in the frequent *romerias* and number of feast

days an influence for evil, whilst we, of the nineteenth century, are convinced that every man who labours has as much right and, *a fortiori*, a stronger right than he who does not, to that leisure in which the hard wrought fibres of the body and mind may have the strain slackened.

I should like to say a few words about the modern literature of Spain, as it has taken a most important and original development, and is destined to take a high place amongst the national literatures of the nineteenth century. Perhaps no country can boast of such a brilliant group of writers—true, I can count them on my fingers, they are as the Spaniards say, "pocos y buenos," few and good. Above them all shines fantastic, impalpable, like a will-o'-the-wisp or a gleam of pale moonlight on the sward, the strange furtive genius of Becquer, who in his weird fantastic legends and subtle verse seems to have inherited and transmitted to us the very spirit which produced the mysticism of the Middle Ages, and inspired a San Juan de la Cruz. He died at thirty of a broken heart.

Perez Galdos, the melancholy and reserved Canary Islander, is the realistic student of modern Spanish society; of those violent contrasts caused by the struggle between the old national life of Spain and the disturbing influences of modern and ultramontane thought and life.

If you would conceive some idea of modern Spain, Spain as she is in this fleeting moment, you will find it portrayed to the life by an artist, whose brush omits no detail however insignificant, dissected by the scalpel of a skilful anatomist in " Gloria ; " " Leon Roch ; " " El Amigo ; " " Manso ; " "el Doctor Centeno ; " " Tormento," etc. The nature and historic reality of the *Episodois Nacionales* have already made them integral parts of the national literature of Spain, in which the dramatic events which constitute the history of Spain from the conclusion of the last century are knit together in a series of fictions, in which already the eye of the treasure-seeker might have predicted the coming glory of the Leon Roch. In the characters which live in the pages of this monumental fiction, we shall find the same delicate portrayal of character, the vivid light and shade, the dramatic and real interest, which have since made their author famous.

Pereda, a native of Santander, has dedicated himself to describing with a master hand the customs, aspects, the lives full of hardship and picturesqueness, of the laborious mountaineers and rough fishermen of his native province.

Firmly every touch is laid on the canvas until some little village, nestling in the slopes of a hill, covered with chestnut woods, or buried in the shade of the valley beside some brawling trout-stream; and the lives, secrets, and thoughts of its inhabitants, woven into a humble drama, lie exposed to our view. Galdos paints an ephemeral phase of society, the elements of which, even as he paints, are dissolving; which will within twenty, at the most forty years, be antiquated—as antiquated as that depicted by Balzac. Will he live? Is there in his books that quality, that reality, which for its innate truth will defy time and public opinion to lessen and conquer immortality? We cannot tell. That Perida will live—will live under the shadow of Cervantes, as being next to him one of the greatest of European novelists—is, I think, indubitable. He has described a state of rustic society and manners historically true—a state of manners unimpaired for ages. He deals with realities, not with psychological problems; he sees more beauty in the rural tasks, in a country feast with its vivid life and colour, than in the mental aberrations of a weak-kneed and unstrung social life in Madrid. The one deals with man face to face with, and acted upon by, a Nature eternally the same—a patriarchal simplicity of life as true to-day in the mountains of the Asturias as in the pastoral days of ancient Greece; the other with the human character disturbed by the conflicting influences of a temporary moment of an artificial social life, its harmony and balance destroyed or greatly impaired. As we read " El Sabor de la Tierruca," " Pedro Sanchez," "Sotileza," we hear the lowing of cattle, the slow tinkling of the bell as they are driven slowly home through the dusky village streets; we watch the autumn advance stealthily and sadly; we see the naked trees streaming with dew or rain; the flocks of sea-birds, driven inland from the coast by the cold and storm, settling on the stubble fields amongst the dried stalks of maize. We see the peasants crouch around the blaze as the hailstones rattle against the walls, the cattle ruminating despondently, dripping with wet, in the " corral;" we hear the slow, melancholy wind of autumn, which, increasing in fury, tears the tiles off the humble roofs, whirls the dried leaves from the chestnut trees, and brings down the old decayed bell-tower of the village church. We follow fascinated the incidents which chequer the lives of the humble *dramatis personæ;* the guileless character of the simple-minded village priest, whose peasant shrewdness is still keen enough to see through the wiles of his parishioners; the greed of the rich labourer who lends out money and sucks his poorer neighbours into terrible toils from which there is no escape ; the poor, proud, and simple-minded hidalgo, whose grey escutcheons, which moulder over the gateway of his old dilapidated house, do not drive hunger from the door ; the superstitions,—innocent, often terrible, of the villagers,—all these live and breathe in pages which bear the very reality of truth and the love of an enthusiast.

We may also count Valera, the ambassador and scholar, the dainty literary dilettante, amongst the pre-eminently great novelists of Spain. Pepita Jimenez for artistic form, and absolute harmony between the idea and form which clothe it, would be a gem in any language.

Leopoldo Alas towers in criticism. In a style simple, terse, so unaffectedly natural, that we can say of it as Fraz Luis de Leon did of Sta. Teresa's, that it is elegance itself, *la misma elegancia ;* he gives vent to a mordant satire which bites like acid, or a delicate and subtle humour which is fascinating and delightful. He is terribly truthful, terribly in earnest, and he uses his weapons mercilessly. Such a critic must exercise an almost incalculable influence for good on the formation and heightening of the standard of a current literature. No one in Spain at this moment writes a Spanish so free from mannerism and bombast. From this point of view, the slightest fragment he has ever written is invaluable. He has written a great novel, a novel so powerful that it places him in the foremost rank of modern novelists. We might compare it, had it been shorter and more concentrated, with the greatest work that mediæval Spanish realism produced, the great tragi-comedy of " The Celestina."

One critic leads me to another. Any account, however brief, of modern Spanish literature would be incomplete if it did not include the name of Menendezy Pelayo. He has written a work on the *Progress of Esthetic Thought in Spain from the Earliest Times*, in which he shows how and to what degree it has been influenced by the ideas imported from foreign sources. Besides the German and French, he traverses an immense cycle of English literature ; the Scotch School of Philosophy, Reid, Stewart, etc. ; Cowper, Pope, Dryden, Carlyle, Ruskin, which he criticises with a precision and appreciation that only a long and continuous study of English literature could ensure. This book, full of erudition and research, of earnest and careful thought, of keen acute criticism, would, if it had been written in English or German instead of Spanish, at this moment have been translated into every other European language as a great and monumental work. He has set himself the task of vindicating and resuscitating the literary and scientific glory of Spain in the fifteenth and sixteenth centuries, a period in which all foreign critics have affected to find a singular dearth of philosophical and original thought. He has gone far to prove that in spite of the trammels cast on thought by the Inquisition, Spain could boast in those centuries of schools and teachers of Philosophy as original, as great, and as glorious as any other country of Europe; that in their works may be found the germ of those great ideas, of those revulsions of thought, which it was reserved to other nations to develop. He has vindicated the glory of Gomez Pereira, a Cartesian before Descartes; of Vallés, the terrible adversary of the Aristotelian Cosmology; of Huarte, the father of Phrenology; of Servet, the discoverer of the circulation of the blood; of Fernan Perez de Oliva, who spent his life in experiments as to how two people, separated by distance, could be made to communicate with each other by the means of the magnet; of Luis Vivés, who advocated that method, afterwards indelibly connected with the name of Bacon. And a woman must not forget to mention the greatest female writer in Spain, perhaps in Europe— there is no writer of her sex that I could name in England to approach her—Emilia Pardo Bazan, whose article on the " Position of Spanish Women " lately attracted so much attention in the pages of the *Fortnightly Review*. Her literary life has been crowded with work. From the study of the legends, philosophy, and historic movement of the Middle Ages, which she gives us in her life of *San Francisco de Asis*, to a pamphlet on the question which for a time convulsed all literary Spain, viz., *Realism and Idealism in Art*, Zola *versus* Victor Hugo, she has explored the most diverse fields of literature with brilliant success. She has lectured on Nihilism, a movement which she considers full of vitality and vigour, for the very good reason, as she told me, that she knew nothing whatever about Russia, and therefore was the better able to form an impartial opinion. She has written much, but, undoubtedly, what she has given us of most artistic value are one or two novels, *Los Pazos de Ulloa*, and Mother Nature, *La Madre Naturaleza*. These two books alone place her far beyond any writer of her sex I know of in England. In them she describes, with loving truth and unerring exactitude, the scenery and primitive manners of the province where she was born and has lived the greater part of her life—Galicia. They are full of dramatic and sustained interest, of life and colour.

Amongst a number of novels and other works, let me signalise a volume of charming essays on her native province, *Mi Tierra*, and another of short stories, *La Dama Joven*, in which I can trace a faint perfume of Bret Harte, and which will, perhaps, take as high, or a higher place, when the history of the present literature of Spain comes to be written, than even the more sustained novels I have mentioned.

It is to her, possibly (I hope so), that Spain may owe the higher education of its women. Clever, witty, full of initiative, belonging by birth to one of the noblest families of Galicia, she has already done more towards that object than could reasonably have been expected from that alternately idolised, alternately despised, long-suffering and very patient creature, they call a woman.

Amongst dramatists and poets, Spain can number names like Zorrilla, Campoamor, Ayala, Echegaray, who, besides being a powerful dramatist, is a scientist of note.

Secondary names throng to my mind; but those I have quoted, for original genius can compare with advantage to themselves with the exponents of the current literature of any other country in Europe.

An indescribable pathos and melancholy hangs around modern Spain which cannot fail to impress a thoughtful mind. In the midst of its beautiful and harmonious decay, a happy but poor people, an industrious peasantry, might have lived unenvied, unenvying.

But she has felt the restless and accursed influence of the great industrial revolution, or rather evolution, which has transformed the bulk of the people of Europe into work slaves and manufacturers of fortunes; the fungus growth of a few years, a middle-class, ostentatious and vulgar, is increasing in Madrid, Barcelona, and the trading towns; a cheap veneer of modern bourgeoisism is spreading, utterly alien to the national life and instincts, which it modifies but cannot alter;—this, combined with other causes, the altogether disproportionate taxation of the peasantry, squeezed to the limits of possibility to gratify the greed of the needy politicians, who swarm like locusts in Madrid; a Government, whose sole object seems to be to extort the last pound of flesh from the agriculturist, for the sole object, as it appears to me, of maintaining a large and useless standing army;

—these are the vampires which suck the blood from the children of the soil.

A Spaniard never tires of declaiming against the universal corruption which extends down to the very lowest branches of the administration, but never seeks to remedy it—*Cosas de Espana.*

The soldier swarms. True, he no longer sits fishing with a piece of string tied to his bayonet at the seaport town. No longer on guard in the dilapidated castle, does he sleep under the shade of his coat, stuck upon his musket, through the supposed hours of his vigilance. No longer, when you pass him, does his brown hand steal out from a tattered greatcoat, and silently implore your charity. Seldom, to-day, shall you see him asleep guarding stalwart prisoners, who in the public square with cutlasses fell the grass as it were trees. He has a uniform—boots too, which he replaces with sandals when on the march—but his pay remains of the slenderest, and his rations of the scantiest.

The Artillery, corresponding to the Household Troops in England, are the flower of the Spanish Army; the Cavalry, of small account, well horsed but badly drilled, equipped, and designed apparently for no other purpose but to squander public money; the Infantry, patient of hardship to an incredible extent, still preserves the tradition of untiringness on the march, which was its characteristic in the Middle Ages. The officers, ill-paid and ignorant in the lower grades, become ambitious, and remain ignorant, when they attain the rank of Colonel. Their first idea, to advance themselves by political scheming; their amusements, the bull fight, the card table, and intrigues with the women of the town where they are quartered. Both soldier and officer, one of the plague spots of the country ; one of the causes, together with the others I have mentioned, of the increasing emigration to the River Plata and Chile, which has taken alarming proportions of the backbone of the country, and without which it must dwindle into absolute ruin—the peasantry.

A large Spanish proprietor said to me the other day, "I don't know what we are all to do in the face of this increasing emigration. We cannot cultivate our lands ourselves, and all the labourers are going. We shall find ourselves face to face with ruin." I have passed lately through villages in the north of Spain, where on every door was painted a rude red cross, the sign of abandonment and departure. When I listened for the accustomed and well-remembered song of the peasant, as he dug between his vines, the silence was pathetically significant. The men have all left a country which has proved such a bitter mother, and only women and children are left.

It is strangely sad and oppressive to see, as in Spain, a grand ideal, which has inspired centuries of thought, and art, and life, lying vanquished, buried, crushed, annihilated under the material ruins of its grandeur.

The coldness and neglect which brood over the Church of San Marcos of Leon, the celebrated monastery and hospital of the wealthy Knights of Santiago, which contains the cell where Quevedo was confined, one of the most magnificent monuments of early Renaissance that Spain possesses, penetrate to our very marrow. The monastery has become a museum of bad antiquities. The ragged urchins of the doorkeeper play about amongst the grand old carved stalls of the "Coro Alto" (the raised choir). The organ is silent. Had it been moveable, it would long ago have been sold. The immense chests in the sacristy, of a workmanship the art of which seems entirely lost, which contained the splendid vestments of gold tissue and brocade, stand empty, until such time as the porter shall break them up and burn them for firewood. On the promulgation of the decree for the suppression of the monasteries, the two hundred Esculapian friars, who preserved the building and loved it, were turned out in a single night; the altar, stripped and torn to pieces, testifies to their precipitate flight.

As with the convents, so with the people. The Maragatos, that strange and singular race, which cluster in gipsy-like communities amongst the red sandhills of Astorga, the traditional carriers of Spain, their long files of carts, and strings of laden mules, the strangest, wildest, most picturesque sight the country roads of Spain can present; their origin and that of their curious costume and marriage ceremonies lost in the night of antiquity —some say they are descended from the Goths, others from the Moors—are passing away. To-morrow they will have vanished. The railroads make such a race of men superfluous, and you will alone be able to trace the fact of their existence in the legends which linger in the country side; in researches amongst historical antiquities; in the dust and confusion of public libraries.

It would be curious to speculate what would have been the fate of Spain to-day if the idea of political and religious liberty had not waved its tempting lure before the eyes of its Catholic Kings. Had their temper, and the temper of the people they governed (for the stimulus came from the heart of the nation), been more tolerant and less exclusive, Spain and her colonies would probably have been preponderant in the world. Instead of the God-like English-speaking man of Mr. Stead, we might have had to reckon with the Spaniard. Her agricultural capabilities would have been exploited by the Moors; the Jews would have taken charge of her commercial interests;—all this presupposing a tolerance of thought which would have placed Spain in the foremost rank of the kingdoms of Europe. It is not rash to affirm that to-day she would have been one of the biggest industrial countries in the world; millions of factory chimneys would have been vomiting foul smoke, blackening the radiant sky, which covers the great melancholy plains of Castille or the wild pasture grounds of Andalusia. Her cities, so beautiful in their decay, would not exist; her agricultural life which in its primitive simplicity takes us back to the idyllic days of Theocritus, would have disappeared (as it has in England), and her legends might have become forgotten.

Let me point out that we are too apt to overlook the importance of these retrogade, stagnated, decayed countries (call them what you will); we forget that they are our only visible material connection with the past; that in them only can we study the past; they have not, like England, Germany, France, indissolubly severed their intimate connection with it. Not but that what the handbook (I seem to be fond of handbooks) calls "monuments of art" do not exist in the countries I have mentioned, but they are monuments only, and the link between them and the national thought and life is eternally broken. Looked on with a sort of patronising pity by some—"poor old things, how long they last!" —with genuine admiration by the many, with wistful sadness by the few, still they are emphatically skeletons of the dry bones of things and ideas which have been, but now are not.

Let us remember that these countries, which have stopped short and crystallised, as it were, at a certain point of their career, are of far more importance than any country devoted to industry can be, in the development and continuance of the most important introspective faculties of man. Let us remember that however much they may seem, to a superficial criticism, merely melancholy and beautiful museums of antiquities, that the life of other ages is still warm in them, and that they have played a far more important part in the history of human culture than any state of society possible now.

They open to us other horizons lying behind us; horizons which every year in the world's history makes a little dimmer; horizons in which the mind, weary with railways, surfeited with the ugliness and brutality of material progress and its concomitant miseries, may seek and find rest, refreshment, light !

X.

NORWAY.

H. L. BRACKSTAD.

I WOULD ask you to go back with me about a thousand years, and to picture to yourself a bright, sunny morning on the eastern coast of England in those early times. The ancient Saxons are just bestirring themselves to begin their day's work —men, women, and children are issuing from their primitive huts; they stretch themselves, rub their eyes, and gaze towards the glittering sea, upon which the rising sun is shining in all its glory. Suddenly an old man discovers a speck on the horizon; his experienced eye tells him that it is something unusual; he mounts the nearest eminence; soon he sees a large vessel—a stranger from over the sea—steering towards the coast. The old Saxon runs to tell his neighbours, and before long people are seen hurrying to and fro; the men are talking loudly, the women wail, the children shriek. "It is the Norsemen! Save us from the Norsemen!—save us from the Norsemen!" is the cry that rends the air.

You know what followed. These strangers, these Vikings, introduced themselves in a most rude and unceremonious way to your ancestors, the early Saxons—unceremonious, I say, for not only did they pay you these visits uninvited, but they also helped themselves to everything they took a fancy to, without asking anybody's leave to do so—goods and chattels, gold and silver, sheep and oxen—yea, even your fair-haired Saxon maids did they take unto themselves; and after making merry, and feasting on your good English ale, they set sail for their own fjords and creeks, only to return again next spring to the shores of Albion to fill their galleys again with all the good things they could find, till at last these unwelcome visitors became a source of terror and dread along the whole coast.

This was the way, I believe, in which the old Norsemen and the English first became acquainted with each other—a very barbarous one, I must acknowledge; but, notwithstanding this, I find that, in time, the relations between the two countries became more and more friendly—some of the Norwegian princes were even sent over to England to be brought up; and now, I am glad to say that all feeling of animosity has vanished; in fact, I find that some of your first English families rather pride themselves upon being descendants of these Vikings, or the Normans, who were descendants of Norwegian Vikings that settled in the north of France, and after whom that part of the country was called Normandy. Within the last few weeks a well-known writer, Mr. Du Chaillu, has published a voluminous work, "The Viking Age," in which he attempts to prove that the whole of the English people are descendants of the Scandinavians—that is, the Norwegians, Danes, and Swedes, and not of the Anglo-Saxons, are the real ancestors of the English race. I expect this theory has come somewhat suddenly upon the English, and it will, no doubt, take some time before it will be fully gone into and refuted. Several reviewers have, however, already protested against Mr. Du Chaillu's theory. I may here mention that the other day a clergyman in the north of England actually wept on reading Mr. Du Chaillu's arguments—not from joy, however, but from sheer vexation—on learning that he descended from such barbarians as the old Vikings. It is, however, well known that large numbers of Norwegians settled in the Orkney and Shetland Islands, on the eastern coast of Scotland and England, especially in Yorkshire, and even in Ireland; but I am fully convinced that these northern invaders are not the original ancestors of the English. There must have been, and, as a matter of fact, there was, a race—the old Anglo-Saxons, or Britons, if you choose to call them so—that had been settled, no doubt for centuries, in this country before the Norwegians and Danes first began to visit these shores.

Norway and her people ought, therefore, to be of special interest to Englishmen, not only on account of the blood-relationship between the two peoples, but also on account of the very friendly, as well as the commercial, relations which have long existed between the two countries, and which are now developing year by year.

Having been asked by the South Place Ethical Society to give a lecture on Norway in the series of lectures on National Life and Thought in various countries, which are now being delivered here, I do not think, in doing so, that I need trouble you to any great extent with the ancient history of Norway; it is a very long and complicated one, and a dry historical *resumé* of it would hardly interest you. I fancy it is more about the National Life and thought of the Norway of to-day, about our history and our aspirations of the present times, that you are interested to hear something. To understand this all the better, I must, however, refer for a few minutes to what has taken place before the beginning of this century, and for this purpose I will divide the History of Norway into three epochs :—*The First* being from the earliest times, when the country was divided into a number of small kingdoms, which King Harold the Fairhaired eventually gathered into one, when the Norwegians were known as one of the most warlike and daring of all nationalities ; when they crossed the seas in their galleys, not only to Iceland, England, France, and to the Mediterranean, but even to America, of which country they are the first discoverers ; and when they were ruled by a succession of famous kings, such as King Sverre, King Olaf Trygvason, and King Olaf the Holy, down to the year of 1450, when Norway, after a number of disastrous wars, became a province of Denmark. *The Second Epoch* we will call the time of the *Union with Denmark.* This lasted for nearly 400 years,—from 1450 to 1814. There is a good deal to be said about this period ; no doubt, it was *most disastrous* to Norway, and the best the Norwegians now can do, is to try and forget it. I ought, perhaps, to mention here, that during this period the Norwegian peasantry maintained and asserted their old independence, and would not suffer anyone to interfere in their rights and privileges, and, as long as this was not attempted, they seemed to have cared very little about the management of the rest of the country. This apathy may, no doubt, be explained by the fact that, at the beginning of the union, there were practical men of the old lead-ing chiefs of the peasantry left. King Sverre had, for purposes of his own, tried to crush down and exterminate these bold and independent leaders of the people, but the spirit of those brave Norsemen was not to be quelled altogether ; nay, it has shown itself to be alive to this very day. The Danes soon discovered that these bold and obstinate peasants were not to be trifled with, and an attempt was made to link them more closely to Denmark, by inviting and inducing some of the sons of the old peasant families to visit, and stay for some time in, Denmark. These sons were eventually to be made noblemen, which, however, a good many of them thought they already were. They were at first to go through a course of military discipline, and to learn fine and courtly manners ; but the attempt to make these sturdy Norsemen fine cavaliers and courtiers proved a most miserable failure, for the lads gave the officers and their teachers a sound thrashing, and got up a mutiny, and had at last to be sent home. Another attempt was that of trying to organise a Norwegian corps of Life Guards in attendance upon the king at Copenhagen; but this was just as unsuccessful, and terminated in the same way.

All the officials in Norway during that period were Danes, and were, on the whole, very insolent and overbearing to the people. To show, however, that the old spirit of the Norway peasants did not tamely submit to this sort of treatment, I will relate an anecdote, which will better serve to illustrate the character of the people at that time than all the historical facts I can give you. The Danish officials I have referred to, such as judges, sheriffs, and even clergymen, did not at that time live exactly the life they ought to have led, and often neglected the business of the people to suit their own comfort and convenience. On one occasion—it happened in Valders, one of the wildest mountain districts of Norway—that the sheriff, the judge, under-sheriff, and the counsel who came to the Assizes, and who had been invited to dinner by the clergyman, who lived hard-by, forgot all about the people who were waiting for them outside the court-house. When at last the satiated and inebriated guests came rolling out of the house on their way to the court, they were seized hold of by the people, who had ranged themselves in a row on either side of the door, and judge, sheriff and lawyers were all soundly thrashed in their turn, as they were passed along from man to man.

We now approach the *Third Epoch* in the Norwegian history, the one during which the country regained its independence and the sole control over its affairs.

Many of you will remember that, during the wars of Napoleon, Sweden foolishly joined Russia against Napoleon, and, later on, England, Prussia and Austria also joined this Alliance, while Denmark already had allied herself to Napoleon and his fate. Russia had promised Norway to Sweden in return for the services rendered them by the then Crown Prince, Karl Johun of Sweden. This Karl Johun was the well-known French General Jean Bernadotte, who had just been elected Crown Prince, or successor to the feeble Swedish king, Karl XIII.

Karl Johun invaded the southern part of Denmark, and beat the Danish army, which was stationed in Holstein. The Danish king then lost all courage, and, by the Treaty of Kul in 1814, ceded Norway to Sweden. When this news reached Norway, the old spirit of the Norwegian, which seemed to have been long asleep or enthralled, came to life again. They would not tamely submit to being handed over as mere goods and chattels to Sweden and the ambitious Prince Bernadotte, and preferred the then Danish Governor of Norway, Prince Christian Frederick, whom they elected as their sovereign.

A meeting of delegates from all parts of the country was convened at Eidsvold, not far from the Norwegian capital, where the representatives of the nation framed and adopted the Constitution or Grundlov of 17th May 1814, of which I shall speak later on.

As soon as the Swedes heard that Norway would not submit to the conditions of the Treaty of Kiil, they invaded Norway, with the Crown Prince, Karl Johun Bernadotte, at their head. They met with a gallant resistance, but Prince Christian Frederick, the new king, soon saw the hopelessness of the struggle ; he resigned, and returned to Denmark. A convention was then held at Moss, where the Norwegians accepted the Swedish king as their sovereign, on the condition that their Constitution of 17th of May should remain intact, except such alterations as the union with Sweden rendered necessary. An extraordinary Storthing, or National Assembly, was summoned at Christiania, and on the 4th November 1814, Norway was declared to be a " free, independent, and indivisible kingdom, united with Sweden under one king." The Constitution framed at Eidsvold was retained, forming the present Grundlov, or Fundamental Law of the kingdom. It is generally acknowledged to be the most free and democratic of any Constitution in the world. The people obtained by this such an amount of political liberty as no other nation can boast of, and which, in fact, it has taken the Norwegians themselves some time to understand fully.

It is now well known that Karl Johun Bernadotte only agreed to the Norwegians retaining this Constitution as he found he could not then conquer or subdue the Norwegians ; but he lived in the firm hope that he would soon find a fitting opportunity to establish his power more firmly in Norway, perhaps even to seize it, and make it a province of Sweden. He was especially very anxious that the Norwegian Parliament should grant him an absolute veto, which the king, according to the Constitution, did not possess. On two occasions the sturdy patriots in the Parliament resolutely declined to entertain his proposal, and, to this very day, the merely suspensive veto remains one of the most important features of the Norwegian Constitution. I may here mention an incident which shows the kind of people Karl Johun had to deal with. A few years after the union was entered into, the Norwegian Parliament proposed a bill for the abolition of nobility. The country was, in fact, too poor consistently to keep up and maintain an aristocracy. The few counts and barons that still were found in the country were all Danish, and of very recent origin. The really true and ancient nobility was the leading peasants or bïndes, descendants of the old jarls or earls and chieftains in the land ; but then plain people did not want any titles or handles to their names. Among the many great acts for which we have to thank the patriots of those early years of our independence, I think that the abolition of nobility was one of the greatest services they could have rendered their country. But Karl Johun Bernadotte, who by this time had become king of the two countries, on the death of the old king, Karl XIII., was not of this opinion. He felt that the abolition of the nobility was another blow at his power in Norway, and for two sessions he refused his sanction to the bill. But, according to the Constitution, any bill passed three times by the Parliament becomes law, whether the king likes it or no.

In 1821, the bill came on for the third reading, and the king thought he would try to frighten the Parliament into throwing out the bill, and for this purpose he commanded some Swedish men-of-war to the Norwegian capital. These ships were moored almost outside the very windows of the National Assembly, and, during the debate on the third reading of the bill, he had given orders to fire blank shots from the guns of the Swedish ships. The very windows were rattling from the shots while the discussion was going on, but the brave representatives of the people were not to be frightened into submission. The bill was passed for the third time, and became law, to the great chagrin of the king. I will, at this point, relate another anecdote which also tends to illustrate the independence of the Norwegian peasantry. One of the leading men in the Parliament, who bore a noble name, and who naturally opposed the bill for the abolition of titles and nobility, was remonstrating with one of the peasant representatives about this bill, and told him that, if the bill was passed, he would say " Farewell " to the mountains of Norway. The peasant only replied, "*And the mountains of Norway will echo—' Well !—well !*'" The Constitution of the country was

prepared in a very short space of time—in two or three weeks—
and was framed on the Constitution of France of 1791, or that
of the United States of America and that of Spain of 1812, and
is, no doubt, a very masterpiece of its kind. I have said before,
that it is the freest of any Constitution in the old or the new
world. It has not imposed upon the country an *Upper House*,
a *House of Lords*, a *Senate*, or whatever you may like to call the
august assemblies in all countries, who seem to be appointed
as guardians or nurses to the naughty children in the popular
chamber. Now, here is a lesson for our English cousins! The
hereditary chamber you possess is already doomed! There has
been some talk of mending or ending it. I say, take a leaf from
the Norwegian Constitution, and end it. I look upon the National
Assembly of a country in this way,—The electors of a free and
civilised country ought to elect the *best* men they have to legislate
and manage the country for them, without appointing another
set of men—a sort of a board of guardians—over them, to see
that they, the elect of the country, do not misbehave themselves.
An Upper House in a National Assembly *may* have been useful
in times gone by, but I think the time has now come that an
intelligent nation can do without these guardians over their best
men. I, for my part, think it shows a want of confidence in the
men you elect.

Our Parliament, which we call the Storthing, consists at present
of 114 representatives. As soon as it is assembled, it proceeds
to elect from among its members a fourth part of their number
for a kind of *select committee*, which we call the *Lagthing*, and
which is the nearest approach we have to an *upper house;* but it
will not be right to call it so, for these twenty-eight men are part
of the representatives elected, and if you have a Liberal majority
in the Parliament, the members elected for the select committee
are naturally selected from amongst the Liberal majority. As an
act of grace, a few members of the Opposition are allowed to be
elected on this committee, the lagthing. The remaining three-
fourths of the representatives constitute the *Odelsthing*, where all
legislation is initiated. When a bill has passed the odelsthing, it
is sent up to the lagthing, which, according to the Constitution,
has a limited suspensory power of revising or rejecting the bills
sent up. But you can easily understand that, as this select committee is elected by the men with whom they are in sympathy, much
opposition or obstruction is not met with in the lagthing. If a
bill should be twice rejected by the lagthing, a joint meeting is

held with the odelsthing, at which a majority of two-thirds will
carry the measure. As already stated, the royal sanction can
only be refused twice.

The present king—King Oscar II.—evidently believed, until
quite lately, that he possessed an absolute veto. It will here be
necessary for me shortly to refer to the political crisis we had in
Norway with reference to this very question. The Constitution
of 1814 had one fault. According to it, the Ministers of State
had not seats in the National Assembly, and the Liberal party,
finding this to be a great defect in their constitution, proposed in
1872 what the Conservative press of the country—we have Conservatives even in our Democratic country—pronounced a most
revolutionary and dangerous measure — that of admitting the
Ministers of State to the sittings of the National Assembly, and
to take part in its proceedings. But, mark you, the proposed bill
did not give them the right to vote, so, I have no doubt, you will
find it was not a very dangerous measure after all. The first time
the bill was carried by 80 votes against 29 ; but the Government
at the time, which was a Conservative one, although they only
had a support of about 30 out of 114—we had not yet got real
Parliamentary government introduced—was evidently jealous of
the growing power and influence of the "peasant party" in the
Parliament, and advised the king to refuse his sanction to the
bill. The Government also saw in the proposed reform the
threatened introduction of the Parliamentary system, with the
prospect of their own fall, as they would have to depend upon
a majority in the Storthing to maintain their position. Three
Parliaments, after three successive elections, carried the bill, each
time by an increased majority—the last time, in 1880, by the
overwhelming majority of 93 out of 111. It was then generally
expected that the king and his Government would at length
comply with the wishes of the people, but the king finally refused his sanction to the bill, declaring, at the same time, that
his right to the absolute veto was "above all doubt." He has,
however, since then been obliged to alter this, his conviction, and
he has actually had to sign the bill which involved the question
of the veto. The Norwegians were not, however, going to let
the matter rest with the royal declaration. From that moment
a serious struggle arose between the people and the king, and
centered itself upon the question of the existence or non-existence
of an absolute veto on the part of the Crown. In England it is
generally assumed, and is recognised by such a high authority as

Sir Thomas Erskine May, that an absolute veto is practically *unconstitutional*—that is to say, *illegal.* Although, theoretically, the veto is a prerogative of the Crown, it has in England long ago become effete and obsolete. It was hard, however, to understand how the king of so enlightened and free a nation as the Norwegians could, in these advanced times, set up a claim for such an antiquated prerogative. The Parliament now proceeded to adopt the last resource provided by the Constitution—it impeached the whole of the ministry before the supreme court of the realm, or, as it is called, the *Rigsret*, with a view of obtaining the dismissal of the ministry. The first charge against the ministers was having acted contrary to the interests of the country by advising the king to refuse his sanction to the amendment of the law for admitting the ministers to the Parliament; and to this was added two other charges, one involving a question of supply, and another about the refusal of the Government to appoint two additional members on the Committee of the State Railways.

The result of this remarkable trial can be stated very shortly.

The ministry was dismissed one by one, the king being compelled to accept the judgment of the supreme court. It was, however, very critical times that the Norwegians then passed through. It was rumoured that the king intended a *coup d'etat* by the aid of Swedish troops, and of a few Norwegian military officers; the Norwegian army could not be depended upon, as it was well known that the men sympathised with the Parliament; but wiser counsels prevailed, and although the king attempted to form a conservative government again, which, however, only lasted a few months, he eventually appointed a liberal ministry, with John Sverdrup at its head. The liberal party had then a great victory all along the line, and the question of the absolute veto was settled once for all. It is not likely that any king in Norway will claim this again. It is, of course, in itself absurd to suppose that such a free and democratic Constitution as that of Norway, with no upper house, and the large power vested in the people, should give the king an absolute veto. In this struggle the peasantry and their representatives again played a prominent part, and without their aid this victory would not have been won. Although Parliamentary government has not yet been carried out to perfection, it may be looked upon as the future popular form of government that will be generally acknowledged.

I must next refer to the position of the king in the country.

He represents the executive of the country; but his person is holy, and his ministers alone can be held responsible to the Parliament. The king can declare war and conclude peace with foreign countries, and has the command of the Norwegian army and navy. In an aggressive war he must, however, have the sanction of the Parliament to use them. The king elects his ministry and all higher officials, and he is, besides, the head of the state Church.

In all questions of supply of taxes and customs, the king has nothing to say; his and the royal *upanages* must be voted yearly, and some time ago the Parliament took the liberty to reduce some of these. A few years ago a bill was passed dispensing with the old formula, "To his most gracious majesty, the king," which was used on all state documents and addresses to his majesty. Henceforth the formula is to be only, "*To the king.*" All this tends to show that the true democratic spirit, which the patriots of 1814 imparted to our Constitution, is not slumbering, but that we gradually are developing it in the direction which they, no doubt, intended.

Norway has not yet got *Universal Suffrage;* but it is in the programme of the liberal party, and will, no doubt, be carried in a few years. At present every Norwegian of twenty-five years of age, who (1) in the country possesses freehold land, or has been a tenant of such a property for five years; or (2) who is a burgess of any town; or (3) possesses property in land or in houses to the value of £30; or (4) who has paid taxes to the state on a yearly income of at least £30 in the country, and £45 in the towns, so you see we have already a very extended suffrage.

The elections for members of the National Assembly takes place every three years. The mode of election is, unfortunately, at present *indirect;* but this will, no doubt, be altered in time, now that the communication between the different parts of the country is so much better. At present, the electors first nominate a number of deputies, or an *election committee,* for each town or county; and these among themselves again elect the number of Members of Parliament representing the town or the district. In Norway the Members of Parliament are paid. They are allowed 12 kroner, or 13s. 6d. a day while in session, and their travelling expenses. I think it is only right that the state, and especially a democratic one, should in some way remunerate the representatives for the loss of time they incur in the public service of their country.

Norway has, for the last fifty years, possessed a most perfect system

of local government. It is only a year or two since you introduced
it in England, but I doubt if the powers of the County Councils
are as full and thorough-going as the Norwegian system. I will
not take up your time by going into details of local government
in Norway; suffice it to say that the elected Board, called
"Kommune Bertyrelsi," and which is divided into two—the
Formandskab, or the executive; and the Representantskab, a
larger body, is entrusted with all necessary powers to manage
the affairs of the "Kommune," as it is called.

From the beginning of the next year, the jury system will be
introduced into the country, but in criminal cases only, so, on the
whole, we think we are getting our house into better and better
order for coming generations.

I must next touch upon the position that Norway and Sweden
occupy in the union between the two countries. It will be remembered that, according to the Act of Union of 1814, Norway was
declared to be a free, independent, and indivisible kingdom,
united with Sweden under one king. The king is really the only
thing we have in common, besides ambassadors and consuls
abroad. Each country has its own parliament, its own government, its own army and navy. Each country impose their own
taxes and customs, and are really two distinct kingdoms—a fact
often misunderstood, or not known, in England. The king resides
for the greater part of the year in Stockholm, his Swedish capital,
but comes on two or three visits to Norway every year to open or
close the Parliament, or on matters of State. Three members of
the Norwegian Government are always in attendance upon the
king at Stockholm, and through whom he transacts his Norwegian business.

At present there is a great controversy going on in Norway
about a point in the Union which has been overlooked from the
very first, and never since, until now, has been seriously discussed.
Strange to say, in the Norwegian Ministry, there is no Foreign
Minister. At the time of the Union, in 1814, nothing had been
settled with regard to the share that Norway was to have in the
transaction of diplomatic affairs with foreign countries. Fortunately, Norway is very little troubled with diplomatic affairs; but,
in 1835, a resolution was issued to the effect that, when the
Swedish Foreign Minister was discussing diplomatic matters with
the king, which concerned both countries, or Sweden only, another
Swedish councillor, and the Norway minister at Stockholm, should
be present; but if the matters concerned Norway alone, the Nor-

wegian minister alone was to attend the deliberations of the king
and his Foreign Swedish Minister.   This arrangement has not
always proved satisfactory to the Norwegians; but, in the meantime, this state of affairs have been allowed to drift on, and
gradually the Swedish Foreign Minister has come to be looked
upon as the Foreign Minister to Norway also.   But nothing is
said about this in the Norwegian Constitution, or in the Act of
Union; and, as the Swedish Foreign Minister cannot be held
responsible to the Norwegian Government or Parliament, it is no
wonder that the Norwegians wish to have this point settled.   As
a matter of fact, in the diplomatic relations of the two countries
with foreign powers, Norway has not enjoyed equal right and
share with Sweden, as she, according to the Act of Union, had a
right to expect and demand.   Only last summer we had an instance
of this.   Norway was officially represented at the Paris Exhibition,
while Sweden would not take part in the celebration of the cen-
tenary of the French Revolution.   Before the day of opening, the
Swedish and Norwegian Ambassador in Paris had been requested
by the Norwegian commissioner to be present at the Norwegian
department, and receive the President on his tour of inspection
through the Exhibition, but this the Ambassador flatly refused to
do.   It was afterwards ascertained that the Ambassador had
received instructions from the Swedish Foreign Minister in Stockholm not to be present and represent Norway at the Exhibition.
The Norwegians could not but look upon this as an insult, but
we can neither call the Foreign Minister or the Ambassador into
account; we could only resent it in the public press.   This
occurrence, and many others, in which the Swedes seem to show
that they want to have the upper hand, have given rise to the
controversy I mentioned, and at present it seems that the Norwegians want to appoint their own consuls and representatives
abroad, which they, according to their Constitution, have a full
right to do, and even to appoint their own Foreign Minister,
unless a satisfactory arrangement is arrived at with Sweden.   This
may hereafter give rise to serious dissensions between the two
countries, and I mention it because it is part of our political
aspiration at the present moment to assert our just claim to equal
rights and an equal position in the Union; in fact, it seems that
the discussion and the settlement of the matter will, on the part
of the Norwegians, be carried on on the following lines : " Full
equality, or out of the Union."

    It is especially on this and similar points that there is a feeling of jealousy between the two countries, but otherwise the two nations get on very well together, and I hope the Union may long exist, and that the two sister countries will prosper side by side and in full harmony. Some few still dream of the Union, or an amalgamation, of the three Scand countries—Norway, Sweden, and Denmark. I myself think that this may come to pass, say in five hundred years or so; but, in the meantime, each nation must be allowed to develop independently. I do not think we need to trouble ourselves about this amalgamation in the far future; at present, it is our duty to develop our national characteristics, our political liberty, our literature, our arts, on national lines, and quite independent of one another. Take away, for instance, the national element from our literature, from our arts, our music, and we should not command the attention and respect we at present enjoy. If our authors were to fall into the style of the Swedish or the French writers, our musicians to be influenced by the German or French school, and so on during our present development, as a new-born nation, we should be nowhere. Nothing is more contemptible than a dandified French-Norwegian, a German-struck Norwegian, or an Anglicised-Norwegian with sporting and betting proclivities! I maintain that, in the case of nations, each must, for the present, and for some time to come, develop the national element in their character, in their literature, and in their arts, just as individuals must develop their personal characteristics to make themselves worthy of the respect and friendship of their fellow-creatures. To illustrate more plainly what I mean, I would, as a contrast to the class of individuals upon whom our hope of the future is built, only mention a class of beings we now find in our midst—a class of beings who evidently have no independence of character or independent way of thinking, and who seem to have lost all the characteristics of the nation to which they belong—I mean the *mashers*. They are living proofs of how individuals as well as nations can deteriorate. I suppose the English have their ideal of what an Englishman should be. I think they would hardly present a masher to the world as a representative one! Unless the development of national as well as personal character is carried out on the lines I have referred to, we shall all be mashers, and have nations of mashers, and the decline and fall of the British and other empires will soon follow. We Norwegians are a small nation, and we must not forget that our very existence among the nations of the world depends upon our upholding the national character and

independence of our race. I see in the distant future a time
when the nations and the peoples of the earth have approached
each other more than now, understood each other more than
now, and have even amalgamated with one another more than
now, perhaps in a kind of international brotherhood, but I hope,
even then, that both nations and individuals will preserve and
retain what is great and good in their national and personal
characters.

I must not forget to say a few words about the Norwegian
people themselves, in their daily life and work. The Norwegians
have a hard struggle with nature for their existence. The Norwegians of to-day must be divided into two distinct classes—the
Norwegian bïndes, or *peasants*, and the *townspeople*. The latter
are neither more nor less interesting, neither better nor worse,
than most town populations in Europe. The better classes in
the towns are mostly of foreign origin—Danish, German, and
even English—whose forefathers immigrated into Norway in the
early part of the century, soon after we had gained our independence, when business began to look up and improve, while the
people of the official classes were formerly almost wholly of
Danish origin from the time of the union with Denmark.

The Norwegian peasants, however, are, and have been, the
kernel of the nation. They are the freeholders of the property on
which they live, and where, as a rule, their forefathers have lived
for centuries before them. From the earliest ages the peasantry
have been absolute owners of the land. Even during the long
union with Denmark, the Norwegian peasant was, as I already have
referred to, the free and independent master of his own farm. To
him the English system of leasehold is incomprehensible, and he
cannot believe his ears when he hears it explained to him. I
believe that Norway is one of the few, if not the only country in
Europe, where the peasantry never have been serfs. Their udal
laws trained them in the management of their own affairs, and
produced that feeling of self-respect and independence which
the possession of property, and land in particular, gives. Nature
has not been bountiful to them ; in many cases they have even
to carry up the soil on to the rocks to grow the necessary corn
for their existence, but still there is hardly a happier and more
independent man than the Norwegian bïnde. He is the descendant of the old " jarls," or chieftains of the land, its true and
ancient nobility, and many of the peasant families descend from
the old Norwegian kings. I must here relate a story which

throws a deal of light on the independent character of these
sturdy peasants. Soon after Karl Johun had become king in
1814, he had to undertake a journey through Gudbrandsdalen,
one of the finest villages in the country. In those days travelling
was not so quick and convenient as now, and the king had to
put up at night at the farms of the peasants, who generally
received a message a day or two beforehand to prepare for the
reception of the king. On the occasion I refer to, a wealthy
peasant, by the name of Tofti, in the upper end of the valley, had
received notice to receive the king, and when the king and his
suite entered the room where the dinner was to be served, they
discovered that, at the head of the table, a smaller table had
been placed crossways, and was laid for only two persons. The
king was conducted by his host to this table, and the Swedish
Chamberlain, who was in attendance upon the king, thought,
as a matter of course, that the other seat was for him, and proceeded to take it, when the peasant tapped him on the shoulder
and pointed to a place at the other table, saying, as he sat
down by the side of the king, "This table is only for those of
royal blood." I can hardly imagine a peasant in another country
speaking thus in the presence of a king. The townspeople
address the king as " *Your Majesty,*" or by the polite "de," or
"you," but a Norwegian peasant addresses him with the familiar
"du," or "*thou,*" which is only used when people are intimate
with one another. I have on several occasions heard the
peasants speak to the king, and it has amused me greatly to hear
them address him in this familiar way. During many political
difficulties, the Norwegian peasants have been the saviours of the
country, and from their ranks have sprung some of the most
celebrated men of our day. I am certain that no other country
possesses so many men in official positions, such as doctors,
clergymen, engineers, and teachers, who are peasant-born, and
even often from the farm-labouring and working-classes, and
that no other country has so many eminent poets, artists, men of
science, and statesmen, who have also risen from the peasantry.
Lately we have had three bishops—one is still alive—who were
peasants, and you must take your degree with unusually high
honours if you aspire to be a bishop in Norway. Bjornson, the
well-known poet and dramatist, is the son of a clergyman, who
worked his way up from being a poor peasant lad. Ivan Aaser,
the great linguist, Vinje, the poet, Gurbory, a talented writer,
are all peasant-born. Skredsvig, the well-known painter, is the

son of a working-man, and a great number of our best painters,
and nearly all our sculptors, are of the peasantry. Svendsen,
the well-known composer, is the son of a working-man; one of
our most gifted editors, and three of the members of the late
Liberal Government, were all peasant-born, and several peasants
have been presidents or speakers in the Parliament. Mr Samuel
Laing. an English traveller, and father of the ex-member for
Orkney and Shetland, speaks as follows of the Norwegian peasant:
"The remarkable firmness, and moderation, and judgment with
which these people have exercised the legislative powers which
the Constitution entirely has vested in their representatives, place
them, in the moral estimate of Europeans nations, in a much
higher rank than those who have received a much greater share
of public attention in this country."

Norway ranks high among European countries in the matter
of education. All the peasants, and all belonging to the working-
classes, can now read and write, and they all know the Constitution and the history of their country on their fingers' ends; they
read all new books; the parish libraries all over the country
supply them with sufficient reading, but it is also well known
that the better off among the peasantry buy the modern literature, and lend them out to their neighbours. Thus Bjornson's
and Ibsen's works are read just as eagerly and as early by the
peasantry as by the townspeople. You find a newspaper in
every farmstead, and even in the cottages of the farm-labourers.
Besides the usual national schools, we have the so-called Folke-
hoiskoler (high schools for the people), where instruction and
lectures are given to grown-up people of both sexes.

I said that the Norwegian peasant carries on a hard struggle
for his existence. It is very difficult indeed to understand the
hardships he has to go through, unless you see it with your eyes.
The peasantry may be divided into two classes—the coast population, and the inland population. The people on the coast
live to a great extent by fishing, but they have also small farms
to cultivate. In the winter months the greater part of the
population on the coast proceed often hundreds of miles in
their open boats, or by steamer, to the great fisheries in the
north of Norway. Few people could endure the life they lead
during the time the fishing goes on. They often remain in their
boats out at sea on the fishing grounds for one, two, or three
days, frequently through wet, and hauling in their catch at sea
in a cold of which we have little idea. And when they come

ashore they often fail in getting accommodation for the night, and half of them are not able to get their food cooked, but must content themselves with eating it cold, and with a "dram," and with sleeping in their stiff frozen clothes, packed closely together, like herrings in a barrel, on the floor, or even in a standing position, one leaning against the other, in a close and stifling atmosphere. Sometimes they must go back to their boats, and cover themselves with anything they can find, and, shivering from cold, spend the night under the Arctic sky. Many catch illnesses, with which they are troubled all their life. Rheumatism is a general complaint among the fishermen. A great number every year lose their lives in stormy weather. Often the fishing turns out badly, but they go at it again next year. It is not gain alone which tempts them ; the life itself is so adventurous, they have heard accounts of it from their boyhood, and do not rest till they get off to the great fishing grounds to try their luck.

The Norwegians, as you know, are great sailors, and there are now about sixty or seventy thousand men engaged in the shipping of the country. Next to England, Norway possesses the greatest fleet of merchant ships.

Of the inland population, the people employed in the forest industry of the country undergo the greatest hardships. I cannot enter into detail of their life in the great vast forests, where they sometimes stop for weeks at a time, but I will give you one or two sketches of the kind of life they lead. After having been felling trees in deep snow in the forest the whole day, they return at night to a rough sort of a shanty, built of logs, about eight by twelve feet, with no doors or windows. On a slab in one of the corners they keep up a fire all night, the smoke escaping through a hole in the roof ; but the doorway and the chimney are open, and the hut is exceedingly draughty. Opposite the fire they make a bed, on some logs, of some hay and moss. They never undress; in the evening they pull off their boots and stockings, which they dry while sitting with their bare feet before the fire, but they put both stockings and boots on again before they lie down. In very severe weather, it happens that the clothes, on the side near the rime-frosted wall, become frozen fast to it ; while the other side, which is turned to the fire, becomes smoking hot and steaming.

When the floating begins, in the spring, the men have to wade about in the rivers, often to their shoulders, without changing clothes for weeks. Sometimes they lose all feeling in their feet, and are then obliged to take off their boots and stockings, and rub them until feeling is restored; often they have to lie down to get a little sleep, with nothing over them as a covering except branches of the pine tree.

The occupation of "floating" is a dangerous and health-destroying one. It is a wonder that more lives are not lost. It is this life of adventure and peril, and the solitude in these parts, that attract the Norwegian peasant to it. For every one who meets his death in the cataract, or succumbs from slow disease, there are only too many to take his place. Norway has over 750 sawmills, so you understand large numbers find their livelihood in this industry, and that timber forms a great article of export.

Every year thousands of our English cousins now visit our country, and we bid fair to become the great hunting ground in Europe for tourists and sportsmen, and we, on our part, wish you hearty welcome. I only trust that my countrymen will keep their heads cool at the great influx of visitors from all countries, and on the great praise they and their country receive in the numerous articles and books which continually are being published about Norway. If you will notice, there is scarcely any other country about which so many guide-books and books of travel at present are published here in England as about Norway.

Before I conclude, I must refer for a moment or two to the literature of the country, which has now become such an important factor in the national thought and life of the Norwegians. Time will not permit me to go back to the dawn of our present literature, when the names of Wergelund and Welhaven was on everybody's lips. I will at once mention the two names in our modern literature which have now an almost world-wide reputation. First of all, I must mention the great national poet of Norway *par excellence*, Bjornstgorne Bjornson. He struck, in his very first attempt, a chord in the heart of the people, which gave a new impulse to the national life that was dawning on Norway. The poet became a patriot; he thinks that a poet need not necessarily shut himself up in a room, and, in a velvet jacket, and with long curls, write sweet, sentimental verses to the moon or some fair lady. He mixed with the people, learnt their yearnings and their aspirations; at great risk to his reputation and his financial position, he joined the ranks of the people, he thrilled the minds of his countrymen as he spoke to them of their duty to themselves and their country, and stirred up the old independent spirit of the Norsemen. The part he took in the political struggle between the king and the Norwegian people some years ago, and the part he at present is playing in Norwegian politics, is of the greatest importance to us, and, in the future, when he will be better understood than now, the historian will inscribe his name in the honourable place it deserves in the list of champions for his country's rights. And how could it be otherwise? Look at Bjornson himself! Is he not the very ideal of a Norwegian—the fine, broad-shouldered figure, with the noble head and the lion's mane, looks every inch a jarl, one of the chieftians of old, as fine a representation of the old Norseman as you would wish. He has been called by one of his friends *the political conscience of the Norwegian people*, and I think it very appropriate. Where should we have been during the late political struggle if he, before any one else dared to do so, had not courageously spoken out on behalf of his countrymen, and reminded them of their duties, and what their forefathers had done before them.

No, the Norwegian people have not sung his songs or read his tales in vain; they, at least, understand him and love him, notwithstanding what certain sages and wise heads may say to the contrary. At the same time, his latest work shows him to be the true poet, who finds his way to the inmost chords of the human heart, and shows them the way to a truer and better understanding of our existence here, and of our duty to one another, than all the sermons and goody-goody talk that has been levelled at the heads of humanity for generations. Bjornson is the ideal optimist. He loves life; he loves his country; but he loves humanity above all.

The name of our other great poet is Henrik Ibsen. Until lately, Ibsen was little known in England; but, after the performance of two of his plays last summer, and the many articles that have appeared about him in English papers and magazines, his name is now known to most intellectual Englishmen and women. It would take hours to go into his numerous works, and the general development of his remarkable talent. He also began as a writer of historical plays, which appealed to the feelings of his countrymen; but gradually he became the philosophical poet, and in bitter satires told his countrymen their little follies and vanities, opening up at the same time a new vista of life to them, of which they never dreamt. Ibsen is a pessimist and realist of the first water. How could he, with his knowledge of human nature and human weaknesses, be otherwise? He has been called the poet of woman; and, as far as many of us believe that the salvation of the world is to come from woman, that of society is to rest upon a sounder, healthier, and happier basis than hitherto, woman must step in and take her share in the work of progress, and not be the plaything—the doll—she hitherto has been, then it is right to call him the woman's poet. I prefer to call him the Shakespeare of the nineteenth century, for Ibsen is not for woman alone, not for Norway alone ; he is for all mankind, for all countries where civilisation has left its mark.

Of other authors I will only mention Jonas Lie, the Dickens of Norway, and Alexander Kielland, the great satirist. We have painters and sculptors, and men of science, of European renown ; we have musicians who have made their mark, and of these you well know the name of Edward Grieg. I spoke, at the beginning of this lecture, about the invasions of the ancient Norsemen. I did so purposely. Now, a thousand years later, we are contemplating another invasion of your empire; with our authors, our poets, our artists and our bards in the front, we intend to invade your country again, but not in the fashion of our ancestors. No, we want to make way to your hearts, to gain your sympathy for our aspirations, for our national life and movements, to help us to break down national prejudices, that the nations of the world all the sooner can stand side by side, hand in hand, all working for that great aim of mankind—the happiness of the human race.

XI

SWEDEN.

EIRIKR MAGNUSSON, M.A.

WHEN the veil of myth and legend lifts, and historical light first begins to throw a glimmer over the life of the Swedish nation, we find the country inhabited by two kindred races. The southern lowlands, together with the island of Gotland, are occupied by a people who call themselves Gautar or Goths. But the great central basin, forming the watershed of the vast lake system of Wenern, Vettern Mülaren, and a multitude of other inland standing waters, is held by the race who call themselves Sviar, Svear, Swedes. The Aborigines, the Fins, and the Lapps had already been pushed by the southern invaders far to the north, where the former maintained themselves chiefly by hunting and fishing, the latter by nomadic pursuits, even as they do to this day.

All human civilisation is, in the first instance, a struggle, more or less victorious, with Nature. All races that begin this struggle with the combined forces of land and water at once are generally in advance in civilisation of those races who inhabit vast continental prairie or steppe territories. Hence we find that island populations and lake populations are not only the first to organise themselves into civilised communities; but when they receive civilisation through foreign impulse, are the quickest in adapting themselves to it. Thus, in the very dawn of Scandinavian history, we find that the lake districts of Sweden are inhabited by a people who form not only a civilised community, but have already advanced far in the art of organising a state. The Svear maintain a general supremacy over the whole country, and have managed to establish, in the midst of their settlement, a central temple to which both Goths and Swedes owe one common religious allegiance. At first this central temple was at Sigtuna, on the eastern shore of the Mülaren; afterwards it was removed to Upsala, where in splendour and magnificence it outrivalled every other temple north of the Baltic. On its ruins, speaking historically, towers, at the present day, the largest and stateliest cathedral in Scandinavian Christendom.

The earliest race of rulers that history mentions in Sweden were the Ynglingar, out of whom sprang the so-called overking or imperial head of the land. It followed, as a natural consequence of the close connection which in these early ages was supposed to exist between rulers and gods, that the chief king was also supreme pontiff at the same time. *Ex-officio* also, as it would seem, he was the president of the general assembly which met yearly at Upsala.

But, as in all states struggling through the first stages of organisation, the power exercised by the supreme head is precarious, so the authority exercised by the royal primate of Sweden over the provincial tributaries, the so-called Folk-kings, depended entirely upon the effectiveness of the blows of his sword—on his personal ascendency and bravery in fact. Hence he had constantly to fight combinations among the Folk-kings, which aimed at transferring to some one among themselves the supreme power he wielded. Thus the earliest centuries of the history of Sweden present a picture of perpetual warfare and bloodshed, of one dynasty going down in blood and the next rising out of it to, in its turn, perish in the same way. The most famous of these inter-dynastic conflicts is the fight on the moor of Brávöllr or Bravalla, as the Swedes pronounce the name, about 740, where the mighty warrior Harald Hilditönn, ancient and blind, fell at the hands of his nephew, Sigurd Ring, who thus became the founder of a new dynasty, which counted among its representatives the much-legended hero Ragnar Lodbrok and Bjorn Ironside, both conquerors by sea and land. During this dynasty great changes took place in Sweden. From within the mighty Viking upheaval begins to present to Eastern Europe a threatening front, 750-60. From without Sweden received in Ansgarius, 829, the first messenger proclaiming the principle of peace and goodwill among men—a principle which received a stubborn resistance, as might be expected, not only because of the tenacity with which the people clung to the faith of their forefathers, but especially on account of the Viking policy which at that very time had become a burning question in Scandinavia. By this policy murder and bloodshed were not only a lawful occupation, but constituted an indispensable title to consideration and advancement in society. Hence Christianity advanced in the North pretty much at the same rate that its Viking energy spent itself. And in Sweden it was preached for nearly two hundred years, before the country had a Christian ruler in Olaf Skeetking, A.D. 1000.

The Viking policy of Sweden deserves a moment's attention on account of the radical influence it brought to bear on the destinies of the Slavonic people of Eastern Europe. For West-European students of history the matter receives additional interest by the fact that the modern school of Russian historians is busily at work suppressing, as an idle fable, the story I am going to tell you. In the year 859 the earliest Russian historian, who goes under the name of Nestor, and was a monk from Kijef, who lived in the twelfth century, states that the Varegs or Warangians came over the sea and collected tribute from various Slavonic tribes in Russia. Three years afterwards they were driven out of Russia; but on their departure there arose such an anarchy in the land, that the people agreed at last to send for a prince who should rule over them and protect them. And they went over the sea, says Nestor, to the Warangians, to the Rus, for so these Warangians were called, and set forth to them the anarchical state of their country. And three brothers, princes among Rus, went with all their followers. The oldest, Rurik, settled in Novgorod; another, Sineus, took up his residence in Bêlo-ozero; the third, Truvor, established himself in Izborsk. These purely and exclusively Scandinavian names, which, in the vernacular, have the forms of Hrœrekr, Signjótr, and Thorvarr,[1] are in themselves evidence sure enough of the veracity of the chronicler, which also is borne out by many a corroborative evidence from other independent sources, such as Byzantine chroniclers, Frankish and Venetian annals, and even early Arabic writers, such as Ibn Dustha, Ibn Fadhlan, and others.

We have already seen that these Scandinavians were called Rús by the first Russian chronicler. The Arabs call them by the same name, and the Byzantines invariably Rhos. No doubt the Arabs and the Greeks got the name from the Russian Slavs. They again had got it from their nearest northern neighbours the Fins, whose name for Sweden from time immemorial has been Ruotsi, which by natural phonetic law in Slavonic becomes Rús. The Finnish name is on all hands acknowledged to be of foreign, that is to say, Scandinavian origin. In the Middle Ages the

---

[1] I think it is open to doubt whether this is the original of Truvor. I am more inclined to think that it was Thórdr, pronounced by the Scandinavians, by means of Svarabhakti, somewhat like Turder = Slav-Truvor.

inhabitants of Upland and East Gotland in Sweden were called the Rods-karlar or Rodsmæn, the rowing men, the oarsmen, or seafarers, and the first element of the compound might have been taken up by the Fins and given to the whole nation of Sweden, whom they practically knew as the rowing or seafaring nation. In any case, Rús was the name of Swedes among their eastern neighbours; and from them, as founders and organisers of the Russian state, it passed into a name or title not only for that state, but also for all the nationalities composing it. Hence, historically traced, Russia means the Swedish Empire. For two hundred years, or to about 1054, these Scandinavians were alternately the terror or the mercantile customer of the Byzantians. There is something historically significant in the fact that the ferocious sway of the Scandinavian Vikings should come to an end both in the east and the west at almost the same time, in the course of the eleventh century. This is not the occasion for going into that interesting question; but I may briefly mention that the conquest of the Holy Land by the Seldjukian Turks in the same century, and the incessant current of news to Western Europe by returning pilgrims of the brutal treatment of Christians by the new conquerors, created gradually a new idea, that of saving the Holy Land from the infidel barbarian, and provided for the military energy of Europe a new outlet in the Crusades, which after all are but the Viking movement in another form.

While the Swedes thus became the founders and organisers of the Russian state, the nation at home was passing through gradual changes, constitutional as well as religious. By the opening of the eleventh century the country had a Christian ruler, as I said before, in the person of Olaf Skeetking. And now history exhibits to us for the first time a telling and interesting illustration of the constitutional condition of the country. In the various folklands different and peculiar codes of law had grown up, and the guardianship of the law was chiefly left to the so-called lawman, whose duty it was not only to instruct the people in the law, that is, to give out at the periodical folk-motes the law as it stood, but especially to guard the rights and privileges of the Franklins against infringement on the part of the king. A telling illustration of the vindication of this constitutional right is related as occurring in the reign of this king, all the more telling, because it is an evidence of the indomitable spirit of freedom which at all times, especially at the most serious, has found an exponent among the Franklin class of Sweden. The story tells how Olaf

Skeetking harboured an inveterate grudge towards King Olaf Haraldsson (Saint Ol.) of Norway. The latter, in order to bring about friendship between the two countries, sued for the hand of the daughter of his Swedish namesake; but though she tried with the aid of others to bend her father's temper towards acceptance of the suit, yet all her endeavours proved in vain. But the time of the general assembly of all the Swedes was at hand, and the mighty law-man of Tiundaland, Thorgny by name, was one of the self-chosen members of the assembly. Earl Rögnvald, the ambassador from Norway, seized the opportunity of sounding the great spokesman of the Franklins with regard to Norway's suit. He came to Thorgny's home one day towards eve. The house was great and magnificent, and many people about, who took at once charge of the Earl's caravan, and gave him good cheer. The Earl entered the hall, which was crowded with the law-man's attendants. In the high seat there sat an old man, and a grander-looking magnate they had never set eye on before. The beard was so long that it covered the whole of his front and rested on his lap. And a goodly man he was, and noble to behold.

One day Earl Rögnvald told Thorgny his errand; that his master wanted to put a stop to a state of retaliatory raids over the boundaries of the two kingdoms, and in order to secure peace between them desired to obtain the hand of Ingigord, King Olaf the Swede's daughter. "But I know not how to prevail," said the Earl, "on account of the Swede's implacable hatred towards Norway." Thorgny, after a pause, answered: "Your ways are strange. You hanker after titles; but if you encounter some difficulty, your counsel and forethought forsake you. . . . I deem it no deprivation of dignity to belong to the Franklins, with full liberty of speech, so as to be free to utter one's own mind frankly even in the presence of the King. Now, I shall come to the Upsala Assembly, and you speak out there whatever seems good to you."

At the Thing held in the open the King occupied a seat surrounded by his court. On the other side sat Thorgny with his house-carles, and Rögnvald the Earl with his court. Behind Thorgny stood the crowd of Franklins, while others took up their station about hillocks and mounds to listen to the speakers. When the King had answered, by a most insolent speech, the Earl's errand of peace and wooing, Thorgny stood up, and with him all the Franklins who were seated before, rushing forward, crowding round their tried spokesman to hear what the grand old man had to say. And a great clashing of weapons was the cheer by which he was hailed. When silence prevailed, he said : " Very different is now the temper of the kings of Sweden to what it has been in bygone days. My grandfather, Thorgny, told me how he remembered King Erik, son of Emund, and how he, while he was yet in the free course of manly thew, went every summer out on warfare to various lands, and subdued Finland, Karelin, Esthonia, and Courland, besides other eastern dominions ; and still you may see standing the earthworks and other great fortifications which he made, yet was he not so haughty as not to listen to people who had important matters to bring to his notice. My father was for a long time with King Björn, whose dominion stood firm and fast through life, and he was easy and affable to his friends. I myself may well remember King Eirik the Victorious serving him, as I did, in many a war ; he increased the Swedish power and defended it with manly hardihood ; yet it was easy for us to bring him to listen to reasonable counsel. But this King whom we have now allows no one to be so bold as to talk to him aught but what may be pleasing to himself. In this he shows himself stubborn enough, but his tributary lands he allows to be lost by reason of his want of ability and lack of strength. He aspires to subdue Norway, which no King of Sweden before him set his mind on, whereby unrest and trouble is brought home to many a man. Now we, the Franklins, desire that thou, King Olaf, shouldst make peace with Olaf the Stout of Norway and give him in marriage your daughter Ingigord. So, too, if you are minded to reconquer those dominions in the Baltic which your predecessors and forefathers have had there, we will all follow you on such an errand. But if you will not consent to what we say, we shall set upon you and slay you, and suffer no disturbance and lawlessness at your hands. Such have been the ways of our forefathers. At the Assembly of Muli they plunged five kings into one ditch, who were swollen with pride and insolence against them, even as you are towards us. Make quickly up your mind as to what you mean to resolve." Then the people made great roar with clashing weapons, and His Majesty the Skeetking came promptly to terms with the Franklins.

This digression is long, but it is a key to many a glorious chapter in the history of Sweden. It is the free Franklin class of that country which, at the most threatening periods in it history, has proved the unconquerable safeguard of its liberties against tyranny and lawlessness.

From the accession of Olaf the Skeetking, and for the next two hundred years, Sweden was the scene of internal and ruinous disunion, originating partly in the divergent religious tendencies of the two main races, the Gothic being the willing, the Swedish the unwilling and recalcitrating factor; partly in the ambitious contention between the Swedish royal family of King Erik the holy, and that of the Gothic house of Sverkir. During these internal disruptions the chief sufferer was the class of the Franklins, out of whom there sprang a military aristocracy, boundlessly selfish and reckless of every other interest in the state but its own. It secured for itself at last full immunity from taxes, and from the common jurisdiction of the ordinary courts of justice. And after the elevation of Upsala to an archbishopric in 1163, whereby the hierarchy of Sweden obtained its own metropolis, these two principal parties in the state became on one side the undermining agents of the royal power, and on the other the oppressors of the people. As the military aristocracy in its time had arisen out of free Franklin class, so in time there arose, in their turn, out of the military aristocracy, certain mighty families, who divided practically all power in the state between themselves and the prelates. Of these families the mightiest in the thirteenth century was that of the Folkungs, who were Earls by dignity of birth. The most famous of the Folkungs was the Earl Birgir who in Swedish history figures as the reconstructor of law and right, and who with ruthless cruelty, even against his own kin, whom he destroyed in large numbers by treachery, combined the highest qualities of a patriotic ruler for his time, and brought the country to a height of prosperity which it had not known for generations before him. By abolishing the rights and dignities of Earls in Sweden, and lowering it to that of Dukes, he thought he should contribute an element of stability to the Crown. But he only introduced thereby a fresh danger. His eldest son, Waldemar, † 1302, became King, his three younger sons Dukes; but they soon revolted against their weak and incapable brother, and from among them Magnus not only rose to the supreme power, but proved himself the ablest ruler Sweden had had for a long period. His historical surname, Barn-lock, is a fitting heading to the history of his reign. He was the Franklin's and farmer's especial protector, so that under his reign the robbing baron durst not even touch the farmer's property, though the barn had no other lock than that of the King's law. But with him the series of great Folkung rulers came to an end, and after sad and serious reverses the family died out with King Magnus II., Smek, who, after having wandered about for eleven years a dethroned monarch, was drowned in the Bay of Bergen in 1374. To him, however, the country owed the code of law which was first sanctioned in 1442, and remained the code of Sweden for 292 years.

His nephew and successor, Albrecht of Mecklenburg, was expelled, after an inglorious and anarchical reign of twenty-five years, and Sweden became a member of the confederate kingdom of Scandinavia under the provisions of the union-treaty of Kalmar (1397). That union only brought Sweden trouble and disaster, and was at last blotted out by the fearful massacre of Stockholm by Christian II. of Denmark, in the blood of six hundred of some of the best men of Sweden. It was not, however, without benefit to the country eventually, because it brought to the fore in the persons of the great Stures a family that was to give to the country some of the most famous men of the world. Gustav Wasa was the first of these. After many miraculous escapes from the persecutors of Christian II. he succeeded, by the bravery of the Franklins of the province of the Dalarne, in driving out the Danes and making himself master of the situation at home, and securing his election to the throne in 1523. We should have to go far afield in history to find such a true father of his country as this wonderful man. By prudence and firmness he overcame all internal troubles, destroyed the power of the hierarchy, and established the Reformation, caused the Bible to be translated, checked the aristocracy, and linked it to the crown by judiciously according it a share in the spoils of the dissolved monasteries and other confiscated Church properties. He had to fight with rebellious subjects, and he conquered and won their loyalty. He fought the Hanseatic league, then in the prime of its commercial insolence ; he had to battle with Russia, and out of both struggles he came victorious. When he had ruled as elected king for twenty-one years, the Rigsdag of Wadstena made the succession hereditary in his family in both lines male and female. The property of the crown was largely increased, the exchequer enriched, the laws relating to taxes, customs, and duties were reformed, agriculture, mining, trade, and industry, not to speak of education and learning, were all fostered by the same fatherly hand, the same penetrating wisdom. And never had the people of Sweden before witnessed so great a work and so full of blessing done by any of its rulers as that left by this noblest of kings, when, after a reign of forty-one glorious years, he left the throne to his unworthy son Erik XIV., who, as a madman, lost it eight years afterwards, and his life by poison in prison 1577. But the great qualities of the founder of this dynasty revived again in Charles IX. (1604-1611), and especially in the most illustrious of his successors, Gustavus Adolphus II., who was as great a genius in the organisation of the internal administration and in his legislative activity as he was on the field of battle.

His military successes are matters with which the whole world is familiar. His premature death on the field of Lützen cut short the many plans he had formed for the future, among which not the least eventful would have been that of creating a Protestant Scando-Baltic Empire under the regency of Sweden, as a counterpoise to the Catholic House of Hapsburg, a plan which it was reserved for the Great Brandenburgers of North Germany to take up a century later, in the person of Frederick the Great, to practically accomplish, after the lapse of another century, on the field of Sadowa in 1866, and to give the final touch to by the collapse of the other great Catholic power on that of Sedan in 1870.

In one respect the glorious reign of Gustavus Adolphus redounded to the misfortune of Sweden. The commanding character and personality of the King had prevailed with the aristocracy to lend him a self-sacrificing assistance in order to carry on his war in Germany. Thereby the aristocracy won, both at home as purchasers of state domains, and in the battlefield as plundering victors, an enormous ascendency, which still increased under the successors of Gustavus, Christina, and her cousin Charles X., and came to a disastrous culmination during the minority of the latter's son, Charles XI. For when, soon after his accession, 1672, he was engaged in war with Denmark and Brandenburg, the evils of the previous administration were soon brought to light, and Sweden suffered one serious reverse after another. Having secured for himself almost absolute power by the consent of Parliament in 1680, and more especially in 1682, the gifted and energetic ruler made it his first business to deprive the aristocracy, which, by its selfishness, had all but ruined the country, of an immense amount of its property and of its more dangerous privileges. He left the state in every way in a thoroughly organised condition, 1697, to his son Charles XII., then fifteen years of age, after having four years previously, 1693, received from his Parliament such absolute power as to be free to act independently of Parliament altogether.

At this moment the King of Sweden ruled, besides Sweden itself, over Finland, Esthonia, Livonia, Courland, Ingermanland; further, Pomerania, Rügen, Bremen, Verden, and Wismar. The enormous sacrifices to which the wars of this extraordinary man put his country are probably unsurpassed in the military history of civilised states. In nine years the country, with a population of some 1,800,000 inhabitants, supplied its extremely obstinate young hero with no less than 400,000 soldiers; and even after the disaster of Pattava, managed to put in the field a fresh contingent of 70,000 men well organised and well equipped. That to say, it placed in the field one-fourth of the whole population. But he left it also exhausted and powerless; and worse than that, he had transferred from it the character of a great European power over to Russia, which, three years after the death of Charles, invaded Sweden, and in less than three months laid in ashes 5 towns, 1361 villages, 141 country seats, besides a large number of iron works and mines, and deprived Sweden, by the treaty of Nystad, 1721, of all her Baltic possessions which had not already, the year before, passed into German hands. The consequences of the Charles's wars with regard to the internal condition of Sweden were equally disastrous. The exhausted land, plunged in the depths of the extremest misery, had practically fallen under the sway of the few nobles who had amassed fortunes out of its ruin. They soon made such a compact combination against the Crown, that they not only abolished the absolutism which Parliament had conferred on Charles XI., but, confident of their invincible power, brought humiliation on humiliation on the sovereign, especially during the reign of the conscientious, peace-loving, honest, but passive King Adolph Frederick, 1743-1771. Immediately almost after the death of Charles XII., however, the nobles began to contend among themselves for the lion's share of the spoils which the helpless state of the country held out to them. And eight years after his death (1726) their split was complete, and remained so for forty-six years. The two contending parties were called "Hats" and "Caps." The Hats were the military party, bent on the recovery of the military renown of Sweden and her *prestige* abroad. The Caps were in favour of developing generally the internal resources of the country. But what both had in common was an insatiable craving for all power in the state, and at length so thoroughly sheared the Crown of her prerogatives, that the sovereign had no longer even the freedom to dispose of any state patronage. So unscrupulous were these factions, and so unpatriotic, that to oust each other out of favour at court, they took foreign bribes by turns, and naturally neglected entirely what was most necessary, namely, the internal organisation and the real welfare of the state. To this kind of anarchy Gustavus III. put an end by a *coup d'état* in 1772, when, by the aid of his soldiers, he put the Council of State in prison, and forced the Rigsdag, surrounded by the military, to frame a constitution by which the executive power, the command of the army and navy, the state patronage, the creation of Peers, the right to enter and abandon alliances, to make treaties and defensive wars, was again vested in the Crown. But the brilliantly gifted monarch, the great patron of learning, and founder of the famous Academy of Sweden, was also a light-hearted, wasteful, and unscrupulous prince ; his war with Russia, 1788-90, brought Sweden only loss and no advantage. His hostile attitude towards the French republic and submission to Russian influence cost him his life, 1792. Under his successors, the half-lunatic Gustavus IV., Adolph, who was deposed by a military conspiracy, and Charles XIII., the misfortunes of Sweden came to a final end by the loss of Finland in 1809, a loss which the Swedish nation, in spite of sore regret, has wisely made up its mind never more to repair. It was recompensed to some extent by the acquisition of Norway under the treaty of Keil in 1814, an arrangement which, in spite of a good deal of friction, has proved on the whole beneficial. Since then Sweden has enjoyed a profound peace and made a magnificent use of her opportunity. Not the least important of the innumerable items of progress which during this period have ennobled and adorned the national life of the Swedish people, are the constitutional laws of the country, namely, the Constitution proper of June 9, 1809 ; the Parliamentary regulation of February 10, 1810, radically reformed in 1865, and sanctioned June 22, 1866 ; the Law of Succession, September 26, 1810 ; and the Free Press Regulation, July 16, 1812.

By these laws Sweden is a constitutional monarchy, hereditary in the male line only. The administrative power is vested in the King alone, while the legislative he shares with the representatives of the nation forming the Parliament or Rigsdag. He can propose measures, and has an absolute veto. He is irresponsible and his person sacred, all responsibility resting on his ministers who form the council of state. He is commander-in-chief by sea and land. He has a right to enter alliances and to make treaties with foreign powers. He can, having consulted the council of state, resolve on war and peace as he judges most profitable to the state, in which matter the councillors of state are responsible to the nation for their advice. The prerogative of supreme judge is transferred from him to a supreme court of judicature composed of twelve to eighteen judges.

The Rigsdag is no longer, as in former times, composed of the four estates—the aristocracy, the clergy, the burgesses, and the farmers, but by elected deputies. It is divided into two chambers, called first and second chamber, both having equal authority in all legislative matters. Qualified for the first chamber is a person who has attained his thirty-fifth year, and has at least for three years previous to his election been in possession of assessable real property to the value of 80,000 crowns (£4444), or on capital or labour has paid taxes to the state amounting at least to kr.4000 (£233). The members to the first chamber are elected for nine years by the so-called "landsting," or provincial assemblies; but in towns which are not represented in these assemblies, they are elected by special deputies. The population of each electorate for the upper chamber is fixed at 30,000.

Qualified for the second chamber is every member of a commune having filled his twenty-fifth year, who has a domicile within it, and a vote in its general affairs, provided he has, either in town or country, assessable real property of at least the value of kr.1000 (£50), or farms for life, or at least for five years an agricultural estate of at least kr.6000 assessable value, or pays voluntary tax on a yearly income of at least kr.800. These deputies are returned for three years, and are elected in rural districts by electors, each of whom represents 1000 of the population of the community, one for every jurisdiction, in the towns for every full 10,000 of the inhabitants. When the population of a jurisdiction that returns one member numbers more than 40,000 inhabitants, it is divided into two electorates, and returns two members. Towns, whose populations do not amount to 10,000 inhabitants, are grouped into electoral combinations, each of which shall number not less than six, nor more than twelve thousand people, returning one member. Members for the second chamber must have filled their twenty-fifth year, and have had the right of communal vote for one year at least, before their election to the Rigsdag. These deputies, in contrast to those of the upper chamber, are paid members of the diet, receiving kr.1200 for every session, and having their travelling expenses paid beside.

The diet, which meets ordinarily on the 15th of January, cannot, except at its own request, be dissolved till it has sat for four months, unless, during the session, the King dissolves for re-election one or both chambers.

The King nominates the speaker and deputy-speaker of both houses. The standing committees of every ordinary Rigsdag are : The constitution committee (20), the state committee (20), the tax committee (20), each consisting of twenty members; further, the bank committee and the law committee, each consisting of sixteen members. On all these committees both houses are equally represented. The ministers can, *ex officio*, without being members, attend and take part in the debates of both houses, but have no vote unless they happen to be members of the standing committees. Whatever measure both chambers pass by a majority becomes a resolution of the Rigsdag. Any measure failing to obtain a majority of votes in either chamber is thereby defeated, except such as relate to the budget, for which special regulations are provided. These are some of the most important provisions of the present Swedish constitution, which, unlike the paper constitutions of the continent, is, in common with that of England, one of traditional growth, an organic systematisation of the public life of the people, through which, at last, by heroic endurance and patient trust in their indomitable free heart, the no less gifted than noble-minded tillers of the soil of Sweden have won the day, practically for ever—a very proper reward to those who, through all the thunder-and-lightning period of Sweden's existence in Europe as a great power, had to maintain the show by the only thing which only too frequently was left them, their best and dearest blood.

If an illustration were wanted to bring home the truism that peace is the greatest blessing that any nation can enjoy, let the history of the progress of Sweden in the nineteenth century be attentively studied. The population has already doubled itself. In 1800 it was 2,347,000; in 1885 it had risen to 4,682,000. Of this population just about one-half is engaged in agricultural pursuits. The value of the proceeds of this industry, varying, of course, with varying seasons and harvests, amounts to between twenty and thirty millions sterling. From 1840 to 1880 the exports of cereals exceeded the imports to a considerable extent. But under the present protective system this has ceased to be the case. This protection, I should mention, only extends to cereals, and is the result of the shortsighted policy of the Swedish agriculturists, who command at present a preponderating influence in Parliament. In other respects Sweden continues to be a free-trade state, a commercial policy which it adopted in 1854, and which since then has produced results which are likely to link the nation to that policy for ever. Thus the value of the manufactures of Sweden amounted in 1850 to two million pounds, but in 1883 to more than ten and a half million. In 1850 the aggregate value of exports and imports was calculated at £4,000,000; in 1884 it exceeded £31,000,000. In 1850 the aggregate tonnage of ships inward and outward bound amounted to 858,827 tons, but in 1884 to 5,388,000. Such to Sweden have been the results of free trade.

The mining industry of Sweden is in a state of constant and rapid progress. For a long time, and, in fact, till only very lately, its iron, on account of its good natural quality, has commanded the price of the European market, where even still it ranks high. There are being worked at present more than 500 iron mines. In 1884 the aggregate produce amounted to over 900,000 tons, while cast-iron stood at 416,958 tons, bar-iron at 267,534, and sheet at 66,329 tons. The copper mines at that time produced 650 tons, those of silver 4000 lbs. troy weight. Pit coal has as yet been found only in one province, Malmöhu, but in such small quantity that the output of the mines only amounts to one-eighth of the coal imported from abroad.

Railways have been in existence in Sweden for thirty-three years. In 1856 the first railway of twenty-one miles long between Orebro and Nora was opened. In 1884 the total length of rail was 4194 miles, of which less than half belonged to the state, the rest to seventy-six private companies. At the same time the telegraphic lines extended to nearly 13,000 miles.

With regard to the education of the nation, it is scarcely a moot point that the Swedes are the best educated nation in Europe. Primary education is not only compulsory but free, and has been so for a long time, for every Swedish child. The instruction is conducted on a methodical system under government regulation. For the supply of primary education there were maintained, at the exclusive expense of the state, in 1884, no less than 9925 national schools, with 12,048 teachers male and female. In the larger parishes—some of which reach the size of many a German principality, and one, Gellivare in Lapland, is larger than the kingdom of Wurtemberg—the schools are organised on the ambulatory system, the teacher taking up his abode and setting up his school at one farm after the other, according to the convenience of attendance for the children. For higher education there are provided 96 public schools, attended by 14,617 pupils ; and two universities—one at Upsala, 1375, the other at Lund, in Schonen, erected 1668, for the wise purpose of welding to the Crown all the more firmly the newly-acquired southern provinces. The number of students at Upsala amounts to over 1900, with a teaching staff of 58 professors and 61 docents. At Lund the attendance of students exceeds 800, and the teaching staff counts 86 persons. At both universities, which are largely endowed by the state, the teaching is conducted on the most advanced lines of scientific method. In fact, the Scandinavian universities altogether occupy a position in the very front rank among the universities of the world.

Among the languages or dialects of Scandinavia the Swedish is by a long way the most euphonious and pure-sounding, with a modulating intonation which gives it a peculiarly noble grace. It is from no chauvinism, therefore, that the Swedes are proud of their idiom and name it the metallic tongue. And even when one of their greatest poets calls it the language of honour and heroism, the poetical hyperbole does not far overshoot the mark. For if there is any lesson that the history of Sweden teaches us more than another, it is this, that the salient characteristics of the race are *honour* and *heroism*.

XII

DENMARK AND ICELAND.

EIRIKR MAGNUSSON, M.A.

I SHALL, perhaps, best enable my audience to follow my remarks by at once giving a brief summary of the main points of my discourse.

Rapidly surveying the history of Denmark, I propose to show how, by the inexorable law of readjustment which is inherent in every false position, and not by faults of statesmanship only, Denmark from a great power has come down to her present position. I shall show how, instead of resulting in ruin, the catastrophe of 1864 has proved a blessing to the long-tried and long-wronged nation; how it was due to the troubles in the Duchies of Schleswick-Holstein, at least in part, that the absolute monarchy passed into a constitutional one in 1848; and, finally, how this constitution works, and how the constitutional principle has been applied with regard to Iceland.

It is true that Denmark is a small kingdom, its territorial extent amounting to but 15,000 square miles, or one-half of Scotland, and naturally contributes but little to the political forces now at play on the other side of the North Sea; but it is inhabited by a gifted and a brave race, and its history is full of interest to those who, animated by broad human sympathy, love to take a wide view of the changeful destinies of mankind.

In the very dawn of Scandinavian history, the Dane rises out of the sea, as it were, with an art entirely unknown in Northern Europe—the art of naval warfare. After the sack of Lindisfarne in 793, Alcuin, the most accomplished scholar of the age, wrote, "Who ever heard of such a thing as war made by sea?" So entirely at that time was the peace of the sea trusted in, that, both in Western Europe and in Great Britain, some of the wealthiest religious establishments were erected close to the shore, or out on the islands around it, in order to be as far removed as possible from the turmoil of robbing barons and plundering kings.

217

From the beginning of the ninth century the sea became, as one of their poets has expressed it, the Danes' path to power and glory. Every creek and bay and river bore their keels into the midst of some populous centre in the west of the old world. The Frank, the Gaul, the Spaniard, the Italian, the Moor—not to speak of the Anglo-Saxon in England, and the Celt in Ireland and Scotland—had to yield their blood and treasure to this ruthless ruler of the sea, in ruinous plenty, for three hundred years. The memory of this reign of terror still lives vivid in every Danish breast, and has, unfortunately, always tended to infuse more or less inconsiderate brusqueness into their dealings with nationalities subject to their sway. This, however, is no peculiarity of the Danes; it is the common malady of conquerors.

The conquest of England and the reign of Canute the Great, who even added Norway to his empire, brought Denmark to such an height of power in Europe as it has never enjoyed since to the same extent. That reign may be regarded as the culmination of the Viking conquests, as the century following Canute's death may, in a measure, be considered the period of reaction after the long-sustained strain. During this century internal disorders, and consequent weakness of the crown, rendered the country an easy prey for the Slavonic populations, who were its nearest neighbours on the south of the Baltic. Internal order was first re-established under the able rule of Waldemar the Great (1157-82), who retaliated handsomely on the Vends, seized the island of Rugen, and converted it, after the fashion of the time, to Christianity. The conquests of this monarch were extended by his son Canute VI. (1182–1202), not only to the Vends on the Continent, but also to the territories now called Mecklenburg and Pomerania; and his brother and successor, Valdemar the Victorious (1202–41), extended the sway of Denmark along the whole southern border of the Baltic, winding his victorious progress up with the conquest of Esthonia in 1219. Once more Denmark was a great power in Europe. But the fatal German axe was soon aloft again, and Denmark's ascendency came to a total collapse in 1227, when, defeated in an expedition against a confederacy of North German magnates, Waldemar became a prisoner of the Count of Schwerin, and had to renounce all his Vendish and German conquests. Another century of disasters now opened, during which the selfish disloyalty of the aristocracy and the Church, together with German aggression, so completely beggared the crown that King Christopher II. (1319–33), in order to maintain himself at all against his many foes, had to mortgage nearly the whole of his kingdom, and after a disastrous fight with the Holsatian Count Gert, practically lost it to the Germans. During the anarchical period of eight years that followed his death in 1333, even the old Danish provinces of Sconen, Holland, and Bleking in Southern Sweden passed under the crown of that country.

But for the murder of Count Gert by the Danish nobleman, Niels Ebbeson, 1340, Denmark would now have become a German state. So dark did the Danes regard this long period, that when once more there arose a sovereign of ability, in the person of Waldemar, the son of Christopher, who brought coherence to the state and security to the people, the nation conferred on him the suggestive title of " Day again." He reconquered the Swedish provinces, occupied the island of Gothland, and sacked the wealthy Hanseatic emporium of Wisby. A great drawback to his otherwise successful reign was the disastrous war which, for nine years towards its close, he waged with the Hanseatic towns, whose commercial power in the Baltic had been rapidly increasing ever since the close of the thirteenth century. Waldemar left his realm, however, in a fairly organised condition to his grandson Olaf, then only five years old. He was the son of King Hakon VI. of Norway and Waldemar's exceedingly able daughter, Margaret, the Semiramis of the North. Regent in Denmark for her young son from the death of her father in 1375, likewise in Norway on the death of her husband in 1380, Queen of both kingdoms on the death of her son in 1387, elected sovereign of Sweden in 1389 in recognition of the assistance she had afforded the Swedes in expelling the hated and despised King Albrecht of Mecklenburg, this mighty woman, by dint of personal ability and the fortune of circumstances, was the first person recorded by history as sole sovereign over the whole Scandinavian race. Her great idea was that this union should not only be one *de facto*, but should be secured by substantial guarantees, tending eventually to organic unity, an idea which, if her successors had possessed but a particle of her political sagacity, would probably have changed the history of Scandinavia, especially that of Denmark. She bestowed Schleswig on the Counts of Holstein as an hereditary feud 1386, thereby securing peace in that fatally dangerous corner. And in 1397 she brought about in Kalmar the Act of Union, the main stipulations of which provided that henceforward the three kingdoms should have one king ; that he should be chosen by representatives from all three kingdoms; that they should mutually assist each other against foreign foes; that each kingdom should be governed by its own laws. This Union, though wisely conceived, never worked properly. Sovereigns and people were alike immature for a political experiment of so delicate a nature. National jealousies, aristocratic insolence, hierarchical contumacy, and royal caprice were the chief internal foes. The deathblow was given to it at last by that implacable enemy of the aristocracy and hierarchy, King Christian II., who, but for his ruthless cruelty, was one of the most able and truly patriotic kings that ever occupied the throne of Denmark. In the hope of rendering the Swedes more submissive to his relentless rule, he caused to be massacred, in Stockholm, on the 8th of November 1520, two bishops and thirteen councillors of State, besides some six hundred citizens, and by this act broke off for ever the union of the two countries, after having lasted nominally on paper for 126 years.

By the accession of the Oldenburg dynasty to the throne in the person of Christian the First (1448) there arose on Denmark's political horizon the ill-omened star which went down in the blood of Dübbel, 1864. With this German family German influence in Denmark took up its headquarters at court, and for more than three centuries pervaded the national life, the language, the laws, the literature of Denmark. There were able men among these Oldenburgers; but unfortunately for a small country with a population within a million, trodden down by baron and prelate alike, and with an exchequer in constant straits, they were, most of them, far too recklessly warlike, and still more unfortunately so seldom had really solid victories to boast of. The worst legacy left them from previous reigns was the so-called "Haandfæstning" or capitulation, which at every successive election from that of Christopher II. in 1320, the barons and the prelates extorted from their unwilling sovereigns down to the middle of the seventh century. Every successive capitulation was more and more exacting, more and more destructive to the power of the crown. Out of this suicidal abuse grew eventually its very anti-climax, the absolute monarchy in 1660, when the aristocracy insolently refused all monetary assistance to the defence of the country, which the war of Frederick III. with Charles X. of Sweden had brought to the very verge of ruin. The Reformation had already broken the power of the unpatriotic hierarchy by sweeping out the bishops. Frederick III. therefore allied himself with the united estates of the Burgesses and the Protestant Clergy, who were burning with indignation at the ruinous selfishness of the barons, and succeeded not only in putting for ever an end to the disastrous capitulations, but also in securing an undisputed succession to his heirs, male and female, on the understanding that he should give the kingdom a constitution. Instead of that, however, he betrayed his allies; and in the so-called Kongeloo or King's law of 1665 established absolute government in his realm, an act which remained in force till 1848. Much as this King thus had achieved for the stability of the crown, he lost, on the other hand, a great deal through his war with Charles X. of Sweden, which cost Denmark for ever her ancient possessions on the Swedish continent, the provinces of Sconen, Holland, and Bleking.

A great credit is due to the Oldenburgers for having raised Denmark from an insignificant to an important naval power. Frederick II. (1559-88) was the real founder of the Danish navy, and already in his reign it did good service in breaking down the commercial tyranny of the Hanseatic league. His successors one after the other bestowed on the navy all the attention the exhausted exchequer permitted. And it is with her naval arm that Denmark has achieved her most brilliant triumphs. Niels Juel and Thordenskjold are naval heroes of world-wide fame. And the wonderful engagement off Heligoland in 1864, where three small Danish men-of-war engaged the combined squadrons of Austria and Prussia, which to save itself from utter disaster had to retire at last within the line of England's maritime jurisdiction, showed that Danish tars were still the true chips of the old Viking block.

Not the least of Denmark's many misfortunes was the loss of her fleet to England in 1807, and the ruinous war in which she became then involved for nearly three years. The worst of that disaster was, that it was the result of shortsighted statemanship, of an utter want of insight in the European situation, and of true appreciation of the character of her friends. This event was really the climax of a policy which Denmark had followed for a long time. The Danes have always, by natural instinct somehow, had strong leaning towards France. And, strange to say, the stronger the less France has done for them and the more they have suffered for their Gaulish affection. If Denmark had entered in 1807 the alliance proposed by England, how different would her position be to-day!

But there is another political friendship for which Denmark has suffered even more, and may perhaps suffer irreparably in the end. From the beginning of the eighteenth century (Frederick IV. 1699-1730) Denmark had begun to cultivate closer relations with Russia through her naval ascendency in the Baltic. From that time the Muscovite has kept a close watch on Denmark. His influence in that country has been what it is everywhere where he comes in contact with superior civilisation, reactionary and repressive of freedom ; his policy treacherous. By way of illustration, let me mention, that after the death of the greatest statesman Denmark ever had, Bernstorf the Younger, in 1797, who had given full freedom to the press and introduced such reforms in the administration of the State as to bring it to a really flourishing condition, it was Russia's first care to interfere in the internal affairs of Denmark, to the extent of procuring the abrogation of the press law and to introduce the censure. Further, let me remark that when Denmark, on two occasions, had assisted Russia against Sweden, in 1788 and 1809, and Alexander I. had given Denmark a distinct pledge that, in consideration of her alliance on the latter occasion, he would make good to her the loss of her fleet, he not only did nothing of the kind ; but in 1812, three years after the conclusion of the Finnish war, entered on negotiations with Bernadotte, the successor elect to the crown of Sweden, which had for object the alienation of Norway from Denmark, on condition that Sweden should act the part of an ally to Russia in case of need. In her greatest need, in fact, his Muscovitic majesty had made a miserable dupe of Denmark. You may gauge the ruin of the country with but 1,000,000 inhabitants being burdened with a national debt of over £22,000,000, besides a debt of over £16,000,000 sterling of unguaranteed note issue, with its fleet gone, with Norway torn away from it in 1814 by Sweden, and Heligoland by England. The notepaper debt was cleared off by the drastically, simple process of State bankruptcy, which merely transferred the ruin from the treasury to the holders of the paper, a shift which had the most deplorable effect possible on the country's agriculture and commerce. This was the outcome of Denmark's infatuated policy in leaving her destinies in the hands of Russia and France.

Still, the unfortunate kingdom was not out of her troubles yet. Its weakness meant a proportionate gain in strength to her arch-enemy Holstein. Throughout the whole history of Denmark from its first dawn all her troubles either rose directly from Holstein (Schleswick-Holstein), or were aggravated by the action of those principalities. And now that she had paid the penalty of her warlike follies and fond confidence in fickle friends, she still had to count with her Dano-German Duchies. In the struggle which was now soon to commence, Denmark no doubt did not always act with unimpeachable wisdom and sagacity. She resorted at times to high-handed, at others to underhand dealings. But she had dire provocations to meet. It is perfectly unjust to lay at the door of Denmark the eventual loss of these duchies. It was bound to come about sooner or later, no matter how justly, how considerately Denmark might have acted. Denmark was still in the false position in which fate had put her. The duchies were border lands where two nationalities met. On one side the German, with the immense sentimental Fatherland behind, believing in Germanismus as in God, in German civilisation as a sacred mission, as the salvation of the intellectual soul of the world ; on the other the Danish, downtrodden by its very rulers, with a civilisation which after all was chiefly borrowed from Germany, with precious little but a strongly Germanized language in the way of a Scandinavian back bone about it. It was inevitable, under such circumstances, that the Holsteiners, to whose dukes Schleswig had over and over again belonged as a royal feof, should wish to draw the bonds closer between the two duchies ; and, above all, that they would not stand any attempt at eradicating the German language out of that part of Schleswig where it had become the common speech of the people and driven Danish out of the field. On the other hand, it was not only natural ; it was the duty of Denmark to protect the Scandinavian nationality in Schleswick as best she could. She could not do it in any way without rousing the jealousy of the German neighbours who wanted to have the whole of Schleswick all to themselves. The more masterly Denmark had managed the matter, the more surely she would have exasperated the Germans. By the beginning of this century about one-half of Schleswick was occupied by a German-speaking population. When Frederick VI. in 1810 attempted to take measures for the purpose of arresting the forward march of German in the duchy, it was soon evident what the Germans meant, for the royal word remained a dead letter, so compact an opposition did it meet with from the German officials and the clergy.

It is impossible for me to attempt in the brief space of an hour to unravel the tangled skein of the political conflict which eventually was settled by the sword in 1864. Only the principal events can be touched upon, and that but briefly.

The wave of revolutionary emotion which the July revolution raised in 1830 brought also about in Denmark a national upheaval which led to the first step towards a constitutional monarchy, by King Frederick VI. calling together into four separate consultative assemblies the four estates of aristocracy, clergy, burgesses, and farmers, 1834. At the same time, a common government was given to Schleswick-Holstein with common court of supreme judicature, which helped the Germanisation of Schleswick forward in a large measure. Christian VIII. (1839-48) pursued an exceedingly indulgent and conciliatory policy towards the duchies, appointing his own brother-in-law the Duke Frederick of Augustenburg as viceroy of the principalities. But this only left all the free play to German aspirations in Schleswick. And when his son Frederick VII. succeeded to the throne in 1848-63, the long meditated revolt broke out, and forthwith received military support from Germany.

In this ominous state of affairs, which was seriously aggravated by the outbreak of the French Revolution in 1848, the King, whose motto was, "The people's love my strength," resolved to give to the country the constitution which every one was clamouring for; and on the 5th of June 1849 the absolute monarchy came to an end, and Denmark entered upon constitutional paths. After three years the revolt in the duchies was quelled; but instead of now seizing the opportunity of incorporating Schleswick for good and all, as was strongly urged by the Whole-state party in Denmark, the King, yielding to German diplomacy, gave to the duchies in 1852 a constitution which practically amounted to Home Rule, leaving under imperial control foreign affairs, the army, the navy, the post office, and the national debt. These matters were to be dealt with by the Council of State, in which the duchies should be represented in the same proportion to their population as Denmark was to hers. Seeing, however, that the population of the duchies only amount to two-fifths of that of Denmark proper, and the duchies consequently were left in a perpetual minority, this arrangement was readily seized upon as ground for disaffection, the fire of which was assiduously fanned by the Holsatian and the German press especially on the sore point that the Danes, who had taken measures in 1850 for protecting their language in Schleswick, were in fact suppressing the German. This, no doubt, was in a measure true. The Danish population was loyal, the German disloyal, in the disguise of enforced peace. The consequences must be obvious.

In 1858 the imperial constitution was abrogated in the case of Holstein (and Lauenburg), and the draft of a new constitution was submitted to the representative assembly of the duchy. Instead of discussing this government bill, the assembly simply set up, as a counter proposal, a new constitution for the whole kingdom, demanding that the monarchy should consist of three parts, each on an equal footing with the other—Denmark proper, Schleswick, and Holstein-Lauenburg. The proposal was probably never meant but as an affront, nor was it taken seriously by Denmark. Long-continued negotiations, in which England endeavoured to act the part of a mediator, led to no result ; and at last, tired of the ineffective strife, the King of Denmark, without further negotiations, incorporated Schleswick in the Danish monarchy by a proclamation of 30th March 1863, excluding Holstein and Lauenburg. This step introduced the last act of the drama. The King was called upon by the Federal Diet of Frankfurt to rescind his proclamation. Germany was convulsed by patriotic indignation, and the political outlook grew most threatening. Denmark was inexorable ; an execution was threatened ; and as Denmark did not yield, was carried out in Lauenburg and Holstein. Thus matters stood when the last of the Oldenburgers, King Frederick VII., died on 15th November 1863.

King Christian IX. now ascended the throne, in conformity with the provisions of the London Protocol of 1852, which not only settled the question of the Danish succession, but practically bound the signatory powers to guarantee the integrity of the kingdom. The German powers, so far from acknowledging any such duty, disputed, on the contrary, the King's right to the crown—a dispute which, however, never went beyond a mere utterance of opinion. These were sad times indeed for Denmark and the royal house. Holstein was once more in revolt, supported by an army of execution from the German " Bund." Alone, and abandoned by the guarantors of her integrity, Denmark had now to face the overwhelming forces of Austria and Prussia combined, who soon overran the whole of Jutland ; and, after the storming of the forts of Dübbel, where the Danes fought with dauntless valour (April 18, 1864), and the surprise of the fortified position of Alsen, there was no choice left to the exhausted land but to sue for peace. By the Treaty of Wiesma (October 30), Denmark had to sign away not only the German territories of Holstein and Lauenburg, but also the old Scandinavian territory of Schleswick, with half its population purely Danish-speaking. The provision of section 5 of the Treaty of Prague (1866), providing for the restoration of the purely Danish northern part of Schleswick, is now a dead letter since 1878, when Austria gave her consent to its abrogation.

Thus the last and the bitterest cup of Denmark's misfortunes was drained. But the false position into which she had been placed as a borderland ruling over a population of an alien and a mighty race was rectified, and the real cause of all her most serious troubles was removed, an incurable state disease, in fact, had been cured by amputation. Was the sacrifice worth the cure? I think there are overwhelming reasons for an affirmative answer to that question. It is but natural that the Danes should find it hard to persuade themselves that the greatest wrong inflicted upon them by the ruthlessness of brute force could be anything but an unmitigated evil. Even their Scandinavian brethren on the other side of the sound, at least, take the loss of Schleswick so seriously, that there can never, they maintain, until Schleswick or North Schleswick at least, is restored to Denmark, be a question of an alliance of Sweden-Norway with Germany. With these national susceptibilities it is easy to sympathise; but I think any one who has taken the trouble of attentively following the history of the relation of Denmark to the duchies, any one who knows what the Germanistic propaganda means, especially under the new conditions of that empire, if he is a well-wisher of Denmark, and capable of taking a dispassionate view of a political situation, must hope and trust that Denmark may never again have anything to do with Schleswick. At present the Danes set their heart the more fondly on the recovery of the duchy because they are firmly convinced that the Czar of Russia is going to set the matter right, and on that very ground he enjoys greater popularity in Denmark than even the King himself. Imagine the Czar of Russia compelling the German Empire to give up Schleswick to Denmark. What would that mean? Why this, that on the first opportunity given or taken, the Germans would pick a quarrel with Denmark, and make her pay the penalty of her simplicity on their own terms. Let Denmark fence about and ward the Scandinavian nationality in what is left to her of Jutland with all means in her power, but to return to the course of her old quarrels with Teutonic aggression and Germanistic aspirations is as impolitic a thing as could well be conceived. In this respect, too, we must not forget that the cause of Denmark is the cause of Scandinavia. The strong feeling that animates all Scandinavians is the feeling of solidarity of race.

The fear of the danger of Denmark's absorption in the mighty Teutonic Empire is no idle hallucination. That event, unless the Scandinavians, the Danes especially, are carefully, wisely, coolly on their guard, may at any time come within the reach of practical politics. The surest way of avoiding it is to keep clear, as long as possible, of political entanglement in Schleswick. My advice is, no doubt, unpalatable to my Danish kinsmen, but it does not follow therefore that it is not politically wholesome.

A glance at the material state of Denmark now, as compared with what it has been even at the most favourable times in her past history, so far as comparison is possible, soon convinces us that the country has never been in such a state of sure and solid progress, never so prosperous before. Naturally, for the people and the government can now give their undivided attention to the great material interests and natural resources of the land. The finances of the kingdom are in an exceedingly sound condition, and are managed with ability and thrift. Not only does the annual budget cover current expenses, but leaves considerable surplus for the redemption of the national debt which, though heavy, 170 millions = 9½ stlg., seems to sit very lightly on the tax-payer. The yearly income of the State amounts to about fifty-six million crowns, the yearly expenditure to fifty-three millions.

Denmark being, in the main, an agricultural country, agriculture, stockrearing, and farm produce may be said to be the main springs from which the wealth of the country flows. Nearly one-half of the population is engaged in these trades ; and the progress they have made during the last quarter of a century, both as regards improved methods and as to the gross turn-out of the products, reflects the highest credit on the Danish agriculturist. With great energy and determination fenlands, moors, lakes, and shallow inlets of the sea have been reclaimed for agricultural purposes all over the land. Three-fourths of the whole area of the land is now under tillage, and of that area over thirty per cent. has been properly drained, chiefly of late years. The yearly value of the cereal produce (oats, barley, rye, wheat) is estimated at from 180 to 190 million crowns ; and the whole ground produce, including hay, root-crops, etc., is estimated at 300 millions. Of the cereal produce, the surplus exported abroad amounts in value to thirty-three millions (nearly £2,000,000).

In proportion to the population Denmark rears a larger stock of farm animals than any other country in Europe. In 1876 there were no less than 350,000 horses in the country, nearly

1,350,000 cattle, 1,719,000 sheep, and over 500,000 hogs. And up to that year the three last-named classes of animals had been steadily increasing in number for some time. Along with this increasing prosperity goes a constantly improving husbandry and improved methods in the preparation of dairy produce. Thus Danish butter commands now the highest price in the English market of all foreign butter, and in that market alone Denmark disposes of this one article of a quantity amounting in value to one-and-a-half million sterling. Altogether, the export trade in live animals and dairy produce is estimated at about four million sterling.

Recognising the necessity of Denmark becoming a self-supporting country in timber, instead of importing that article, as at present, to the amount of three-fifths of a million sterling yearly, a powerful association, the so-called Moor Society, has been in existence for some time, which works energetically at extending timber culture in the country, especially throughout the wild moors of Jutland. This Society has done an immense service to the country by scientifically exploring the soil of these barren wildernesses, and practically solving the question how they may be reclaimed both for cereal and forest culture.

The Government, being keenly alive to the importance of the agricultural interest for the welfare of the country, show a praiseworthy liberality in supporting at the expense of the State a High School for scientific, veterinary, and agricultural instruction, which has had a most beneficial influence on the education of the Danish farmer. Great encouragement is also given by the Royal Agricultural Society, which has large means at its disposal, and dispenses them freely, both in travelling, pensions, and otherwise.

In the industrial and manufacturing lines Denmark has not progressed at the same rate it has done in the agricultural business, the reason being want of the requisite capital. But everything tends to progress even in these pursuits also. The distillation of spirits, the brewing of beer, of which the country exports large quantities to India, China, Australia, and South America, and the manufacture of sugar, are all vigorously progressive industries. Still more so is shipbuilding and iron-smelting. Denmark's china is noted for excellency of quality and tastefulness of design, and the art-furniture of Copenhagen enjoys a special reputation in foreign markets. In fact, in art industry Denmark not only leaves the other Scandinavian countries far behind, but competes more and more successfully with foreign countries. Throughout the country great interest is taken in developing the artistic talents of the people, one of the principal things taught in Sunday schools being drawing.

The foreign commerce of the country has also developed of late years very rapidly. The total average value of exports and imports is calculated at 400 million crowns (over £22,000,000). The mercantile fleet numbers about 3000 sailing vessels, and nearly 200 steamers, with a total displacement of over 250,000 tons. The coasts are well lighted by seventy lighthouses, and the more dangerous waters with eight lightships.

Railway and telegraphic communication is in a state of constant improvement. From twenty miles of rail in 1847 the length has now considerably exceeded 6000 English miles. Where practicable the islands have been joined by railway bridges; and Jutland has now, besides a main line running through the whole length of the country, several other parallel bylines, besides cross-country lines, uniting the more populous centres with the main artery of its traffic. Some of the lines have been built by private enterprise, but by far the greater part by State support. I believe they are all paying lines, the lowest rate of dividend being about $2\frac{1}{2}$ per cent. The total capital invested in Danish railways amounts to over £7,000,000. With the extension of the railways has gone that of the telegraphic communication, the improvement of which is being steadily attended to with great zeal. At present the length of telegraphic wire amounts altogether to between eight and nine thousand miles.

But I must pass on from Denmark's material progress, of which my sketch does not form anything like even a satisfactory outline; and, I am sorry to say, I must altogether pass by the literary and scientific position of the country, on which, by predilection, I should have liked to dwell, not only because I myself owe a good deal to Denmark in that line, but because there is so much in the whole educational system of Denmark that is well worthy of notice, and because she is producing so fast men of overtowering eminence in their respective and particular lines.

From these pleasant considerations we pass over to the one great failure of the country—its present politics.

I mentioned before that Denmark became a constitutional monarchy in 1849.

The principal provisions of the Constitution are these: Every king of Denmark, before he can assume the government of the monarchy, must deliver a written oath that he will observe the constitution. He alone is invested with the executive power, but the legislative he exercises conjointly with the Assembly (*Rigsdag*). He can declare war and make peace, enter and renounce alliances. But he cannot, without the consent of the Assembly, sign away any of the possessions of the kingdom or encumber it with any State obligations. Laws and royal resolutions are so far binding that they be signed by the king and the Cabinet minister to whose portfolio they belong. The king's person is sacred and inviolable; he is exempt from all responsibility. The ministers form the Council of State, of which the king is the president, and where, by right, the heir-apparent has a seat. The king has an *absolute veto*.

The Rigsdag (Assembly) meets every year, and cannot be prorogued till the session has lasted for two months at least. It consists of two Chambers—the Upper Chamber, " Landsting," and the Lower Chamber, " Folketing." The Upper Chamber consists of sixty-six members, twelve of which are Crown-elects for life, seven chosen by Copenhagen, and one by the so-called Lagting of Farö. The forty-six remaining members are voted in by ten electoral districts, each of which comprises from one to three Amts, or rural governorships, with the towns situated within each of them included. The elections are arranged on the proportional or minority system. In Copenhagen and in the other towns one moiety of electors is chosen out of those who possess the franchise for the Lower House, the other moiety is selected from among those who pay the highest municipal rates. In every rural commune one elector is chosen by all the enfranchised members of the community. And the election of the representative of the Landsting is thereupon transacted by the electors of the rural communes conjointly with the highest-rated members of the electoral district, as many in number as there are communes within the electoral Landsting's circle. The town electors bear the proportion of one to four to the electors of the communes (chosen and highest rated).

The Lower House is elected for three years, and consists of 102 members; consequently there are 102 electorates or electoral districts. According to the Constitution, every electoral district should number about 16,000 inhabitants. As no revision of the electoral districts has been undertaken since the constitutional charter was given in 1849, many and very considerable alterations have now taken place in respect of the population of the primitive electorates—some having now doubled, others even quadrupled, their population, as compared with 1849. If therefore a revision of the electorate were undertaken now, the Lower House would be increased by between twenty and thirty members. The Lower House is elected by manhood suffrage. Every man thirty years old has a vote, provided there be no stain on his character, and that he possesses the birthright of a citizen within his district, and has been domiciled for a year within it before exercising his right of voting, and does not stand in such a subordinate relation of service to private persons as not to have a home of his own. If he has received poor-rate support, he must have repaid it, or been excused the repayment.

The two Chambers of the Rigsdag stand, as legislative bodies, on an equal footing, both having the right to propose and to alter laws. Should the two Houses disagree, a committee elected by both, and consisting of an equal number of members from each, has to endeavour to settle the matter in dispute. The ordinary, as well as the extraordinary, budget must first be laid before the Folkething; and to that House exclusively belongs the right of impeaching Ministers. No tax can be levied, raised, or lowered, no State loan be negotiated, no domains be sold, without the authorisation of the Rigsdag. No taxes can be collected till the budget is voted.

At present this very Liberal Constitution is not working smoothly. As was to be expected, two parties have gradually come into existence—a Conservative and a Liberal, or, as they are termed after French fashion, the Right and the Left. The country is governed at present arbitrarily against an opposition in overwhelming majority in the Lower House. The dispute between the Left and the Ministry does not really turn so much upon conflicting views with regard to great public interests, as upon the question whether Denmark has, or has not, to have parliamentary government. There are, however, vital questions —fiscal, agrarian, and military—in dispute into which time will not permit me to go. But the one great central question is parliamentary government. The Right represents chiefly the educated and the wealthy classes; the Left the mass of the people, and is looked down upon by the Right. The standing objection on the part of the Right to admitting the Left to the government of the country has been hitherto that that party had no men capable of undertaking the government. This has always seemed to me to be the very reason why the Right should give way to constitutional exigencies, rather than to carry matters on to the legislative deadlock which at present is the order of the day in

Denmark. Surely, for a Ministry in such a minority that the Opposition can stop all legislative work, it is the wisest thing possible to do to let an incapable party come into power, and by its own incapability destroy its credit with the nation. Surely the tenure of office by such a party could only be brief, and come speedily to an ignominious end, with the result that the nation would transfer its suffrages to the Right. But of such a solution there seems to be no prospect at present; and now the Right lives in high hope that the forthcoming elections in January may turn the scale in some manner at least in their favour, because the Left party for the time being is divided in itself.

The technical reason why the parliamentary principle has not yet won the day, lies in the fact that by the charter both chambers, as constitutional factors, are placed on an equal footing. This, the Government maintain, makes it lawful for the King to govern the country irrespective of the state of parties in the Lower House as long as his ministry has a majority in the Upper Chamber. This state of things has led to very unfortunate results, the worst of which is, that the charter of the Constitution has been unscrupulously set aside, and for the last four years the taxes of the country have been collected under a provisory budget, which in no case has been sanctioned afterwards by the Assembly. *De facto* therefore, Denmark is at present governed on the lines of ministerial absolutism, or, which comes to the same thing, by absolutism pure and simple.

In view of the general European situation, I regard it as the supreme duty of the present ministry of Denmark to lose no time in setting their house in proper constitutional order. And seeing that the only possible way of doing it is to resort to the method of parliamentary government, for which really the whole nation is clamouring, the sooner that method is adopted the better it will be for Denmark. Then, first, such a legislative dead-lock as that now existing would be an impossibility. There is nothing so dangerous in the government of States as for the two opposing parties to persevere in the course of mutual exasperation until passion becomes the primary, patriotism the secondary consideration. Denmark has plenty of men among the Opposition able enough and patriotic enough to take the Government worthily in hand. The experiment should be tried while peace still prevails; the excitement of wars and rumours of wars should not be waited for; for then the sufferer would be not so much the copper-headed ministry as the Young Dynasty

I said in the beginning that I would tell you how the constitutional principle has been applied to Iceland. I have only time briefly to touch upon that matter. In 1800 the old Althing (All Men's Assembly, General Diet), which had existed from 930, came to an end. Forty-five years later it was re-established by King Christian VIII. in the character of a consultative assembly. At that time the constitutional question in Denmark had been under consideration for ten years, and had found its first practical expression in the estates' assemblies of 1834, which I have mentioned already. The Althing at once began to direct its attention to the question—What Iceland's proper position should be in the Danish monarchy when eventually its anticipated constitution should be carried out. The country had always been governed by its special laws; it had a code of laws of its own, and it had never been ruled, in administrative sense, as a province of Denmark. Every successive king had, on his accession to the throne, issued a proclamation guaranteeing to Iceland due observance of the country's laws and traditional privileges. Hence it was found entirely impracticable to include Iceland under the provisions of the charter for Denmark; and a royal rescript of September 23, 1848, announced that with regard to Iceland no measures for settling the constitutional relation of that part of the monarchy would be adopted until a *constitutive assembly* in the country itself "had been heard" on the subject.

Unfortunately, the revolt of the duchies intervened between this declaration and the date of the constitutive assembly which was fixed for 1851. The Government took fright, being unfortunately quite in the dark about the real state of public opinion in the distant dependency, 1200 miles away in the North Atlantic, and imagined that there something was brewing similar to what was going on in the duchies. This fear had for a long time a very unfortunate effect upon the progress of the negotiations between Iceland and Denmark. The Icelandic population was then, as it is still to-day, so thoroughly loyal to the Royal House, that State-dissolving aims, as the Government would persist in defining its fidelity to its own national institutions, never had entered their heads. The Icelanders only wanted to abide by their laws, and to have the management of their own home affairs, but the so-called National-Liberal Government wanted to incorporate the country as a province in the kingdom of Denmark proper. This idea the Icelanders really never could understand as seriously meant. How was an island 1200 miles away to be really governed as an incorporated province, and for what purpose? This the Government never explained, and all the more suspicious grew the Icelanders, who soon saw that it must mean for themselves the abrogation of all the traditional privileges of the country. Thus their opposition to the idea became one which numbered every soul in the country except a few crown officials of the highest class who had not the courage of their own opinions. The constitutive assembly was brusquely dissolved by the Royal Commissary when he saw that it meant to insist on autonomy for the Icelanders in their own home affairs. And from 1851 to 1874 every successive Althing (but one) persisted in calling on the Government to fulfil the royal promise of 1848. It was no doubt due to the very loyal, quiet, and able manner in which the Icelanders pursued their case, under the leadership of the trusted patriot, Jon Sigurdsson, that in 1874 the Government at last agreed to give Iceland the constitution it demanded. But instead of frankly meeting the Icelandic demands in full, they were only partially complied with, and from the first the charter met with but scanty popularity. The main fault of it is found to be, that the seat of the Government is left at Copenhagen, and, consequently, the administrative action is so seriously lamed on account of the scanty communication. For some time the successive Althings have been busying themselves with revising the charter of the Constitution, but so far their labours have been futile, because the so-called Upper House, composed of six crown nominees and six national deputies, mostly manages to "put the constitution to sleep," as the parliamentary phrase goes in Iceland. But there is no ill-feeling towards Denmark on the part of the Icelanders on this score. Nor has there really ever been any such feeling in Iceland. The people always draw a distinct line between the Danish Government and the Danish Nation, with which they always feel sympathetically akin, whatever their feelings towards the Government may be. Hence there is no such thing in Iceland as a race antipathy against the Danes. But it is often felt that on their part the feeling is not reciprocated, no doubt because they regard themselves as the ruling race.

There is, however, just now a growing feeling in Iceland that the Government of Denmark is bent upon making the constitution as ineffective as possible. This feeling, unfortunately, has been seriously roused within the last few years, in consequence of a very unfortunate financial scheme having been launched by the minister for Iceland upon the financially utterly ignorant community in 1885, by which a so-called "Land's Bunk" was set up for the country, for the purpose of "facilitating monetary intercourse in the land and of promoting its industries." For this purpose the minister for Iceland, advised by the directors of the National Bank of Copenhagen, issued in 1886 half a million of inconvertible, unguaranteed treasury notes, ranging in nominal value from five to fifty crowns. This paper was, by the Bank Law of September 18, 1885, made legal tender in the country. Lawfully it could only circulate in the county itself. But that principle has been disregarded by the administration who have allowed people to depose the paper in the Danish Post Office at Reykjavik against orders on the Danish Treasury which, of course, have been paid out in good Danish currency of the realm. By this manipulation all the treasury paper that has passed into the Post Office has naturally ceased to be legal tender, and has become valueless, having been taken beyond the boundaries of its circulation and negotiated in a foreign market, where it has no value. To recoup itself, the treasury of Denmark has made the Icelandic exchequer redeem its absolutely worthless notes in gold, the consequence of which is that on every Post Office Order the Icelandic treasury loses exactly 100 per cent. In this manner the poor country has lost already in less than four years nearly a millions crown (between £50,000 and £60,000). The affair is creating a great sensation in the country, and an exceedingly bitter feeling against the Government, who, though they are well aware of the iniquity of the transaction, silently persist in their mad career.

XIII

LESSONS FROM THE DUTCH REPUBLIC.

PROFESSOR J. E. THOROLD ROGERS.

A S men become civilised, and as they become acquainted with the history of their own and of other countries, the habit of association grows upon them; that is to say, they are anxious to see, or, if they cannot see, to read accurately of those parts of the world in which great events have happened, and in which great deliverances have been wrought.

I should not think much of a man who, knowing at all the facts of the case, gazed without emotion on the Pass of Thermopylæ or the field of Marathon, where, at critical periods of the world's history, the march of Asiatic despotism was arrested by the valour of a small State, not so big as some of our English counties. Everybody knows the feelings of interest—I might even say of affection—with which persons representing every variety of religious thought, and some of them unassociated with any form of religious belief whatever, visit and look over those sites in Palestine, which are hallowed to memory as the scene, as I think, of the greatest deliverance that ever happened to the human race, because, at any rate, whatever else we may admit about Christianity, it declares unfalteringly and unansweringly the doctrine of the natural equality of man.

And in the same way there is a small, storm-vexed part of Europe, rescued with difficulty from the sea, and preserved from the incursions of the ocean by zealous care and anxiety, in which one of the greatest deliverances that modern Europe has ever witnessed, or ever been interested in, was waged through a war which lasted for close upon forty years. This is the country of which I am going to say a little to you to-night—the country of Holland; and if there are places in Greece which could be named, if there are places in Palestine which could be recounted, which fill one with sympathy and that kind of faint, but, at the same time, real feeling of wonder and thankfulness, so I have always looked upon the Binnenhof at the Hague as one of the holiest spots in modern Europe, because there the great deliverance was planned, and there it was successfully carried out.

Now, before the struggle in Holland, of which I shall have to say a few words, there were attempts made with more or less success to shake off the yoke of the aristocracy of idlers and murderers, and to put in their place a body of men united in a common purpose indeed, but who also knew that the conditions of human life were labour. The Swiss, as early as 1307, at the battles of Sempach and Morgarten, gave a taste of their quality to the chivalry of Austria; and let me tell you that in my conviction, who have studied, perhaps, more deeply than any living Englishman the doings of the chevaliers, that they were the most portentous of shams. The Swiss vindicated their independence, and, with one short interval, have preserved that independence from the days in which they met the armed knights of the Duke of Austria to our own time.

There was a similar struggle carried on in England a little over five centuries ago. It has been my advantage to be able to point out to this audience—and you know that most English historians are excellent compilers of other people's knowledge—to point out to writers of history what was the real meaning of that struggle, which came apparently to a sudden and tragical conclusion, not a mile from the place in which we are. I refer to the so-called insurrection of Wat Tyler. The insurrection of Wat Tyler was a determination on the part of the whole industrial population in this country, from Scarborough in the north, to Southampton in the south, and throughout the whole of the eastern counties (where alone, at that time, textile industries were carried on), to resist the encroachments of the feudal aristocracy. It is true that the multitude who rose against the landowners were cajoled; it is true that the leader of the insurrection was murdered by an eminent supporter of law and order, the Lord Mayor of the time. But the efforts of the insurgents were successful. Never afterwards did the great landowners in the country try to constrain either the peasant or artisan to forced labour, till such time as the fruits of the victory having passed away from memory, a conspiracy between the king and his nobles led again to the enslavement of the English working man.

And, just in the same way, there was an uprising—and the echoes of it are still in our ears—in Bohemia, when John Ziska led the peasants against the columns of an arrogant, and apparently overwhelming aristocracy, and for more than two centuries his descendants—his representatives in political union—held sway there.

Similarly in Flanders, at the beginning of the sixteenth century, the industrial population was so determined to resist the pretensions of the Roman Church—with what was associated with it, the authority of monarchs, and of aristocrats, as long as they remained in allegiance to the Roman Church—that the particular industry which characterised what is now called Belgium, that of the weaver, was taken as synonymous with a heretic. But although a weaver was always a heretic, our monarchs in England were exceedingly anxious to naturalise the arts of the weaver amongst us, so as to turn to account that produce for which England was famous in the Middle Ages, the wool of the country, and being occasionally disposed to be rather indifferent to the pretensions of the Court of Rome, actually welcomed these industrious heretics, if so be the English people might learn their craft from them.

Now, in three of the countries that I have mentioned—England in 1381 and onwards, Bohemia in 1410 and onwards, and the Low Countries from the beginning of the sixteenth century, owed the whole of the inspiration which determined them to resist what they conceived to be unwarranted opinion and unwarrantable authority, from the teaching of a single Englishman. Latterly, a society in England has been printing the works of Wycliff. From inquiries I have made among the leading members of this society, it appears to me that the gentlemen who publish the works of Wycliff do not read what he wrote. If they did, they would discover that John Wycliff was not only the most remarkable Churchman of his age, but the most remarkable statesman and the most singularly far-seeing economist. Wycliff found the doctrine which was very prevalent, very orthodox, and, I regret to say, very harmful, that kings and rulers were responsible to God alone. Wycliff expanded this doctrine by saying they were also responsible to men ; and the responsibility of kings and rulers to men is, I need not tell you, the very centre of modern constitutional government. It is the basis of all our liberties. As long as men were supposed to be responsible to God only, they did not mend their ways. As soon as they became convinced that they were to be made responsible to man also, they began to improve.

Now, the form in which Wycliff put his argument may seem

strange to us. He laid down the doctrine—and this was all that was known about his opinions till his great work was recently published — he laid down the doctrine that "dominion was founded in grace." He used, that is to say, current theological expressions to indicate his political and economical meaning.

Now I will tell you what his interpretation of this was. It was alleged, he said, against his view, that kings and rulers are responsible to God only; but, he said, under no conception except that which is utterly heretical, can God be the author of evil; but the practices of these persons plainly show that their deeds are evil, and, therefore, their authority cannot be derived from so high a sanction. All allegiance, says Wycliff in explanation of his doctrine, is due only to proved worthiness. That doctrine he inculcated; that doctrine he taught the emissaries of his religion. This doctrine was taken over the whole of the civilised world—was put down in most places by the strong hand of power, but was remembered as an important and real fact among the obscure sectaries that followed his teaching, and who are much more the authors of the English Reformation— the weavers, I mean, in Norfolk and other parts of England— than the miserable caitiffs who yielded to the caprices and whims of Henry VIII. It never passed out of the minds of these people, and in our day it has borne fruit; for assuredly, as I said but now, the doctrine that all human authority is responsible to man—I do not deny that it is responsible to God also—has had a marvellously sweetening influence upon the conduct of public men.

The system is not perfect yet. There are a good many people who want the salt rubbed in still. But, at any rate, the doctrine is admitted, however little the practice may accord with the doctrine in certain individuals. I am afraid that we have got into a strange position with regard to one of these doctrines—the doctrine of ministerial responsibility. It seems to me that in these times nearly the whole responsibility which a wicked man getting into office has to suffer is that of being turned out again. If I had my way, and, I believe, if morality had its way, something else would be in store for him besides this exceedingly moderate reprobation.

Now, we have recently had a question raised as to what constitutes nationality; and without any definition being given of that term, we have had the minor premiss in the nationality of particular peoples abundantly criticised. We are told that one of the nations comprising the United Kingdom is a nationality, and that another is not a nationality, without much evidence being accorded on which to substantiate the distinction that is drawn between the two. Now, if you come to look at it in the light of origin, the Swiss are the most mixed of nations. A considerable portion of them is distinctly Italian, derived, probably, from the most ancient tribes which settled on the borders of Italy. A considerable portion of them is German, not a little of them is French,—that is to say, has been brought in ancient times distinctly under "Latin influences;" but, if you go from one extreme of Switzerland to the other, and all through its breadth, you will find that the whole of the cantons are united in the same determination to maintain, as far as possible, their individuality and their nationality. No more mixed race can be conceived than the Scotch. The northern part of Scotland, from the Tay upwards, with the exception of some intermediate settlements, is distinctly of Celtic origin. The southern part of Scotland is more Anglo-Saxon than England itself, and represents a purer Teutonic dialect than we speak, yet the whole of the Scotch have been fused into one race. No doubt sentiment played a little part in it, but the fact and the result remains.

I remember a very distinguished man some time ago said that the crowning blessing of the Scotch people was the battle of Bannockburn—it made them a nation—and the crowning misfortune of the Irish people was the battle of Athenry. They were fought in the same year; the Irish never virtually made head again, and the Scotch remained an independent nation till they were taken into the English Constitution by a treaty, as well as a union, and on terms of absolute equality, besides the fullest respect being shown to their local institutions.

Now, nobody knows what was the origin of the ancient inhabitants of Holland. They speak, as you know, a dialect of German, which goes by the name of Low Dutch, but there is reason to believe that all sorts of nationalities, from the earliest times, were united, and inhabited that country. They constituted themselves, as I shall point out to you, a new race.

Now, let us look for a moment at what the situation was when the Dutch, in 1572, ventured upon a conflict with Philip of Spain. Philip of Spain was a monarch who dreamed, as other monarchs have before and after him, of universal empire, and he filled some of the most powerful states of Europe with dread. He was lord, practically, of the New World. The donation of Alexander VI., Pope and profligate, had bestowed upon him the whole of what is

now called America, just as he bestowed on the House of Portugal
the whole of the Eastern world.   The famous bull of the Pope
might not have meant it, but some of the captains who had been
brought up under the discipline of Ferdinand and Isabella, succeeded in adding vast kingdoms to the Spanish branch of the
Austrian family, and the whole of the richest metalliferous districts
of Central and South America passed under the sway of Spain.
The resources of the monarch of Spain appeared to be inexhaustible.   He had entirely overset the whole machinery by which the old
world was supplied with money, and was himself part owner and toll-
taker of all the great stores of precious metals which were being mined
in the new world.   He was also the king over a country which
supplied the most redoubtable and the best-disciplined soldiery in
Europe.   The Spanish infantry was the type of all that was courageous, of all that was resolute, of all that was ferocious and cruel.
The power of Philip II., the heir to these vast dominions, comprising also the principal industrial centre of the world, then the
Low Countries or the Netherlands, and now Belgium, seemed to
be greater than any other person could venture on encountering.
On the other hand, was a small country not very much larger
than Yorkshire, defended by incessant care from the encroachments
of the ocean, without manufactures, without trade, without commerce, and deriving a scanty substance from the fields which they
rescued from the deep.   These men dared on the ground of
liberty and conscience to revolt, always under decent forms, and to
resist the overwhelming power of Spain.   It is impossible to conceive any conflict, the elements of which seemed more unlike and
more unequal ; the one the richest and most powerful state of
Europe, the other the poorest and apparently the most helpless.
From 1572 to 1609 the Dutch carried on their struggle with
Philip and his successor ; they growing stronger and healthier
every day, he weaker and more contemptible.   Of course this was
not the beginning of the struggle.   The commencement of it was
twenty-two years earlier, with the establishment of the Spanish
Inquisition in the Low Countries, and it was against this establishment of the Spanish Inquisition in the Low Countries, and the
entire control of the political system of what, for a short time, was
called the United Netherlands, that the conflict had its origin.

Now, in these days it would puzzle us why the monarchs of
Europe should have been so alarmed at religious dissent or discontent, why these powerful monarchs should have expended so
much resolution, so much money, and so many lives in subduing

so remote a portion of the earth. The reason was they knew that freedom in religious opinions involved the development of political freedom also.

When James I. said, "No Bishop, no King," he was uttering a more sensible adage than he generally thought proper to lay down. I do not mean to say that our Puritan forefathers more than two centuries ago were perfectly wise and blameless in their actions and in their policy because they were still infected with a mad passion for securing uniformity, but at any rate they truly connected the doctrine of political liberty with the doctrine of religious liberty, and they fought for both. And then, you see, there permeated these people that strange and undying proposition that "Dominion is founded in grace," which is, being interpreted, "Allegiance is due to the leader only on proof of his worthiness." Now, he must have been a very astute courtier who could have discovered that Philip II. was worthy, or Henry IV., or, for that matter, Lewis XIV., all of whom aimed at universal empire, the second having had his career cut short when he was just going to precipitate the hideous Thirty Years' War, the last war of religion in Europe.

Well, these Hollanders—inhabitants of a small country—a poor country, with very few natural defences, except those which could be adopted to their own apparent ruin—entered into this gigantic struggle. The work was all done by themselves. It is perfectly true that some help was accorded by our Queen Elizabeth. She was a much wiser woman than some of her biographers make her out to be. She was a very shrewd woman. She knew perfectly well that the independence of Holland was a fortress against the designs of Philip II. upon England; but then Elizabeth was desperately poor, and very shifty. Her father had stolen everything he could lay his hand upon, and squandered it in a way which does seem to me quite incredible and quite inexplicable; and she was left miserably poor. The Dutch had little help from her. I am not certain whether they did not get more mischief than help from the people she sent, for two of the captains that went over, rejoicing in the historic names of Stanley and Yorke, turned papists and traitors, and betrayed the towns that were put into their hands and the standards. The Stanleys have always been on the winning side; they thought they were then; perhaps they think themselves there now. I will not attempt, even in your minds, to disabuse them of any impression of the kind. There was a little help pretended to them by France—the brother of the King of France went there as a commander-in-chief, just as our Elizabeth sent her favourite Leicester, who made nothing but a fool of himself during the time he was in Holland. Anjou tried to seize part of what was then within the control of the Dutch republic, and was deservedly shown up as a traitor and a knave. But, almost at the very time when the Dutch fishermen gained their first victory in the seizure of Brill, these reputed friends of Dutch freedom were planning the massacre of St. Bartholomew, and William the Silent knew, all the time that he was trying to get help from the French royal family, that the designs of that family were—and I do not find fault with them from the point of view of their own personal interests — to extirpate patriotism and freethought over the whole world. Nothing was really done by France—the Dutch did everything themselves.

The form, then, which the resistance of the Dutch to their liege lord—that is the phrase the lawyers use ; lawyers are always inventing terms which are intended to obscure justice—the form which the opposition of the Dutch took was a claim for freedom of conscience. When they achieved their independence, after a severe struggle, one of the stipulations which Philip III. of Spain wished to press upon them was that they should show toleration to Roman Catholics—that is to say, they claimed for persons of their own religion that which they had been fighting nearly forty years to refuse to the Dutch themselves. Of course there is a good deal of inconsistency in human nature. The Dutch naturally refused. If I were a diplomatist, and, on making peace with a neighbouring power, the neighbouring power introduced a clause into it that every inhabitant of the country I represented should read the Ten Commandments and say the Lord's Prayer every day, I should repudiate so preposterous a condition. You have no right to impose it—however important it may be to keep the Ten Commandments and to say the Lord's Prayer. The Dutch, therefore, refused to be bound by the terms of a treaty to toleration. But directly the treaty was granted in a grudging way in 1609, the Dutch instantly granted toleration. They took care, of course, that the public manifestations of the religion, which had striven to put them down by violence, should not be such as should cause offence to those who were liberated from such attempts, but the reasonable enjoyment of every religion was accorded. And many of you know the Dutch gave a harbour and a refuge to the Jews when they were almost expelled, or, at least, put under serious disabilities in the rest of the world. In other words, the Hollanders, at the very beginning, learned that, when they had fought for their own freedom, it was right for them to grant freedom to others. You know those who had opposed the working out of that. It has always struck me that one of the grandest acts the democracy has ever done—that is, a form of government in which there is no privileged class—was when the inhabitants of the northern part of the great American Republic, smarting with what they thought to have been an unjustifiable and wanton rebellion, aggravated by its attempt to maintain the greatest of all immoralities—personal slavery—had conquered, they put a curb on themselves, and pardoned the arch-traitor, who only died the other day.

Now, the old doctrine of Europe was that all subjects should be of the religion of their rulers ; and it must be admitted that the heads of the Anglican Church—the community to which I am proud to belong—showed a marvellous alacrity in following the will of their rulers. I use the expression clerical caitiffs of the bishops who surrounded the throne of Henry VIII. Hardly one sacrificed himself against the overweening haughtiness of that monarch. Now, during the time of Henry VIII., you know that there occurred a great reformation in Europe ; but this doctrine, that the subject should be of the religion of his monarch or his ruler, was not attacked. All that Luther did was to kick out the Pope, and put the king in his place, and the consequence is that, to me, the Lutheran reform is, of all religious reforms, the most hollow and contemptible that I know. He put the king in the place of God. He gave no liberty to man whatever. There seems to be some discontent with what I say. When the peasants rose in revolt against the insupportable tyranny of their lords, the man who goaded these lords on to take the bitterest revenge on the peasants was Luther himself. He was not made of the stuff that Wycliff was. He was not made of the stuff of the Lollards, who held to their own view, although outward manifestation of their opinion was suppressed. He handed over the inhabitants of Northern Germany from the Pope to the king, and I am not certain that they did not make a change for the worse when the transfer came.

Now, what the Dutch laid down was the very reverse of this position. We have followed in this matter—imitating them without much gratitude. They laid down that the ruler should be of the religion of his people, and there is a good deal to be said for that. We found it was impossible in England that the monarchy of this country, even with very limited powers, should be of a religion which was antagonistic to the mass of the people, and we sent a certain monarch flying because he was obstinately determined, and we kept his descendants out of the throne because they were obstinately determined that they would not be of the religion of the people. I do not mean to say that it does not look like a certain violation of what may be called the principles of absolute toleration, but if a person takes upon himself the extremely comfortable and well-paid office of king, I think, on the whole, he may be expected to submit to the conditions that are involved.

Now, the Dutch won their independence by deeds of valour, which would take me, not one evening, but the whole of the Sunday evenings from now to midsummer, to recount. And what was the result? They became the first commercial nation in the world. They excited the envy and admiration of all other people—I regret to say, envy and admiration that were turned into bad and unjust intrigue. They were the source of nearly all the learning that was developed with the revival of letters. They invented all the principal arts of life. Among other things, they were the principal persons who developed a scientific agriculture, which was an object of admiration to our own writers in England long before the English people had the courage or the skill to adopt such a system of agriculture. I regret to say that, in my opinion, the English nation was for a long time the very stupidest in creation. There was no change in its agriculture from the time of Edward III.—no improvement—to the time of Charles I. You do not find a single painter in England till centuries after the art had been developed first across the water. You had Flemish and Dutch schools of painting when the only persons who plied the art in England were foreigners. Where did all your great artists come from? Where did Holbein come from? Where did Vandyck come from? They were from foreign countries, and the first native-born English artist you had was Thornhill, who painted those stupid pictures in St. Paul's Cathedral. I always say that the English school of art does not begin till the middle of the 18th century. Well, we were just as backward in agriculture, we were just as backward in letters. There was one thing, I admit, in which the English people were very much to the front. They tried conclusions over and over again with bad rulers, and then deposed them, and were not curious to inquire what became of them after they were deposed. The whole of Western Europe was the debtor of Holland in the arts of life. Its universities were frequented up to the middle of the 18th century by numbers of people, not only those who, by a narrow policy, were excluded from? our own universities, but by men who themselves received the benefit, such as it was, of some training in those ancient places of education.

No doubt the Dutch committed errors. One of their gravest errors — they sinned in good company — was their attempt to maintain a sole market; that is to say, to get hold of certain portions of the earth's surface from which they excluded the ships and the sailors of every other country. We were just as unwise. All our wars in the 18th century were for the maintenance of a sole market. We went into the war of the Austrian succession with a view to improve our Colonial possessions.

The Seven Years' War was entirely for the purpose of a sole market, and the war with the American Colonies was waged in order to secure and maintain the same sole market that we had got by the war that ended with the Peace of Paris. Not a doubt the Dutch fell into this error. But it is an error which is being fallen into now. Why do you think the French people want to retain and to extend their African dominions—Algiers, Tunis, Tripoli, if they can get it—but to maintain there a sole market, and to exclude the goods of every other country? What do you think induced the illustrious Prince Bismarck to encourage Colonial Empire in Germany, but to carry into it the German tariff, and to exclude everybody else from the country? These same follies are being perpetrated by statesmen at the present day, and if you look to see what the result is, I will warrant this, that it costs the German taxpayer the whole of twenty marks in value for every twenty marks of goods he imports or exports. He gets nothing by it. The Dutch fell into this error indeed. They strove to exclude other people from the markets that they had discovered and appropriated in the old world, and the result was that the nations met them with jealousy, and nowhere more than by the Governments of this country.

I think one of the most scandalous pages in our national history is the conspiracy of the English Government—Stuart and Hanoverian—against the integrity of the Dutch Republic. In an evil hour, and against the remonstrances of the Dutch themselves, the Princes of the House of Orange intermarried with the Stuarts. They only got one good Prince out of the lot of them,

and he was quite as serviceable to us as he was to them—
William III. Then afterwards the House of Orange were intermarried with the Hanoverian family, and from that day they
have steadily declined. We did everything we could to check
their trade, to destroy their influence, and to do them harm.
We passed, for example, the Navigation Acts, with the sole purpose of crippling and damaging the Dutch trade, and even so
great a man as Adam Smith, commenting on the Navigation
Acts, knowing that they were commercially mischievous, justified
them on the ground that defence was better than opulence.
They never gave one or the other ; they were no use to us at
all.

Whether one looks at the resources on the side of the two
Commonwealths, or whether one looks at the utter want of
military skill on the part of the weaker of the two, one is filled
with amazement at the courage and resolution of the Dutch.
Their first victories were on the sea—which was very natural, so
to speak, because they were expert fishermen, and finally they
became expert in more important maritime undertakings. If you
look at the benefits that they have conferred on modern Europe by
the development of the sciences and the arts—for they challenged
almost all the great discoveries that have been made in modern
times ; they have claimed, for instance, the invention of the telescope, and yet the man I spoke to you about just now—Wycliff
—knew all about it, for in the very book to which I have been
referring, he gave a description of the telescope, and of the
wonders that it effects ; and then, as would be natural to the
theologian, he said, at the conclusion of his description of the
process by which a telescope was made, the function of this
instrument is like the function of faith, it brings things remote
near to us, and makes things small clear to us. But in those
days you must know that, if any man had any exceptional knowledge, he ran the risk of being accused of sorcery, and that was
even worse than heresy.

But it always seems to me that the greatest lesson that you can
derive from the history of the Dutch—for it is from these facts in
history that one should gather lessons—is that you should never
despair of being in a minority. No minority ever seemed more
hopeless than the minority of the Seven United Provinces when
they threw down the gauntlet to Philip of Spain. Minorities
have constantly been, to all appearance, hopelessly weak, and yet
are on the high road to victory. I remember, when I was a young

man, and took my part as an undergraduate at Oxford in the liberation of the poor man's cupboard from the oppressive bread tax, at which time I knew the eminent man who used to lecture in this chapel, the body that supported this measure of justice to the English people seemed very small and very feeble ; and yet, within three years after the youngest of the party who advocated the reform in Parliament went into Parliament, those laws were irrevocably abolished. Never despair of a minority ! If your conscience convinces you you are in the right, stick to it. To stick to a minority is constantly a high act of religion. Do not take the wicked advice of Lord Melbourne, and stick to the unpopular side till the other get the upper hand, because, said the old cynic, in this way you get an advantage from both sides : but, even though it seem to be hopeless, if you are convinced that a thing is right, stand to it.

I do not say that any of us in this day can win the well-deserved reputation which Holland won among all those persons who study impartially and wisely the course of European history, but the strength of great movements is not made up by counting the units of the force which compose it, but by adding one's own force to that which already exists. Of all the pitiful kinds of vanity, none, I think, is more pitiful than that of the man who wants to have measured for him by his fellows what has been the part which he has played in doing good to mankind. Let him work for his own hand, for his own conscience, to the end which he puts before him. The best heroes of the Dutch War of Independence were obscure men. They had no great place, and they wanted no great place. But they felt they should live, if not in the memory of their countrymen, in the constant endurance of that great work to which they had put their hand, and from which, unlike the miserable aristocracy of Holland, they never flinched. That at least, the doing of one's own work in one's own generation, for what one holds to be a high and noble, and righteous purpose, is in everybody's hands, and a man at least knows, when he carries out these ends, that he is, if not seeking for a niche in the Temple of Fame, doing that which is much better than all the reputation which individual man can ascribe to individual motives and individual aims.

XIV

BELGIUM.

ALFRED WATHELET.

IF Belgium has been for the last sixty years an independent and free nation, the fact should not surprise any one acquainted with her past history. Her present existence as a well-characterised nationality, and the advanced development of her political life, are better understood when one remembers the many efforts and struggles of the old Flemings and Walloons for conquering and maintaining their free charters, and for shaking off the yoke of foreign domination. What Belgium at present enjoys of liberties of all kinds, which many a greater country must envy, is deeply rooted in her provincial and communal institutions of the past centuries; while the brave citizens who brought about Belgian independence in 1830 had received from their forefathers many an example of a stern, if not so successful, resistance against foreign masters. It will therefore be rational to study Belgium as it is now in the light of the history of her old times.

The name of Belgian is of Celtic origin. The Belgæ of Cæsar, whom he calls the bravest in Gaul, were Celtic-speaking tribes, who inhabited the territories between the Rhine, the Somme, and the North Sea. During the first centuries several irruptions brought in their midst numerous German tribes, who became the majority; among these arose the power and dynasty of Clovis. From Belgian soil also—from the banks of the Meuse—sprang afterwards the greatness of the race of the Pepins and Charlemagne.

Then, from the ruin of the great empire of Occident, we see Belgium dividing itself into a number of small sovereignties. They were the duchies of Brabant, Limburg, Luxemburg; the counties of Flanders, Hainault, Namur; the Prince-Bishopric of Liége, and others. The county of Flanders became superior to all others, while flourishing by its industry and commercial activity. At the end of the fourteenth century, the main line of the Counts of Flanders being extinct, their possessions passed into the hands of the Dukes of Burgundy.

Duchies and counties were not the only power which had sprung in Belgium from the darkness and chaos after the dissolution of the empire of Charlemagne. If here we see small sovereign houses, there we see, in antagonism with them, free communes, like distinct republics—each defending itself, having its charters, its guilds, its courts of justice, its finances. Where the communes are mighty, the dynasties are powerless ; where the dynasties are strongly established, the institutions of the commune remain undeveloped. We see the influence of the commune predominate in Flanders and Liége ; while the reigning houses rule over Hainault, Namur, Luxemburg. The communes of Bruges, Ghent, Louvain, Liége, produce heroic tribunes like Van Artevelde, Breydel, and De Coninck ; the Belgian dynasties, after taking a brilliant part in the Crusades, give kings to many a great throne—Godefroid of Bouillon, King of Jerusalem ; the Baldwins of Flanders and Namur, Emperors of Constantinople ; John, Count of Luxemburg and King of Bohemia ; Charles of Luxemburg and his descendants, Emperors of the Romans.

Among the numerous charters by which the communes obtained recognition of rights eagerly vindicated, the Charter of Albert de Cuyck, granted by that Prince-Bishop to the citizens of Liége at such an early date as the end of the twelfth century, the Great Charter of Bruges (1304), and the *Joyeuse Entrée* of Brabant (1354), stand like monuments of liberal guarantees, proclaiming individual freedom, right of association, judging of the citizens by magistrates chosen from among their ranks, free administration of the commune by the citizens. In Liége, so inviolable was the domicile of any citizen, that there was a saying, *Pauvre homme en sa maison roy est ;* nobody could be arrested but by an order of the echevins ; no taxes levied without the consent of the city ; no military service required but for the defence of the territory. In 1312 another charter established in Liége the principle of separation of the three powers—legislative, judicial, and executive ; and afterwards the "Tribunal des XXII." was instituted as a sanction to the responsibility of all public officials. At that time already the democratic spirit was triumphing in Liége definitely, and Michelet can say that the Commune of Liége from the fourteenth century gives the standard of the most complete political equality that ever existed. In Brabant, the Charter of *Joyeuse Entrée* openly proclaims the right of citizens to refuse obedience to the sovereign who would not observe the communal liberties. So we can go back to the free traditions of the communes for the origin of many an enlightened principle of which Belgian institutions can boast nowadays. That communal movement which brought about the intervention of the burgess element in public affairs, is intimately connected with the development of the numerous guilds or *corps-de-métiers*, which, while bringing honour and power to artisanship, had the happiest influence on trade prosperity in the communes. Nor did the social progress restrict itself within the walls of the cities ; for there dates also from that time a great amelioration in the condition of the rural masses by the alleviation or complete abolition of serfdom. The history of the communes is not less characterised by their patriotic resistance against foreign interference than by their free spirit ; and the victory of the Flemish citizen-troops over a powerful French army near Courtray in 1302 (battle of the Golden Spurs) may be recorded, among others, as a glorious feat.

Frequent intercourse and treaties of the communes with each other and with the sovereigns began to prepare the unification of Belgium, which was to be accomplished under the Dukes of Burgundy. That House succeeded, by wars and alliances, in destroying the local dynasties, and partly in doing away with the franchises of the communes, though these were to leave traces in the institutions of the country down to the present day. While the Dukes were centralising in their own hands the power over the whole of the Netherlands, industry and commerce in Flanders were enjoying a singular prosperity ; Bruges, Ypres, Ghent, were the market places of half the civilised world. Charles the Bold was the last Duke of Burgundy ; he had the passion of conquering, without the qualities of a monarch ; he could have been the creator of an important kingdom, his disorderly ambition made him only an adventurer. The daughter of Charles, Mary of Burgundy, married in 1477 Maximilian, who was to be Emperor of Germany. That union made the Netherlands the accessory of other States, and so they were to be for centuries.

The ten years that Maximilian had the regency over the Belgian provinces after the death of Mary were years of struggles between that Prince and the States of Flanders and the communes of Ghent and Bruges, and these patriotic bodies then showed admirable tenacity and fortitude in the defence of their privileges. By the help of a powerful army Maximilian could be master of Ghent and tear into pieces the charter of its privileges; but, King of the Romans as he was then, the proud Commune of Bruges kept him for several months a prisoner, until he would swear on a public place of Bruges, before an immense assembly, to observe the peace consented by the States of Flanders. This solemn oath did not refrain him from bringing again a foreign army, with which he at length humiliated the Commune of Bruges as he had done that of Ghent.

However, when the grandson of Maximilian, Charles V., came into possession of the Netherlands, which he united to that of Spain and the Empire, it may be said that the Flemish race was at its apogee, having attained a degree of commercial prosperity which was only to be equalled by her splendour in the arts. Charles V. was born a Belgian himself, and remembered it; he associated the Belgians to all the great events of his long reign; Belgians were in his council and at the head of his armies; but he was fighting for a dream of universal dominion, never to be realised. When Protestantism began to spread in the Low Countries, Charles persecuted it implacably, and many artisans from Flanders fled to Germany and England, where they brought with them much of the Flemish trade and industry. Yet Charles used a mild treatment if compared with the cruelties to which religious exaltation led Philip II., who had nothing Belgian, no heart for Belgians, but all the hatred of fanaticism in his soul. These were the darkest pages of the history of the Netherlands, when, the practices of the Inquisition tribunals having driven the people into rebellion, Philippe sent the Duke of Alva to devastate the country and erect scaffolds everywhere.

At length the northern portion of the Low Countries established its independence as the Republic of the United Provinces. Belgium, which had much greater difficulties to resist, having no natural defences when the Dutch had the water of the rivers and the sea to protect them, remained under Spain. Philippe granted the sovereignty of the Belgian provinces to his daughter Isabella and her husband Archduke Albert, who attempted to restore prosperity, and partly succeeded; but after thirty-five years of a peaceful reign, they died without issue. And again Belgium was in the hands of Spain, sharing her declining fortunes, always exposed to the first attack in the wars of Spain with France, and of France with Holland, and paying for peace at the expense of her own territory.

In 1713 Belgium was assigned to Austria, and governed thence sometimes smoothly, but with indifference by princes who lived elsewhere. Dutch garrisons were in Belgian fortresses, and the Scheldt was closed to Belgian navigation, and Antwerp entirely separated from the sea. However, under the mild rule of Maria Theresa, Belgium enjoyed a wiser administration and more happiness than it had known for a long time. But this period of calm was not to last under Joseph II., who, superior in knowledge to those he was to govern, and more of a philosopher than of a monarch, pretended to rule over his people as he would, says a historian, have made a book. He attempted to curb the power of the priests, but he excited the religious feelings of one of the most Catholic countries that were. Then he gave much offence to the States by trying to overturn the government. A few weeks after the beginning of the French Revolution, a revolution broke out at Brussels, mainly prepared by the monks who had been deprived of their convents. But the success of this revolt did not last, discord being among the leaders of the movement; nor was the return of Austrian soldiers endurable. The forces of the French Republic soon invaded Belgium, and had no great difficulty in conquering a country exhausted by interior divisions. It is worth mentioning that with the French domination there came to an end the temporal power of the Prince-Bishops of Liége; it had lasted for many centuries through an eventful and interesting history, which would deserve special treatment, and highly testifies to the free and patriotic spirit of the citizens of Liége.

The generous ideas proclaimed in France in 1789 soon made a deep impression in the Belgian provinces. The new spirit of equality, of tolerance and progress which they introduced among populations well prepared for it (this especially true of Liége), was not the only beneficent influence of the French *régime* in Belgium. Though its excessive centralisation met, especially in Flemish provinces, with a latent force of resistance, the fact that Belgians were then submitted to a common legislation and a uniform administration did much to prepare them for national unity. With a civil organisation which was a great improvement on the complicated system of the past, Belgium also owes to the French period the benefit of civil and criminal laws, of which the greater part has remained in force till the present day.

In 1814 no national dynasty could present itself to claim for Belgium, and the Treaty of Paris gave it, as a heritage vacant,

to the Stadtholder of the United Provinces, who was raised to
the dignity of a king. Under several respects that reunion
seemed to be a reasonable arrangement. The industry of the
Belgian provinces was to find in the colonies and the large trade
of the Dutch an immense opening. Also a fusion existed already
between Flemings and Dutchmen, who had the same origin,
the same language, and had only been separated by the feudal
divisions of territories, and afterwards by the religious quarrels.
But how were the Walloon provinces, of French language,
customs, and sympathies,—how would these submit to the new
rule? The fundamental law of the new kingdom was a liberal
charter, but that is the only praise deserved by the Dutch
supremacy. The new monarchy represented in Belgium the
foreigner; a mild and conciliatory policy would have made
Belgians forget this; but during the fifteen years of their rule,
neither the king nor the Dutch nation did what was necessary
to render themselves tolerable, and fault after fault was committed which rendered the necessity of a rupture unavoidable.
The use of the French language was not allowed in the public
and judicial acts; an iniquitous electoral system secured the
political preponderance of the northern provinces, which had
only half the population of the southern; in the north was the
seat of all the great public establishments, in which nearly all
places were given to Dutchmen; also there was an anti-catholic
tendency in the laws, which was no small factor of discontent
among Belgians. A few unhappy incidents made the measure
full, and a revolution broke out at Brussels in August 1830,
which caused the whole of the Belgian provinces to rise in the
vindication of their independence. By driving Flemings and
Walloons into a common resistance, King William had greatly
helped them to bring together the elements of a nation.

Brave and able men were the chiefs of that movement, which
improvised in a few weeks of struggles an independent Belgium—
Rogier, Devaux, Lebeau, de Mérode, de Potter, J. B. Nothomb,
and others—and seldom was seen a more remarkable assembly
of men of talent and eloquence than that National Congress
which gave Belgium its Constitution. A few months after the
Congress had met, Prince Leopold of Saxe-Coburg, proclaimed
King of the Belgians, swore before them to observe the fundamental pact. The independence of the new State, however, was
only recognised by the great Powers after very difficult diplomatic

negotiations, in which the Belgian delegates, Van de Weyer, Nothomb, Devaux, played their part with energy and skill. The election of Prince Leopold was no small help to their endeavours for winning the goodwill of the Powers. The young kingdom was much indebted to France for the intervention at a critical moment of a French army which successfully operated at the siege of Antwerp and took the place from the Dutch. The sympathy of England under the ministry of Lord Grey and Palmerston also greatly contributed to bring the recognition and guarantee of Belgian independence and neutrality by the Treaty of London of the 15th November 1831. Holland only acknowledged the accomplished facts in 1839.

The Belgian Constitution is the pride of the movement of 1830. It has attributed to civil society all the liberties that could be brought by the republican system, while keeping the guarantees of monarchical heredity. It proclaims the equality of all citizens before the law, the suppression of all privileges attached to nobility, the liberty of the press, the liberty of teaching, the right of free petition, the inviolability of home, the trial by jury for all criminal and political charges and for offences of the press, the free exercise of all religions and their equality, the exclusion of all interference of the State in religious matters. No other European country has fully enjoyed so many liberties.

The executive power belongs to the King, who exercises it through his Ministers responsible before the two Chambers—the Chamber of Representatives and the Senate. This principle of ministerial responsibility is one of the most important innovations of the Belgian Charter compared to the fundamental law of 1814. The King convokes, prorogues, and dissolves Parliament. The throne is hereditary by order of primogeniture in the male descendants.

The House of Representatives is elected for four years by citizens above twenty-five years of age, and paying 42 francs in taxes to the State. The Senate is elected for eight years by the same body of electors, but only those who pay 2000 francs in direct taxes are eligible, and they must be over forty years of age ; while the minimum age of twenty-five years is the only condition for eligibility to the Chamber of Representatives. Parliament is re-elected by half every two years for the Chamber, and every four years for the Upper House, which arrangement greatly contributes to make the political system work smoothly, and to avoid the peril of too sudden changes. All revision of the constitutional law must be demanded by the two Houses acting separately, and can only be discussed after re-election of Parliament.

All judges are chosen by the King, on lists presented by the Law Courts and the Senate and the Provincial Councils.

The national charter, of which we have thus given a brief summary, has remained unaltered ; it can be called a monument of rational freedom and liberality, and has had a great and felicitous influence on the progress and prosperity of the nation.

The provincial and communal laws are also deserving of great praise. They leave to the provincial and local councils a considerable authority, and the solution of many important questions. Each of the nine provinces is administered by a governor, with the assistance of a permanent delegation of six members of the provincial council. This council meets every year to deal with all matters of provincial concern ; its members are elected for four years. Each of the 2500 communes has its administrative body, with a burgomaster, several echevins, and a more or less numerous communal council, elected for six years. Burgomasters, like the governor of the province, are appointed by the King, generally in agreement with the majority of the Council. Echevins, or assistants of the burgomaster, are chosen by the Communal Council. The burgomaster and his echevins are the local Executive Board, and share with the Council the gestion of all municipal interests.

Under the beneficial effect of such laws, the Belgians have now been for sixty years consolidating their national existence, and working their politics in a most regular way ; not without very acute controversies and agitations, but these were only the natural outcome of the free play of institutions which are and will remain dear to the nation.

Catholics and Liberals, the two parties, very nearly of equal strength, which divide Belgian politics, have had several times in turn the management of public affairs. They are respectively much of the same nature as the Conservative and Liberal parties in other countries ; but a special and important factor in Belgian politics is the considerable influence of the Catholic clergy. The Belgian populations being in majority intensely Catholic, the clergy have kept a strong hold on the conscience of the people, and, naturally enough, give their full support to a party whose first purpose is to maintain the supremacy of the Church. Within the last twenty years the antagonism between Catholics and Liberals has become more and more acute; Liberalism has been many a time treated on the other side as heresy; and though the Liberal leaders denied that they were hostile to religious ideas, declaring they only wanted the independence and neutrality of the civil power, the tendency has been towards making political matters more and more mixed with religious ones, so that leading Liberals are nowadays nearly all out of the pale of the Roman Church, and in fact of any Church, Protestantism having hardly made any progress in Belgium.

During the first years of the Belgian government, predominance belonged to the Catholics, though the two parties were then for a time, so to say, in a latent state. The success of the Revolution had been due to the union of both elements; while the eyes were still turned towards the frontier, the safety of the country commanded to maintain that Union. In the Government, Catholic and Liberal members were meeting on a friendly footing, brought there more by the ascendency of their talent and their devotion to the country than by a political party. However, as the nation was beginning to feel reassured against the external dangers, parties were soon organising themselves, and that struggle was beginning, which is now more ardent than ever. On the Liberal side were Devaux, Rogier, Lebeau; on the other, as an enlightened and tolerant Catholic, J. B. Nothomb. The ministry headed by this remarkable man saw the last years of the Catholic-Liberal Union. Fifteen years after the establishment of the kingdom, that Union was banished from practical politics. Under M. de Theux a real Catholic ministry was formed, of which young M. Malou was the heart and soul. The Liberal ideas, eloquently defended in Parliament, were then advocated through the country with great talent and success at the Liberal Congress in the same year. Laying down the programme of a new policy, claiming the independence of the civil power, and obligation for the heads of the clergy to remain within the limits of their special functions, the Liberals carried so unanimously the opinion of the great towns, that M. Malou had to give way, and a new Cabinet was formed, with Messrs. Rogier and Frère Orban; the influence of the last soon became preponderant. It was due to the confidence which the country professed for the Government, as well as to the wisdom and great popularity of King Leopold, that Belgium could pass in tranquillity through the storm which in 1848 shook all Europe. By wise and opportune concessions

to the democratic spirit, especially by reducing to the constitutional minimum the tax required qualification for parliamentary
franchise, and by organising the civic guards in the country, they
prevented all excesses and disarmed demagogy.

The grave event which, on the 2nd December 1851, placed
France once more under a despotic rule, produced its reaction
in the small neighbouring country. The great difficulties which
were created in Belgium by the government of Napoleon III.
on account of the attacks of the Liberal party against the man
of the 2nd December, the presence of so many French refugees
on Belgian territory, the threats of semi-official French papers
against the safety of Belgium as a nation, all that turned to the
profit of the Catholic opposition, and contributed to the retreat
of the Liberal administration.

The Catholic ministry under Messrs. De Decker and Vilain
XIIII. came to power with prospects of moderation and an omen
of interior peace and prosperity, which soon proved deceiving.
Led by the exigencies of the Ultramontanes to present a bill
bringing privileges to the convents, namely, withdrawing from
the control of the State all legacies and endowments by private
persons in their favour, the ministry saw such an agitation spread
through the country against that measure that they had to
adjourn it, and soon after to retire.

Again in power after elections in favour of the Liberal party,
M. Frère Orban signalised his administration by important
economical measures, such as the abolition of the octrois and
the establishment of a system of customs tariffs approaching free
trade, and by organising at great expense the defence of the
country through an extended line of fortifications. After the
lamented death in 1865 of King Leopold I., the Liberal ministry
remained in power for five years under Leopold II. It should
not be forgotten to give credit to M. Frère Orban for having at
that time successfully resisted the perfidious designs of Napoleon
III. in the affair of the Luxemburg Railway, a railway through
Belgian territory, which the French government, knowing its great
strategical importance, wanted to get into their own hands ; but
the sagacious diplomacy and decisive action of M. Frère Orban
were able to counteract the plans of the French Emperor, which
would have brought upon Belgium an invasion during the
following war.

Since that time, Belgium, as if obeying a periodical wish for a
change in her politics, has had a Catholic ministry for eight years,

a Liberal Cabinet during six years, and now has had again, since 1884, a Catholic administration.

The question of popular education is the one which has for many years been the greatest object of division and eager discussions in Belgian politics. Under Mr. J. B. Nothomb in 1842, a law on elementary education had been passed which was inspired by a spirit of compromise, leaving to the Catholic clergy considerable prerogatives and influence in the schools. While enacting that there should be at least one primary school in every commune, that bill gave freedom to the communes to adopt one or more private schools, possessing the legal qualifications, so as to occupy the place of the communal school; it placed the primary schools under the surveillance of the communal authorities and Government inspectors, while the imparting of moral and religious instruction was to be superintended by ecclesiastical delegates. In the great towns, where Liberal ideas were predominant, the schools under the law of 1842 were kept more independent from the influence of the clergy, but it is true to say that in the greater part of the rural districts the Church was master of the primary schools. When the elections in 1878 brought M. Frère Orban to power, it was the general expectation of the Liberal party that there should be a new law of primary education, based strictly on the constitutional principle of independence of the State towards the Church and equality of all creeds. The Bill which was passed in 1879 stated that religious instruction would be given in all schools either by the clergy of all creeds, or by a special teacher chosen by the communal council. A special room in the school was to be put at the disposal of the clergy to give their religious teaching before or after school hours; ecclesiastical inspection of the schools was suppressed; communal authorities were deprived of the faculty of adopting, unless by Government permission, private or denominational (Catholic) schools instead of the official ones. So the schools were taken away from the influence of the clergy, to pass entirely under that of the State, independent of all creeds. The events did not allow this system of lay schools to show lasting results. The bishops and clergy undertook against the new law a campaign of resistance, which, so to say, terrorised peasants and inhabitants of small towns. From the pulpit, the schools of the State were condemned as atheistic; the bishops refused their priests the authorisation to give religious teaching in the room offered them in every school; sacraments were refused to teachers and children of these schools; under the threat of excommunication, hundreds of teachers left the State schools. The Liberal Cabinet defended itself with great energy; however, they had met more than their match, and the agitation of which their bold innovation was the subject throughout the country is one among the different causes which brought the fall of the Frère Orban ministry in 1884. It was only to be expected that the first result of the great Catholic reaction at the general elections of that year would be some new organisation of elementary education so as to replace it under ecclesiastical influence. The new law by which the Catholic majority realised their purpose is in many respects different from the law of 1842: the schools have been put under communal autonomy, with the faculty for the burgomaster and his council, whenever they have the approval of the Government and the Committee of the Provincial Council, to abolish the official school and adopt in its place a private or denominational one; religious teaching, under ecclesiastical direction, can be inscribed or not by the municipality in the programme of the schools; if it is not inscribed in the programme, and twenty heads of family claim against it, the Government may oblige the municipality to adopt and support a private school for the minority. In several large towns, the communal authorities having refused to organise religious teaching to be given by the Catholic clergy, they have had to provide for private schools belonging to Catholic congregations, which compete most eagerly against the official schools. The authorisation granted by the Government to hundreds of rural communes to adopt private schools instead of the old State schools has created in the Liberal camp an irritation which can only be compared to the anger among Catholics a few years before.

Another section of Belgian politics upon which parties have been for many years most busily engaged is the question of electoral franchise, whether for Parliament or for the province and commune. The restricted suffrage, based upon a certain amount paid in taxes, has been, especially for the last ten years, the object of violent attacks from the more advanced section of the Liberal party. Though it cannot be denied that to the restricted " *suffrage censitaire* " and to the parliaments it elected are due all the great reforms enjoyed by Belgium since her first days of independence, and though every notable diminution of the electoral franchise has proved an ultimate loss to the Liberal party, the Radical minority among Liberals have been most eager in claiming for a revision of the constitutional charter with a view to abolish the tax-paying privilege. One cannot see, however, that there is anything like a great desire in the nation at large for such a serious innovation, advocated by a body of politicians much more noisy than numerous. The policy of M. Frère Orban, foreseeing that universal suffrage at present in Belgium would be most certainly Catholic, has been to resist with all his energy the idea of promoting any too sudden change in the lowering of the franchise. It has, however, been to the honour of that statesman, in his last administration, to introduce into the electoral laws the new principle of an educational qualification for the provincial and communal franchise : to the body of electors by virtue of tax-paying has been added a large number of electors by virtue of professions or positions (persons exercising liberal professions, holders of diplomas, officials in public services, officers in the army or the *garde civique*, etc.), and also by virtue of an electoral examination passed successfully, according to the requirements specified by the law. More than 100,000 citizens have been thus endowed with the franchise. It is a very interesting experiment, which may lead later on to an extension of the franchise for Parliament.

A singular fact in Belgian politics is that, by the turn of elections, it is not infrequent to see in Parliament a majority which does not correspond to the real position and strength of the two parties. The larger constituencies have a rather important number of representatives, who are elected with the *scrutin de liste* by majority. As in districts like Brussels, Ghent, and Antwerp, of which alone the members occupy a quarter of the seats in Parliament, Liberals and Catholics muster often nearly the same total of electors, it may happen that 200 voters or less have it in their power to turn the scale and return to the Chamber thirty-two Catholics or thirty-two Liberals, as they choose. Thus one comes to results such as these : The Liberals having in 1878 the majority in Parliament when the total number of electors who had voted for them in the various districts was actually the minority, and now there is in the House of Representatives a number of ninety-five Catholic members against forty Liberals only, when the strength of the two parties in the electoral body is nearly equal. Such a system, in which the strongest majorities depend upon a minimum of uncertain voters, is a wrong system ; and fair-minded men on both sides, among whom the present Prime Minister, M. Beernaert, and the eminent economist, M. Emile de Laveleye, are now advocating representation of minorities, which would render the direction of politics less a matter of chance and give more stability to the Government, while securing it a more solid and true basis in public opinion.

A study of Belgian affairs ought not to omit reference to a question which has of late grown in importance—the question of languages. Since the kingdom of Belgium existed, French has always been the language of the cultured classes; and, in fact, it is now more than ever understood, if not exclusively spoken, among the great majority of Belgians. But since a few years there has been a reawakening of the friends of the Flemish tongue, who pretend theirs is much more a national language than the French, for this peculiar reason, that it is hardly spoken anywhere else than in Belgium. Flemings are certainly deserving of sympathy when they think they must keep with a kind of veneration the language of their brave forefathers, of their poets, and their great novelist Conscience. But when they claim for and obtain the use of Flemish in all public documents, on coins, and street corners—more than that, in the law courts and public assemblies —and want the obligation of knowing Flemish to be imposed upon all officers in the army, it seems doubtful whether they are pursuing a very useful and patriotic course. The future belongs to the great languages spoken by millions and millions; it does not belong to the Flemish language. For the good of Belgium, as well as for the peaceful union of her populations, it is to be hoped that the practical preponderance of the French tongue will not suffer too much from the pious zeal of a few Flemish men of letters, who, as it seems, would like to create a barrier between Flemings and Walloons. That barrier is not to be. Exaggerations on either side have not provoked, so far, any serious friction of feelings between the two elements; and one may trust that the good sense of the nation will always give reason to the words of the poet, a Walloon: "Fleming, Walloon, are but Christian names; Belgian is the name of the family!"

With its large population of working men in the rich industrial provinces of Liége, Namur, and Hainault, Belgium has seen for some years an eager tendency develop itself among the working classes to claim a better state of things for themselves. The great strikes, which were not always without justification, have impressed upon the public at large the necessity of doing something to better the material and moral life of the workman. While wages were raised to a fairer level, both parties have met to promote beneficial laws in the popular interest, namely, securing arbitral decision of differences between the workmen and their employers, protecting the miners against underground accidents, forbidding the employment of children and women for heavy work, resisting the evil of intemperance, and so on.

If we take a general survey of Belgium at the present time, we may consider her as a remarkable country for her great civic liberties of all kinds, and the development of her political life. Belgians love their institutions and national independence, which have been bought at the cost of such hard times in the past centuries and struggles on so many occasions. No doubt, if ever the hour of danger should come, Belgian patriotism would give a good account of itself. If there is a fault in the way Belgians understand and practise politics, we should say it is that the partisan spirit is too much infused in the life of the people; that a fair tolerance of adverse opinions is often left to be desired; and that the animosity between Liberal and Clerical interferes in social as well as in public life, reducing sometimes political warfare to miserably petty and narrow strifes.

It has been said that Belgians have inherited many a good quality from a singularly mixed ancestry; in fact, with a steadiness of their own, there is frequently to be found among them something of the quickness and adaptability of the Frenchman; they are good-tempered and energetic, men of patience and industry, fond of hard work. While they have shown a remarkable progress in the agricultural art, their industrial works have made them rivals of many greater nations; and the fact that Belgium, with her small territory of 11,000 square miles, occupies the fourth rank among the nations of Europe by the importance of her industrial production, is the best eulogy of her activity in the material sphere.

In the happy development of independent Belgium, no small praise is due to the two sovereigns who have presided for the last sixty years over her destinies. When the National Congress in 1831 sent a delegation to the Castle of Claremont in Surrey to offer the crown to Prince Leopold of Saxe-Coburg, they could not have made a better choice. With his experience of men and things, his deep knowledge of politics, his tact and wisdom, Leopold I. proved a most beneficent ruler to Belgium, while being a model of a strictly constitutional king; it is well remembered to what a prestige he had attained in the council of European sovereigns; he was a great friend of this country, and enjoyed the sincere veneration of Queen Victoria. King Leopold II. has been worthy of his father, being, like him, a popular and enlightened sovereign, faithful observer of his constitutional duty, impartial between the parties, and deeply attached to his people. His earnest desire of opening new fields to Belgian interests contributed to bring him to undertake his great enterprise in Africa, which will ever ensure him a noble fame before all nations.

Last year, in the House of Commons,[1] the name of Belgium happened to be mentioned in debate, and Mr. Gladstone pronounced these words of sympathy, which were gratefully noticed in Belgian circles : "There is not in all Europe a monarchy of more untainted honour; there is not a government of more beneficent operation; there is not a spot on the map where constitutional principles have been more faithfully and more beneficially observed, from the time when that remarkable man, Prince Leopold, was chosen the first King of Belgium, down to the present moment, when the present King of Belgium has for so long been engaged in treading in the steps marked out for him by his father to the immense benefit of his country. (Loud cheers.) I believe I am speaking the sentiment of the whole House when I say that that monarchy has our sympathy (cheers); and should the necessity arise, it would, I believe, on all proper occasions have our support." (Renewed cheers.)

We could not look for a more appropriate conclusion than such a precious testimony. Belgians could see in it, and in the way the graceful utterance was received, a fresh proof that this country will remain for them, as she has been, a powerful friend and steady guardian of their independent position.

---

[1] 29th May 1889.

XV

SWITZERLAND.

HOWARD HODGKIN, M.A.

PROBABLY a very small proportion of the many thousands of English tourists who every year spend their summer holiday in Switzerland have realised that there are other interests in that little land beside the grandeur of its mountains, the verdure of its valleys, the beauty of its lakes, and the excellence of its hotels. These last are the interests that engross the multitude, while the soul-stirring history of the Swiss Confederation, and the pure and simple democracy of its existing political institutions are, in general, suffered to remain unnoticed; yet knowledge such as this could not fail to add to the enjoyment of the traveller in that land of freedom. The picturesque scenery of Switzerland is world-famed; but the history of Switzerland is as picturesque as its scenery. And the present Constitution, or rather Constitutions, of Switzerland are as interesting to the student of politics as is its history to the historian.

That history may be said to have begun about six hundred years ago, when, in the year 1291, the three forest cantons of Uri, Schwytz, and Unterwalden entered into a perpetual alliance for mutual protection against their foes. But before summarising their history from that day to the present, I propose to explain shortly what it is that now gives a peculiar interest to Switzerland, from a political point of view.

Switzerland is a very small country, one of the smallest in Europe; and there are some people who are tempted to ignore it, to say that so small a country can achieve nothing that is great and glorious and worthy of observation. They think upon it only as the holiday ground of Europe.

It is a small country, with an area about a quarter of that of England and Wales, a population of under three millions—about the same as Yorkshire—and hemmed in on west and north and east and south by the four great European powers of France,

Germany, Austria, and Italy. Yet it has an interest quite apart
from that of any other small European country such as Belgium
or Portugal; for, small as it is, there are within it twenty-two (or, if
we count the three divided cantons, twenty-five) separate states,
generally called cantons, having distinct sovereign powers of their
own, which they can exercise free from the control of any other
state or authority whatsoever, thus differing entirely from our own
counties, and being very similar to the separate states of the
American Union, only with a more strongly-marked individuality;
and these separate and independent cantons are now allied
together under one of the most perfect systems of Federal
Government that has ever been devised.

Professor Freeman gives the following definition of federal
government: "A union of component members, where the
degree of union between the members surpasses that of a mere
alliance, however intimate, and where the degree of independence
possessed by each member surpasses anything which can fairly
come under the head of mere municipal freedom."

The present Swiss Constitution dates from 1874, in which year
there was a total revision of the previous Constitution of 1848.
The object of the Constitution is declared to be: "To ensure
the independence of the country against foreign nations, to maintain internal tranquillity and order, to protect the liberty and
rights of the confederated citizens, and to increase their common
prosperity."

The cantons are declared to be sovereign in all respects so far
as their sovereignty is not limited by the Federal Constitution, so
far, that is, as the cantons have not given over a portion of that
sovereignty to the Federal authority, which is elected by them.

Now, what are the matters—the attributes of sovereignty—
which these five-and-twenty free and independent states have volun-
tarily relinquished, and deposited with the Federal power at Berne?

The most important of these are :—

1. The right of declaring war and concluding peace, and of
making alliances with foreign states. But the cantons still retain
the right of concluding conventions among themselves on administrative matters, and treaties with foreign states on commercial
matters and frontier relations.

2. The control of the army; though each canton may maintain
a very limited number of troops of its own.

3. The entire postal and telegraph service is also under direct
Federal control.

4. The Confederation has the sole right of coining money; determines the system of weights and measures; has the monopoly of the manufacture of war powder; and (recently) the manufacture and sale of spirituous liquors.

5. In order to meet the expense of carrying on the Federal Government, it has the sole right of levying export and import duties; but it levies no direct taxation.

6. Certain other matters which strictly ought to be under the control of the cantons, have been placed under the control of the Confederation, because they affect the whole or a considerable part of Switzerland, such, for instance, as the preservation of forests, dykes for keeping in the big rivers, railways, and great through roads, etc.

But you will see that, in spite of this subtraction from cantonal sovereignty, a great deal of sovereign power is left to be exercised by the cantons themselves. The government of the cantons is the rule, the government of the Federal body the exception; and in all other matters than those which by the Constitution have been entrusted to the Federal body, each of these little Republics is as sovereign, as independent, as England or France, or any of the great powers of Europe.

The following are some of the matters in which the cantons are still supreme :—

1. All civil and all criminal law; and the administration of civil and criminal justice.

2. Cantonal and local police.

3. Land laws.

4. The organisation of the communes, or small local communities or districts.

5. The organisation of education.

6. The levying of taxes, except on imports and exports—for instance, graduated or proportionate taxation both on property and income—has now been imposed in a majority of the cantons.

You will see that these are very large and important powers which the cantons still exercise; and yet consider the smallness of some of the communities which exercise them. Two of them have a population of 12,000 each. Thirteen, or more than half of the cantons, have a population of under 100,000 each.

I have used the words "the powers which the cantons *still* exercise;" for you must understand that these powers are not new but old. Indeed, the tendency of modern times has been and still is to curtail these powers, not to enlarge them.

This will be seen more clearly if at this point we take a brief retrospect of Swiss history.

It may be said to have begun, as already mentioned, towards the end of the thirteenth century.

At that time Switzerland did not exist as a country, but the germs of it were to be found in three little communities living in three valleys, which ran down to the Lake of Lucerne, and in the forests and mountains surrounding them. The names of these three districts were Schwytz—from which the whole country afterwards took its name—Uri, and Unterwalden, which, even earlier than the time we are speaking of, was divided for some purposes into the half-cantons Upper and Lower Unterwalden. No one but the Emperor rightfully claimed any sovereignty over the people; and, thanks to the remoteness and inaccessibility of their homes, their life was an independent one. But the house of Hapsburg had considerable territorial rights within these districts, by virtue of which the Hapsburgs were constantly endeavouring to increase political sovereignty; and when in 1273 Rudolf of Hapsburg himself became Emperor, there was naturally much confusion of rights, which would have been much more serious but for that prince's high qualities.

On his death, in the year 1290, the people of Uri, Schwytz, and Unterwalden met, and, in self-defence, concluded a perpetual alliance, agreeing on oath to protect each other, their persons, families, and goods, against all comers, and to aid each other in council and in arms, and each state put its common seal to the document. From this date they styled themselves Confederates or Eidgenosun (*i.e.* companions of the oath). They did well. Albert of Hapsburg became Emperor in 1298, and, according to tradition, he came into Switzerland anxious to incorporate the three cantons with Austria, and on their refusing he sent among them Austrian bailiffs or stewards (notably Gessler and Landenberg), who exercised a despotic power over them, oppressed and maltreated them, levied exorbitant taxes from them, and imprisoned them for the slightest offences, real or imaginary.

This treatment led to a renewal of the oath. In 1307, on the green plateau of Rütli, on the shores of Lucerne, there met at night some ten men from each of the three cantons (under the leadership of Steuffacher, Fürst, and Melchthel), and with hands raised to Heaven they swore to live and die for the rights of the oppressed people, neither to suffer nor commit injustice, to respect the rights of the Count of Hapsburg, but at the same time to place some check on the arbitrary acts of his tyrannical bailiffs.

They fixed the 1st January 1308 for the execution of their design. Before that date, however, Gessler, as tradition goes, had been killed by William Tell. When the day arrived the plot was successful; Landenberg was driven from the country; the castles of the bailiffs were destroyed or taken; and without loss of blood the liberties of the cantons were restored, and once more their alliance was renewed.

I must refer to Schiller's "Wilhelm Tell" for a poetical description of the somewhat obscure and traditional events of these years. But history soon takes the place of tradition. Albert had been slain in 1301, and in 1315 Leopold of Austria invaded Switzerland with a large army, and for the first time the League proved its power in battle by completely defeating him at *Morgarten*, and driving forth from their country the Duke and the remnants of his vanquished army of nobles. This struck a great blow at the exercise of political rights by the house of Hapsburg. Henceforth the Confederates are known as Swiss. And the next few years are marked by several important additions to the League. As early as 1332 Lucerne joined them, and the four forest cantons made a perpetual alliance. In 1351 Zurich, threatened by Albert of Austria, appeals for help to the Confederates, and then joins the Confederation. In the following year Glasus and Zug are both admitted, and in the year 1353 the League was greatly strengthened by the accession of Berne. For more than a century these eight cantons alone formed the Confederation. The sixty years from 1291 to 1353 had worked wonders in this little land.

But the Swiss had not yet won for themselves freedom. Europe had not yet realised the united strength of these little Republics which were thus growing up in their midst; while the dwellers in mountain and in valley were still suffering oppression at the hands of the tyrannical and tax-collecting Austrian land-stewards. This oppression led to further resistance; and the destruction of the castle of Rothenburg by a party from Lucerne was the immediate cause of the advance of young Leopold of Austria, whose avowed object was to crush for ever the rising vigour of the Confederates. He was nephew to the Leopold defeated at Morgarten. Leopold's hostility was primarily against Lucerne; but the other cantons (apparently with the exception of Berne and Zurich), remembering their oath, decided to join their forces in resisting him. He advanced, 5000 strong, against Sempach, which lies ten miles north-west of Lucerne, intending, after having subdued the town, to pass on and attack the city.

But on the morning of the 9th July 1386 he found opposed to him the army of the Confederates, numbering barely 2000. By Leopold's orders his cavalry dismounted, and, closing their ranks, they formed with their shields one solid iron wall, which was defended by their long lances. Against this wall the little Swiss army poured itself in vain, but with most disastrous results to itself. All seemed lost, when, according to tradition, which is neither proved nor disproved, Arnold Von Winkelried of Unterwalden, declaring that *he* would open a way for freedom, cast away his weapons, and, rushing forward, gathered into his breast as many of the Austrian spears as his arms could encircle. This device opened a space in the great armed wall of the enemy through which his comrades could enter. The Swiss victory was complete. Leopold and hundreds of his Swabian knights were slain, and Winkelried, by his heroic self-devotion, won for himself the everlasting gratitude of the Swiss people.

Two years later (1388) the Austrians were again defeated, this time by Glasus, almost without help, at the battle of *Noefels*. In the early years of the next century we find Appenzels bearing the chief brunt of the Austrian attack. Assisted by the Confederates, she several times successfully repulsed Frederick of Austria, and the latter proposed and concluded a 'fifty years' peace with the Confederates, in the year 1412. This peace was broken not by Austria but by the Swiss, who were urged on by the Emperor Sigismund, also by the Church, to attack Frederick's territory in Aargau. In spite of the protestations of many of the cantons, who condemned this breach of faith, Berne, and at length all the Confederates, conquered Aargau. Berne took the greater part of it, and the remainder was governed in turn by the other cantons, except Uri, who declined, from conscientious motives, to have any share in the spoil.

But, alas! "the love of money is the root of all evil" in Switzerland as elsewhere. When the Swiss had been fighting in self-defence and for freedom they were united. Now there were jealousies about this property they owned in common again. A few years later a disputed claim to territory led to a quarrel between Zurich and Schwytz. The Confederates offered to separate, but Zurich declined, and this led to actual civil war between the Confederates and Zurich. After much fighting and bloodshed peace was restored in 1450.

Then for a time the Swiss are once more united in having to face the terrible attacks of Charles the Bold of Burgundy, who came against them with great armies. And thus united they defeated him in 1476 at *Grandson*, and took from him enormous spoils of gold and precious stones. And later, in the same year, he was once more completely defeated at *Morat*, and the year after defeated and slain at *Nancy*.

But, alas! when they were thus saved from their dangers and peace was restored, the Swiss quarrelled once more amongst themselves over the booty they had taken in war. The unsettlement caused by so much fighting led to brigandage and internal disorder. Many Swiss hired themselves out to foreign countries, to fight as mercenaries. There were disputes also between the towns and the country districts. The condition of Switzerland at this time was far from satisfactory.

Several Diets or Assemblies of the cantons were held without success; discord usually prevailed at them. The same fate seemed to be awaiting the Diet which was being held at Stans in the year 1481; but an old hermit, called Nicholas de Flue, suddenly came among them, and preached to them peace and concord. His venerable dignity told upon them, and harmony was restored. By the Convention of Stans the points in dispute were settled, and Soleure and Freiburg were admitted to the Alliance. The effect of the Convention was still further to increase the Federal sovereignty, and to lessen the individual power of the cantons.

A few years later the Austrian attacks were renewed, but in many engagements they were successfully repulsed by the Swiss, whom this danger had again united. These incidents led in 1501 to the admission of Bâle and Schaffhausen, and, in 1513, of Appenzell, into the Confederation, which now numbered thirteen states, and this number was maintained until the year 1798.

I need not dwell long on this period of nearly three centuries. It is not marked by great victories or triumphs; rather is it marked by great internal discord, due primarily to religious wars, which troubled Switzerland, as they did most other countries of Europe, during the sixteenth and seventeenth centuries, for both the old faith and the new had many adherents in Switzerland; due also to present revolts and political disturbances, for the town states, such as Berne, Lucerne, etc., treated the rural population as sub-jects, in this differing from the old country cantons of Schwytz,

Uri, Unterwalden, etc., where the whole population were on the same equal terms.   The fact that these thirteen states held together during all those troublous times, is itself a strong proof of the national feeling in Switzerland.   That there was so much discord, arose from the want of a strong central executive.   Much of the remaining territory which now forms part of Switzerland, was at that time connected with the Confederation, either as subject states, such as Aargau and Thurgau, or bound to it by treaties, such as the Grisons, the Valois, Geneva, etc.

The spirit of the French Revolution reached Switzerland, and there was a rising of those who were being denied the privilege of citizenship.   In 1798 France interfered, and having defeated the Swiss, she put an end to the old Confederation, and introduced one united Republic for the whole of Switzerland, which destroyed the old sovereignty of the cantons, and was most distasteful to the majority of the Swiss.   It could not last long.   In 1803 Napoleon drew up a form of Constitution, called the Act of Mediation, which nearly restored the old Confederation, except that a more regular Constitution is given to the Diet, and that six new cantons were admitted, viz., St. Gale, the Grisons, Aargau, Thurgau, Ticino, and Vaud.   They had been subject or allied cantons ; now they exercise sovereign rights as members of the Confederation.

Then came the fall of Napoleon, but the great Powers recognised the neutrality of Switzerland, and in 1815 approved of a new Constitution, known as the Federal Pact, and three more cantons, Valois, Neuchâtel, and Geneva, making twenty-two in all, were admitted.

The Federal tie was firmly maintained ; there was a Diet for general affairs, meeting in alternate years at Zurich, Berne, and Lucerne.   Each canton had one vote, but there was little unity of purpose.

It was found that the central authority was not strong enough to cope with agitation and discord throughout the country.   The cantons were too independent.   The deputies they sent to the Diets were delegates only, and could only vote according to their instructions, and these instructions were varied and conflicting.

The spirit of revolution prevalent in Europe reached Switzerland, and by the year 1847 the Constitutions of nearly all the cantons had been modified and made more democratic.   It became evident that a change in the general Constitution was necessary. It was precipitated by religious troubles.

Unfair treatment, as it was thought of the Catholics, especially in Aargau, led to seven Catholic cantons forming a separate League, known as the Sonderbund, in the interests of their religion. This was clearly a violation of the Federal Pact. A committee of the Diet, to whom the settlement of the disputes was intrusted, declared the Sonderbund dissolved, and by a short three-weeks' campaign they soon reduced the seceding cantons to submission.

Then followed the work of drawing up a Constitution, that of the United States being largely taken as a model. Two months sufficed to complete it. The new Constitution was at once accepted by thirteen-and-a-half cantons, and was finally promulgated with the assent of all in September 1848.

It was a compromise. A stronger central power was created. This gave compactness to the country, which better secured peace both without and within; but it lessened the sovereignty of the cantons.

In fact, a new epoch in Swiss political history began in the year 1848. The lower form of Federal Government, known as a *system of Confederated States*, had previously existed. Now the full idea of Federal Government is for the first time introduced, which Professor Freeman describes as "the most artificial production of political ingenuity."

According to Professor Dicey, "The sentiment which creates a Federal state is the prevalence throughout the citizens of more or less allied countries, of two feelings which are to a certain extent inconsistent—the desire for national unity, and the determination to maintain the independence of each man's separate state. The aim of Federalism is to give effect as far as possible to both these sentiments."

Both these sentiments were prevalent in a marked degree in Switzerland at the time of the Sonderbund war, the latter being perhaps the stronger; and effect was successfully given to both of them by the new Federal constitution which was then introduced.

There were now for the first time to be two Legislative Chambers, together composing the Federal Assembly, in which the supreme authority of the Swiss Confederation is vested, subject nevertheless to the rights of the people and the cantons as hereinafter mentioned.

Of these two Chambers, the *National Council* is elected proportionately to the whole population, one deputy being chosen for each 20,000 inhabitants, and it represents the Swiss people as a whole.

The *Council of States*, on the other hand, keeps alive the sovereignty of the cantons; for each canton, great or small, sends two members, and the mode of their election (whether directly by the people or by the Cantonal Parliaments) and the terms of their office is fixed by each canton individually. The deputies of the National Council, on the other hand, are all elected for three years; and every Swiss, on attaining his twenty-first year, is qualified to vote.

These two Chambers generally sit separately. But sitting together, they constitute the Federal Assembly, and have power to elect the members of the Government, or Federal Council, as it is called, and to choose the chief Federal officers.

Such is the general outline of the present Swiss Constitution. There is one striking fact to be drawn from the history of this country, which should not be without its lesson to us, namely, that in Switzerland the constitutional movement throughout several centuries has not been one of disintegration, but of gradual cohesion, not of weakening the central authority, and giving greater powers to the separate governments; but the separate communities, starting with practical independence, have been gradually giving up more and more of their authority to the central power, and especially has this been so in the last century.

Up to 1798 the Federal tie binding the thirteen cantons was a very loose one, not amounting to much more than an alliance. Other cantons were bound to them only by alliances. Then came the short-lived Helvetic Republic, which in 1803 gave way to Napoleon's Act of Mediation, when a regular Diet, but with limited powers, was created. Then came the Federal Pact in 1815, and also with a regular Diet; but the central authority was still nearly powerless. This has had to give way in 1848 to a much closer union of the cantons in a Federal Constitution. And again in 1874 a revised Constitution binds them still more closely together. Even since that date there have been some partial revisions; and in the matters of marriage laws, factory laws, the sale of spirits, and patent laws, the Confederation has been encroaching upon the cantons. And it seems certain that more power must gradually come into the hands of the Federal authorities, for convenience demands it; the diversity of legislation in different cantons, on common subjects, such, for instance, as bankruptcy and crime, being clearly productive of much inconvenience and even confusion.

Professor Freeman's axiom that Federal Government must be closer combination of States, not a separation of United States, is certainly true of Switzerland.

Personally one cannot help feeling sympathy for the smaller and older States who, having been nearly sovereign for the last five or six centuries, desire still to retain as large a portion of that sovereignty as is compatible with a strong, united Switzerland. But the Constitution is on the whole popular—both with those who desire further centralisation, and think it will come gradually, and with those who, favouring the sovereignty of the cantons, think this is fairly secured to them under the Constitution. This is the view of the late Sir F. Adam, British Minister at Berne, to whose most interesting book on the Swiss Confederation I am indebted for much material of this lecture.

The Constitutions of the several cantons, the manner in which they exercise those sovereign powers which remain to them, differ enormously; and subject to certain Federal restrictions, each canton regulates its own constitution according to its own devices. In olden times, the form of government in some of the cantons, such as Berne and Lucerne, though republican, was intensely aristocratic, the power being in the hands of a close corporation or a few patrician families. In others, such as Zurich and Basel, though all the townspeople had a voice in the government, the country people were excluded. But the three original cantons and the other rural cantons had all along been purely democratic. Now, however, the sovereignty of each State must, according to the Swiss Constitution, reside in the people of that canton.

But that sovereignty is very variously exercised. In some cantons the people elect a representative Pact, it may be for two years, as in Geneva; or for three, as in Zurich; for four, as in Vaud; or for five, as in Freiburg. These Parliaments not only pass laws, but in most cantons choose the members of the Government. In some cantons, however, such as Zurich and Zug, the members of the Government are chosen directly by the people.

I need not, however, weary you with more examples of such diversity. Enough if I call your attention to one of the most striking and one of the most picturesque features of Swiss political institutions, namely, that in some of the smaller cantons there is no need for any representative Parliament at all. There are half-a-dozen of these communities so small, numbering only from 12,000 to 50,000, that instead of electing a Parliament to pass laws and vote taxes and choose ministers, the sovereign powers of the canton are directly exercised by all the adult male citizens assembled once a year in some historic spot in meadow or in market-place, and there they transact all the necessary business for themselves.

In the spring of 1886 I had the privilege of being present at two of such gatherings—one at Stans, the capital of Nidwalden, and the other at Altdorf, the capital of Uri.

In both cases the proceedings of the day were begun by High Mass in the Church, which was attended by the Landamman, or Prime Minister of the canton, and the remaining members of the Government, and other officials, all of whom in Nidwalden wore their robes of office. After Church the officials went in procession, accompanied by a military guard and a band of music, to the place of meeting; for in both the cantons the actual meeting place is in a green meadow a mile or two out of the town. In Uri there is nothing special to mark the spot; but temporary hustings are erected, forming a large ring, in the centre of which sits the Landamman and the Land-schreiber, or Secretary of State. In Nidwalden, on the other hand, there is a permanent earthwork enclosure, of course with no other roof than the sky, surrounded by a fine grove of chestnut trees, just then in their freshest green. But in both cases the more distant surroundings, the green châlet-covered slopes in the foreground, and giant mountains rising in the background, whether the snow-capped heights of the Busin or the rugged outline of Pilatus, formed an amphitheatre which it would be hard to equal for beauty or for grandeur.

Passing over the brief and less exciting scenes at Stans, I will give a short outline of the proceedings at the Landesgemeinde of Uri. My companion and I obtained without difficulty front seats on the hustings.

The Land-haibel, or chief of the ushers, whose duty it is to count the voting, opened the business by a declaration as to the qualification of electors. Then the Landamman, Herr Maheim, made his retiring speech. He addressed the Assembly as " Dear fellow-countrymen" (Liebe mit Landlente), and told them that meeting them here at the end of his year of office, his heart was, as ever, full of love for their little Heimatland (Home-country). He then spoke of the great evils of spirit-drinking, which had been on the increase in Switzerland, referred with satisfaction to the recent Federal law (already alluded to), which placed the manufacture and sale of spirits under the control of the Federal authorities, and concluded this portion of his speech by appealing to his fellow-citizens to live a self-controlled and moral life.

He then proceeded to recall the famous memories of early times, and to make this, the five-hundredth anniversary of Sempach, the keynote of his speech, which continued somewhat as follows :—

"Faithful and dear fellow-countrymen," said he, ."on the 9th of next July,'it will be just five hundred years since the famous battle of Sempach was fought, which secured to us our liberties. Important as were the League at Rütli and the fight at Morgarten, that which was achieved by them was but dim and insecure. Later, in the same century, came young Leopold of Austria against the four forest cantons to crush them ; but they went forth to meet him, and Uri sent out her illustrious Conrad der Fraven. It was a glorious and complete victory which the Confederates achieved over a much more numerous enemy ; and it is only since that famous battle of Sempach that our League has been strong, respected, and feared. Dear, faithful fellow-countrymen, we hold our Landesgemeinde to-day on the same spot where our ancestors decided to fight for their liberties and for ours. Let us follow their great example. It is true that the character of our warfare has changed ; we have peaceful work to perform instead of waging war. But we have our vigour and our existence to maintain, and it is only through a childlike devout trust in God that we can do this. Let future generations speak well of us too ; and though they will not say that we have won victory in battle, may they be able to say of us that we have preserved our religion and maintained the State, and have handed down to them the same glorious inheritance.

"Let us now ask God's assistance, and that He will guide our work aright. Let us each say five Ave Marias and five Pater-nosters."

He ceased. The whole assemblage, numbering probably upwards of two thousand, then rose to their feet, bared their heads, and prayed in silence. During the time thus occupied in prayer, which could hardly have been less than two minutes, and seemed much longer, perfect stillness prevailed amongst that great throng. The scene was a most impressive one.

Then followed the regular business. The Landamman was re-elected, so were most of the other retiring officers. Most of this business was formal, but the matter became animated when a

certain Herr Müller, whose turn it was to retire, begged not to be
re-elected. A member of the Government receives as salary only
3f. (or 2s. 6d.) for each time the Government meets to
transact business. It is therefore not surprising that men should
often shrink from rather than seek after the labours of office. But
a man chosen by the people to fill a certain office in the State is
bound to serve. Hence Herr Müller's difficulty. He pleaded
the claims of his family, said he must consider their interests, and
felt that he could not attend further to public affairs. Two others
were against their wishes nominated to fill the office, and the
names of the three unwilling candidates were successively put
before the meeting. There was a close contest; three times a
show of hands was demanded, but eventually Herr Müller was
re-elected. And thus for three years more this poor man must
needs neglect his family to serve the State. Would that such
unselfish patriotism were common among our own politicians !

The exciting business of the day was yet to come, viz. the
consideration of the Government Bill, which besides other fiscal
amendments, introduced progressive taxation, both on the capital
value of property, and on income,—the tax on income increasing
from a quarter per cent. on the lowest incomes to two per cent.
on the largest.

The debate was animated. It was clear from the cheers and
cries of disapproval what the issue would be. But if members
were on the side of the tax, one could not help thinking that the
arguments were against it, but perhaps this was prejudice. One
witty opponent said he thought the people did not understand the
principle of progression. He would explain. Suppose a cobbler
made a pair of boots for some one whose foot was six inches long,
and then another whose foot was twelve inches long ordered a pair
of boots, and the cobbler, instead of making the second pair twice
as long as the first, made it three times as long, that would be
progression, that is the principle of progressive taxation.

The Landamman wound up the debate, supporting, of course,
his own measure. It was carried by an acclamation, and by an
immense majority of votes, and this brought the meeting to a
close. It had lasted about four hours.

If it be thought that this is too hurried a way for determining
important questions of State, it must be borne in mind that a few
weeks previous to the meeting a printed official programme is
sent to every citizen. The laws to be proposed are set out in
full, a list of the offices to be filled, and details of the taxes to

be asked for. Thus the citizens have ample opportunity of considering and discussing among themselves in private the questions upon which they will shortly be called upon in public to decide.

I trust you will not think too much time has been devoted to those Landsgemeinden. They are not the *important* feature in Swiss political life to-day; but, on the other hand, they are of great historical and antiquarian interest. They are a perfect survival of the oldest institutions of our race, and probably represent what used to take place in the early year of our own country. Through storm and revolution, through wars without and discords within, these primitive institutions have been maintained, and form an integral part in the practical working of the Swiss Confederation at the present day.

The striking feature in Switzerland is to be found in the extraordinary success which so far has attended the close form of Federal Government which has existed since 1848, a period of more than forty years.

It has on a move made Switzerland strong and united, as the smaller Switzerland used to be when, in the fourteenth century, she had to contend against the might of Austria, and has thus enabled her to take up a stronger position towards the nations without, and to prevent discord between the various cantons within; and yet through all it preserves the identity, the peculiarities, the local sentiments of the canton.

Little Catholic Nidwalden, with its 12,000 inhabitants, holds its yearly Landsgemeinde. Her great Protestant neighbour Berne, with more than half a million inhabitants, has the complete machinery of a representative Parliament. The most extra-ordinary differences of language and religion exist among the cantons of Switzerland. Some German cantons are all Catholic, others practically all Protestant, others half and half. In Berne, a Protestant canton, we find both Germans and French. In Freiburg, a Catholic canton, we find both French and Germans. Ticino is Roman Catholic and Italian. In the Grisons, where the religions are about equally divided, we find a preponderance of German, but also Italian, and the old-fashioned Romansch and Ladin languages. Again, some of the cantons are violently Conservative, other advanced in their Liberalism. Some are almost wholly pastoral and agricultural, others have a large manufacturing and urban population. Truly, then, the Swiss may claim for their Constitution a great success, when without destroying the individualism of the cantons it effectually and amicably binds together such contrary and diverse elements.

But it is not only in this successful binding together of diverse elements that the Federal Constitution has achieved a great success. Both it and the individual constitutions of the majority of the cantons satisfy the two requirements of good government laid down, which I think we may safely adopt. In the preface to the Constitution which he framed for Pennsylvania, William Penn stated that in his view the perfect form of government was one " when the laws rule, and the people are a party to those laws."

Let us see how far these two tests apply to Switzerland. The laws rule in Switzerland, because the people who made the laws naturally expect them to be obeyed, else where were the good of making them. And they intrust the administration of those laws to a government which is elected for a definite term of years and holds office independently of the subsequent approval or censure of the electing body. This is true whether of the Federal Council, which, as before said, is elected for three years by the Federal Assembly, or of the governments of individual cantons which are similarly elected for a term. If the Federal Government proposes some measure which is rejected by the Assembly, that measure does not become law ; but the Government accepts the rejection, it asks for no vote of confidence, nothing ensues in the shape of a ministerial crisis, nor does it dissolve the Assembly, for it has no power to do so. The Government having been elected for a fixed term, remains at its post, and everything goes on as before. The effect of this is to make the Swiss Government during those three years that it lasts a strong Government. And the Republican Swiss, like the Republican Americans, know well, what we in monarchical England seem too often to forget, that a strong executive is absolutely essential to the good government of any country.

Bearing upon this, there are some further points about the Swiss Federal Council which are well worthy of note. Their salaries are small, only £480 a year each. It is an almost universal practice to re-elect the members of the Council when their term of office expires, provided, of course, that they are willing to remain in office. There have hitherto been only two exceptions to this practice. The country therefore does not lose the services of a capable, honest, and devoted administrator because his own political views happen just then not to be in the ascendant. This rarely is an excellent principal.

It follows almost as a corollary from the last proposition that men of different political views sit and work amicably together in the same Council. They may take strongly divergent views on individual questions. It has even happened that two of their body have risen in succession to support opposite sides in the debates in the Assembly (which they are permitted to address, but of which they are not members), and yet they will work harmoniously together all the time in the administration of the country. The majority in the Council generally belong to the same party as the majority in the Assembly. But the majority in the Assembly does not exercise its strict rights ; there is a certain feeling of fair-play which leads them to concede the principle that other parties should at least be represented in the executive government.

Would that such a state of things existed in England, that our politicians might, especially when in opposition, forget the petty claims of party for the welfare of our common country ! Would it not be for the benefit of the whole United Kingdom if the Government thereof could be intrusted for a term of years to good and capable men and administrators of whatever party. We should eliminate from either party its less able and less trusted members, and we should not have the ablest members of the opposition perpetually thwarting the ablest men in office.

We see, then, that in Switzerland "the laws rule;" and more than that, there is no other country in which it may so safely be said that "the people are a party to those laws."

I have already explained how purely democratic is the composition of the Federal Assembly ; and have stated that "in it the supreme authority of the Swiss Confederation is vested, subject nevertheless to the rights of the people and the cantons as hereinafter mentioned." We now come to consider what are the rights of the people and the cantons which impose limitations on the power of the Federal Assembly. They are to be found in the peculiar Swiss political institution known as the *Referendum*, which means "the reference to all vote-possessing citizens of the Confederation for acceptance or rejection of the laws passed by their representatives in the Assembly."

If any charge is proposed in the Swiss Constitution, there *must* be a Referendum ; but if any ordinary laws or general resolutions are passed by the Assembly, a Referendum takes place only if such be demanded either by 30,000 citizens *or* by eight cantons. When a change in the Constitution or any new law or resolution is put to the Referendum, such change or law only comes into force if a majority of the citizens participating the vote pronounce in the affirmative, *and* if a majority of the cantons are also in favour of the change.

Thus the new Constitution of 1874 was agreed to by 340,000 citizens against 198,000; and by fourteen-and-a-half cantons in favour, and only seven-and-a-half cantons against. Now supposing that twelve of the smaller cantons had voted against the Constitution, and ten of the larger in favour of it, the reform would not have been carried out, even though a majority of Swiss citizens were in its favour. In this way something of the old sovereignty of the cantons is secured. The voting is very simple. All that the voter has to do is to deposit in the ballot-box his voting-paper with either Yes or No written upon it.

This ultimate reference of important decisions directly to the people secures a more purely democratic form of government than anything that can be obtained by the necessarily defective system of representation. It gives back to the Swiss people something of that direct share in legislation which they possessed before representative Parliaments were introduced, and which the six small cantons still possess in regard to their own affairs, as we saw when speaking of the Landsgemeinde.

The result of the system is said to be excellent. It makes each citizen feel his own individual influence and responsibility; it strengthens national and patriotic feeling; extreme measures on one side or the other have no chance of passing, and measures that are passed naturally carry greater weight, having thus the direct sanction of the majority of citizens. Radicals like the system, because it is essentially democratic. Conservatives have become its earnest supporters now that they find it acts as a check upon hasty and radical law-making.

Not only does this system prevail in the Confederation, it prevails in most of the cantons also. The cantons which have a Landsgemeinde do not need it; the others acquire many advantages of the Landsgemeinde by means of the Referendum.

In seven of them the Referendum is compulsory; that is, the people must express their opinion directly on all important matters as defined by the Constitution. Thus, in all these seven cantons, any single expenditure above a certain limit, or increased annual expenditure, must be submitted to the popular vote. In Berne the limit is £20,000. In Schwytz it is as low as £2000, or £400 additional per annum.

In seven other cantons there is an optional Referendum only;

that is, that a certain number of citizens have a right to demand the Referendum.

Freiburg is the only canton where there is *no* Referendum as to laws or expenditure; but even there it prevails as to the revision of their Constitution.

It is evident that the Referendum, both federal and cantonal, affords to the Swiss people a certain guarantee that they cannot be governed by laws to the making of which they have not themselves been parties.

There are many other phases in the political and social life of Switzerland to which time will only permit a brief allusion.

Among such are the *Communes*, the units of political life in Switzerland, which may be considered as the base from which first the canton and then the Confederation is formed. They are purely democratic. Two or three times a year a general assembly is held of all male citizens belonging to the commune. The assembly elects an administrative council of six or eight members, votes the communal taxes, and decides important questions. The council so elected looks after the roads, the police, the poor, public instruction, and so forth. Most of the communes have property, especially woods and pastures, in high Alps; and this communal property is also administered by the council in conformity with the wishes of the commune.

It is this communal life which is, in some respects, the strength of Switzerland. By it the Swiss nation has been trained from its infancy—and each individual Swiss from his infancy—to habits of law-making and administration. And when we add to this the training which so large a proportion of the Swiss have for centuries had as members of cantons—especially in the old free cantons— it is not surprising that, at the present day, every Swiss is born a statesman, and that the Swiss as a nation are pre-eminent in the art of government.

With a population about two-fifths Roman Catholic, and three-fifths Protestant, it is not surprising that the Constitution of 1874 declares liberty of conscience and belief to be inviolable, and guarantees the free exercise of worship within the limits compatible with public decency and order. It must be admitted, however, that this limitation is somewhat strictly enforced. The order of Jesuits is not allowed in Switzerland; new convents cannot be founded; and in some cantons no religious processions are allowed to take place in the streets. Considering this strictness against Roman Catholics, we can well understand that the Salvation

Army should so often be interfered with as being likely to cause a breach of the peace. All these limitations on religious worship are remarkable in so free a country as Switzerland. They no doubt arise from the remembrance of so much religious discord in the past; a discord perhaps due to the fact that the Swiss are earnest in their religion, and feel their differences keenly.

The Swiss are the best taught nation in the world. The Constitution makes primary education compulsory, and it is given at public expense; but each canton has its own system. In some cantons Catholic and Protestant children receive religious instruction together in the communal schools; in other cantons it is given separately. The best sites in town or village are chosen for the schools, and public money is ungrudgingly spent on education. As a result, every child in the Confederation, not mentally incapacitated, is able to read and write.

But one must not prolong the description of all these various phases of life in Switzerland, or tell of her marvellous success in manufactures and in agriculture—a success obtained nevertheless by the utmost skill and industry, and insufficient to obviate a considerable annual emigration to America. This is no place for a detailed description of the little Republic. My aim has been rather to give you a brief outline of its history and development, especially in connection with the existing forms of government; and to rouse, if it may be, some enthusiasm such as the Swiss feel in their country and its institutions.

They are all proud of their history—which, nevertheless, as we have seen, is not common to all the cantons; they delight in celebrating centenaries of its important events, and yet the ancestors of many of those who in 1886 were joyfully celebrating the five-hundredth anniversary of the battle of Sempach, suffered defeat in the army of Leopold. But that matters not now. These ancient feuds are forgotten. Federalism has done its work; it has succeeded in binding together very diverse and even jarring elements, while preserving the sovereignty of the cantons. It has succeeded in enlarging the borders of Switzerland, and freedom within her borders has thereby been enlarged also.

The principal object of this course of lectures is stated to be "to modify our insular prejudices respecting foreign countries.' There is no European country to whose history and institutions Englishmen ought to be more alive than the Switzerland in which they spend so many a pleasant holiday; none in which they can learn better the advantages of a strong yet popular executive, freed from the tyranny of party warfare ; none in which they see better the full ideal of Federal government; yet few, perhaps, whose history and institutions have received less attention from the British public. To travel for the sake of historical or political research is one thing, to travel for the sake of beauty of scenery is another, but it is nowhere possible to combine these two pursuits so effectually and so delightfully as in Switzerland.

Yet who considers for a moment when he takes the boat from Lucerne to Fluelen, touching at Beckenried and Brunnen on the way, that he has in those two-and-a-half hours been in four successive Republics, each of them semi-sovereign and independent? How many of the English travellers who daily in summer are crossing the Brunig Pass, or winding with amazement through the circular tunnels of the S. Gothard railway, dream for a moment that at Sarnen and at Altdorf they are passing green meadows where the whole manhood of a free state still yearly meets to choose its ministers, to vote its taxes, and to make its laws?

As one who has found intense enjoyment in the natural beauty of Switzerland, and has felt that enjoyment quickened by the study of the history and politics of her people, it is but discharging a debt of gratitude if I have been enabled this afternoon to inspire some keener interest in Swiss freedom—in the story which tells how that freedom has been won—and in the political institutions under which it is safeguarded.

XVI

MODERN LIFE AND THOUGHT AMONGST THE GREEKS.

J. THEODORE BENT.

I DO not propose in this lecture to confine myself to the narrow limits of the kingdom we now call Greece, but to give an account of the condition in which we now find the whole of the Greek race scattered through the towns, villages, and islands on the Eastern seaboard of the Mediterranean. Somehow the enthusiasm for the Greek which was so keen during the first half of this century, an enthusiasm which was fostered by our poets and our classical students, has of late years cooled down into something like indifference, as far as the modern Greeks are concerned. Theories like that of Fallermayer have been widely discussed, namely, that the modern Greeks are all of Albanian blood, and that the descendants of the old race of heroes is extinct ; this theory is doubtless in a measure true, on the mainland and in the mountainous districts it is undoubtedly the case. The Greeks were never a pastoral race, but gregarious, wedded to the sea and commerce, hence we must look for the race always along the seaboard, either in the big towns of the Levant, or in the islands to which the barbarian races never penetrated. But into this question of race I will not go, for it is an inexhaustible and unsatisfactory one ; suffice it for our purpose that we have now existing a kingdom inhabited by people who call themselves Greeks, and a much larger area inhabited by people speaking the Greek tongue, a language much more closely akin to the language spoken at the beginning of our era than the English which we speak to-day is to the language spoken in the time of Chaucer ; and it is a curious but well-ascertained fact that the language of the New Testament is much more akin to the language spoken in Greece to-day, than it is to the language of Plato and Demosthenes, that is to say, a period of eighteen centuries of turmoil and oppression has had less effect on the language than four centuries of prosperity and literary activity.

T

Let us first glance at the progress made by the present kingdom of Greece during its sixty years of emancipation from Turkish oppression.   It is true that Europe is somewhat disappointed with the position it has taken up amongst nations.   It was expected to develop itself like Italy has done, to become a power in the East, to eventually take up the reins of government in the Balkan provinces, with its capital at Constantinople.   That is to say, we are disappointed that a tiny, mountainous country, without resources, for the most part sterile, the inhabitants of which, from long disuse to government, look only to local interests, and on whom the idea of patriotism is only just dawning, has not as if by magic blossomed forth into a ruling power.   We might as well set Ireland adrift by itself in the middle of the Atlantic, and expect it to rival the British Empire, as expect the tiny Greek kingdom, with its two million inhabitants, to take her position as a power in the East. On a close examination, however, I think Greece, especially now that it is becoming more united in a common cause, will be seen to have done everything that any one in reason could have expected of it.   The first of the many difficulties it had to contend with was want of union.   Every town and every island scrambled at the outset for its own separate advantage; patriotism was a quantity entirely unknown to them ; then again, a national Greek failing was that everybody sought to be a politician, everybody talked, and nobody dared to act.   The outcome of this is still evident in Athens, the smallest capital in Europe, yet the one which produces the greatest number of daily newspapers in proportion to its size.   Governments rose and fell with a rapidity that would be startling even in a South American republic, until at last one man, by his firmness, his ability, and his uprightness, has at last stemmed this disastrous current, and is moulding Greece into a steady system of practical politics.   This man is Mr Tricoupis, who spent most of his youthful days in England.   He was educated at Harrow, and made himself thoroughly master of our system of legislature, and under his guidance it is being brought to a successful issue on the old soil of Hellas.

Let us glance at the capital.   Athens is all modern, and the pity is that King Otho, out of sentiment, reconstructed it where it is.   If he had kept the ancient city with its Acropolis as a museum, and built his capital at the Piræus, it would have been infinitely superior, both for those who wished to pursue commerce, and those who wished to study archæology.   The rows of white houses, the trim, clean streets, the public buildings and palaces,

are all the growth of the last half century. In 1832, as Professor
Jebb tells us, 'the inhabited dwellings in Athens consisted of
a few wooden houses, one or two more solid structures, and the
two lines of planked sheds which formed the bazaar;' and when
Otho became the first King of the Hellenes, not a single house
in his capital could be made fit for his accommodation. Now
the town contains a king's palace, an university, which, I think,
is one of the most perfect and elegant modern buildings I have
ever seen, three national museums, free schools, hospitals, boule-
vards of fine marble palaces, squares and streets, and a population
of nearly 60,000.

No country, in proportion to its size and wealth, has spent half
as much on archæological research as Greece has done during
the last twenty years. Excavations on a most elaborate scale have
been conducted on the Acropolis and elsewhere; large museums
have been constructed to contain the treasures found in these
excavations, and those found by French, German, and American
excavators, for the Government now forbid the exportation from the
country of any works of art; and no country has spent more on
education. Education would seem to be one of the first instincts
of returning life amongst the Greeks, an instinct even still more
remarkable in unredeemed Hellas, where the difficulties attending the advance of education have been infinitely greater, and
which we shall presently discuss at greater length. Young Greeks
swarm in the universities of Germany and France, where they
have gone to complete the already sound education given them
by their university at home, and it surprises all travellers who
visit Athens to see the multiplicity of book shops in the city.
Translations of the best known foreign books, histories, poems,
and novels written by modern Greek authors, and the evidence
of an exceedingly high state of mental culture pervades the
country. Mentally, the Greeks have made the most rapid strides
during their period of freedom; they are a clever, far-seeing race,
amongst whom the brain power is far in excess of the physical
energy.

The development of railways in Greece is one of Mr Tricoupis'
pet schemes, and it is one which will have much to say to the
future of the new kingdom. The railway along the northern
coast of the Peloponese, from Athens to Patras, has already been
constructed, bringing the capital into closer communication with
the west; but the great line of rail which is, in five years, to
unite Athens with the main systems of Europe, has only just

been commenced this winter by English engineers. It will pass up the classical valley of the Kephissus, and cross the mountain ridge which divides the plain of Attica from Bœotia by the Phyle Pass; thence it will run to Thebes, skirt Parnassus by Livadia, Daulia, and the Lake of Orchomenos, penetrate into the plain of Thessaly by the pass of Thermopylæ, and reach the Turkish frontier fifty miles beyond Larissa. This will leave a short gap between the Greek system and the line down to Salonica, and when this is finished it is confidently hoped that the line to Athens will be the great overland route to the East, and that the harbour of the Piræus will succeed to the traffic which has for so many years found its headquarters at Brindisi.

The town of Hermoupolis, on the Island of Syra, in the Cyclades, is, perhaps, one of the most interesting specimens of modern Greek commercial enterprise. During the Turkish days, it was the seat of a Roman Catholic mission, and was under the direct protection of the Kings of France. At the time of the revolution, Greek merchants and labourers flying from Chios, Psara, and other points where the Turks perpetrated wholesale acts of cruelty, took refuge here, as on neutral ground. Syra in itself is a mere barren rock, and at that time had not more than 1000 inhabitants on it. By degrees the Greek merchants gathered round themselves the nucleus of trade, and even before the declaration of independence, Syra was a prosperous place. In 1825, the first two-storied house was built; a few years later a barn-like church and barn-like storehouses were erected on the beach; Luke Ralli christened the infant town Hermoupolis, and after the war of independence, Syra grew with the rapidity of the mushroom towns of the western hemisphere. To-day it has a population of 25,000 souls, fine warehouses, factories, a theatre, a town-hall, and quays. Its harbour is one of the busiest in the Levant, it is the central depot of the eastern telegraph in this part, and of the Greek Steamer Company; most of the outward and home-ward bound steamers call here, and, next to Athens and Patras, it is the most imposing place within the realms of modern Greece.

From these points it will be seen that the little kingdom of Greece has done well during its half century of emancipation, but its resources are so limited that, unless it can get accession of territory, it cannot hope to do better. 'Without Crete, Epirus, and Macedonia,' writes one of the best modern Greek politicians, 'Greece has no future;' and wealthy Greeks, the representatives of Greater Greece, we might call them, have recognised the impossibilities of their country by withholding their support from it. They continue to live in Constantinople, England, France, Egypt, and elsewhere, carrying on their commerce and enriching their adopted countries, a race as scattered almost, and as commercial, as the Jews; but at the same time they are by no means unpatriotic. Far from it; large sums of money find their way into proper channels for the education and elevation of the Greek nation still in bondage. They realise the fact that education is the one weapon with which to fight Turkey, and to check the advance of Russia in the East, and when it is a question of money for the building of schools for Greeks in remote parts of the Turkish Empire, the purse-strings of Greater Greece are always open. Let us now glance at the component parts of the Turkish Empire, Asia Minor, Thrace, Macedonia, and the islands. Here it is that we shall find the majority of the Greek-speaking population, and all, until quite lately, living in a state of the grossest ignorance. Here has been a field for generosity far more deserving than the self-supporting institutions of free Hellas, and into this channel we shall find that the money of rich Greeks flows ever freely.

During the dark ages of oppression, the Greek Church was the only community which contributed in any degree towards education; the monastic bodies and the village priests, too, did a praiseworthy work in keeping alive the Greek nationality and the Greek religion, but this was almost all they could do. After the revolution there came a thirst for a more extended system of education, the spirit of patriotism was aroused, and central societies were formed at Constantinople with a view to elaborating some scheme for the elevation of the masses of the Greek population. scattered through the Turkish Empire. For many years the progress made towards this end was exceedingly slow, owing to the keen opposition of the Turkish Government, and it was not till 1861, when the Porte found itself in a hopeless condition of finance, that the Greeks were able to step in and literally purchase from their rulers concessions for schools, and a concession for the existence, in the very centre of the Ottoman empire, of a central educational body. At first a so-called " central college " was formed by the Greeks of Constantinople, which drew up for itself a wide line of action, and established as the basis of its work the patriotic motive of raising the Greek masses out of the depths of ignorance into which they had fallen during the Ottoman rule. But this college failed, for reasons which we need not here discuss, and finally handed over its programme to a Society, which rejoices in the somewhat high-sounding title of the " Hellenic Philological Syllogos," and which three years ago tried to celebrate its twenty-fifth anniversary, but the Turks would not permit the demonstration.

To this Society is alone due the great advance in education which has been made amongst the Greek population in the Turkish dominions during the last twenty years. The influence which has been effected by it over the masses is only now beginning to be felt, and if its area of usefulness develops with similar rapidity during the ensuing quarter of a century, little will be left to be desired on the score of education.

This Society was not, as its name would almost lead one to imagine, a literary society founded by a collection of literary men —far from it. The men who in 1861 joined together with a view of developing and spreading education amongst their compatriots were, for the most part, bankers, shopkeepers, doctors, and priests, not one of whom had at that time any special predilection for literature or art ; and up to the present time it is from these classes of society that the ranks of the Syllogos are filled. Hercules Basiades, for example, who was for many years president of the Society, is by profession a medical man.

The Society is distinctly patriotic, and has for its chief object the instruction in letters of a vast population, of whom, fifty years ago, only five per cent. of the males, and one per cent. of the women, could either read or write.

The branches of the Society are manifold; there is the archæological branch, pure and simple, presided over by its own chairman and directed by its own committee. This branch has done admirable work in the preservation of ancient monuments in and around Constantinople. Then there is the scientific branch, likewise under the direction of a separate committee, which has done all it can towards the advancement of scientific research, and towards the amelioration of the sanitary condition of one of the most unsanitary cities of Europe. Thirdly, we have the financial committee, which looks after the internal working of all the branches of the Society ; this branch has the onerous duty of soliciting and collecting subscriptions, and of attending to the demands made on the Society's resources by the other committees ; but the most active and useful branch is the educational, the committee of which has adopted the work which the former college set itself as its own, namely, that of spreading education through the Levant. It is with this branch of the Society that we are now more especially interested, so we will at once set out its scheme, which is as follows :—

(*a*) The spread of education amongst the orthodox peoples of the East, paying especial attention to female education, whereby the mothers of the future Greek race may be enabled to undertake the instruction of their children from their earliest infancy.

(*b*) This object is to be brought about by the erection of boys' and girls' schools wherever necessary, and by assisting already established schools to increase their usefulness.

(*c*) Special attention is to be paid to the publishing and distribution of good educational books for the use of these schools.

(*d*) Efficient schoolmasters and schoolmistresses are to be sent from Constantinople to superintend these schools in remote districts of the empire, where the same cannot be locally provided.

(*e*) And lastly, the Society is to endeavour to establish colleges for the better education of the lower clergy, whose immediate work it is to cope with ignorance and superstition.

The carrying out of this scheme has naturally called for the greatest liberality on the part of the wealthier Greeks, and the substantial success which has been already achieved during the short period of twenty-five years is the greatest testimony that can be found to illustrate their genuine patriotism.

Throughout the period of four centuries of darkness which succeeded the fall of the Eastern Empire, there always existed amongst the Greek-speaking population an attempt at education solely conducted by the clergy; their schools were known as "simple" or "elementary schools," and the education therein given to the boys who attended them was limited in the extreme ; specimens of these "simple" schools may still be found in outlying districts, where the central educational system has not yet penetrated. The classes are generally held in the vestibule of the church, or in a house close by, and are only opened at those seasons of the year when the priest, who is usually the master, is not obliged to be working in his fields. The scholars learn the letters of the alphabet from written tablets, and when they can read correctly a verse of the Psalter, they are sent home to their work, and to forget the very shape of letters. Some few only are permitted to prosecute their studies until they are able to read the Psalms and the Gospels; two or three at the most ever attain to such a pitch of excellence that they are allowed to read a portion of the service in church. When such a paragon of intellect adorns a family, the grateful parents and relatives will make a great feast in honour of the occasion; they will bring handsome gifts to the instructor as a testimony of their gratitude, and the successful pupil is considered to be so superior to the rest of his family, that he takes the name of Diakos or Deacon, which name is treasured in his family for generations. If such a youth feels inclined to take up literature as his profession in preference to the tilling of his ancestral fields, he may proceed to the higher branch of writing, and from being the secretary of the schoolmaster in his capacity of village scribe, he may attain to the proud rank of schoolmaster and village scribe himself.

It is on such material as this that the Syllogos had to build its educational structure. Of course in some of the larger towns there existed schools of a higher class; these were at once incorporated into their scheme, and this was done by constituting them as the heads of branch brotherhoods and societies incorporated with and constructed on the same principle as the Syllogos at Constantinople.

Fifteen years after the foundation of this Philological Society, there sprang into existence no less than eighty-four of these independent branches, scattered all over the empire, which recognised the educational committee in the capital as their central head. By degrees, in some towns—such as Adrianople, for example—reading-rooms were opened and libraries formed, and the several branches of archæology and science were added to the already existing educational one, so that the constitution of the mother society was reproduced at Adrianople in all its departments.

Now there are many more of these branches, and the work is steadily advancing. Some of these offshoots have taken to themselves appropriate names; that at Philippopolis was known as "The brotherhood of good works," that at Smyrna is called "The Homer," that in Patmos "The regeneration." It is required of each of these societies and brotherhoods that they shall send periodical accounts of the work done and of the necessities of each place for the beneficial extension of the system; and in the journal, which the Central Society publishes periodically at Constantinople, side by side with accounts of archæological discoveries and scientific research, we read the minutes of the Educational Committee, which proves at the same time the extent of the generous help already given, and the immense field that there is for future development.

We will now proceed to take examples of the educational work that is in progress from various points of the Turkish Empire. Where the monastic resources are sufficient, and where help is not urgently required, matters are allowed to pursue their old course. On the island of Nisyros, for instance, we found the Archimandrite Cyril, of the monastery of the Holy Virgin of the Cave, the chief mover in the diminutive society on this island; besides acting as banker for the peasants and issuing cardboard notes, an inch and a half square and of the value of one penny each, signed by his name, as a medium for exchange, and, besides paying for a doctor, who attends the poor people free of charge, he has likewise, with the income of the monastic property, established a boys' school and a girls' school at Mandraki, the chief village on the island, which are presided over by efficient teachers, who have been sent out thither through the agency of the Society; the books of instruction have likewise been provided from the same source. But all this has been done at the expense of the monastery, which is a prosperous one; and to realise the real benefit of religious institutions on mankind, and the readiness with which even effete monastic institutions work for the advancement of the Greek race, one ought to travel in the out-of-the-way corners of the Turkish Empire.

In Greece proper, the work of the monasteries is practically over, since the Government has taken upon itself the sole superintendence of education, and is alone responsible for the improvement of the people. What monasteries once were, and what good they have done, can now only be realised in Turkey; the smaller ones, as the one in Nisyros, for example, have provided education for the masses; the larger ones, as Mount Athos, have provided instruction in the higher branches of learning, and act as universities; and it is a question open to much doubt, as to whether the Greeks have benefited by the transfer of education from the priests, who have acted for ages as their protectors from annihilation and barbarism, to the Government schools; in Turkey, as we have seen, they provide for the better education of the clergy, and, if this can be effected, the priesthood will continue as the natural instructors of their flocks.

On the neighbouring island of Telos, which is inhabited by

semi-barbarous Greeks, living in a state of shocking ignorance and superstition, the monastery, in a similar fashion, has of late years commenced to work for the good of the people. Five years ago, the monks decided to expend £25 per annum on the maintenance of a schoolmaster, who gave us a lamentable account of the ignorance he found there, and which still exists among the elder inhabitants; but when we visited the school, each boy had in his hands the books which the Society has printed for educational purposes, and the elder ones could read Xenophon quite fluently, and translate it into modern Greek. The monastery of Telos is far from being as rich as that of Nisyros, so the inhabitants have to die without physic, and the girls have to grow up without instruction; but doubtless, in good time, the Society will step in and see to the rectification of the latter deficiency, for such ground as this is the field on which the Society has done such admirable work elsewhere. But the island of Telos is only thinly populated, and as remote a spot as well could be found from any centre of civilisation.

In Macedonia, the Society can now boast of over twenty affiliated branches, the chief of which are the "Educational Brotherhood," at Kozane; the "Educational Society," at Drama, and the "Pieria," at Naousa; and from Macedonia we may select an instance of the beneficial work which has already been carried on. At the mountainous village of Deliachova, when the Society commenced operations, it had most lamentable difficulties to contend with. Here the mother tongue of the Greeks and the Slavs alike was a barbarous Turkish *patois;* and as none, even of the better class, understood Greek, the great difficulty was to obtain local assistance in the schools, and even those available would only teach when there was nothing to be done in the fields; the population was considerable, and the church could only manage to advance £30 a year towards educational purposes. This position of affairs was duly represented to the Syllogos at Constantinople, and, through the Society's instrumentality, not only have proper Greek masters been provided, and the necessary educational books, but also a girls' school has been opened, that the future mothers of unborn Greeks may be able to speak to their infants in the language of their ancestors.

Fifteen years ago a valuable branch of the Society was established at Adrianople, with the object of forming a central head for the furtherance of education in Thrace; it started with a subscribed income of 30,000 grossia, partly advanced by the Syllogos, and partly by the richer inhabitants of the town; ever since then this income has been steadily on the increase, and the advantage of a public reading-room and library are now enjoyed by the Greek inhabitants of this large city, where not so many years ago the exception was for a man to be able to read or write. One of the most flourishing branches in Thrace is at Heraclea, on the Propontis, where previously, even though it was within easy reach of the capital, the greatest ignorance prevailed, and immense benefit has been conferred on a people who hitherto have known nothing of patriotism and their own nationality; whereas now, thanks to the efforts of the Society, the fact has been brought home to them that they are Greeks, and that the main object of their rulers has been to keep them in ignorance of this fact.

In Asia Minor the war against ignorance has been waged by the Society with equal success; here many villages existed and still exist where the Greeks are only recognisable by their religion, the language and customs of the dominant race having been universally adopted; to these villages the Society has sought, to the best of its abilities, to send instructors to teach the children their ancestral tongue. We will briefly detail the history of the foundation of the brotherhood of Argyropolis, near Trebizond— it is a peculiarly interesting one, and one which serves to illustrate the method adopted by the Society in carrying out their work.

Argyropolis is a town in Armenia, and was founded and chiefly colonised by Greeks who fled thither from Trebizond for greater security after the Ottoman conquest; it is situated in a wild and sterile district, the land around is unproductive, and timber is exceedingly scarce; but the town grew rapidly in importance, and took its name from the discovery of gold and silver mines in the neighbourhood, and in the sixteenth century Argyropolis presented the appearance of eminent prosperity—churches, schools, and other fine buildings were erected, and in addition to the wealth that accrued to them from the working of the mines, the inhabitants carried on a large carrying trade with the Asiatic tribes from the East. After the lapse of years the mines were exhausted, and the caravan trade from Eastern Asia found its way into other channels, so that, owing to loss of employment and the want of natural productions for sustaining life, those who continued to live on at Argyropolis were reduced to the greatest state of destitution; the result being that, at the commencement of this century, the once flourishing town was reduced to a mere village, and of the numerous Greek families only a few hundreds remained, and for these there was no education, their language degenerated into an almost incomprehensible *patois*, and their only livelihood was gained by depredations and other acts of dishonesty.

About twenty years ago a few of the respectable Argyropolitans, who had settled at Trebizond for purposes of commerce, met together and expressed their distress at the condition of their native town ; they accordingly determined on making an applicacation to the Philological Society at Constantinople, which was then in its infancy, for assistance in forming a scheme for ameliorating its condition ; and shortly afterwards, their statements having been duly considered at headquarters, a brotherhood of Argyropolitans was formed at Trebizond, and enrolled as one of the Asiatic branches of the Society. With the generous assistance which was obtained from Constantinople, this brotherhood was enabled to open in Argyropolis, in the year 1870, a boys' school, and three years later this was followed by the opening of a girls' school ; and now, not only in Argyropolis are there good schools, provided with efficient instructors and books from the central head, but also the brotherhood has been enabled to establish branch schools in some of the neighbouring villages.

Instances of the beneficent effect of the work done by the Society might be enumerated indefinitely, but those I have given will serve to prove the progress which has been made during the last few years. As it at present exists, the Syllogos has representatives amongst its members of the best and richest Greek families in Constantinople ; it possésses a large building in Pera, containing a good-sized lecture hall, reading-rooms, and a library, which is at present unfortunately small, owing to the fact that their original building was burnt in the great fire of Pera in 1872, when many valuable books and manuscripts were destroyed. They have a literary reunion every week, at which scientific and archæological papers, and they have periodical business meetings, at which the secretaries of the several sections read minutes, which are published in the journal under the head of Πρακτικὰ.

On realising this intellectual activity on the part of the Greeks, one cannot help thinking that, if left to themselves, they would soon settle the Eastern question in their own peaceful way ; meanwhile, the fear of Russia, the jealousy of the Powers and other causes, have led politicians to give a helping hand to the expiring Turkish nation, whilst at the same time they distrust and despise it, and now it is Western Europe, and England more especially, that is the greatest check to the development of Greater Greece. We call ourselves humane, we abolish slavery, we are the champions of liberty all over the world, and yet we support a nation which is tyrannising over the rightful owners of the soil to an extent that in many cases is worse than slavery.

The Island of Samos has been an independent principality for fifty years; it has only a population of 25,000 Greeks, and the progress which Samos has made, and the contrast it forms to the neighbouring islands, is a proof of what the population of Greater Greece could do if left to themselves. When they obtained their freedom, the Samiotes were little better than mountain shepherds; there was not a rich man amongst them. Now the capital Vathy, which has been entirely built in this period, has good houses, presenting as their frontage an excellent quay over a mile in length. The Samiotes govern themselves by a council of four. She has her own code of laws; nowhere in the world is property safer than it is on Samos. The Greek prince who is sent from Constantinople to look after Turkish interests and collect the small tribute is absolutely powerless, and dare do nothing without the consent of the council; if he does do so, as happened a short time ago, the Samiotes send him back to Constantinople in disgrace.

An hospital has lately been opened, and an university called the Pythagoras, after the ancient Samiote philosopher. New roads are in course of construction all over the island, and at three different points around the coast, breakwaters are being built to supply the one deficiency of the island, namely, the want of harbourage.

It is like going out of paradise into purgatory to cross over from free Samos to poor ruined Chios, which, before the war of independence, was one of the most prosperous marts in the East. Of course the contrast has been intensified by natural causes, the earthquake and the subsequent paralysis of trade. But in spite of this overwhelming misfortune, no part of the Turkish Empire has been subjected to more tyranny than Chios. After the earthquake, the Turkish government magnanimously proposed to remit the taxes for five years. Europe heard of this, and praised the Turk, but Europe did not hear how the following year double taxation was imposed, and double was established as the rate for the future. I have been an eye-witness myself of this tyranny, more marked in the outlying villages, where the cry of the oppressed is not so easily heard. Some of the villagers are wild with hope when they see an Englishman amongst them. They remember the generosity displayed by our nation after the earthquake, and they somehow believe that to England alone have they got to look for help. Even now, in the ruined villages where relief was distributed, prayers are offered up every Sunday in the churches for Queen Victoria and her nation. Little do these poor creatures realise that it is the English nation and English politicians who are the chief props and mainstay of their oppressors.

XVII

THE OTTOMAN EMPIRE.

H. ANTHONY SALMONÉ.

THE present mode of thought and condition of learning in a great part of Turkey and the Mohammedan world may be considered to be in exactly the same state as it was in Europe some four or five hundred years ago. Notwithstanding this general statement, it is still true that in certain portions of the Ottoman Empire there have been during the past fifteen or twenty years rapid strides in the paths of progress and advancement. Turkey might have been at the present day equal to any of the great European Empires had her progress not been handicapped in many ways. Probably the main causes may be found in the want of unity amongst her subjects, and the lack of general education.

There is, unfortunately, in the greatest part of the Empire, this lack of a national spirit, and the lack of that unity and concord which so much helps to raise a people in spite of opposition and rulers. It is because the people of Turkey have not sufficiently striven to find that stepping-stone to greatness, that their lot is not a hundredfold better than it is.

Those who have studied the question will, I think, agree with me, that there hardly exists a more intelligent and more industrious people than those races which now inhabit the Turkish Empire. And it is to be hoped that with the spread of education and an improved administration, the sons and daughters of Turkey will be enabled ere long to vie with their European brothers and sisters.

When speaking of European civilisation, it is impossible to dissociate the progress which it has wrought in the way of knowledge, and the improvement and development of the higher instincts of mankind from the customs of society which it has given rise to in late times. Although it cannot be denied that much refinement and good taste are displayed in the modern

303

customs of civilised Europe, still it is to be hoped that the Eastern races of Turkey will retain the picturesque customs of their forefathers. Every country has its own laws, institutions, and customs; and I maintain that it is far better for each race with the spread of education to improve that which requires improvement, rather than for them to adopt the customs of another nation which are unsuitable to their characters and country. So far, the introduction of European civilisation into the East, and particularly into Turkey, has been in reality productive of more evil than good. There are two reasons for this; the one is, that it came too suddenly upon them; and the second is, because the said civilisation was not through the effort and work of the people themselves, the result of this being that the majority of the people, instead of selecting and culling, so to speak, the finest flowers and immortelles, as they should have done, trusted to the forced and hothouse fruits, which they greedily ate and which disagreed with them. A great number learned all the vices and shallownesses of modern European civilisation, and ignored all the immortal blessing, which it has created in the form of science, learning, and knowledge.

The date of the first appearance of the Turks in Europe has never been clearly ascertained. Some assert that Turkish tribes were settled in Southern Russia as early as the beginning of Greek history. It is generally agreed, however, that they were known to the Chinese long before the existence of any European historian.

The founder of the present Ottoman Empire was Othman, who reigned from 1288 to 1326. From his early youth, Othman proved himself to be a daring warrior, and his power grew gradually but surely, forming, as it were, the basis of the succeeding glory which fell to the lot of the Ottoman dynasty.

During the reign of Urkhan, his son, a standing army was established called yeni-cheri. In common with many other Oriental words, this word was corrupted by Europeans into Janizaries. The title of "Pasha" also came into existence at this time, and several of the provinces were governed by them. The origin of the word is from the Persian Paï-Shah, meaning "the foot of the King." The power of the Ottoman Empire now grew very rapidly, and the conquest of Constantinople was attempted by several of the Sultans, but unsuccessfully. But in May 1453, Mohammed II. met with greater good fortune; for, after a siege of nearly two months, Constantinople fell into the hands of the Turks. This great victory was quickly followed by several important conquests, that of Servia, Peloponnesus, Trebizond, Kaffa, and several provinces in Asia; and in Europe, Scander-beg, Herzegovina, and Otranto also fell into the hands of the Turks.

But the most glorious epoch in the history of the Turkish Empire was during the reigns of Selim I. and his son Sulaiman.

Selim, who reigned in the year 1512 to 1520, was the first Sultan of Turkey who received the title of Khalif, *i.e.* chief of all Mohammedans, and successor to the Prophet. He was acknowledged such by the Sheriff of Mecca, after the conquest of Egypt and Syria, and Al-Mutawakil, the last Khalif of the Arab dynasties, was deposed from his rank. The Sultans of Turkey have been acknowledged ever since by almost all the Mohammedans in the world as "Amir-ul Muminin," or chief of the believers. Turkey possessed during the reign of Sulaiman the finest navy in the world, and Europe trembled before the conquerors of Constantinople.

Although the reign of Sulaiman marked the most brilliant page of Turkish history, the decline and fall of the Ottoman Empire may be dated from the closing days of this monarch's life. Nevertheless, the Empire continued to maintain her power, and towards the end of the sixteenth century, in the reign of Murad III., was still the terror of Europe. Besides European Turkey, Greece, and the greater part of Hungary, she possessed all Asia Minor, Armenia, Daghistan, Georgia, Western Kurdistan, Mesopotamia, Baghdad, Syria, Cyprus, Arabia, Egypt, Algiers, Tripoli, and other places.

A severe blow was dealt to Turkey during the reign of Othman III., who, owing to the rapid rise of the power of Russia, was induced to declare war against Catherine II. This proved disastrous to Turkey. She lost several towns and fortresses, and her fleet was destroyed by the Russians in the bay of Chesme. Through the working of Russian agents, insurrection broke out in Greece, Herzegovina, and other parts of the Empire. It might be truly said that ever since that time, the troubles of Turkey with Russia have never ceased.

Let us now inquire into the causes which led to the decline of the power of the Ottoman Empire.

During the reign of Sulaiman I., the Turks had arrived at the summit of their glory, but it was an altitude that they were unable to maintain, for from this time dates the commencement of their retrogression.

Among the many factors which led to this retrogression may be mentioned :—

1. A too great indulgence in luxuries.

2. Internal factions. The Viziers or Ministers by reason of the continued absence of the Sultans (who were invariably at the head of their armies abroad) obtained considerable power. The direction and management of all state affairs were left to their charge. This aroused jealousies and intrigues

3. Demoralization of the army. Love of luxury becoming widespread, engendered love of gold. The passion which ruled amongst the soldiers was gain and plunder, not love and glory, or a sense of duty.

The main factor probably was the baneful influence which the Imperial harem (the ladies) exercised.

The progress of the Empire was also checked by the apathy of the rulers towards commerce and trade. They little suspected that liberty, wealth, and greatness are the blessings of industry. All conquering races that have not consolidated their triumphs with labour and commerce have fallen into decay. Their fate was such, because they looked upon industry and trade as servile, trusting to the sword to gain them riches and independence. This was precisely the fate of Turkey. Two or three hundred years ago she was wealthy and powerful, feared by her enemies and respected by her allies. Turkey was elated with pride after her conquests. She thought but little of working out her resources, of encouraging art and commerce, and of affording to her subjects (whether Christians or Mohammedans) that protection which was indispensable to their welfare. She left to all the nations of the world a vast field for commercial enterprise, and a free market for their productions. Hence such arts, sciences, and commercial spirit as Turkey once possessed, were soon outstripped by the gigantic development and the rapid improvement of the Western world. The result to Turkey was a general financial embarrassment. Having lost all her arts, and most of those immense productions of industry which she at one time brought into the market, she had to apply to foreign marts for all her needs, exporting thither her gold and silver.

Two distinct populations inhabit the Turkish Empire. The one (comprising many nationalities) is the native or aboriginal population whose lot has been, for many generations, one of subjection. This population is numerous, industrious, and intelligent, and is made up of Christians, Jews, and Mohammedans. The other, the dominant Turk, is an alien population, which looks upon industry with disdain. These two constituent elements of the population, productive and unproductive, contending one with the other, kept the country in a state of immobility for nearly four hundred years. The fatal jealousy and hatred which existed between the governing and the governed classes, together with the supineness of the rulers, subverted the native and caused the introduction of foreign industries. Hence arose two directly opposite political tendencies: the first, a combined foreign interference in all matters of internal policy; and the second, a partial and selfish protection by alien powers of interests inimical to Turkey. Europe, for the last sixty or seventy years, by introducing all the products of her art and commerce, has been, from a material point of view, the mistress of the Turkish Empire. Europeans monopolised all profitable undertakings, such as steam navigation, postal communication, etc. Thus between the combined and partial interference of foreigners, and the struggle of the two populations, the Turkish Government has to divide its attention, its subjects meanwhile becoming more and more neglected.

It must be remembered that there is a sharp distinction not only between the races, but also between the classes of the people in the Ottoman Empire. Many people designate any one who happens to have been born within the limits of that Empire as "a Turk." Now there are many subjects of Turkey who are as little Turks as Osman Digma is a Frenchman, or the Mahdi an Englishman. There is equally a vast difference in the customs and ideas which prevail in different parts of the Empire. Amongst the upper and educated classes of the Turks—I allude particularly to the Pashas and Beys who swarm in Constantinople—there are many who have either been brought up in the West, or received a Western education. These, no doubt, would be glad to introduce Western improvements into the Empire, but are prevented from doing so by the opposition of a vast majority who are very conservative, and averse to modern European customs and institutions.

Colleges and schools, comparable to the finest institutions of the kind existing in Europe, are established in various parts of the Empire, either by Europeans themselves or through European influence. The establishments of the American missionaries and those of the Jesuits are among their number.

The system of native education, under which the great mass of the people is brought up, is still exceedingly poor, especially among the Mohammedans. These have their Kuttab school, which consists of a large dirty room under the care of a teacher. On entering one of these schoolrooms, one sees a number of children squatting on the floor, and rapidly swinging their bodies to and fro, repeating, in a monotonous chant, passages from the Koran. Their teacher, who probably may be dreaming of houris and future bliss in Paradise, corrects their exercises.

One word as to the influence of the Mohammedan religion upon the life and thought, not only of the people of Turkey, but of the whole Eastern world. Whatever faults and evils are attributed to Mohammedans, it must yet be allowed that they are probably more sincere in their faith, and more true to the dictates of their religion, than the believers of any other religion throughout the world. A proof of this is that there are fewer Mohammedans converted to Christianity than followers of any other religion.

There are a number of people who think that nothing said against Mohammedans is bad enough ; but impartiality requires of us to give Mohammedans their due.

The Koran, it should be understood, is regarded by them not alone as a book of Divine inspiration. The Koran is their rule of faith, their code of civil and criminal law, and their universal directory in all matters intrinsic and extrinsic to themselves. Although its dictates are simple, so far as the principles of the doctrine go, nevertheless there is great diversity of opinion, owing greatly to the complexity of its language. Mohammed laid down strict rules as to pilgrimages, fasts, and other things to be done ; but it does not appear that he enumerated and enlarged upon those things which should not be done. Besides the Koran, they have a great many traditions of which some have been accepted and others rejected. One of these traditions, or rather legends, is very amusing. It runs as follows :—" At the end of time, when everything will be in confusion, the Prophet will appear to the faithful in the form of a huge sheep. Then, by a special miracle, his followers will be transformed into fleas, and crowd into the wool of the sacred sheep, and be carried by him up into Paradise."

Mohammedanism has had a remarkable influence on the laws

and institutions of every country into which it has spread. The Arabic language, the language of its sacred book, has similarly influenced the tongues and dialects of many nations. Turkish literature is by no means poor; but it cannot be compared to the literature of the early Arabs. The ideas of the majority of later works, especially in Turkish, are borrowed from the West.

The study of Arabic opens to the Western student a vast field of literary research. Let me quote the following passage on the subject from the pen of Mr. Bosworth-Smith of Harrow:—

"During the darkest period of European history the Arabs for five hundred years held up the torch of learning to humanity. It was the Arabs who then 'called the Muses from their ancient seats;' who collected and translated the writings of the great Greek masters; who understood the Geometry of Apollonius, and wielded the weapons found in the logical armoury of Aristotle. It was the Arabs who developed the sciences of agriculture and astronomy, and created those of algebra and chemistry; who adorned their cities with colleges and libraries, as well as with mosques and palaces; who supplied Europe with a school of philosophers from Cordova, and with a school of physicians from Salerno."

Before concluding my lecture, I should like to say a few words with regard to the relations of this country with Turkey.

England is most assuredly the one European power whose relations with Turkey should be closer, and whose interest in her must be greater than that of any other foreign nation. The reason is that England possesses the greatest Eastern Empire in the world, the Queen ruling over a greater number of Mohammedans than any other potentate. Hence, necessarily, her interests are of unparalleled importance in the East in general, and Turkey in particular, because the Sultan is the Khalif of Islam, and the recognised head of the Mohammedan world. The Sultan should, therefore, be the natural ally of England.

It would be advantageous to England to help Turkey in the readjustment of her internal affairs. England could win the confidence and friendship of the Eastern races by greater intercourse with the people, and by pointing out, in a gentle and reasonable way, the advantages that would accrue to them from an improved state of things. It is by thus proving that England is the friend and ally of the Eastern world, that she can constitute and maintain her position as the undoubted mistress of the East.

The Oriental mind requires leading, not driving. One cannot make a horse drink, but once led to the water he invariably does so. Let us, then, whenever an opportunity occurs, help by our sympathy and our interest to lead the people of Turkey to the fountain of knowledge, enlightenment, and advancement.

APPENDIX.

WHY DOES NOT THE SICK MAN DIE?

C. D. COLLET, EDITOR OF "DIPLOMATIC FLY-SHEET."

THE proximate dissolution of the Ottoman Empire has been a fertile theme for poets, theologians, and politicians for more than four hundred years. Waller made it the subject of a poem, which he presented to James II. But the Revolution of 1688 swept away the Stuart dynasty, and left the descendants of Othman reigning at Constantinople.

William Eton, many years resident in Turkey and in Russia, wrote, in his "Causes of the Decline of Turkey," that Turkey must very soon be overwhelmed by the Empress Catherine of Russia, and the followers of Mahomet be entirely driven from "the countries in Europe which they have usurped;" and in the advertisement to his fourth edition, published in 1809, he declared, of a new chapter in the book, that "it will show that the awful crisis I foretold is nearly arrived."

This was in 1809. In 1807 the British fleet, under Admiral Duckworth, had made an unsuccessful attempt to bombard Constantinople, while another fleet, in the same year, bombarded Copenhagen, thus aiding Russia in the straits which both in the north and the south most circumscribed her power of aggression. In 1809, England made peace with Turkey, but in 1812 she terminated her bloodless five years' war with Russia by the Treaty of 1812. Then she commenced the character of the candid friend of Turkey, which she has ever since kept up. The Treaty of Bucharest (1812) robbed Moldavia of the province of Bessarabia, which introduced Russia to the Danube, where in 1883 her position as one of the Danubian European Commission was finally and triumphantly established.

In 1827 England's friendship for Turkey, which was manifested by constant advice to submit to the demands of Russia, was somewhat disturbed by the "untoward event" at Navarino, where the Turkish fleet was destroyed by the combined fleets of Turkey's three allies—Russia, England, and France. This cleared the way for Russia to invade Turkey, which she did in 1828. The first year of invasion was far from triumphant; the second brought the peace of Adrianople, on the 14th September 1829. But fraud assisted the Russians even more than force. Colonel (afterwards General) Chesney, in his "History of the Russo-Turkish Campaigns of 1828 and 1829," page 245, says:—

"It is pretty certain that he (Sultan Mahmoud) would have continued the war at all hazards, had he been aware that at that moment the Russian commander, now Marshal Diebitsch Zubalkouski, had not more than from 15,000 to 17,000 bayonets. A defective commissariat, and a still worse medical department, caused disease to commence its work as soon as the invaders reached Adrianople; at a grand review which took place on the 8th of November 1829, and at which the author was present, there were scarcely 13,000 men of all arms in the field."

The British Ambassador at Constantinople, Sir Robert Gordon, advised the Sultan to sign the Treaty of 14th September, and, on the 31st October, his relative, Lord Aberdeen, despatched to St. Petersburg a quasi-protest, which was hidden in the archives of the Foreign Office till, on 30th June 1854, the House of Commons, on the motion of Mr. Layard, requested a copy of it. Only then was it given to the world.

This hypocritical protest was addressed, according to the usual form, to the British Ambassador at St. Petersburg, who was to read it to the Chancellor, Count Nesselrode, "and, if desired, to give his Excellency a copy." In it Lord Aberdeen told the Czar, in the most affectionate manner, that, as a matter of fact, he was a violator of his word, and that the stipulations of the Treaty were inconsistent with the desire which he had expressed for the independence of the Ottoman Empire.

This protest, like Waller's poem and Eton's history, contained a prediction. Lord Aberdeen referred to the anxiety on the part of those Powers, who have always felt a deep interest in the preservation of the system " of the European balance established by the Treaty of Paris (1814), and at the Congress of Vienna (1815);" and he said:—

" This anxiety must be greatly increased when, in addition to the unavoidable weakness and prostration of the Turkish Power, it is found that fresh causes are brought into action which are obviously calculated to hasten and ensure its utter dissolution."

This was twenty years after Eton's prophecy. Greece at this epoch became separated from Turkey, and the Mahometan inhabitants were expelled from Wallachia and Moldavia, to strengthen by their loyalty those parts of the Empire to which they might repair. Turkey, however, was not "overwhelmed," nor were the followers of Mahomet driven across the Bosphorus.

If we were to inquire into the details of the Crimean war, we should find that the Turks, after having driven the Russians out of the Danubian Principalities of Wallachia and Moldavia, were handicapped by the assistance of England, France, and Sardinia.

The essential agreement, between Russia on the one hand and the Allies on the other, is established by the despatch of Count Nesselrode, 29th June 1854, in which he said that, as regards the civil and religious rights of the Sultan's Christian subjects, the Czar "would be ready to give his concurrence to a European guarantee for these privileges;" and by the reply of M. Drouyn de L'Huys, in his despatch of 22d July 1854, in which he agreed that "France, Austria, Great Britain, Prussia, and Russia shall lend their co-operation to obtain" these privileges for the Christians "from the initiative of the Sultan."

This alliance of the five Powers, afterwards increased to six, by the admission of Sardinia, succeeded in obtaining a further separation of the Danubian Principalities from Turkey and the exclusion from the Black Sea of the Turkish fleet, which was stronger than that of Russia. This was effected under the pretence that it was an insulting restriction upon Russia's power. Turkey observed the treaty religiously; Russia armed her merchant vessels and mail packets, and thus compelled the Circassians to leave their country, whose blockade by Russia deprived them of the means of subsistence. Then Russia tore up the Treaty— running the risk of having one day to meet the Turkish fleet in the Black Sea, but gaining the prestige attaching to the power of being free from all restrictions, even when made by a solemn and an equal treaty.

The gain of Russia by the Crimean war cannot be accurately estimated by any who are not aware of the efforts that Turkey was making to emancipate herself from the restrictions, commercial and otherwise, under which she laboured. But Russia had undermined the Turkish power in the three Danubian Principalities, and, although she had not expelled it, she was able— through England and France, who, with Austria, Prussia, and Sardinia, joined Russia in the European Concert for the regulation of the Principalities—to facilitate the process of disintegration. The war of 1877-8 accomplished the severance of the three Danubian Principalities, and of that of Montenegro, from the

Ottoman Empire, and, for the purpose of their future severance, created the Principality of Bulgaria and the Province of Eastern Roumelia.

But the effect of this disintegration has not been entirely unfavourable to Turkey. Roumania, which still recollects the devastation of the Russian armies which occupied it "like a cloud of locusts" in 1848-52, and which she contrasted so unfavourably with the contemporaneous occupation by the Turks, is not disposed to become a Russian province, and does not consider herself called on for gratitude to a Power which, as she now sees, deceived her into the belief that she was acting as a liberator.

It is different with Montenegro and with Servia. But it remains to be seen how far Russia will succeed in her glaring attempts to incorporate these provinces.

From the time that Bulgaria and Eastern Roumelia were constituted, Russia set to work to unite them into a Russian province; but, though they have pretty nearly accomplished their union, it is as a Turkish province. Roumania, Bulgaria, and Eastern Roumelia do not yet form a flowery path for the march of the Russian troops to Constantinople.

In 1688, and in 1809, and again in 1829, Turkey was about to be overwhelmed by Russia. Now, after 61 years, 81 years, 202 years, in which Russia has gradually secured the aid of all the European Powers, the Sultan still rules at Constantinople, the Moslem has not been driven across the Bosphorus.

Why have the predictions of the Christian prophets failed of accomplishment? Why has the diagnosis of the European doctors not penetrated the secrets of the Asiatic Constitution? Why has not "civilisation" driven "barbarism" out of Europe? Why does not the sick man die?

Among many causes of this persistent vitality, three are pre-eminent. The first is the fraternal spirit of the Mahometan religion, which is fully embraced by the Turks. The simplicity of the Monotheism of Mahomet must have been a refreshing breeze to all senseful men whose priests were engaged in disputes about the nature of Christ, and the rank of the different persons in the Trinity. The Mahometan religion recognises the substantial equality of all Mussulmans, and the Turks know no hereditary rank except in the family of the Sultan. The conquered Christians who accepted Islam were at once invested with all the privileges of the governing race. These privileges included the duty of national defence. Honour and duty thus went hand in hand, and the purity of their morals is still evinced in the noble disinterestedness which encourages Turkish soldiers to go on serving without mutiny, while their pay is many months in arrear.

The second cause has been the liberty and the self-government accorded to those who refused to accept Islam, and continued to belong to one form or another of the Christian faith. The usual system in the Turkish provinces, where religions are mixed, is to recognise the religious chiefs as the municipal rulers of their congregations. The archbishops and bishops of the Greek Church, of the Roman Catholics, of the Protestants, Jews, Romanist Armenians, and Gregorian Armenians, instead of being subject to disabilities, or proscribed the realm by the Government Church of Islam, as they would have been in this country at the Reformation, are all invested with authority. Of course every election has to be sanctioned by the Sultan, just as in England the Lord Mayor, after election, is presented to the Lord Chancellor for the approval of the Queen. But no creed is imposed on any of their churches by any government authority. The Christians, too, in consideration of a money payment, have generally been exempted from military service.

In Greece, before the Revolution of 1821, the organisation was different. In the continent, in the Morea, and in the islands, the communal system was more secular, and in each of the three the forms varied infinitely, but the principle was everywhere the same. The councils were elective. Henry Headley Parish, Secretary to the British Legation in Greece from 11th November 1830 till May 1834, in his " Diplomatic History of the Monarchy of Greece " (1838), gives a chapter on the communal rights of Greece under the Turkish rule, which shows how erroneous is the ordinary opinion on that subject. We can afford only one extract from this chapter, which was extracted from a Greek journal called " *Le Sauveur*," published at Nauplia in 1834, under the Royal Regency.

" Each province had a *Baluk Bashi*, or chief of the *gendarmerie*, under the orders of the Voyvode and the provincial council.

" The council might displace him whenever it thought proper, without referring to Turkish authority.

" No tax of any kind, which was called for by the wants of the government or of the country, could be levied without the express consent of the provincial council, as well as that of the mayors of towns, burghs, and villages. The mayors assessed this tax proportionally amongst the families."

At the end of this chapter Mr. Parish remarks :—

"Such was the simple and beautiful system of administration which the Greeks had enjoyed until the year 1820, and under the shade of these institutions they had advanced in population, commerce, administrative knowledge, and mental cultivation beyond any conquered or tributary people of modern times. In 1820 their merchant vessels covered the Mediterranean. When the revolution broke out, the merchant navy of Greece consisted of 600 vessels, mounting, in all, 6000 guns. The cities of Hydra, Spezia, Ipsara, Scio, and others were rapidly rising to the fame of the Hanseatic, Venetian, and Genoese Republics, when it suited the purpose of the Cabinet of St. Petersburg, for the third time, to revolutionise Greece." [1]

Mr. Parish says that, under the Venetian rule, the population of the Morea was 190,653; under the Turks, in 1820, it was 458,000. It was much diminished during the war of independence. Mr. Frederick Martin, in his "Statesman's Year-Book" for 1880, puts it at 743,494.

At the conferences of Poros in 1828, under the influence of Sir Stratford Canning, afterwards Lord Stratford de Redcliffe, the envoys of the three protecting Powers—Russia, France, and England—declared that :—

"In the establishment of a hereditary government in Greece, it would be both unjust and dangerous to deprive the Greeks of the representative principle, for even under the Turkish rule they elected their municipal magistrates, and their 'Notables' were generally invested with the right of apportioning the taxes imposed by the Porte." [2]

In the process of constructing the Greek monarchy, the representative system was, by great exertions, planned by Russia, and carried on by her in conjunction with her satellites, England and France, very much weakened. Mr. Stillman, a celebrated Phil-Hellenist, who, when American Consul in Crete in 1866, gave considerable assistance to the insurrection against Turkey, bore testimony to this in an article in the "Fortnightly Review," November, 1880, when he said that, "under the Turkish rule the municipal liberty is much greater than in the kingdom of Greece." He draws a picture which is well worth the consideration of all who think that they are doing good service by detaching provinces from the mild sovereignty of the Sultan, and placing them under the bureaucratic government of some petty sovereign under Slavonic protection. From this article we extract the following. The article was written at the time that the Berlin Conference was adding territory to Greece in Epirus and Thessaly :—

"As a friend of Greece, and especially as an admirer of its courageous, in-

---

[1] Parish's "Greece," p. 44.   [2] Ibid, p. 74.

domitable, and warm-hearted people ; not blind to its vices, but knowing that its virtues far surpass them, if those of any people can be said to do so, I ask myself the question others have asked me, and will ask now—What can be done, if Greece is in this desperate condition, to make her fit for the new responsibilities Europe proposes to bestow upon her ? The answer is in one word—Decentralisation—a radical change of the constitution to one on the Swiss plan, with the fullest administrative liberty to the commune, entire abandonment of the system of nomarchs,[1] re-establishment of the original States as provinces, and the remission of the provincial affairs to elective provincial governments ; in short, the most complete separation of the general Government at Athens from the affairs of the country consistent with keeping a firm, federal bond, the maintenance of the army, navy, and diplomacy under a common direction, and, as far as possible, the removal of the central administration and the civil service from the vicissitudes of an ignorant universal suffrage or unreasonable changes.

" That the Government is not strong enough to bring about complete assimilation is shown by the fact that it has been obliged to leave the Ionian Islands in the condition, in most respects, in which it got them. It has never been able to establish uniform taxation, or to abrogate special laws or institutions. It has generally planted the seeds of great discontent when it has done anything in the way of centralisation there. In a voyage through the Ionian Archipelago last spring-time, I found everywhere increasing discontent with the Government of Athens, and a growing regret for English rule, as well as a contempt for Athenian law. Ten years ago I could find nothing of the kind. And not only from the islands, but from almost every part of Greece where I have been, or where I have friends, I hear the same growing complaint against the absorption by the Government of the liberties and prosperity of the provinces, and the same outcry against over-centralisation. Even the poor semblance of municipal liberty is not respected, for the demarch, or mayor, though elective, is utterly powerless for good, as he cannot even construct a road without the consent of the Central Government, while even illegal infringement of the prerogatives of the municipality are not uncommon. As to the elections, woe to the Demarch who acts against the will of the Ministry.

" Decentralisation will remove the great objection to enlargement of the kingdom, and will even make it practicable to a greater extent than will be found possible under the present form of government. It will permit the new provinces to come in with their local administration unchanged ; and it is a curious fact that, under the Turkish rule, the municipal liberty is much greater than in the kingdom of Greece. There is a great and substantial danger that in annexing a population so large and so habituated to that particular kind of liberty which will be denied it by the Greek Constitution, Greece may find itself in the position of a gun that fires a shot heavier than itself—the gun will go farther than the shot. If, for instance, Crete were to come, as the Greeks all hope it will, into the assembly of the Greek States, and the Islanders, accustomed to an extraordinary amount of provincial independence, and even to an insular autonomy within certain limits, were to experience the operations of a Greek administration, with nomarchs appointed from Athens, etc., etc., I am certain that two years would not elapse without a revolution and a separation. And the plain truth is, that Crete is to-day better and more intelligently

---

[1] The nomarchs are appointed from Athens.

governed than the Hellenic kingdom has ever been, and is, indeed, a model of government for populations so situated."

The Greek nation has increased in population since there have been no Turks in Greece against whom it could rise in rebellion, but it is far from possessing the energy, the patriotism, or the habit of self-government which it displayed seventy years ago. The municipal liberties which the Roman and the Turkish conquerors respected has been destroyed by the protection of Russia, France, and England.

The municipal liberty so remarkable in Greece was not confined to that country. When, in 1880, the Secret Societies in Bulgaria were endeavouring to eject the Greeks from the Church of St. Marina, in Plovdiv, they addressed letters to the Bulgarian villages, calling for evidence that, thirty years before, the Church had been constructed chiefly by the subscriptions, not of Greeks, but of Bulgarians. The letter commenced as follows :—

" Call a meeting of the members of the Council of Elders, and summon to that meeting the old men of your village who, thirty years ago, were at the head of affairs in the village. You will then question them minutely, in order that each may recollect what you have contributed from the village towards the restoration of the Church of St. Marina in Plevdiv."[1]

If the spirit of the Greeks has been broken by the seventy years' persecution of Russia, it must be remembered that, during the whole of that time, Russia was supported by England, sometimes by design, sometimes by inadvertence. It has yet to be seen whether the Bulgarians will meet with a similar fate. Since the brigand-like kidnapping of Prince Alexander, England has not *actively* assisted Russia in Bulgaria.

In order to appreciate the encouragement given by the Sultans to commerce, it is necessary to recollect the many impediments to commerce enacted in England, and in particular the prohibitions made for the protection of English manufacturers, and even agriculturalists, against the commerce of Ireland. During the reign of William III., it was even proposed to make it felony to import Irish cattle into England.

The Hatti Sheriffs of the Sultan according liberty of trade to the Rulers of England, France, Venice, and Poland, are indeed couched in an Oriental style of imperial condescension.

The Emperor and Conqueror of the earth, who by Divine grace is the King of Kings of the world, and the dispenser of crowns to

---

[1] Turkey No. 5 (1880). Correspondence respecting the condition of the Mussulman, Greek, and Jewish populations in Eastern Roumelia, p. 268.

monarchs, granted them to the most glorious among the great Princes professing the faith of Jesus, and the most conspicuous amongst the potentates of the nation of the Messiah, and every time that the Hat was renewed it was mentioned that the exalted Christian potentate who had made professions of sincerity and friendship, had demanded and received permission for his subjects to come and go into these parts, "in addition to other special commands, to the end that, in coming or going, either by land or sea, in their way, passage and lodging, they might not experience any molestation or hindrance from any one."

But the provisions were really liberal, and protected the merchants from all that petty system of annoyance by which it is possible to destroy the effect of general regulations. It is true that the custom-house officers often tried to override these liberal regulations, and that the merchants, through the governments, had to remonstrate. But the original grants of permission were always repeated on demand. To the number of seventy-five, including the repetitions, these capitulations are given in Mac-Gregor's Commercial Tariffs, No. 8, "The Ottoman Empire," published by command in 1843.

We can give only four :—

"No. 30. That the English merchants, having once paid the customs at Constantinople, Aleppo, Alexandria, Scio, Smyrna, and other parts of our sacred dominions, not an asper more shall be taken or demanded from them at any other place, nor shall any obstacle be interposed to the exit of their merchandise.

"No. 39. That customs shall not be demanded or taken on the merchandise brought by them in their ships to Constantinople, or any other part of our sacred dominions, which they shall not (of their own free will) land with a view to sale.

"No. 51. That the merchants of the aforesaid nation, having once paid the customs on the merchandise imported into Constantinople, and other ports of our sacred dominions, and on those exported therefrom, as silks, camlets, and other goods, and, being unable to sell the said goods, are under the necessity of transporting them to Smyrna, Scio, and other ports ; on their arrival there, the governors and custom-house officers of such ports shall always accept their teskares, and forbear exacting any further duty on the said merchandise.

"No. 54. That the English merchants, having once paid the duties on their merchandise, at the rate of three per cent., and taken them out of their ships, no one shall demand or exact from them anything more without their consent ; and it was moreover expressly commanded, that the English merchants should not be molested or vexed in manner aforesaid, contrary to the capitulations."

These permissions are called capitulations because they are heads of what is granted only on one side. They are not treaties, for they stipulate nothing on the part of the Sovereign to whose subjects they were given.

In 1809 we made a Treaty of peace with Turkey, whom we had attacked without reason. Article IV. renewed what is called " The Treaty of Capitulations of the Turkish year 1086 (A.D. 1675)," and declared that they shall continue to be observed and maintained as if they had suffered no interruption.

The following is Article V. :—

" In return for the indulgence and good treatment afforded by the Sublime Porte to English merchants, with respect to their goods and property, as well as in all matters tending to facilitate their commerce, England shall reciprocally extend every indulgence and friendly treatment to the flag, subjects, and merchants of the Sublime Porte which may hereafter frequent the dominions of His Britannic Majesty for the purposes of commerce."

The return for the restoration of the capitulations which the Turkish Plenipotentiary expected was that three per cent. *ad valorem* should be the highest duty on Turkish trade with England; but Mr Adair said that this was not a proper thing to consider in a treaty of peace, but only in a treaty of commerce; and he said something about its being impossible under the Navigation Laws. This was true, but showed the injustice of England. The first part of Mr Adair's argument did not prevent him from accepting the confirmation of the capitulations in the Treaty.

There were other capitulations which, after the time of Charles II., were so extended that not only British merchants, but their descendants, are exempted from Turkish jurisdiction. This is no part of the reason why the sick man does not die. On the contrary, it is a most important part of the European Concert or conspiracy against the Ottoman Empire. We must, therefore, quote an anecdote which shows the extent to which this abuse has been carried :—

" The dragomans of the consulates go every day to the chief police office, and claim their respective subjects who may have been taken up during the night on their predatory excursions. On one occasion the British or the Austrian dragoman, it does not matter which, claimed a thief, who, in the usual course, was released. Two days later, a merchant had a large sum of money in his house, and, having been warned that his house was likely to be attacked, he applied for and received four Turkish policemen to guard his premises. An attempt to break in was made in the night by a band of burglars who did not know the house was guarded; resistance was made, pistols used, and two of the burglars killed. The dead bodies and the captured survivors were brought to the public station; and next morning, when the dragomans came to claim their own, the Zabtieh Pasha conducted one of them to the dead burglar, and said:—

"'There is your subject; you had better have left him in my hands two days ago, and he would not have had an opportunity of returning to his evil ways, and be in the state in which you now see him.'"[1]

A people that survives such a system as this must contain a principle of immortality.

Such a people are the Turks.

---

[1] "The East and the West," by the third Lord Stanley of Alderly, page 37.

XVIII.

EGYPT.

A LTHOUGH the events of the past eight or nine years—to say nothing of the modern fashion of Eastern travel—have familiarised most of us with the geography of Egypt, it may be convenient to introduce the necessarily rapid sketch of its history and present condition which is to form the subject of this afternoon's paper, by a brief notice of its physical area and limits.

A glance at the map will show that it occupies the north-eastern corner of the African Continent, where it is linked to Asia by the Isthmus of Suez, and separated from Europe by the Mediterranean Sea. Its shore-line along the old historic sea extends from Cape Hazaïf to El-Arish, the frontier of Palestine, and includes the three ports of Alexandria, Rosetta, and Damietta, to which has now to be added Port Saïd, at the entrance to the Suez Canal. Westwards, it is separated from the Fezzan and Tripoli by the Libyan Desert; and, eastwards, is bounded by a line drawn from El-Arish to Akabah, at the head of the Red Sea Gulf of that name; and thence, enclosing the Peninsula of Sinai, across to the western coast of the Red Sea down, at present, as far as Suakim; and, on the south, by the First Cataract at Assouan, about 400 miles as the crow flies from the Mediterranean, or nearly 600 if measured by the windings of the Nile.

The area thus enclosed was computed by the French survey, made during Napoleon's short occupation of the country, to be 115,000 square miles; but of this only some 10,000 were then cultivable, the rest being rocky and desert waste. Since then, improved irrigation has added nearly a fifth to this arable total; but owing to still defective methods of distributing the river water —on which the fertility of the whole depends—only some 5000 square miles are now under actual tillage. From Assouan, the old, mysterious river winds without an affluent—with, indeed, only two farther south, from its far-away source among the Equatorial lakes—down, nearly due north, through a narrow valley, which, though spreading at parts into spacious plains, closes in at others to the river's banks, and so averages a width of only about seven miles. Twelve miles below Cairo the great stream divides into two branches, which, forking north-east and north-west, form the great plain called, from its shape, the Delta, and empty themselves into the Mediterranean at Rosetta and Damietta. The five other ancient mouths of the river have long ago silted up, and their courses can now be hardly traced over the great alluvial flat and through the network of canals and lakes which interpose between the sea and this point. Strictly, Alexandria lies outside the Delta, but in common phrase the latter includes the whole of the cultivable land, as well east and west as within the two branches of the river. Few or no monumental remains of remote antiquity have as yet been found in this vast triangular tract of nearly 5000 square miles; but it is now the most densely populated and, with its great port of Alexandria, the most commercially active section of Egypt. In fertility, too, it is surpassed by only one other—the splendid valley of the Fayoum—which, formed by a deep sinuosity in the Libyan Mountains some 80 miles south-west of Cairo, and abundantly watered by an artificial cut from the Nile, blooms over 700 square miles with the most varied and luxuriant vegetation.

There remain only to mention the five Oases, those

"——— Tufted isles
That verdant rise amid the Libyan wilds,"

varying in size from the Great Oasis, of 200 miles long by 20 broad, to the small Wah-el-Sirvah, or Oasis of Ammon, famous as the site of the great Jovian temple and oracle, whose priests proclaimed Alexander's sonship to the god and foretold his mastery of the world. Without these, however, the upper river valley to Assouan, the Fayoum, and the Delta give a total area of about 12,000 square miles, which—*plus* the strip of Red Sea coast from Suez to Suakim, and the almost "no man's" wilderness of Sinai down to Akaba—may now be said to form the Egypt of the Khedive. Less than a dozen years ago Ismaïl Pasha claimed sovereignty from the Mediterranean to the Equator, but with the sacrifice of Gordon at Khartoum that bubble burst; and, although we now garrison an outpost at the Second Cataract, the Egypt proper of modern politics and trade—as that also of the Exodus—lies within the limits I have roughly sketched.

A couple of miles beyond this southern boundary of the First Cataract lies the sacred island of Philœ, the mythical burial-place of the great god Osiris. To the ancient Egyptian this was the most sacred spot on earth, more than Mecca to the Mussulman, or Calvary to the Christian, and the most solemn oath he could swear was, "By Him—the Un-named and Un-nameable—that sleeps in Philœ!" The temple ruins of this gem of the Nile are amongst the finest in Egypt; but as they lie beyond the strict frontier line, they can receive only this passing mention.

Such, then, are the present limits of Egypt proper—nearly as they were 6000 years ago—enclosing a cultivable area about equal to the square mileage of Belgium, or to that of our own four counties of Hertford, Lancashire, York, and Lincoln. Yet, small as this was and is, in historic interest and in the measure of its influence on human civilisation, this Valley of the Nile transcends every other country in the world. Historically, it is unique. While China and India were still wrapped in legendary mist, and long before even legend began the story of Europe anywhere between the Mediterranean and the White Sea, Egypt had a settled government and an advanced civilisation. Britain and Gaul were covered with primeval forest, and their inhabitants were nearly, if not altogether, as savage as are now the cannibals of New Guinea and the Solomon Islands; the semi-mythical War of Troy was yet 1000 years in the future, and both Buddha and Confucius were unborn for still 500 years later, when great cities, arts and sciences, an established religion, and a matured civil polity whose surviving monuments still excite the wonder and admiration of the traveller, already flourished in the realm of the Pharaohs. However chronologists may differ by not merely hundreds, but even thousands of years, certain it is that the antiquity of Greece and Rome is but a thing of yesterday as compared with the hoar antiquity of Egypt. From the Nile Valley it was that Greece derived the first inspirations of her art, her sciences, her literature; and improving them in the light and fulness of her own exquisite imagination, handed them down to imperial Rome, whose mission it was to diffuse them over Western Europe. Egypt was, in fact, the cradle of the world's civilisation, whence, over the great "Mid Sea," spread the influences which even yet are operative in redeeming the farthest parts of the earth from barbarism.

The historical evidence on which this claim to advanced civilisation in a remote antiquity rests is based on hieroglyphical

inscriptions on the Nilotic monuments, on papyri discovered
among their ruins, and on passages in the Hebrew Scriptures.
On many points, of course, the knowledge thus derived is vague
and imperfect ; but a collation of the whole authenticates Egyptian
annals nearly up to a level with those of Greece and Rome. So
far back, however, do these links in Nilotic history extend, that
chronologists differ, as I have said, in fixing their commencement,
not by centuries merely, but by more than 3000 years—Boëkh
reckoning it at 5702 B.C., and Sharpe at 2000 B.C. ; but Lepsius'
nearly mean computation of 3892 B.C. is generally accepted as the
most proximately accurate ; and from that sufficiently far back
point in the track of time, or near to it, we may date the beginning
of the first of the five eras into which Egyptian history divides
itself.

How and whence Egypt herself derived the earliest germs of
her civilisation, has much exercised and divided antiquarian
opinion.   But what seems to be the best supported conjecture is
that, far back in pre-historic time, an Aryan migration from
Western India, travelling from the Indus to the Persian Gulf, and
thence along the coast of Arabia to the shores of the Red Sea,
found its way into Abyssinia and Nubia, and there sowed the
seeds of arts and institutions which thence spread later down the
narrow channel of the Nile Valley, where they took root and
ripened into the cultured civilisation that glorified Memphis and
Thebes long before Cecrops laid the first crude brick of Athens,
or Abraham drove his flocks from Chaldea.   This hypothesis is
supported by the striking resemblance which is known to exist
between the usages, the superstitions, and the mythology of the
ancient inhabitants of Western India and those of the first settlers
on the Upper Nile.   Thus the temples of Nubia exhibit the same
features, whether as to style of architecture or the form of worship
to which they were devoted, with the similar buildings near Bom-
bay.   In both countries large masses of rock have been excavated
into hollow chambers, the sides of which are decorated with
columns and statues of men and animals carved out of the same
stone ; and in both are found solid blocks weighing many hundred
tons, separated from the adjoining mountain, and lifted into the
air by mechanical methods, the secret of which puzzles the ablest
of our modern engineers.   Nor are these architectural resemblances
the only features in common between Western India and the long
strip of country watered by the Nile.   Others of nearly equal
historical value have been recognised by archæologists, which

similarly support this conjecture of early connection between the two countries.

But whatever may have been the genesis of Egyptian civilisation, we reach its historical commencement somewhere about 4000 B.C., near to which Manetho, a native priest who wrote in Greek about 300 B.C., placed the beginning of the first of the thirty dynasties which, with three hundred or more sovereigns, filled the long span of time down to B.C. 527, when the first of the five eras was closed with the conquest of the Persians under Cambyses. Agreeing with Herodotus, who visited Egypt 150 years earlier, Manetho—probably founding his "Chronicle" on documents then in existence—named King Menes as the first of the native monarchs who throughout that long chain of sovereignty ruled this Land of Egypt. To Menes or his immediate successor is ascribed the foundation of Memphis, at an easy day's donkey ride from where Cairo now stands, and the sole relic of whose long-dead magnificence is a prone statue of Rameses II., the greatest of all the Pharaohs. It is not, however, till towards the end of the third dynasty, some 500 years later, that Pharaonic history begins to be inscribed on the monuments, and that we have in them, except during two great gaps, definite, if not indisputable, records of what followed. On this authority we know that the great Pyramids of Ghizeh, near Cairo, were built by Pharaoh Shufus—the Cheops of Herodotus—who reigned conjointly with his brother during the fourth dynasty, any time between B.C. 3200 and B.C. 2300, as chronologists differently reckon. Of these oldest and grandest of human monuments, which by book and picture are now familiar to the most untravelled, I need merely say that the slightly higher of the two called "Great" occupies an area of eleven acres— about equal to that of Lincoln's Inn Fields—with a height of 480 eet, or 127 feet higher than the cross of St. Paul's. Like most visitors to these colossal "memorials of the world's faith," I have explored the interior and climbed to the summit of the larger one ; but while the long crawl inwards and upwards to the mortuary chamber in its centre was rewarded only by the sight of Pharaoh's empty sarcophagus, the view from the top a hundred times repaid the fatigue of the ascent. Seemingly close below, though nearly ten miles off, lies Cairo in all its Oriental picturesqueness, its domes, minarets, and feathery palm-clumps rising clear and sharp in this most pellucid of atmospheres ; behind it the range of the Mokattem hills, trending in broken links to the Red Sea ; north-wards, beyond the lonely obelisk of Heliopolis, the luxuriant vegetation of the Delta stretching away to the lakes that separate it from the Mediterranean; while east and west flows the sacred and mysterious Nile, dotted far into the distance with sails that flash in the sun; nearer, the palm-groves that wave over buried Memphis; beyond these, the scattered smaller pyramids of Sakara and Dashour; and, farther away, the winding valley of Upper Egypt losing itself in the hazy distance half-way up to Thebes. There is, indeed, no other view in Egypt, and few in the world, to compare with that which delights the eye and feeds the imagination from this Great Pyramid top. The second of these huge mountains of stone is some forty feet lower, with proportionately narrower base; but as it stands on higher ground, the difference in size is hardly perceptible. On the same plateau cluster six other smaller pyramids—the whole, it may now be taken as proved, forming part of the great royal necropolis of Memphis. They are the grandest graves in the world, but—despite the ingenious theories of Professor Piazzi Smyth—they are nothing more.

In a sand-hollow a few hundred yards south-east of the Great Pyramid, stands, or rather crouches, the colossal Sphinx—"gazing straight on with calm eternal eyes" across the vista of seven thousand years, for, according to Mariette Bey, the famous French Egyptologist, it was already old before the stupendous gnomon of Cheops was built. But of this again no description need be attempted. From Pliny to the latest book-maker on Nile travel, its solemn and majestic presence has been the theme of a hundred pens. The prophetic rhapsody of Eothen may, however, be once more quoted: "Upon ancient dynasties of Ethiopian and Egyptian kings, upon Greek and Roman, upon Arab and Ottoman conquerors, upon Napoleon dreaming of an Eastern Empire, upon battle and pestilence, upon the ceaseless misery of the Egyptian race, upon keen-eyed travellers—Herodotus yesterday, Warburton to-day—upon all and more this unworldly Sphinx has watched, and watched with a Providence, with the same earnest eyes, and the same sad, tranquil mien. And we, we shall die, and Islam wither away; and the Englishman, straining far over to hold his loved India, will plant a firm foot on the banks of the Nile, and sit in the seats of the Faithful; and still that shapeless rock will be watching and watching the works of the new busy race, with those same sad, earnest eyes, and the same tranquil mien everlasting."

More than mere allusion to the other great monumental antiqui-

ties of Egypt would be beyond the scope of this paper; and I
need, therefore, only say that they nearly all lie south of Cairo,
scattered along the river from the rock-tombs of Beni-hassan to
Abydos, Denderah, Thebes, Esneh, Edfou, and Philœ—the
shattered but still splendid memorials of a dead faith and civilisation
with which the world can nowhere else show anything to compare.
To those who care for scholarly and picturesque description of
nearly the whole, I can recommend no better guide than Miss
Amelia B. Edwards's *Thousand Miles up the Nile*, a book which
is most valued by those who know Egypt best.

From reference to these relics of far-away time, it is hardly
a transition to return to the chronological point at which I
digressed—the fourth of Manetho's thirty dynasties, which ended
somewhere about 2000 B.C. The records of the fifth and sixth
offer little that is of modern interest, except, perhaps, the fact of
Abraham's visit to the Egyptian Court during the reign of Pharaoh
Phiops (of the sixth), about 1900 B.C. Of the next four dynasties,
which covered some 500 years, nothing is certainly known, as the
monuments are again silent, and Manetho's names and dates,
unless based on papyri which no longer exist, can at best be
conjectural. During the twelfth it was that Joseph the Hebrew
was "found in a pit," and was, some years afterwards, when
"learned in all the wisdom of the Egyptians," promoted to be the
prime minister of Pharaoh Osirtesen I., somewhere about B.C.
1700. From the thirteenth to the seventeenth dynasty occurs
another long monumental blank, during some 500 or more years
of which, it is believed, occurred the invasion and rule of the
Hyksos, or shepherd kings, who were apparently of Arab race.
These aliens were at length got rid of by a rebellion promoted by
the native Prince Aáhmes I., of the eighteenth dynasty. During this
and the following dynasty, Egypt attained perhaps her highest point
of civilisation. Then it was (in the nineteenth) flourished the great
Rameses, whose colossal statue, as already remarked, is now the sole
relic of Memphis. Seventeen centuries after this greatest of the
Pharaohs had been interred in the superb temple which his genius
and power had erected at Thebes, Germanicus visited that famous
capital, and the Egyptian priests, as Tacitus relates, read to him from
the monumental records the deeds and victories, the treasures and
tributes, the resources and the subject realms of this great king.
His empire stretched northward to the shores of the Caspian,
southward beyond the Second Cataract, westward to the interior
of the desert, and eastward it included Arabia. His son and

successor, Pharaoh Menephta, is generally identified as the
Pharaoh of the Exodus. And here may, perhaps, be conveniently
mentioned the explanation now accepted by the best modern
criticism of the alleged miraculous passage of the Red Sea by the
flying Israelites and the destruction of their Egyptian pursuers.

Brugsch Bey, a German *savant*, who spent several years investi-
gating Egyptian archæology during the reign of the late Khedive
Ismail, and whom—as also the late Mariette Bey and Professor
Maspero, along with Brugsch, the greatest of modern Egyptologists—I have had the pleasure of meeting more than once at
Cairo, has given special attention to this subject, and has, it may
fairly be said, demonstrated the route taken by the Israelites, and
rationally shown how their passage of the Red Sea took place.
There is evidence that even in historic times what is now called
the Gulf of Suez extended as far north as, and included, Lake
Timsah, now nearly about midway in the Suez Canal. By the
time of the Israelites, however, it had, through evaporation and
other physical causes still in slow operation, receded to the Bitter
Lakes, and a shallow had been formed between those deeper
depressions and the present northern extremity of the Gulf. Up
south-eastwards of Lake Timsah travelled the Israelites from the
Land of Goshen to this ford, and here, during a favourable wind
which left it nearly dry, they crossed to the other side of the
Gulf. The pursuing Egyptians, endeavouring to follow at the
same point, were caught by a change of wind which swept the
southern waters up over the ford, with the result of engulfing
Pharaoh and his host before they could pass. That the Hebrew
writer, full of belief in the special providence of his tribal God for
his people, should have regarded and recorded this as a miracle
expressly wrought in their behalf was natural enough, and the
modern orthodox acceptance of this view has been consistent
with—indeed necessitated by—the now generally obsolete dogma of
plenary inspiration. But with the surrender of this, miracle in the
matter loses its *raison d'être*, and the most religious mind may well
accept an explanation of the event which is at once sufficient,
rational, and naturalistic. The date of it, I may add, is generally
fixed about 1650 B.C.

The records of the next three dynasties furnish little of
modern interest, but early in the twenty-third Egyptian and
Hebrew history begin to synchronise during the reign of Pharaoh
Shishak, who, as recorded on the propylon of the great temple of
Karnak and in the twelfth chapter of Second Chronicles, besieged

and captured Jerusalem about 970 B.C. His successor, Osorthen, is also probably the Zerah of the Bible, who was defeated at Mareshah by Asa, King of Judah. Again, some 350 years later, after various alternations of friendship and hostility between the two kingdoms, the twenty-third chapter of Second Kings similarly confirms the Theban hieroglyphs in recording the defeat of Josiah, King of Judah, at Megiddo, by Pharaoh Nechoh, and his own subsequent overthrow by Nebuchadnezzar. Less than ninety years later, the Pharaonic era virtually ended with the twenty-seventh of Manetho's dynasties, when, in 527 B.C., the Persians under Cambyses invaded Egypt, and for nearly 200 years reduced it to the rank of a Persian province. During most of this time, however, a native revolt was kept alive in Upper Egypt by the princes of three further dynasties until, in 350 B.C., Nectanebus II. was driven into Ethiopia, and with him—the very last of the Pharaohs—closed this longest and grandest era in Egyptian history, extending over more than 3500 years.

Here, perhaps, would be the point at which to say something about the religion of the ancient Egyptians, which coloured and gave their character to the whole polity and social life of the nation during this long span of time. But as much has yet to be sketched, I must content myself with saying that it is still an unsolved problem whether the Egyptians believed in one supreme God, whose attributes were merely symbolised in their numerous deities, or whether the whole structure of their faith resolved itself into a solar myth with many ramifications. Amoun-Ra, the Sun god, is certainly the most ancient object of worship found upon the monuments; but whether the great luminary was merely regarded as the visible type of a supreme and invisible deity, or was itself adored as the paramount divinity of an extended Polytheism, is what the most authoritative Egyptologists much dispute. Be the theological fact what it may, Herodotus describes the Egyptians as "extremely religious, and surpassing all men in the worship they rendered to their gods." But on the religious belief and worship of this remarkable people, as on much else respecting them, I cannot do better than refer any curious hearer to Dr. Birch's admirable *Guide* to the Egyptian Rooms of the British Museum, in which a concise but most scholarly statement of our existing knowledge on the subject will be found.

The second, or Persian, era of Egyptian history lasted less than 200 years, when, in 332 B.C., the Greek era began with the easy conquest of the country by Alexander the Great. The mission of Egypt in the great economy of the world's history may now be considered to have terminated. The spirit of the ancient race, long a flickering flame, died out completely with the appearance of the great Macedonian. The nation was well prepared for the change. A long commercial and military intercourse with Greece had saturated it with Greek ideas; just as the literature, art, and religion of Greece had already been largely coloured by the literature, art, and religion of the land of the Pharaohs. Hellenic colonies had sprung up along the Red Sea. The Thebaid had been traversed by Greek historians and philosophers. Greek soldiers mustered in the Egyptian court. Greek settlements were planted in the Delta. In fact, the condition of things in Egypt in the fourth and fifth centuries before Christ may be compared to that which, 1500 years later, prevailed in England during the reign of Edward the Confessor; so that the people in both countries underwent a long preparation for the introduction of a new dynasty and an alien government. Just as England was Normanised before the conquest, so was Egypt still more Hellenised before its subjugation by Alexander.

Of this third era of Nilotic history I have time to say little more than that the Macedonian conqueror introduced no violent changes into the laws and local government of the country. While garrisoning it with a Greek force, he restored the privileges of the priests and repaired the temples of the deities. His chief work was the founding of Alexandria, in B.C. 332—a monument which, even if he had no other, will sufficiently perpetuate his name. At his death, in B.C. 322, the vast empire constructed by his genius fell to pieces, and Egypt fell to Ptolemy Soter, one of his generals, under whom the country was still further Hellenised. The abstract religion of the priests of Osiris and Pthah was dethroned, and a misty philosophical theurgy with a poetical mythology of Egyptian gods with Greek attributes, reigned in its stead. Alexandria gathered within its walls the learning of the age. Ptolemy Philadelphus, the second of this Greek line, founded the celebrated Alexandrian Library, encouraged the Septuagint version of the Hebrew Bible, and patronised the labours of the historian Manetho, already mentioned. Under his two successors, the intellectual and industrial activity thus promoted still further expanded, and commerce developed until the merchants of Alexandria supplied half Europe with corn, linen, papyrus, and all the rich products of the East. Time compels me to pass over the remaining eight of the twelve sovereigns of this time (three of whom were women) who ruled Egypt for 300 years, till we reach the last of them, the famous Cleopatra, whose beauty and passion—as wildly reciprocated by the great Roman—wrought ruin for herself and Antony. With much of her history Shakespeare has familiarised all readers of our tongue ; and I need say nothing, therefore, to remind any one of how, after beguiling Julius Cæsar himself, she next, after his death, threw the magic of her beauty and her address over Mark Antony, or of how, after her cowardice or treachery had lost him the battle of Actium and the dominion of the world, he followed her to Alexandria, and, there for love of her, found death on his own sword. Shakespeare makes her in turn kill herself by an asp-bite, to escape the humiliation of figuring in a Roman triumph ; but, in strict history, there is no proof of how she ended her wild and passionate life by her own hand, B.C. 30.

With the death of Cleopatra, Egypt ceased to exist as an independent kingdom ; and, except during the brief interlude of a second Persian occupation, was for 670 years ruled as a province of the Empire by Roman prefects. Although disturbed by several native revolts, the Romans, with their usual energy, largely developed the revenue and resources of the country, until it became the rich and abounding granary of the Empire. But the chief modern interest of this period lies in the rise and growth of Christianity in Alexandria, where a fierce warfare was maintained during the third and fourth centuries between the partisans of the new faith and the decaying influences of Paganism. Then followed conflicts as bitter beween the victorious Christian factions themselves, one swearing by Arius, and the other by Athanasius (the latter, by the way, not being the author of the creed which goes by his name). In A.D. 379, the Emperor Theodosius gave its official deathblow to the old native religion by an edict prohibiting the worship of idols, and ordering as many of the temples as had not already been converted into Christian Churches to be closed. And thenceforth the splendid fanes with which the piety and the magnificence of the Pharaohs and the Ptolemies had crowded the banks of the Nile, fell into the decay in which the modern tourist finds them. But the old religion died hard, and for more than a century later numbered amongst its adherents most of the learned and scientific classes, and the students of the

schools of philosophy for which Alexandria had become famous
One of the best remembered incidents of the persecution which
was waged against these was the savage murder—at the instigation
of Cyril, the bishop of Alexandria—of the beautiful Neo-Platonist
philosopher, Hypatia, the daughter of Theon the mathematician,
and familiar to us all as the heroine of Kingsley's fine novel that
bears her name,—one of the thousand historic illustrations that
between so-called Christian and Pagan fanaticism there has never
been much to choose.

With its conversion to Christianity, the history of ancient Egypt
may be said to close. Over its later annals, until quite modern
times, I must pass rapidly. In A.D. 640 the Greco-Roman
dominion came to an end with the invasion and conquest by the
Arabs, under Amrou, the lieutenant of the Caliph Omar, the
second successor of Mahomet. The conqueror offered the
Prophet's usual terms to the vanquished—conversion, tribute, or
the sword. A large proportion of the Coptic (or old native)
population, whose Christianity was only skin-deep, accepted the
first, and readily embraced Islam, while the remainder and the
Greco-Romans elected to pay tribute. To this great apostasy of
Christian Copts was in a few years added a large Moslem immigration from east and west; and thus, besides the ruling caste, chiefly
Arabs of pure blood from the Hedjaz, was formed the great
labouring class whom we call the fellaheen, and who now number
nearly four-fifths of the whole population of Egypt. Of these, the
majority, especially in Upper Egypt, have preserved the closest
feature resemblance to their sculptured and pictured ancestry on
the monuments; and, as Champollion and later Egyptologists
have proved, the Coptic language, which now survives only in
their Church liturgy, is as unmistakably the old Pharaonic tongue.
In it, therefore,. we have still a link with the far-off time of five,
six, or seven thousand years ago.[1]

---

[1] The clue to this lingual mystery was supplied by the discovery, in 1799,
of the Rossetta Stone, near the little Delta port from which it takes its name.
This basaltic block, which now forms one of the treasures of the British
Museum, bears on its polished front a tri-lingual inscription in Hieroglyphical,
Demotic, and Greek characters, purporting to be a decree of the priests of
Egypt in Council at Memphis, in honour of Ptolemy V. (about B.C. 196).
This guided Dr. Young in 1818 and Champollion three years later (quite
independently) to the true principles of hieroglyphic interpretation, and became
in fact the key to the whole hieroglyphic literature on monument and
papyrus which has been so fruitfully studied by later Egyptologists.

For more than three centuries after the Mahometan conquest, Egypt remained a province of the Baghdad Caliphate until, in 970, Moez, the fourth of the rival Fatimite Caliphs who reigned in North Africa, conquered the country, built Cairo, and made it the seat of government. This dynasty ruled Egypt for two hundred years, when, in 1171, on the death of its last sovereign, his Vizier, the famous Saladin, the chivalrous hero of the Crusades, seized the vacant throne.

Not being a descendant of Mahomet, he could not assume the Caliphate, and so took merely the title of Sultan, thus severing the secular from the religious sovereignty, which continued to be represented by a son of the late Caliph. As the theatre of this great prince's main achievements lay outside Egypt, I need say nothing of his successful resistance to the combined forces and the best military genius of nearly all Europe in the Holy Land. For is it not all written in Mill's *History*, Gibbon's *Decline and Fall*, and a score of other chronicles of the time?

Saladin died at Damascus in 1193, and then, sixty years later, followed the revolution of the Mamelukes, a numerous body of guards composed of Turkish and Circassian slaves whom the great Sultan and his successors had organised and drilled beyond any other Eastern soldiery of the time. For about 130 years these mixed mercenaries ruled Egypt, till, towards the end of the fourteenth century, the Circassians overthrew the Turkish Mamelukes, and for another hundred years monopolised the anarchical government that followed. Then came the Ottoman conquest, under Sultan Selim I., in 1517—the next, and as yet the last, dynastic land-mark in Egyptian history.

In historical justice, and to avoid the baldness of mere chronology, I should here say a word as to the indebtedness of Egyptian literature and art to these Saracenic dynasties. First at Alexandria, and afterwards at Cairo—as in Syria, at Baghdad, and in Spain, the Caliphs fostered learning and the arts with a munificence unequalled by either their Greek or Roman predecessors, and which stands in still more marked historic contrast to the neglect of both by their Tartar successors of Stamboul. Besides themselves founding many great libraries and colleges for the higher education, they encouraged the endowment of secondary and primary schools by private liberality, till almost every town and village of the country had its *medreeseh* or *kouttba*. Thus it was that while Europe was sunk in the intellectual gloom of the Middle Ages, Egypt again became the home of science and

philosophy, which flourished there as, after the decline of the
Baghdad Caliphate, they flourished nowhere else but in the
Moorish colleges of Spain. With the fall of the Fatimites, this
splendid patronage ceased, and thence on through the turbulent
Mameluke reigns and the still more anarchic times which followed
the Turkish conquest, Egyptian learning steadily declined, till the
savants who accompanied Bonaparte's expedition found even in
Cairo hardly a trace of the letters and art that were rivalling those
of Cordova and Seville when Peter preached the first Crusade.
If learning and the arts, therefore, have declined in Egypt, it is
but fair to note that not Islam, but the rule of the Turk, which
blights wherever it falls, is to blame for the fact.

For two hundred and fifty years Turkish Pashas, commissioned
from Stamboul, exercised from Cairo a fitful vice-sovereignty over
the Delta and the Nile Valley.   But the power of the Mamelukes,
who still constituted the military force of the province, had been
only scotched ; and during the latter years of this period they
recovered much of their former authority, with the result of such
anarchy as rendered the country an easy conquest for Napoleon
in 1798, when, in the historic battle of the Pyramids, he crushed
the force of all the Mameluke Beys, and made himself master of
the country, till driven out of it by the British under Abercromby
and Hutchinson in 1801.   Then, on our retirement, came to the
front Mehemet Ali, the son of an Albanian petty trader at Cavalla
in Macedonia, who had come to Egypt as one of a small Turkish
contingent in time to be badly beaten by the French at Aboukir.
His courage and energy had, however, so distinguished him that,
soon after the British left, he had won such popularity with the
army and the Cairene skeikhs that, in 1805, these together
proclaimed him Viceroy, and the Porte deemed it politic to recall
its own nominee and ratify the nomination of the young Albanian
brigadier.

How the new *vali*, or governor, as his official title was, in turn
baffled the intrigues of the Stamboul divan to effect his overthrow,
how he made himself sole master of Egypt by exterminating the
Mamelukes, rescued the Hedjaz from the Wahabees, organised a
powerful army and navy on the European system, annexed the
Soudan, conquered Syria, and, after annihilating the Turkish army
at Koniah in 1832, would have carried his victorious standards to
the Bosphorus if Russia had not interposed, I need not tell.   As
little need be said of the hollow treaty which recognised his
feudal sovereignty over Egypt, Crete, Syria, and the large district

of Adana in Asia Minor, on the sole condition of his paying tribute. Fresh complications followed in 1839, when the total defeat of the Turks by Ibrahim Pasha at Nezib reopened the defiles of the Taurus to the victors, and but for the speedy intervention of the European Powers would have placed Asia Minor and Constantinople itself at their mercy. But here our own Government interfered, and the operations of Stopford and Napier on the coast of Syria forced Mehemet Ali to surrender that province and content himself with the international recognition of his own and his family's right to Egypt only. This was guaranteed by the treaty of 1840 between the Porte and the European Powers; and his title to Egypt having been thus affirmed, by the public law of Europe, Mehemet Ali devoted himself during the next seven years to the social and material improvement of the country, with an aggregate of results which has fixed his place in history as the " Peter the Great " of Egypt. Indeed, except some additions and further reforms made during the reign of his reputed grandson, Ismail Pasha, the whole administrative system, up till less than ten years ago, was, in the main, his work ; and notwithstanding many admitted defects, it was at his death incomparably the most civilised and efficient of then existing Mussulmen Governments.

In 1848, this great satrap, then verging on his eightieth year, was attacked by a mental malady, induced, as it was said, by a potion administered in mistaken kindness by one of his own daughters, and the government was taken over by his adopted son, Ibrahim Pasha, the hero of Koniah and Nezib. He lingered till August 1849, but Ibrahim had already pre-deceased him; and Abbas, a son of the latter, succeeded to the viceregal throne. Though born and bred in Egypt, Abbas was a Turk of the worst type—ignorant, cowardly, sensual, fanatic, and opposed to reforms of every sort. Thus his feeble reign of less than six years was, in almost everything, a period of retrogression. On a night in July 1854, he was strangled in his sleep by a couple of his own slaves,—acting, it was variously said, on a secret order from Constantinople, or at the behest of one of his wives.

To Abbas succeeded Saïd, the third son of Mehemet Ali, an amiable and liberal-minded prince who retrieved much of the mischief done by his predecessor, but lacked the vigorous intelligence and force of character required to carry on the great work begun by his father. His reign will be chiefly memorable for the concession and commencement of the Suez Canal, the colossal work which, while benefiting the trade of the world, has cost so much to Egypt. Saïd died in January 1863, and was succeeded by his nephew Ismaïl Pasha, the second son of Ibrahim.

As most of the leading incidents of this Prince's reign, as also the chief features of his character, are still fresh in the public memory, I need merely recall a few of the more salient of both. Amongst the former, history will give the first place to his creation of the huge public debt which forms the main element of a problem that still confronts Europe. But, for this the same impartial judge will at least equally blame the financial panderers who ministered to his extravagance, with exorbitant profit to themselves, but at ruinous cost to Egypt. On the other hand, it is but historical justice to say that Ismaïl did much for the material progress of the country. He added more than a 1000 to the 200 miles of railway in existence at the death of Saïd. He greatly improved the irrigation, and so increased the cultivable area of the country; multiplied the primary schools, and encouraged native industries. For so much, at least, history will give him credit. As memorable, though less meritorious, were the magnificent fêtes with which, in 1869, he opened the Suez Canal, the great work which England had so long opposed, but through which—as if by the irony of history—the first ship that passed flew the English flag, and to the present traffic of which we contribute more than eighty per cent. In personal character, Ismaïl was of exceptional intelligence, but cruel, crafty, and untrustworthy both in politics and in his private relations. At length, when no longer able to pay the usurious interest exacted by the bondholders, our own and the French Governments— moved by Messrs. Frühling and Goschen and the other influential loanmongers—in 1879 induced the Sultan to depose him and set up his son, Mehemet Tewfik, in his stead. It may be mentioned that Ismaïl Pasha was the first of these Ottoman Viceroys who bore the title of "Khedive," which is a Perso-Arabic designation signifying rank a shade less than regal. This he obtained in 1867 by heavy bribes to the Sultan and his chief ministers, as he had the year before by similar means ousted his brother and uncle from the succession, and secured it for his own eldest son,—in virtue of which the latter now nominally reigns.

Of Ismaïl since his fall, a word or two will suffice. Carrying away with him an enormous private fortune, he settled for a time in Naples, and thence, for some years, made frequent and lengthened visits to Rome, Paris, London, and elsewhere, on errands of unsuccessful intrigue, to recover his lost throne. Then, having everywhere failed, in 1888 he shook the dust of the West from his feet, and turned in hopeless resignation to the Mecca of fallen Pashas—Stamboul—and there, in a palace by the Bosphorus, he now lives a virtual State prisoner. Had he played his part better, he might, with the full sympathy of Europe, have been the independent sovereign of a restored Arab kingdom. As it is, he is politically as dead as the Pharaohs.

Before, in conclusion, rapidly reviewing the decade since Ismaïl's fall, a word may be here conveniently said as to the actual social and religious condition of the country which he so wastefully ruled for nearly seventeen years. Its population—which includes Arabs, Copts, Turks, Nubians, Greeks, Jews, Armenians, and Levantines of every shade of mixed Eastern and European blood—numbers in all about 6,000,000, of whom the settled Arabs (or fellaheen) exceed 4,500,000, who are all Mussulmans. The Christian Copts reckon about 500,000; the Nomad Bedouin acknowledging allegiance to the Khedive (who are also Mussulmans), about 350,000; the Turks, chiefly descendants of the official class since the Conquest, about 15,000; the Nubians, hitherto mostly slaves, but now practically freed by quite recent law, about 50,000; native Greeks and Jews, each about 20,000; Abyssinians, 5000; Armenians, 15,000; and Syrians and various foreigners, about 100,000.

Of this total, the felaheen almost monopolise the agriculture. The Copts, also in part farmers, are mainly handicraftsmen and clerks in the Government Offices. The Nubians and Abyssinians are mostly domestic servants; the Jews, Greeks, and Armenians, shopkeepers and traders; and the foreigners anything and everything for which such a field offers an opening. Thanks to recent English administration, the revenue of about £10,000,000 raised from this mixed aggregate now leaves a small surplus over expenditure; and but for the exactions of Mr. Goschen's clients, the bondholders, the taxation which this entails might be greatly reduced. As it is, the fellaheen—for the first time in Egyptian history—if still heavily taxed, are no longer fiscally plundered and oppressed.

Of the religion of this large majority of the Egyptian population, I have the courage to say that I esteem it much above the pseudo-Christianity of the minority. As the result of long residence and wide travel in the East, I do not hesitate to testify that Islam—away from the corrupt administrative centres—is, in point both of faith and morals, a higher religion than the debased Christianity of nearly all the Eastern Churches. I go farther, and say that the Mohametanism of most of these Egyptian fellaheen, as of the moral Turks of Asia Minor, embodies more truth and less error than did the Papacy in its grosser form. Thus, the faith of Saladin was essentially more Christian than that of Cœur de Lion, and Mecca was the shrine of a purer worship than mediæval Rome. Little is it to be wondered at that, in Egypt and throughout the East generally, with such illustrations of Christianity before their eyes, both Arab and Turk have been proof against the Western missionary.

The virtual bankruptcy in which Ismail left the country speedily bore fruit in administrative collapse and military revolt, the latter headed by the notorious Arabi, now a State prisoner in Ceylon. Of our own inglorious bombardment of Alexandria, in the alleged interest of restored order, the less said the better; even though the commanding Admiral received a peerage, the thanks of Parliament, and £30,000 for silencing a few old-fashioned forts with a fleet of modern iron-clads, and the burning of Alexandria thrown in. As rapidly would I slur over our subsequent not more glorious operations on land, in which a British army corps routed Arabi's rabble at Tel-el-Kebir— with similar extravagant reward to the General in command. These, and our subsequent costly but futile campaign on the Upper Nile, culminating in the tragical failure to save Gordon at Khartoum, will form a chapter in Egyptian history of which no Englishman, of any party, can be proud. But, in spite of all this honourless blundering, the stars in their courses have been too strong for our so-called statesmanship; and although, in 1883, I heard Lord Hartington, in reply to a question in the House of Commons, promise that our last redcoat should have cleared out of Egypt within six months from that time, our flag (as I then ventured to predict) still floats over Cairo, and from Alexandria to the Second Cataract our protectorate is now an accomplished—if as yet diplomatically an unacknowledged— fact. Mehemet Tewfik reigns, but we rule; and great has already been the gain to Egypt. For the first time for more than six thousand years, a just, merciful, and uncorrupt Government is being established—such as from Menes to Ismail has never ruled the Nile Valley before. Although in party politics my own vote is not given to Lord Salisbury, I frankly admit that much of the credit for this is due to the policy of more courage and greater regard for our national interests in Egypt which he has followed during the past four years. But *Kismet*, Fate, the Providence which shapes events, underlies and directs it all; and, so far as human prescience can forecast, the Englishman *has* planted a firm foot on the banks of the Nile, and will keep it there until, in turn, the star of our own Empire sets. Having put our hand to the plough, we cannot now draw it back.

XIX.

SERVIA AND MONTENEGRO.

J. C. COTTON MINCHIN.

MY lecture is styled "Servia and Montenegro," but the people that inhabit the two territories known on the map as Servia and Montenegro are one and the same. If you ask a Montenegrin what language he speaks, he replies, "Serb."

The last of the Serb Czars fell gloriously fighting at Kossovo in 1389. To this day the Montenegrin wears a strip of black silk upon his headgear in memory of that fatal day.

In the present lecture I shall endeavour to trace the history of the Serb race from the earliest times, and to describe the fall and resurrection of this brave but unfortunate people.

Early in the seventh century, in the reign of the Emperor Heraclius, the Asiatic provinces of the Eastern Roman Empire were overrun by the Arabs, and adopted the Mahommedan religion. In the same reign the Serbs settled south of the Danube in the regions where they are now found. These countries are to-day severally known as Servia, Old Servia, Bosnia, and Herzogovina. Roughly speaking, the north-western slice of the Balkan Peninsular has been inhabited by Serbs from the seventh century after Christ. Montenegro was then and for many centuries later without any permanent population. Even as late as the fifteenth century the Black Mountain was only visited by herdsmen during the summer season. If we take a bird's-eye view of this primitive Servia, we see a race of shepherds inhabiting the banks of the Drina, the Bosna, and the Morava, and driving their flocks in summer weather to those lofty mountains, where, as the national songs relate, the darkness of the forest is relieved by white rocks or perpetual snows. For centuries the Serbs lived under the rule of native chiefs, solely of their own election. This government was patriarchal, but not national. The scattered tribes did not yet constitute a State. A national King was yet to come. In the ninth century the Serbs and

343

Bulgarians were converted to Christianity. The Apostle of the Slavs, "*Mithodius*," was one of the world's greatest men. He was not only the missionary of the Slavs, but the greatest of Slav patriots, for he is credited with creating the Slavonic alphabet. Although the creed adopted by the Serbs was that of the Eastern Church, they always remained attached to a national as opposed to the Greek Church of Constantinople. To the Western Division of Christianity they were ecclesiastically opposed; to the Eastern, politically.

It is the fashion in some quarters to disparage monastic establishments; but the fact remains, that it is mainly to the monasteries that the Serbs owe the retention not only of their religion, but of their nationality. When the waters of Turkish oppression covered Servia, the monasteries formed the arks of Christian faith and freedom. There seems no reasonable doubt that the conversion of Bosnians to Islamism was due to the few religious Houses in their country. It has been the misfortune of Servia to have suffered at the hands of her neighbours. Greeks, Venetians, Turks, Austrians, and Russians have each in turn been a thorn in her side. The earliest records of her history are a record of attempts by the Greek or Eastern Empire to absorb her. These attempts commence with the fourth century, and proved unsuccessful. Three hundred years later (1353) the Turks crossed the Hellespont. The Eastern Empire was then sunk into absolute impotence. The Bulgarian kingdom was "nodding to its fall." Servia alone of the Balkan lands was prosperous and powerful. During the thirteenth century the aim of a Serb king was to acquire a firm footing on the Adriatic. His title was, "By the grace of God, King of all Serbian lands and to the sea coast." With the fourteenth century his ambition took a wider flight eastwards as well as westwards. Stephen Dushan, the most famous of Serb emperors, could not as such ask for the obedience of the Greeks; he therefore called himself the Macedonian Christ-loving Czar. A monarch so powerful as Stephen Dushan, Emperor of the Serbs, Bulgarians, and Greeks, seemed destined by Providence to check the advances of the Turks. The Osmanli entered Europe in 1353—Stephen Dushan died on his march to Constantinople in 1355. His death was followed by anarchy in Servia. On the 15th June 1389 was fought between the Turks, the Serbs, Bosnians, and Albanians the battle of Kossovo. Both the Serb "Krajl" and the Turkish Sultan were slain. Further details are lost, but the result is only too well known.

Near Vranja, in a gloomy mountain pass, there stand the ruins
of a Roman fortress. Such they are to the antiquary, but to the
peasant they are the ruins of a castle of Kralevitch Marko.
The rocky mountains which stand on either side of the castle are
called the Hill of the Cross and the Hill of Weeping, because
there the hero of Serb legend first heard the news of Kossovo.
Ever since that day till within the memory of living men, the Serbs
may truly be said to have borne the cross and wept. They have
been the scapegoats for the sins of Europe. As Mr. Gladstone
once expressed it, they were the barren beach upon which the wave
of Ottoman conquest broke, while behind them flourished the
harvests of culture and of commerce. To continue the metaphor,
so strong was the wave that it carried all before it—even up to the
gates of Vienna. We only know Turkey in its decrepitude; in
Nisch we have a reminder of what a power she once was. The
bridge across the Nischava bears the following inscription :—

"Constructed by Vizier Mehemet Pasha, Governor General of Buda
Pesth, 1611."

The Norman Conquest of England was effected by a race not
more numerous than the English. Servia was overwhelmed by a
race that could boast of an empire that stretched from Adrianople
to [Bagdad, and from the Caucasus to the Straits of Gibraltar.
But even to this mighty wave of Conquest there were limits.
Bulgaria, Constantinople, Greece, and Bosnia all in turn suc-
cumbed to the Turk. The brave Serbs who escaped from
Kossovo found a sanctuary in the mountains that overlook the
Bay of Cattaro. Their leader, Ivo, surnamed Tsernoi (Black),
gave the name of Tzrnogora (Montenegro) to these desert rocks.

I well remember entering Montenegro from Dalmatia. We
had no sooner crossed the frontier than my guide (who was an
Austrian subject) slipped from his horse, and knelt and "kissed
the consecrated earth." The soil of Montenegro may well be
called consecrated; for what higher form of consecration can the
fatherland receive than the blood of his sons shed in his defence?
Servia having become a Turkish province, her colonists created
in Montenegro a new and independent Servia. The memory of
Ivo the Black is still green in the country. Springs, ruins, and
caverns are called after him, and the people look forward to the
day when he will reappear as a political Messiah. But Ivo's
descendants proved unworthy of him; they committed the un-
pardonable sin of marrying aliens, and early in the sixteenth

century the last descendant of Ivo the Black retired to Venice. From 1516 to 1697 Montenegro was ruled by elective Vladikas or Bishops; from 1697 to 1851 by hereditary Vladikas. For the Montenegrins the sixteenth, seventeenth, and eighteenth centuries formed a period of incessant warfare. No wonder that Danilo Petrovitch at first refused the honour of being their Bishop. The throne of Montenegro nearly proved to him a martyr's throne. He was condemned to be crucified by a Turkish Pasha, from whom he had purchased a safe-conduct. He bore the cross a day's journey, and must have already felt the agony of death, when he was ransomed. This happened in 1702. Up till 1703 the Serbs of the mountain were no more absolutely independent of the Sultan than their enslaved kinsmen of the plain. The Havatch or Sultan's slipper tax was levied on the mountaineers. In 1703 Danilo Petrovitch celebrated his consecration as a Christian Bishop by ordering the slaughter of every Mussulman who refused to be baptized. This massacre took place on Christmas Eve 1703. It is easy for us enjoying all the blessings of civilisation to rebuke the Montenegrin for returning in kind on his pitiless persecutor the very cruelties which he suffered himself at his hands. It is one of the accursed results of oppression that it begets oppression. The slave of to-day is the enslaver of to-morrow, thus realising the poet's words—

> " Nos nequiores, mox daturos
> Progeniem vitiosiorem."

While the Montenegrin was wading through blood to peace and freedom, the Serb of the plain was ground down by exactions of every kind. His fate was rendered even worse by the intervention of Europe. The only freeman left in Servia was the brigand or *heyduc*. Veliko, a leader in the Serb War of Independence, was a typical *heyduc*. When the Russians, of whom Veliko thought so highly that he could never believe Napoleon to have advanced as far as Moscow, told him not to call himself *Heyduc*, which signified a robber, he replied, " I should be sorry if there were any greater robber than I am." Yet Veliko, who would risk his life for a few piastres, was as generous as he was rapacious. " If I possess aught," he would say, "any one may share it with me ; but if I have not anything, woe be to him who has and does not permit me to share it with him." He used to pray that Servia might be engaged in war so long as he lived, but that after his death she might have peace. His prayer was granted.

He fell gloriously defending Negotin against the Turks. His last words were, "Stand firm." This was in 1813, and we are anticipating.

In 1804 Kara George, or Black George, headed a rising in Servia, and drove out the Turk. In this he was unaided by the foreigner, and succeeded, thanks to native valour and his own indomitable will. Kara George was by calling a swineherd, and by the grace of God a hero. It may seem ridiculous to compare him to his great contemporary Napoleon; yet if we consider the means that were at the disposal of the two men, and the results of their labours, we must admit that the Servian overcame greater difficulties than the Corsican, while the good Black George did in his lifetime has not been interred with his bones. When Napoleon died at St. Helena he left behind him the legacy of Imperialism which was to cost France so much blood and treasure. When Kara George died, his mantle fell on Milosch. To these two men Servia owes her great idea, which means the independence and freedom of her people. If Kara George is the Achilles of Servian story, Milosch is the Ulysses, and to the wisdom of Milosch his countrymen owe even more than to the valour of Black George.

Kara George was a most extraordinary man. He was very taciturn, and would sit for days without uttering a word. Pomp and display he despised, but was not insensible to the charms of gold In peace he lived as a peasant; in war he was a warrior who for years passed as invulnerable and unconquered. His very justice was terrible. His only brother violated a maiden. Kara George ordered him to be hung at his own door, and forbade his mother to wear mourning. If we consider his services to the cause of Servian independence and European freedom, his character assumes heroic proportions; but the age in which he lived rendered the growth of gentler qualities impossible. It is an astounding fact that the deliverer of his country was the slayer of his own father. In 1787 Kara George took part in a rising, and found himself compelled to flee. Not wishing to leave his father behind, he took him with him; but the nearer he approached the Save River, which divided them from Austria, the more averse did his father become to cross it. At last the old man positively refused to go further. "How," exclaimed Black George, "shall I live to see thee slowly tortured to death by the Turks? It is better that I should kill thee myself," and seizing a pistol, he shot him dead. Such, then, was the man who summoned his countrymen to arise from Turkish oppression or be for ever bondmen. They obeyed his summons, and for nine years acknowledged him as chief.

In 1813, when the rest of Europe was engaged in settling the Western question with Napoleon, the unhappy Serbs were engaged in their own eternal Eastern question. We have no written evidence on the subject; but it is generally thought in Servia that Black George acted on the advice of Nedoba, the Russian consul at Belgrade, when he fled the country. However this may be, Kara George, the invincible warrior, deserted his country in its hour of danger. Such conduct, in such a patriot, must ever remain one of the psychological mysteries of history, but the unexpected characterises all the actions of this extraordinary man. Forgetful of Veliko's dying words, "Stand firm," Kara George, with Nadoba and most of the Voivodes, fled across the Danube. The Turks again repossessed the whole country. In this reign of terror the downtrodden Rayahs had but one man to look to, and that man was Milosch. "Among the faithless, faithful only he." In his country's direst need he remained true to her, and Servia has not proved ungrateful. The descendants of Milosch Obrenovitch are now the Royal House of Servia.

On Palm Sunday 1815 Milosch raised the standard of revolt in the village of Takovo. Milosch was a despot, but he was one of those despots to whom his countrymen look back with grateful recollection. He first made his country independent, and then prevented her dismemberment. I should require more time than is at my disposal to trace the close connection between the struggle in Europe against Napoleon and the struggle in Servia against the Sultan. Suffice it to say, that when France was dominant in Europe, Turkey was dominant in the Balkan Peninsula; and Wellington's victory at Waterloo secured not only the independence of the West, but the freedom of the Christian Rajah of Eastern Europe. It is a curious but little known fact that on the return of Napoleon from Elba, subscriptions were raised among the Christian traders of several towns in the Ottoman Empire with the object of preventing Napoleon again becoming Emperor. In addition to these foreign and external causes for the overthrow of the Turkish power in Servia, there were other reasons most honourable to Milosch which explain his success. There is a principle of retribution in the affairs of nations as of individuals; and the victories of Kara George, accompanied as they were by cruelty, brought no lasting peace. To the honour of Milosch, he not only

kept faith with the defeated Turk, but treated him with signal cle-
mency. On one occasion some Mohammedan women who fell into
his hands were so touched by his generosity that they exclaimed, "A
religion which commanded such conduct must be the true one."

It is now my duty to refer to one of the blackest incidents in
Serb history. In 1818 Kara George crossed over the Danube to
Semendria in Servia. He came at a most critical time, when
divided councils would have again brought the country under the
Turkish yoke. It is the opinion of the best authorities that it was
not by the order of Milosch that Kara George was put to death,
but the ugly fact remains that the Leader of the first Serb
Revolution was murdered by a Serb, and on Serb soil.

In 1817 Milosch was proclaimed hereditary Prince of Servia
by the National Assembly. Milosch was never a favourite with
Russia, and even as late as 1820 the Russian Ambassador at
Constantinople used to speak of the elect of the nation as M.
Obrenovitch. Nil Popov, the Russian historian, admits that
Russia "feared that Milosch would secure for Servia a position
like that of Moldavia and Wallachia; and that having once
obtained freedom of internal legislation, he would aspire also to
an independent foreign policy." The government of St. Petersburg have doggedly adhered to a plan of action long ago laid
down. Their motto is not, "The East for Eastern People," but,
"The East must either be subject to Russia, or become the prey
to endless strife and discord.'" The history of Servia forms a sad
sermon to that text. In 1830 the autonomy of Servia was at
length solemnly recognised by the Porte, and Milosch proclaimed
"the father of the Fatherland."

One incident only marred the triumph of Milosch. It was
stipulated by the Hatti-scheriff that the Mahommedans should
leave the cities. The Governor of Belgrade, who was a corrupt
man, demanded a price before withdrawing his troops. Milosch,
who thought he had already paid the Pasha enough, refused to
concede this last demand. The matter was referred to the arbi-
tration of the Czar, and Nicholas decided in favour of the Turks.

If asked why the descendants of Milosch still rule over Servia,
and not the descendants of Kara George, my answer is that every
step in Servian progress is connected with the Obrenovitch
dynasty. The liberation of the country, the creation of a peasant
proprietary, the final withdrawal of the Turkish troops from
Belgrade in 1862, the independence of the country, the extension
of its territory, and the making of its railways,—all of these are

among the results of Obrenovitch rule. The founder of the dynasty had in 1830 a great opportunity of making his people free as well as independent. But Milosch had lived too long with Turks to be a lover of freedom. "Am I not the master?" he was heard to say, "and shall I not be at liberty to do what I please?" Acting on this principle, he burnt one of the suburbs of Belgrade, because he wished to erect new buildings on the site. He exacted bond-service, and the tradesmen of Belgrade had to close their shops and assist the Prince in his hay harvest. Milosch, however, rendered one splendid service to posterity. His followers urged him to perpetuate in Servia the Turkish system of large landowners. This had been done in Wallachia, when the Mahommedan had been replaced by Christian landlords. The Spahis had been driven out of Servia, and there were specious arguments in favour of giving their large estates to the leaders of the War of Liberation. It would also have facilitated the collection of the revenue. Milosch resisted the temptation, and distributed the estates of the expelled Turkish landlords among the peasantry. Peasant proprietorship has proved an unmixed blessing to Servia, and Serbs are most zealous of retaining it. Nowhere else in Europe, not even in France, has the cultivator so firm a grip of the land. It might be thought that one who had freed his country from the invader, and its soil from the landgrabber, would have reigned secure, but this was not to be. In 1839 Milosch abdicated. The reason for this step was that he refused to accept a constitution which Russia and Turkey had concocted for him. This charter vested the actual government of the country in a Senate composed of Milosch's rivals, and entirely independent of that Prince. The vice of this foreign constitution was that it was anti-democratic, no less than anti-dynastic. Milosch was succeeded first by his son Milan, and on Milan's death by Michael. Michael was too gentle for the troubled times in which he lived, and after a two years' reign he too started upon his travels. History repeats itself, and the fall of the House of Obrenovitch in 1842 was mainly due to its own dissensions. Wife worked against husband, brother against brother, and thus their adversaries prevailed against them.

Louis Philippe brought the bones of Napoleon from St. Helena and interred them at the *Invalides*. The Napoleonic legend was thus revived, and France was cursed with the Second Empire. A similar result followed from similar causes in Servia. In 1842 the widow of Kara George died Michel, who was the very soul of chivalry, buried her with great pomp and state by the side of her husband. The intriguing Senators, or Defenders of the Constitution, as they styled themselves, who had exiled Milosch, felt their position insecure while a son of their old master remained on the throne. They therefore utilised this public funeral to revive the Kara George legend, and pointed to his son as the hope of the nation. Accordingly, when Michel crossed the Save, Alexander Kara Georgevitch was elected Prince of Servia. From 1842 to 1858 the son of Black George lived— he .can scarcely be said to have reigned—in Belgrade. During these seventeen years this feeble son of a strong man did absolutely nothing for his country. His reign was a blank. Late in 1858 he fled from Servia, and Milosch ruled in his stead. Milosch is the Grand Old Man of Serb history. His mere presence in Servia checked the intrigues of foreign powers. He died peacefully in his bed. If you wish to read his epitaph, look around at the prosperous peasant proprietors of Servia. The creation of these forms a varnish which (in the eyes of his countrymen at least) covers all his faults. Michel succeeded his father. Never were father and son more unlike. Milosch could neither read nor write, and his virtues were rather of a public than a private order. Michel possessed a cultivated mind, and was great enough to forgive his enemies. Milosch was an intensely personal ruler. "*L'état c'est moi*" might have been his motto. Michel had a nobler device, "The law is the supreme will in Servia." The one blot on Michel's character was his determination after thirteen years of marriage to divorce his wife. Her barrenness was her only fault. In moral turpitude the conduct of Michel cannot for one moment be fairly contrasted with that of his successor, yet here again history repeats itself. Michel's prime minister Garaschanine resigned rather than countenance this step. Garaschanine's son, as prime minister to King Milan, acted exactly as his father had done. In both cases misfortune overtook the faithless husband. Prince Michel was murdered by convicts in the park at Topschidera near Belgrade. There seems to be no reasonable doubt that these wretched murderers were tools of the Kara Georgevitch faction, if not of Kara George-vitch himself. The son of Kara George was condemned by a Hungarian Court to *twenty years' imprisonment* as the instigator of the crime ; and a special clause, that was promulgated in the Constitution by the Regency under Prince Michel's successor, excluded for ever from the throne of Servia the family of Kara

George. Michel was succeeded (1868) by Milan, the grandson of Zephrem, the brother of Milosch. As Milan was barely fourteen years of age, a Regency of three was appointed. Of these three Regents, one was the famous Ristitch, who after an interval of twenty years again finds himself the Regent of a boy king.

We must now return to the Serbs of the Black Mountain. The seventeenth and eighteenth centuries were for Montenegro a struggle for existence. In the nineteenth century began their struggle for an outlet to the sea. The fall of Venice would naturally have given the mountaineers the bay of Cattaro, had not the French stepped in and annexed Dalmatia. Marmont was in command of the French troops, and he reproached the Vladika Peter I. with the national practice of cutting off the heads of their enemies. "We do so," replied the Bishop, "and why not? Which is worse, that we should take off the heads of the French who are our enemies, or that the French should take off the heads of their King and of their fellow-citizens. We do so to our foes, you to your fellow subjects." But Peter did not hold his own merely in wordy warfare. In 1813, with the aid of the British fleet, he took Cattaro from the French, but (pursuant to an arrangement between Russia and Austria) was compelled subsequently to relinquish it to the latter power. One word must be said about the new territory which has been given Montenegro by the treaty of Berlin. Confined to her former small limits, Montenegro had done great things in the past; but she might have become a source of danger in the future, standing, as she did, like an entrenched camp in the midst of Europe. All this had been remedied by the cession of Dulcigno to Montenegro. There may, indeed, have been more brilliant strokes of policy; but seldom has the foreign policy of England been more just to all concerned, or more fraught with good to the whole of Europe. In giving Dulcigno to Montenegro, Mr. Gladstone has given the principality a window through which it can peep into Europe, and with seeing it may come to imitate. Montenegro has now given hostages to fortune. She is no longer a little mountain State with nothing to lose and everything to gain from going to war, but a State with a seaboard and a territory that lies outside the charmed circle of her rocks.

Peter I. of Montenegro, the brave but obscure antagonist of Napoleon, died in 1830, at the age of eighty. So simple were his ways of life, that in his last illness he had not even a fire in the cell that served him for a bedroom. His nephew, Peter II., was a wise ruler, ruling by the true divine right of being the best man in his country. At his own wish he was buried on the summit of a lofty mountain, a fitting spot in which to bury a poet. For there, "On the Crown of the Mountain," the name of his greatest poem, he peacefully slumbers in the calm moonlight, and there he receives morning's first beam. The glorious rulers of the Black Mountain might, if urged to take rest, have given the famous answer, "Rest above;" they took none on earth. On the death of Peter II., Prince Danilo, the uncle of the present Prince, went to Russia to be consecrated Bishop of Montenegro. The Czar seems to have laughed him out of this ancient practice ; and the late Prince, instead of converting himself into monk and bishop, returned to his own country and married. Of course, there was a great uproar among the Conservatives, but it is a very grave question whether they were not right. Up to 1851 the Montenegrins had been wont to look up to the Prince of Servia as the head of the Serb race, while the Serbs of the Danubian principality looked up to the Vladika as the head of the Serb Church. All this was changed in 1851. The Prince of Montenegro became the rival of the Prince of Servia. Danilo was, however, so great a man that he could afford to take a second place. He declared himself the first soldier in the army of the Prince of Servia, and he recognised in Michel the head of his race.[1]

The close alliance of the two Serb princes would have been fruitful in blessings to their own subjects, and would have strengthened a hundredfold the prospects of European peace. Soon after his famous utterance of goodwill and union with Servia, Prince Danilo was assassinated at Cattaro (1860). The secret springs of this crime will never be disclosed until that day when all secrets will be revealed. It is at least significant that prior to Danilo's murder Russia withdrew the annual allowance she had been in the practice of making to him. The withdrawal of this allowance produced a deficit in the national revenue, which Prince Danilo endeavoured to cover by fresh taxes. These taxes

---

[1] A treaty existed between Prince Michel and Prince Nicholas of Montenegro, by which the latter recognised the Prince of Servia as the leader of the " Serb Movement," and bound himself to support any plan Prince Michel might form for the delivery of Bosnia and Herzegovina. But after Prince Michel's murder, on a hint from St. Petersburg, Prince Nicholas declared the treaty to be no longer in force.

For another instance of Russian mischief-making, *see* Minchin's *Growth of Freedom in the Balkan Peninsula* (John Murray), page 88.

caused disturbances, and the disturbances were followed by Prince Danilo's assassination. He was succeeded by his nephew Nicholas.

Our brief history has now been brought down to the reigns of two living Serb rulers—the ex-King Milan and Prince Nicholas of Montenegro. It would be impossible within our limits to narrate here the story of the two Serb campaigns against Turkey (1876 and 1877), of the occupation of Bosnia and Herzegovina by Austria Hungary (1878), of the extension of territory and founding of the kingdom (1882), of the abortive Radical rising in 1884, of the disastrous campaign against Bulgaria in 1885, of the divorce and abdication of King Milan. To pass over this last event without comment would, however, be cowardly and unjust to the Serbs themselves. The mistake Nicholas Christitch and his Cabinet committed was that they believed in their King. It is the old cry of him "that hangs on princes' favours," "Had I served my God with half the zeal I served my King, he would not in mine age have left me naked to mine enemies."

King Milan said he would abdicate if he did not get his divorce. To save the country from the dangers attending a prolonged minority, the King's wish was gratified; and when Milan found himself relieved of his wife, he quickly relieved himself of his kingdom. In all history you can find no instance of a monarch purchasing his own ease at such a price to his country. I recently received a letter from a Serb statesman. I regret that I cannot quote from it. If you can imagine a letter from Lord Chancellor Clarendon, written after his fall, to an intimate friend, you will gather but half the bitterness of that letter. It was the outpourings of a loyal soul which has found out that the idol of his life was a fraud. To compare Milan to our own Charles II. is to do injustice to our own sovereign. He at least did not spend the taxes of his country in a foreign capital. He kept up some semblance of royal self-respect, and died in the country of his birth. The spectacle of their ex-King a voluntary exile in a strange land is to a Serb the very quintessence of baseness and corruption. It was not a Radical, but Garaschanine, who described Milan's abdication as "a flight from the battle field."

Before this lecture closes a few words must be said about the present government and condition of the two Serb countries. The Montenegrin government is soon described; it is purely despotic, untempered by regicide, and, it must be added, is as popular as it is absolute. The Serb of the mountain is intensely national, and will always fight against a foreign despot. The Serb of the kingdom goes further than this—he would be free not only from foreign but domestic tyranny. He is the Frenchman of the Peninsula, and is always ready to fight for an idea. Of all European countries, Servia should be to the political observer of to-day the most interesting, because in Servia alone is Socialism the keystone of the arch. You are aware that before his abdication King Milan gave the royal assent to a new Servian constitution, of which I will now give you some of the leading features.

There are two National Assemblies or Skupshtinas. The one is the Ordinary Skupshtina, and the other the Extraordinary or Grand Skupshtina. Under the old Serb constitution every arrondisement and every chief town of a department returned one deputy to the Ordinary Skupshtina for every 3000 taxpayers. For arrondisement or department towns, if under 3000 taxpaying inhabitants, one member was allowed. If, after an election in the bigger places, a group of under 3000 remained unrepresented, this group was allowed another member. For instance, if the town of X had 9000 odd taxpayers, it would return four members to the Skupshtina, one for each 3000, and another for the surplus. Thus the number of members in Skupshtinas under the old Constitution was an accident dependent upon the distribution of population. Under the new constitution this minority representation has been slightly limited. In addition to the popular representatives, the King had a right of nominating to the ordinary Skupshtina a member for every three elected. The Grand Skupshtina is elected entirely by popular vote. Now, under the new constitution, each department elects a member for each group of 4500 taxpayers; and if a group of less than 4500, but over 3000 electors, have no representative, they are allowed to count one member more. Just as four members were formerely given to London on account of the city's past services in the cause of English liberty, so the two villages of Dobrinje and Takovo are allowed a member each, as being the birthplaces of Kara George and Milosch Obrenovitch. Every male Serb (whether a Serb by birth or naturalisation) who is twenty-one years of age, and pays fifteen francs a year in direct taxes, is entitled to a vote. And here may be mentioned a patriarchal survival that we find in parts of Servia existing along-side of manhood suffrage. This is the Zadruga. The great poet whom we have just lost was not blind to the ills and calamities of

life, but he looked at trouble as motes in the sunshine of God's
love. The Turkish conquest was indeed a fiery furnace, but it was
a furnace that has purged the democratic ore of Serb society from
the dross of feudalism. After Kossovo the Serbs reverted to the
patriarchal form which the Slavonic settlers had carried with them
into the Balkan Peninsula when they settled there in the times of
Heraclius. Equality and fraternity reign within the paling of the
Zadruga or house community. It is forbidden, as far as possible,
to alienate their property, or to subdivide it among their members.
No superiority is recognised save that of age and parentage. The
Serb Constitution gives a vote to every adult male member of a
Zadruga, although the head of the family does all the taxpaying
for his clansmen. The chief democratic feature in the new
Constitution is that the King no longer has a right to nominate
members to the Ordinary Skupshtina. Under Article 100 of the
new Constitution (an article on which I have reason to believe
King Milan insisted) two of the members elected by a Department (*not towns*) must be the holders of a foreign university
degree or Serb "faculty." This article does not apply to the
Grand Skupshtina ; in other respects the mode of election to
both is identical.

A Grand Skupshtina contains twice the number of members
that an Ordinary Skupshtina contains. A Grand or Extraordinary
Skupshtina is now sitting. It was called together under a pro-
visional law of the Council of State to remodel the laws, which
have in many cases been strained in direct opposition to the
spirit of the new Constitution. For instance, the Constitution
appears plainly to intend that if the voting power of Department
X be four members, and if the voting power of the town Y two
members, that the total representation of X and Y together shall
be six. The Radicals, however, will it otherwise. To increase
the power of the county electors, who plump for the Radicals,.
the votes of Y are added to the votes of X, and thus X returns
six instead of four numbers, and X and Y together return eight
instead of six numbers.

Every elector is eligible for election to either Skupshtina under
the following conditions. He must be a resident in Servia,
unless he be a State employé in a foreign country ; he must be
thirty years of age, and pay thirty francs a year in direct taxes.
No criminal, nor bankrupt, nor that very useful public servant—
a policeman—can sit. A Government employé, if elected, loses
his post and any benefit from past services unless he be—

1. Either an actual Minister or one *en dispensabilite.*

2. A member of the Council of State.

3. A Minister Plenipotentiary, Diplomatic Agent, or Consul-General.

4. President or Member of the Tribunal of First, Second, or Third Instance.

5. Professor of High and Superior Schools, Engineer, and Doctor in the State Service.

6. Retired Employé.

Ministers have *ex-officio* seats in the Skupshtina, and have no necessity for election or selection on taking a portfolio. There is no right nor left of the President's chair, but each member sits where he pleases, save that the front bench is reserved for Ministers.

Payment of Members and Triennial Parliaments are both in force in Servia. Members of the Ordinary Skupshtina are given their travelling expenses and a daily allowance during Sessions. The amount of this allowance will be fixed by the present Assembly, and used to be between ten and twelve francs a day. The Grand Skupshtina is always elected for some particular purpose, viz.:—

1. To settle matters relative to the Dynasty and succession to the Throne.

2. To elect the Regents.

3. To deliberate on a change in the Constitution.

4. To examine questions relative to a modification of territory.

5. Whenever the King thinks fit to summon it.

A Grand Skupshtina is dissolved when the particular object for which it was summoned has been attained.

The local government of Servia is on the following lines : In villages where the taxpayers number 200, the Mayor will have a Municipal Council of ten members ; where the taxpayers number over 200 and under 500, he will have sixteen Councillors ; where there are over 500 taxpayers he will have twenty Councillors. Belgrade has a Council of thirty-two. Councillors are unpaid, but Mayors and Sub-Mayors (Kmets) are elected and paid by the taxpayers. Any elector is eligible to be a Kmet, unless he be an employé whose duty brings him in direct touch with the Mayoralty. If a Mayoralty is composed of several villages, the President or Mayor is elected by the entire Mayoralty, while each village elects its own Kmet. Mayors and Kmets discharge the duties that in England are intrusted to our paid and unpaid magistrates. They are elected for a term of two years. The number of Kmets for each village is determined by the amount of work they have to get through, and their salaries, as well as those of the Mayors, are settled by the Municipal Councils. Two Councillors are attached to each Kmet, or failing them, two honest peasants as assistants. I cannot tell you in what the difference between the two classes of assessors consists, unless the test of honesty is not to be applied to a County Councillor. What we should call police cases are tried by the Mayor and two Kmets. The accused is given no choice as to the manner of his trial, and must go before a jury on three charges only, viz.—arson, murder with robbery, or robbery with violence.

The new Press Law is all that it should be—in theory. It would be well if in practice it were half as perfect. The correspondents of the *Standard* and the *Daily News* have both been expelled from Servia; the former has been allowed to return, but the latter is still an exile at Semlin. Some hundred lawsuits are said to be hanging over various Opposition newspapers, and fifty of them over the celebrated Peter Theodorovitch, who has wisely betaken himself to Italy. This whilom Radical leader was charged with writing and speaking against the ex-King, and when acquitted on that charge, was imprisoned *"par voie correctionelle."* A power of giving a month's imprisonment was vested in the Prefects under the old law, but has (they say) been repealed by the new Constitution. Let us hope so.

The daily wages of skilled labour in Servia may be reckoned at from 5 to 6 francs a day, and unskilled from 2 francs to 2·50 a day. The best miners are Italians, who nearly all prefer piecework. In fact, except with navvies and farm labourers—a *rara avis* in Servia—piecework is the rule. A working man can live well in Servia on a franc a day; but, there is no denying it, he is most heavily taxed. On this, as on so many other topics, you cannot do better than refer to the Report on the Trade of Servia for the years 1887 and 1888, made by Mr. Macdonald, our Consul at Nisch, which is the best account of Servian trade that it has ever been my pleasure to peruse. What a peasant lives on is a bit of bread, black and hard like sunburnt mud, and an onion, and such fare as this does not cost him more than twenty or thirty centimes a day. A good deal more goes in *raki*. The Serbs are not teetotallers; but, so far as my observation goes, they are not drunkards.

The National Debt of Servia amounts to fourteen millions or £8 per head of the population. The chief exports of Servia are pigs, dried plums, and wine, and for the year 1888 scarcely exceeded in value one-and-a-half million sterling. The exports from Servia into this country for 1888 only amounted to £3259, and the imports from Great Britain for the same year to about £110,000. In the commercial dependence of Serbs on their powerful neighbours across the Save and the Danube, no less than in the occupation of Bosnia, a country inhabited in the main by the same Serb race, you must seek for the causes of the unpopularity of Austria in Servia. There are 458 miles of railway, and on these railways you pass through a land of the most varied scenery—a land whose soil is extraordinarily fertile ; whose plains team with cattle and swine, and are yellow with maize and wheat ; whose orchards are blue with the plum ; whose rivers abound with fish ; whose hills are vineyards ; and whose mountains are covered with oaks, ancient enough to have witnessed the march of the conquering Osmanli.

Young as Servia is, she is already cursed with "sweating." A new well was made for a friend of mine. The contractor charged him 175 francs, but the Italian who dug it out to a total depth of eight metres told my friend he only got twenty francs for the job. Consul Macdonald, on the 24th page of his Report, gives a striking instance of "sweating." The peasant women who make the carpets of Pirot are mostly in the hands of taskmasters, who pay them, as a rule, the sweating wages of 3¾d. and a little bread per day. Our Consul offered a Pirot peasant the town price for a large carpet. Had his offer been accepted, the whole of the profits (instead of being divided with the middleman) would have gone direct to the producer. Not only was his offer declined, but so unreasonable a price was demanded, that he was compelled to buy from the retail merchant. Apparently this Serb bondsman preferred to be "sweated" by his countryman to selling at a profit to an alien. The hatred of a Serb for a foreigner is an unfortunate fact. It is the honourable distinction of the Progressist that he alone among Serb politicians has never pandered to this foible.

The only strike I have ever heard of in Servia occurred quite recently at Nisch, when eighty mechanics at the railway station struck work on account of delay in payment of their wages. They also demanded the expulsion of all foreigners from the lines. There are, however, so many holidays in Servia that workmen might stay away without being missed. There are no Trade

Unions, as we understand them, but there are Trade Guilds or Esnafs. These are a curious survival of the Middle Ages. They form the Guilds of the various trades, and regulate the condition of apprentices and the privileges of master and workmen. They receive no State support, and are maintained by employers and workmen for the following purposes :—

1. To help old and sick members incapacitated from work.

2. To help destitute members.

3. To help widows and orphans of members, especially in educating the latter.

4. To pay the travelling expenses of members in search of work.

5. To give alms in church on feast day of Patron Saint of Esnaf.

The Esnafs exist independently of each other in the towns of Servia; there is no federation among them. There is no Employers' Liability Act, and damages for accidents are privately arranged. Education is the bright spot in the social system of the Serbs. It is both compulsory and free, and in the case of a promising lad includes his studies both at the Belgrade and a foreign university. In 1834 there was not a school in the country, except in the chief towns—in all, perhaps twenty-five. In 1884 scarcely a village was without one. This subject has been fully dealt with by me elsewhere.

There are three political parties in Servia—Liberal, Progressist, and Radical. There are three Regents—Ristitch, Belo Marcovitch, and General Protitch—who are all practically Liberals. Ristitch is the former chief of the party called Liberal. His admirers call him the Bismarck of the Balkans. No one can deny his patriotism, nor his desire to make Servia the Piedmont of the Balkan Peninsula. Belo Marcovitch is a dashing soldier, who took Nisch and Vranja from the Turks, but grave doubts exist as to his integrity. He was impeached before the Skupshtina for embezzlement, but was acquitted. General Protitch belongs to no political party, and may fairly be described as a King's Friend. He is a brave soldier, an indefatigable worker, and an honourable man. If the " Liberals " are the Conservatives of Servia, the Progressists might be called her Whigs. They are unrepresented in the present Grand Skupshtina, which consists of—

Liberals, 15.
Progressists, *none*.
Radicals, 102.

The Progressists held office from 1880 to 1888; great, therefore, has been their fall. It is, however, noteworthy that at the Communal elections of last December the Liberals and Progressists coalesced. Party feeling runs very high; and only last year a peasant told a friend of mine that his house had been burnt over his head by his fellow villagers merely because he was a Progressist. The Radicals are now in office, but their power is not absolute. The Regents and the Cabinet agree together about as well as our House of Lords and a Radical House of Commons. A Serb, who knows Ristitch well, said to me, " Yes, he is Regent again, but this time he is like a tiger behind bars." Besides the Regents there are other rocks ahead of the Radical ministry—their inexperience of office and the high hopes that have been excited by their promises. The Progressists say, and with some force, that the culture and intelligence of the country is with them. On the other hand, the present Radical Government are showing a vigour and an honesty which may falsify the prophecies of their opponents. The cleavage between the two parties—Radical and Progressist—is twofold, one foreign and one domestic; the cleavage between the Radical and the Liberal is mainly domestic. The Radical was for Russia, and in this supported Ristitch; the Progressist was for Austria. Whether this will remain so is doubtful, as the St. Petersburg Cabinet has always hitherto supported the Opposition in Servia. The principle which divides them in home politics is the objection of the Radical to the foreign capitalist. The Radical wishes to keep Servia an agricultural country; the aim of the Progressist, when in power, was to open up the resources of Servia by aid of foreign capital. To the Radical this means the degradation of native labour. He fears that large fortunes will create a prolétariat. At present Servia is a land of very moderate incomes, where wealth does not accumulate, and where men do not decay. Every rood of land maintains its man. There are no poor laws, because there are no poor. If a beggar accosts you, you may be sure he is a foreigner. The mass of the Serb nation is wealthier than any other. This was shown a few years ago, when two-thirds of the capital of the National Bank was subscribed by Serbs, who took from one to five shares each. The sunshine in which the peasantry bask is not without its shadow—flattery. Entire parts of verbs, such as gerunds, have been discarded by some Serb writers, who in their desire to show their sympathy with the masses, have imitated their uncultured language to such a degree as themselves to become uncouth and unintel-

ligible.   Let us not however fall into the opposite error of dispar-
agement.   The energy with which the Serbs have surmounted
difficulties in the past give us grounds for believing that they will
show the same energy in the future.   Freedom is the only thing
in this world for which too high a price cannot be paid.   The
Serbs have lived up to this principle, ay, and died for it.   They
have worked out their own salvation.   Blotted out from the map,
Servia has again appeared, her boundaries marked out by the
swords of her own sons.   Let us extend the hand of good fellowship·
to a race which, "through a cloud, not of war only," has at length
taken its place among the free nations of Europe.

XX

JEWS IN THEIR RELATION TO OTHER RACES.

THE REV. S. SINGER.

I WOULD like to express to you, however imperfectly, the sense of obligation under which I feel at having been invited to take part in this series of discourses on National Life and Thought. Your course of lectures would certainly have lacked one element of completeness if it had, even by implication, excluded from the community of nations one of the oldest, toughest, most virile, and most distinctively marked of races. "The amount of information which people do not possess" about Jews "is really prodigious." In an age of insatiable inquiry, when the electric light of publicity plays upon almost every phase, and illumines almost every nook of the inner life of nations and families, there is no race on the face of the earth at once so ubiquitous, and therefore so open to observation, and at bottom so little understood. You may not go all the way with what Heine wrote in his Confessions; to the main idea, however, contained in one of his remarks, you can hardly withhold your assent: "Neither the conduct nor the essential character of the Jews is understood by the world. People think they know them because they see their beards; but more than that never was perceived of them; and as in the Middle Ages, so they continue in modern times, a wandering mystery."[1] But whose fault is it if they remain a wandering mystery? The more people, and especially our own countrymen, know about Jews, the more they will find that the greatest of all mysteries in reference to them is that there is no mystery. Unlike the shrines of other nations, even our Holy of Holies contained no secret. What of mystery need there be then about us, unless it be the riddle, as insoluble to us as to you, of our existence, and of the dual current, about which I shall presently have to say more, that can be traced along the whole channel of our lives.

---

[1] Heine's *Werke*, xiv. 296.

With the particular doctrines, positive or negative, held by the majority of those who are in the habit of assembling here, I need hardly say I do not in any way identify myself. But your action in regard to my own particular community seems to me to claim some recognition. If I were to go this afternoon into a place of worship of any of the numerous sects into which Christendom is divided, I should hear the Jews spoken of eloquently, dully, learnedly, ignorantly, wisely, absurdly, lovingly, angrily, as the case might be : the only thing which the greater part of the statements there to be listened to would seem to me, as a Jew, to lack, would be an approach to verisimilitude. Among public bodies the distinction is in an eminent degree yours—that in your search for truth you have gone on this, as on former occasions, to those who may be presumed qualified to speak with authority upon subjects with which they personally are best acquainted.

On Wednesday evening last, in all the Synagogues of Jewry, there was read aloud to the congregations there assembled an old story, to which, whatever else Bible critics may have to say about it, they will not deny the merits of dramatic force, and, as regards the major part of the book at least, literary skill. It was the account of the perils and deliverance of that remnant of the house of Israel which, after the fall of the first Temple, found a home in lands, later on to form part of the Medo-Persian empire. One of the neatest passages in the book is the preamble wherewith the Grand Vizier of Ahasuerus introduced to the King his project of what might be called "a short way with Jews." Many such "short ways" have been proposed at various times. During the height of the anti-Semitic fever in Berlin, about the wittiest thing that emanated from our opponents was the issue of a mock railway-ticket, marked "To Jerusalem. Single ticket. No return tickets issued." This was not Haman's method ; but what he had to say was interesting for another reason. It was not all falsehood ; that would have been too clumsy. Haman knew his master too well to offer even such a gobe-mouches, a dish of undiluted lies. It was by no means all truth ; it was a deft mixture of the two, with the evident object that the untruth might pass current by reason of its being in good company, just as those who utter counterfeit coin are generally found passing genuine pieces along with the others in order to cover, and divert suspicion from, the spurious ones. "There is one people," said Haman, "scattered abroad and dispersed among the peoples." Undeniable,—the solidarity of the Jewish race is a fact as patent as their dispersion; they are *one* people, though scattered. "And their laws are diverse from those of all other people." That is only fractionally true. "And they do not keep the king's laws." That is distinctly false, and the inference drawn therefrom, that "it is not to the king's profit to suffer them," is consequently baseless and invalid.

Severe as the accusation sounds, one might assert that these words express not inaptly the sentiments with which, until comparatively recent times, most of the nations among whom it has been Israel's lot to be divided regarded them. They have resented that singular and tenacious union among Jews, which no geographical distribution seems able to break up; they have blamed them for a spirit of separateness, which is both good and evil;—good in so far as every race has to work out its own destiny on its own lines; evil in so far as it is the result of the treatment to which their persecutors have subjected them. They have declared them to be a burden and a misfortune to the State, with no more grounds than confident ignorance, envy, and the desire to have "their spoil for a prey," require to justify themselves.

In the history and literature of the Jews a very different tale is to be read. When once the work of the conquest of Canaan was effected,—and not many European nations have the right to sit in judgment upon Israel in such a case,—no State of ancient times was more hospitable to the stranger. On the basis of certain fundamental principles of morality, there was one law of right, of protection and love for him and the native. In the very Temple of the God of Israel, the prayers of the stranger were welcome. The aboriginal races lived side by side with the conquerors on terms of good-humoured tolerance. When the Jewish State fell, though they neither forgot Jerusalem nor gave up the hope of a return thither, it was in no rancorous spirit that the Jews lived among their captors. "Seek the peace of the city whither I have caused you to be carried captive," was the Divine message which Jeremiah delivered to his exiled brethren, "and pray for it unto the Lord, for in the peace thereof shall you have peace."

Their Temple a second time destroyed, and their land a prey to the enemy, the Jews once more found a home in Babylon, where the Parthians presented an invincible front to the passion of Rome for universal empire. Congregations and schools arose, the produce of whose labours forms to this hour the chief intellectual food upon which Rabbinic Judaism is fed all the world over. Yet so completely did affection for their new country become rooted within them, that one of their leaders of that period could maintain that "he who quits Babylon for Palestine transgresses a positive command."[1]

The language of the country became not merely the vernacular of the Jew; it acquired a quasi-sacred character, and prayers composed in the Aramaic dialect found their way into the liturgy of the Synagogue, and have been retained there to the present time. Then, too, the principle was established which is expressed in the Talmudic maxim, "The law of the State is everywhere binding law for the Jew"[2]—a principle that ever since has regulated the relation of the Jew towards the Gentile communities among whom he has been domiciled, and is itself an explanation of the singularly law-abiding character of the whole race.

Without loosening his hold upon his own distinctive laws and customs, the Jew never at any time was lacking in the consciousness of a union with a larger world outside his own race. He read the lesson of the unity of mankind in the first pages of his Bible. The central doctrine of his religious system—the Unity of God—drove that belief still deeper into his heart. The brotherhood of man was the logical consequence of the fatherhood of God. "When God created Adam," says the Talmud, "He gathered dust from all parts of the earth, and with it formed the parent of the human race."[3] Stripped of its garb of allegory, the saying means that the whole world is the home of man, that the very diversities in the families of mankind are within the original design of the Creator, and, as complementary one to the other, help to establish their essential unity. It was no empty rhetoric that spoke in these words. One practical result of such a theory was, for example, the doctrine: "To rob a heathen is worse than robbing an Israelite, because, in addition to the breach of the great moral law, there is the profanation of the name of God."[4] Where will you find a broader and loftier spirit of religious tolerance than that which is contained in this comment of the Midrash on Canticles: "'My beloved went down to feed in the gardens, and to gather lilies'—'the gardens'—these are the Gentiles throughout the world, and 'the lilies'—these are the righteous among them"? Or in this, from a work that was the offspring of

---

[1] Berachoth 24b. [2] Baba Kama 113a.
[3] Sanhedrim 38a. [4] Tosefta Baba Kama 10.

one of the darkest periods of Israel's fortunes: " I call heaven and earth to witness that, whether it be Israelite or Gentile, man or woman, everything depends upon the deeds that are done, how far the Holy Spirit shall rest upon a mortal?"[1]

That not all utterances concerning non-Israelites are conceived in the same strain, will be readily imagined. The relation of Jews to other races has, of course, been regulated to some extent by the relation of other races to the Jews ; and the one will never be properly understood and be done justice to until the other has been thoroughly grasped. It is, however, no part of my purpose this afternoon to recite to you a chapter out of the Romance of Jewish Martyrdom. Read only what Christians, like Döllinger and Schleiden, have written on this subject, and you will not need to listen to the grim and ghastly record from Jewish lips. This only I will say, that in nothing has Christianity been so un-Christ like as in its treatment of the Jew, from Church fathers, and popes, and grand inquisitors, and Catholic emperors, to Pro-testant reformers, statesmen and rulers, and that there never was a religion which suffered so little as Christianity during its estab-lishment compared with the suffering it has itself caused since— two centuries of intermittent persecution endured, against sixteen centuries of incessant persecution inflicted.

Until the end of the last century, all attempts on the part of the more tolerant among the Gentiles to assert for the Jewish race the status of full brother to other races proved abortive. Even the British Parliament, which, in 1753, passed the Jews' Naturali-sation Bill, was led to revoke its own righteous action the follow-ing year, in obedience to clerical prejudice, commercial jealousy, and popular clamour. It is to the French Revolution that the Jews owe their improved position in the modern world. That prolific parent of good and evil has at least deserved well of *them*. It was the first to do justice, full and unequivocal, to those whom every other great political movement passed over as too insignificant or too contemptible to be taken into account. Mirabeau and the Abbé Grégoire, the one in his desire to secu-larise the State, the other in his policy of Christianising the Revolution, as our historian Graetz[2] puts it, both urged on a move-ment which, in an incredibly short space of time, succeeded in effecting the complete emancipation of all the Jews under the rule of the Republic. On the 17th September 1791, the National As-sembly decreed the abolition of every exceptional enactment pre-

---

[1] Tana d'be Elijahu 9.　　　[2] See vol. xi., ch. 5.

viously in force against them, and thus made them by law what they had previously been in heart, citizens of their country. He who started as the child, afterwards to become the master of the Revolution, proclaimed the same great principles of religious equality wherever his victorious eagles penetrated. Since that dawn of a better time, the light has spread more and more, though even now it is only here and there that it has shone forth unto the perfect day.

If, now, you direct your attention to the attitude of Jews towards their neighbours, you are made aware of a most extraordinary, and, in its degree, unique combination; you perceive a national individuality of singular strength and distinctiveness, side by side with an equally remarkable power of adaptation to the varying circumstances of their existence. I admit it sounds like a contradiction; but reality is often a potent reconciler of theoretical impossibilities, and here, at all events, is a contradiction which is being acted out before our very eyes, one that in the play and alternation of forces furnishes all the elements for one of the most impressive dramas of humanity. One side of the national character has been depicted by Goethe in words to which all the greater weight may be attached, seeing that they breathe anything but a spirit of partiality towards the Israelitish people: "At the Judgment-Seat of God, it is not asked whether this is the best, the most excellent nation, but only whether it lasts, whether it has endured. There is little good in the Israelitish people, as its leaders, judges, chiefs, and prophets a thousand times reproachfully declared; it possesses few virtues and most of the faults of other nations; but in self-reliance, steadfastness, valour, and, when all this could not serve, in obstinate toughness, it has no match. It is the most perseverant nation on earth; it was, it is, it will be to glorify the name of the Lord through all ages."[1] True as much of this undoubtedly is, it is not the whole truth regarding the Jewish people. The other side of their character is not less recognisable. They have the power of adapting themselves to their surroundings with a rapidity and completeness that is altogether unparalleled. I do not propose to enter into the philosophical inquiry, What constitutes a nation? But I do venture to contest the assumption that it requires so many generations of residence on the soil, and the ability to show that your ancestors, upon arriving on these shores, slew the ill-prepared natives, and took violent possession of their land and other effects,

---

[1] Wilhelm Meisters Wanderjahre, II. 2.

in order to constitute you a true Englishman. A man's country is the place where he enjoys the protection of the laws, where he pursues his vocation without let or hindrance, where his home is fixed, hallowed by the tender ties of family life, where the interests and the welfare of his neighbours have become interwoven with his own, where he can worship God according to the dictates of his conscience, and where his life is able to perfect itself in every direction. Given these conditions, or the chief of them, and the Jew not only becomes soon mentally acclimatised, and assimilates himself to the society by which he is surrounded, but reproduces its distinguishing characteristics in an accentuated form in himself, becoming, as at this day he is often found to be, more German than the Germans, more French than the French, more English than the English. By way of pendant to the judgment of Goethe, let me cite a noteworthy utterance of one of the most gifted women of our race, a valued friend of Emerson's, one whose brilliant career closed far too soon for her people's good, though not too early for her fame. "Every student of the Hebrew language," says Emma Lazarus in her Epistles to the Hebrews, "is aware that we have, in the conjugations of our verbs, a mode known as the *intensive voice*, which, by means of an almost imperceptible modification of vowel points, intensifies the meaning of the primitive root. A similar significance seems to attach to the Jews themselves in connection with the people among whom they dwell. They are the intensive form of any nationality whose language they adopt."

Is it well to have kept a people like this at arm's length? It is not alone the Jews who have been sufferers by such a policy. What monasticism did in one direction by withdrawing for many centuries many of the best intellects and noblest characters from the active business of life, that was done in another by the systematic repression of the special genius of the Jew, and his exclusion from all national fellowship. Both systems have tended to the world's own impoverishment.

Leaving generalisations, however, let us regard the Jews in their relation to some of those countries where they have found a home. As types, let us take three, as widely varied as possible —Russia, Germany, England.

It is, of course, notorious that the Jews of Russia are, with comparatively few exceptions, but loosely attached to their fellow-subjects, and to the country which is to them in the place of a fatherland. But the marvel is not so much that they are loosely

attached, as that they are attached at all.   It is not easy to form
a conception of the wretchedness in which a system of legalised
inhumanity has steeped the lives of between three and four millions of our fellow-men.   From his birth upwards, the Russo-
Polish Jew is the object of a persecution which, were it not that
he has inherited a vast capacity for endurance from generations
of luckless ancestors, would soon suffice to crush the whole man
within him.   Almost every avenue to an honourable livelihood is
closed against him.   Barriers are put up in his own country,
beyond which he dare not pass.   Certain provinces are set apart
for his domicile—they are an enlarged ghetto, outside whose
boundaries he strays at his peril.   The whole of the interior is
shut against him, as though he were a leper.   When he sets foot
in it, it is on his way to Siberia.   He is enough of a foreigner to
be denied the rights of other Russians ; he is just Russian enough
to be heavily taxed.   If he has sufficient means to pay for it, he
may purchase at a high price the privilege of being allowed to
establish himself in the capital, or in a few other important towns.
But this elevation has no power of raising his wife to the same
status, and should he leave his property to her, the State will not
lend itself to so unnatural a proceeding, and takes charge of the
inheritance in perpetuity.   If he is drawn for the army, and dis-
appoints the string of hungry officials by not bribing them to
secure his exemption from military service, he and his family bid
each other farewell, without much hope of meeting each other
on this side the grave.   With his fellow-recruits he is drafted off
to the other extremity of the colossal empire ; for it is the Russian
principle—and in this it is quite impartial in its treatment of Jews
and Christians—not to foster anything like local attachments in
its soldiery.   Needless to say that he has no chance of rising
from the ranks, whatever his military qualities may be.

But what is resented with especial severity is the thirst for
knowledge which, despite all repression, the Jew so often manifests.
He presents himself, perhaps fully qualified in all other respects,
for admission into a Russian University.   The chances are that
the doors will be closed against him, as the percentage fixed by
law of Jewish to other students has already been reached, or has
been lowered by a recent Ukase.   That the Jew should become
more cultured than his taskmaster is not to be thought of.   He
cannot even be a Christian any longer in peace.   The temptation
has been, and still remains, very strong to rid one's self by a
single effort, a single concession (the greatest, however, which

a man of honour can make) of all these galling disabilities. With this object, and in order to ease the transition to their own conscience, a few Jews have occasionally gone over to Lutheranism, such a step being deemed not so gross a breach with former habits of thought as joining the Russian Church, with its image and relic worship. Within quite recent years, however, Lutheranism has been declared no resting-place for a Jew who wishes to be considered a Russian, and there is now, in a very mundane sense, no salvation for him outside the pale of the Orthodox Russian Church. Add to all this, that a persistent scorn, more biting and degrading than the knout, dogs him at every turn and movement of his life, and that the knowledge that there is one section of the populace against whom all manner of crimes can be perpetrated without disgrace and with comparative impunity, is apt to demoralise the most virtuously disposed of people, and it will be seen that the fate of the Russian Jews is about as melancholy and as desperate as that to which any portion of the human race is at this moment condemned. The hardest thing about the whole business remains to be spoken : these despised outcasts are in many ways, intellectually and morally, the superiors of their tormentors. If any one considers this a mere piece of racial or religious bias, let him read the address of Archbishop Nicanor at the University of Odessa in September last. No professional advocate of the Jewish cause could have more effectively contrasted the Russian and the Jewish characters, or could have spoken in more glowing language of the industry, the sobriety, the self-denial, the parental and filial devotion, the love of learning, and the unswerving attachment to their faith of these same Russian Jews.

But they are charged with displaying an invincible spirit of exclusiveness, and with taking to ignoble pursuits, to the vocations of the usurer and the innkeeper, who make their profit out of the follies and the vices of their fellow-men.—You shut up a man in prison without cause, and accuse him of being unsociable. You take from him every serviceable brick and stone, and bid him build his hut of mud, and then you are surprised that he has soiled his hands.

What an opportunity now lies before the Autocrat of all the Russias and his ministers ! True, there is danger in making concessions to an awakening people : is there no danger in refusing them ? By a single exercise of his authority, the Czar could break every chain that has so long fettered and disfigured his Jewish subjects. And he, or whoever may do it, would have his reward in the bursting forth of a pent-up spirit of loyalty and patriotism, for there is not a people on earth more quick to forgive injuries, and more grateful for kindnesses, than the Jews. But truth makes its way slowly to a monarch's ear. Have not others also long been crying for justice in that land where the east and the west have met, and barbarism and civilisation are so strangely mingled? We must not complain if their claims take precedence over ours. The Sun of Freedom has always shone last into the gloomy recesses of the Ghetto.

Turn now to Germany. The problem there is different in kind, but in certain respects even more acute. The Jews are accused, strange to say, of diametrically opposite faults. On the one hand, they are condemned for hemming themselves in with a tribal exclusiveness which nothing can pierce, for placing around them an icy barrier no warmth of neighbourly love can melt; on the other hand, they are charged with being too much *en évidence*, with wanting to take their share and more of public affairs, with desiring to make themselves indispensable to their country. It would, perhaps, not be a bad thing to let the objectors settle their differences, which seem to fairly cancel each other, and then to deal with the remainder, if any.

The attitude of the Teutonic anti-Semite recalls a grim story narrated of the Emperor Hadrian in an old rabbinical work.[1] A Jew, happening one day to meet the Emperor, greeted him respectfully. "Who art thou?" said Hadrian. "A Jew," was the humble reply. "And thou, a Jew, art so bold as to greet the Emperor! Thou shalt pay for it with thy head." Aware of the luckless fate of his brother Israelite, another Jew, who chanced to cross the Emperor's path, thought it wise to show more discretion, and omitted the customary sign of homage. Hadrian stopped him, and again asked, "Who art thou?" "A Jew." "And thou darest to pass the Emperor without greeting him! Off with his head!" The counsellors who accompanied him, perplexed at this strange procedure, expressed their astonishment that such punishment should be dealt out alike to him who did and to him who did not greet the Emperor. "Think you," said he, "Hadrian needs to be taught how to rid himself of those whom he hates?" Something of the same spirit prevails among those who, in their hostility to the Jews, are utterly

---

[1] Midrash Echah.

regardless of the inconsistency and even the absurdity of their charges against them. It is enough that they hate them. Need those who hate be logical as well?

Nominally, indeed, all Germans are equal before the law. But, during the last fifteen years or so, anti-Semitism, that hideous recrudescence of the worst passions of the middle ages, that "stain upon the German name," as the Emperor Frederick called it, has striven to place and to keep the Jew under a relentless social ban. There is no more cruel instrument of torture than social persecution and contempt can become in unscrupulous hands. One illustration may suffice. In Germany, the army is everything. The empire exists for the army, though in official parlance the army is said to exist for the empire. Under the law of conscription, the Jews have to render their period of service exactly like the rest of the population. Perfectly just. But of all the Hebrews who have ever served in the army, and they are to be numbered by tens of thousands, one or two only have been permitted, and that with the utmost difficulty, to rise to the rank of officer. They may shed their blood on the battlefield, may make the heaviest sacrifices for the good of the fatherland, as they did in the great war of Liberation as well as in 1870; they may render the most heroic, though less conspicuous, services in giving medical aid to the wounded on the field and in hospitals; but that they should wear the epaulettes of an officer would be a not-to-be-thought-of enormity. Not even baptism can wash the old Adam out of the Jewish soldier. The corps of officers will have none of him in any shape or colour.

The Jews of Germany have their faults—faults that especially offend because they are so conspicuously within view of all the world: they do not know how to bear with becoming modesty their recently acquired wealth and power. But their worst fault is that they are too clever, while they lack the grace which Mr Lang's Prince Prigio acquired after many adventures, of being clever without *seeming* so. In England, when the proletariat was enfranchised, the cry among sensible politicians was: "Now let us educate our masters." In Germany, even before the first instalments of liberty and equality were doled out to them, the Jews began to educate themselves. With the widening of their opportunities in our own time, there has gone an educational development that has in it something truly astounding. With a total population, including Prussia, of about 45,000,000, Germany had, in 1887, 562,000 Jews, or 1 Jew to 80 of the general population. One would expect something like the same proportion to be maintained between Jews and non-Jews in the educational world. What, however, is the actual case? Among 1326 University Professors (exclusive of those who hold chairs in theology) in the German Empire, there are 98 Jews, or about one-fourteenth instead of one-eightieth of the total: of 529 Privat-Docenten, 84 are Jews, or about one-sixth. In these capacities they hold distinguished positions in the various faculties of medicine, law, philosophy, arts, science, and agriculture. A similar state of things is observable in the High Schools. Taking Berlin as an example, with a population of 1,400,000, including 67,000 Jews, we find that the total number of students, boys and girls, in the gymnasium, Real - Schulen, Fach - Schulen, and Höhere Töchter - Schulen amounts to 23,481; of these 18,666 are Christian, and 4,816 are Jewish students—that is, the Jews are four or five times as numerous as their proportion to the rest of the population would lead one to expect; or, to state it in another way, every thousand Christian inhabitants of the Prussian capital furnish 14 students to these schools; every thousand Jewish inhabitants supply 72 students.

I take these statistics not from a Jewish, but from a Christian source, the Anti-Semiten Katechismus, published in Leipsic in 1887—a book cunningly designed to provide Jew-baiters with all weapons of offence in a handy form, and to rouse the animosity and indignation of German Christians against everything Jewish. Its most triumphant passages are those that point to the status of the Jews in the educational world as a peril to the State. Surely we may be pardoned if, while accepting the figures cited by our enemies as accurate, we desire no higher praise than is involved in a condemnation based upon such grounds.

Now, contrast the position of the Jew in both Germany and Russia with that which he holds in England. The English are slow to move in the direction of any political change, but when the time is ripe for it, and the change is made, it is made generously, ungrudgingly, and without irritating reservations. It is not surprising to those who know how to read the Jewish character that, among the many races and religions contained within the limits of the British Empire, there is none that has more completely identified itself with the national sentiments and aspirations than the Jews. Making allowance for the difficulties of undoing the results of long periods of misrule, and of inherited tendencies consequent in great mea-

sure upon such misrule, the transformation has been astounding
at once in its rapidity and in its thoroughness. In every walk
of life, Jews are taking their share : in professions, in commerce, in
handicrafts. They have developed a degree of public spirit and
a civic excellence for which they were little credited before the
experiment had been made. They are to be found among the
the foremost in every philanthropic and educational movement, in
every undertaking tending to the national welfare and honour.
It would be difficult to find within the whole range of modern
history a more perfect realisation than the Jews of Great Britain
present of Mr. Freeman's theory concerning the influence which
an adopting community is able to exercise upon its adopted members : " It cannot change their blood ; it cannot give them new
natural forefathers ; but it may do everything short of this—it
may make them in speech, in feeling, in thought, and in habit,
genuine members of the community which has artificially made
them its own." [1]

Perhaps the clearest proof of the manner in which the Jews
have assimilated the national life of this country is their attitude
in regard to politics. On the supposition, into the merits of
which this is not the occasion to enter, that the division into
political parties is a good thing for this country, the Jews contribute in their measure to the general benefit. They are the
appanage of no political party ; they are to be found in every
one, reflecting not unfairly the differences of opinion prevailing
in the various constituencies themselves. Of course this would
be impossible if their emancipation here had been an incomplete
one. As it is, their interests are identical with those of the rest
of the population. There is, fortunately, no Jewish question to
distract their attention from the wider duties of citizenship. Ill
would it fare with a Jewish clergyman who should venture, from
his pulpit or elsewhere, to dictate to his congregants how they
should or how they should not vote.

Just now, indeed, the public mind is strangely agitated by an
industrial question in which the mass of immigrants of the Jewish
race and faith are mainly concerned. I believe the agitation
will, before long, die a natural death. The saving common
sense of the British people will not suffer fresh disabilities to
be invented for, and to be imposed upon, one of the most law-
abiding sections of the population. It is one thing to protect
them against themselves, as others have had to be protected,

---

[1] " Race and Language," by Edward A. Freeman.

by improved factory legislation; it is another to condemn them
and their fellows to the dismal fate which certainly will befall
them if England for the first time reverses its traditional policy
in their case. It is not conceivable that the land whose boast
it used to be that it afforded an asylum impartially to kings
fleeing from their fickle subjects, and to subjects fleeing from
tyrannical kings, will shut its gates upon those who are drawn
hither by the same law of nature as that which bids a plant
seek the light and the air.

But you ask, perhaps, apart from the present relations of the
Jews towards other races among whom they have found a home,
have they any thought or hope of ultimate independence as a
nationality with a territorial base and a political centre? Is
Palestine still the Land of Promise to the house of Israel? I
wish I could answer that inquiry in the name of all my brethren
with a single voice. Upon no question, unfortunately, are
opinions more widely divided, though upon none has the teaching
of the Synagogue from time immemorial been more unanimous,
decided, and emphatic. Leaving aside those vacant souls, whose
conception of happiness is to be saved the trouble of thinking,
and the responsibility of believing, the Jewish camp is divided
into two parties. There are those among us who have neither
heart nor mind for a restored Jewish state and a revived Jewish
nationality. The whole notion is uncongenial to them. They
will not pray for it, nor hope for it. The ancient memories have
died within them, stifled by the weight of their new prosperity.
They dispose of the bare suggestion with a smile, and quote the
well-worn jest of the wealthy Parisian Jew who declared that,
when the throne of David was re-occupied by one of his descendants, he would make application for the post of ambassador
of his Judaic majesty at the Court of Paris. But it would be a
grave error to suppose that such a method of regarding the
destiny of Israel had altogether displaced the faith of centuries—
a faith sealed with blood and tears, a faith that lent the one
poetic charm to the dark and dreary lives of fifty generations of
our fathers. There is still a goodly band of brethren in whom
that faith is as full of vitality to-day as ever it was in Israel's
history. Every time they open their Bible or their Prayer-Book,
the sacred flame is fed within them. With a keen eye they watch
the progress of events in the East, note with glad satisfaction that
the Jewish population of Palestine has trebled within the last
half-century, that agricultural colonies are springing up on all

sides, and that the exiled children of Judah no longer seek the land of their fathers merely to let their bones mingle with the hallowed soil. Tears of genuine sorrow and of passionate yearning still flow at the recital on the anniversary of the destruction of the Temple of elegies like those of the Castilian Jehudah Halevi :—

> Zion,
> Hast thou no greeting for thy prisoned sons,
> That seek thy peace, the remnant of thy flock ?
> I would pour forth my soul upon each spot
> Where once upon thy youths God's spirit breathed :
> Prostrate upon thy soil now let me fall,
> Embrace thy stones, and love thy very dust.
> Shall food and drink delight me, when I see
> Thy lions torn by dogs ? What joy to me
> Shall daylight bring if with it I behold
> The ravens feasting on thy eagles' flesh ?
> But where thy God himself made choice to dwell
> A blest abode thy children yet shall find.

If you ask me, Where are the men to come from who are to bring about this revolution, not in the career alone, but within the very hearts of a nation, who are to vanquish the indifference, to purify the sordid aims, to enlarge the narrow hopes, that make up the lives of Jewish as of other Philistines, I answer, I do not know. But I know that the same question would have remained unanswered if it had been put before the stirrings of the pulses of the national idea was felt in Greece or in Italy, before the genius of a Byron or a Mazzini rekindled the extinguished hopes and ambitions of these nations.

Nor is it easy to say how this end is to be brought about. Two oaths, says a doctor of the Talmud, God imposes upon Israel,[1] First, that they shall not seek the restoration of their land by means of violence, and next, that they will not rebel against the nations among whom they dwell. That is to say, it is not to physical force, but to the growth of moral influences, that we are to look for the realisation of our ideals. " Not by force, nor by might, but by My Spirit, saith the Lord." It is in the Jewish race itself that the breath of enthusiasm is needed, without which no nation ever worked out, or deserved to accomplish its own regeneration. If, in contemplating the actual condition of mind of multitudes of his brethren, the believer in the destinies of Israel does not always meet with a sympathetic response, he is not dis-

---

[1] Cethuboth 111 a.

mayed or disheartened; he looks to a higher than earthly source for the vivifying impulse, and, face to face with the apathy and the ridicule of the world, he prepares to fall in with the train of thought to which the poetess, who has already enlightened us on one side of the Jewish character, gives utterance in the "New Ezekiel:"—

> What! Can these dead bones live, whose sap is dried
> > By twenty scorching centuries of wrong?
> Is this the House of Israel whose pride
> > Is as a tale that's told, an ancient song?
> Are these ignoble relics all that live
> > Of Psalmist, priest, and prophet? Can the breath
> Of very heaven bid these bones revive,
> > Open the graves, and close the ribs of death?
> Yea, Prophecy, the Lord hath said again:
> > Say to the wind, Come forth and breathe afresh,
> Even that they may live upon these slain,
> > And bone to bone shall leap, and flesh to flesh.
> The spirit is not dead, proclaim the word.
> > Where lay dead bones a host of armed men stand!
> I ope your graves, My people, saith the Lord,
> > And I shall place you living in your land.

And the other peoples of the earth, have they anything to fear from the realisation of these hopes? Which of them will be losers? Will not all of them rather be gainers by the reconstitution of a community which, without abandoning either its own character or its mission, "carries the culture and sympathies of every great nation in its bosom," and which has no heart for a future of national glory apart from the glory and the welfare of mankind?

XXI

THE GYPSIES.

F. H. GROOME.

I CONFESS I was somewhat amused at being asked to lecture on the Politics and National Aspirations of the Gypsies. For the Gypsies have no politics ; they have less than no national aspirations. What *is* the Gypsies' fatherland? Egypt, say the Gypsies; India, say Gypsiologists—of Egypt and of India the Gypsies are equally ignorant. And yet with something Indian they are thoroughly conversant—their mother-tongue. Is there any man here who has served in India as soldier or civilian? Let him, on leaving this hall, walk southward to Battersea, westward to the Potteries in Notting Hill, or far eastward to Wanstead Flats, and go into any tavern there ; the chances are, sooner or later, he will light on some tawney-faced men, discoursing in what at first may sound like gibberish, but in which, if he listen closely, he will presently recognise familiar Hindustani terms, as *chúri*, "knife," or *páni*, "water." Those tawney faced men will be Gypsies ; their speech bewrayeth them. Yet tax them with being Gypsies, they will surely deny it ; for there is, they know, a prejudice against Gypsies, even as in Scotland there is a prejudice against natives of Paisley. Two Scotchmen were travelling in a railway carriage. One of them, a Glasgow man, said presently, "Ye'll be frae Greenock, I'm thinkin'?" "Na, I'm no frae Greenock." "Ye'll be frae Renfrew, then?" "Na, I'm no jeest frae Renfrew." "Man, ye'll no be frae Paisley?" "Ay; but, sure as deith, I couldna help it." That is pretty much the Gypsy's feeling, only he will be more reticent ; for barely a century since it was death, by law at least, to have been born a Gypsy.

People ask me sometimes, "What is a Gypsy? Is not everyone a Gypsy who lives in a tent or a caravan?" Certainly not ; no more than a cat who takes up her quarters in a dog-kennel becomes a dog. True, tent-dwelling is the typical Gypsy manner of life; still, there are thousands of Gypsies who pass all their lives within four walls; as also there are thousands of vagrants who are not Gypsies who have not a drop of the blood or one word of the language. "Well, then," I am asked, "but are not all Gypsies dark?" To which I answer, Certainly, the typical Gypsy, the full-blooded Gypsy, *is* dark; still, I have known unquestionable Gypsies who are fair, even red-headed. Thus, the ultimate test is the Gypsy or Rómani language, a language unwritten in books, but handed down by word of mouth from generation to generation; a language whose secret has been jealously guarded, so that few, very few, but Gypsies can speak it. Hence, if a Gypsy is accosted by a stranger in Rómani, he jumps at once to the conclusion that that stranger must be a Gypsy.

A friend of mine, a clergyman, who has long been a student of Rómani, was a master, some years ago, in a public school. One day he was walking from the schoolhouse to his home, arrayed in college cap and gown, when he saw an old Gypsy woman sitting outside his gate, with a pile of baskets. "*Kúshto dívvus, Dya*" (Good day, mother), he said to her. She looked at him reproachfully, exclaiming, "Pretty Gypsy you, to go dressed that monkey fashion! But there, Gypsies have took to queer ways nowadays!"

I was myself at Scarborough once. I was going out to a picnic, rather a big affair; and I was walking on the Esplanade, waiting for the carriages, and smoking a cigar, when I saw an old knife-grinder, grinding away at a pair of scissors. I had a good look at him as I went past, and then I turned again, and had a better look. He certainly *was* a Gypsy. So, "*Shar shan, bor?*" (How d'ye do, mate?), I said to him. He dropped the scissors, crying, "Lord bless us all, and I thought you was a gentleman. How de do, boy?" And then we fell into discourse.

Another time I was at Westminster, when I saw two tinkers, and a look was enough to tell me they were Gypsies. One was tall, hook-nosed, and elderly; the other a slim, good-looking young fellow; but both were the colour of a copper tea-kettle. So, coming up by them presently, "How d'ye do?" said I in Rómani. And the tall one answered, "And how are you, my brother? I haven't set eyes on you since I don't know when." Which seemed likely enough, because he had never seen me in his life. "No," I said, "it *is* a goodish while." And as we walked on talking, I learnt they were two of the Lovells, living at Battersea. By-and-by Mr Hooknose says, "You'll take a glass with us, brother?" So we went into a bar, and first he paid for glasses, and next I paid for glasses. And then : "You haven't been long out, brother?" "No; not very long." "Seven years, wasn't it, brother?" "Seven years it was." "About a horse, brother?" "Ay, about a horse." After which I came away, leaving my two acquaintances persuaded that I was some Gypsy or other (to this day I know not who) that had got seven years' imprisonment for horse-stealing. Not wholly flattering to myself; still, they did not mean it unkindly.

But I wouldn't have you go away with the idea that a Gypsy takes every strange Gypsy for a horse-thief. There are Gypsies and Gypsies, good and bad, rich and poor, well-educated and ignorant. I know of one who is a clergyman ; another, in the Staffordshire Potteries, has founded a rival to the Salvation Army ; in the United States there are Gypsy landowners of great wealth and intelligence (one recently left a fortune there of a million sterling) ; in the south of France there is a Gypsy horse-dealer, who has sent all his sons to the university ; in Wales, in Hungary, and in Russia the Gypsy musicians are *the* musicians of the country. Nor, though, as I said before, the Gypsies are reticent as to their Gypsy birth, must you fancy they are at heart the least ashamed of it. Nothing of the kind. From his cradle upwards —if ever he possessed a cradle—the Gypsy child thus might parody some well-known lines :—

> " I thank the goodness and the grace,
> That on my birth hath smiled ;
> And made me in this Gentile land
> A happy Gypsy child."

No saying is oftener in the Gypsy mouth than this :—" There's nothing worse than nasty *gaûjoes* "—*gaûjoes* meaning "Gentiles," or all who have not had the privilege of Gypsy birth.

Isn't it strange, then, to reflect that, less than two centuries since, the Gentiles were hanging the Gypsies for the mere fact of their birth—nay, even hanged Gentiles who dared to consort with Gypsies. Here in England, at Aylesbury, in 1577, Rowland Gabriel and Katherine Diego—a woman, mark you—were hanged for " feloniously keeping company with other vagabonds, vulgarly called and calling themselves Egyptians, and counterfeiting, trans-forming, and altering themselves in dress, language, and behaviour." At Durham, in 1592, five men were hanged for "being Egyptians." At Bury St Edmunds, thirteen Gypsies were executed shortly before the Restoration, and others at Stafford shortly after it.

So late even as 1819 (only seventy years ago), it was carried unanimously at the Norfolk Quarter Sessions that all Egyptians are punishable by imprisonment and whipping. In 1827, the judge at Worcester Assizes announced the determination of himself and his brother judges to execute horse-thieves, *especially Gypsies;* and in 1864, at Hayle, in Cornwall, seven Gypsies were charged before the Rev. Uriah Tonkin with the heinous offence of "sleeping under tents," and were sentenced to three weeks' imprisonment with hard labour. These criminals were a mother and her six children, aged twenty, sixteen, fifteen, thirteen, ten, and eight years.

In England, however, a pardon was granted in 1591 to Robert Hilton, and in 1594 to William Stanley, Francis Brewarton, and John Weekes for the felony of calling themselves Egyptians; and England throughout was almost merciful compared with Scotland. Witness the following jottings from Scotch records. Four of the Faas were hanged in 1611; two Faas and a Bailie in 1616; six Faas and two others in 1624, when also, "some days later, there were brought to trial Ellen Faa, widow of Captain Faa, Lucretia Faa, and other women, to the number of eleven, all of whom were in like manner convicted, and condemned to be drowned in the Nor' Loch of Edinburgh," where to-day are the beautiful Princes Street Gardens. In 1636 the Sheriff of Haddington passed doom on a whole company—"the men to be hanged, and the women to be drowned; and such of the women as has children to be scourged through the burgh of Haddington, and burnt in the cheek." Then, in 1698, seven Bailies were executed, as were two more in 1714; and in 1701 James M'Pherson, James Gordon, and Peter and Donald Brown were hanged at Banff, the sheriff further ordaining that "the three young rogues now in prison this day have their ears cropt, be publicly scourged through the town of Banff, be burnt upon the cheek by the executioner, and be banished the shire for ever under pain of death." This James M'Pherson was rather a notable character. He had been leader of twenty-seven armed followers, with a piper playing at their head; and his target and huge mediæval two-handed sword are preserved at Duff House. His fiddle-neck is an heir-loom in the Cluny-Macpherson family. Burns tells us how—

> " Sae rantinly, sae wantonly,
>   Sae dauntingly gaed he ;
> He played a spring, and danced it round
>   Below the gallows tree."

And relics more precious than either sword or fiddle-neck are his rude, reckless "Rant," and the beautiful air to which he set the same. He played it as he walked to execution, and, at the gallows foot, proffered his instrument to who would take it, but, no man venturing, snapt it across his knee.

Now observe, I pray you, that in all these cases the crime was not murder or pillage, but the being what God had made them, or, as the law put it, being "called, known, held, and reputed Egyptians." So late as 1770, those words formed part of the indictment brought against two Gypsies, who were hanged on Linlithgow Bridge. When I think of that pitiless legislation. I am reminded of the cruel old Norfolk gardener. He was hoeing one day, and a frog hopped out before him. "I'll larn you to be a frog," said crabbed Roger, and hoed it forthwith in pieces. So "I'll larn you to be Gypsies," said British lawgivers, and the gallows was their means of education.

It was ten times worse on the Continent. In Roumania, till 1856, the Gypsies (200,000 in number) were slaves, cruelly and barbarously treated. "In the houses of their masters," wrote the British Consul, "they are employed in the lowest offices, live in the cellars, have the lash continually applied to them, and are still [in 1855] subjected to the iron collar and a kind of spiked iron mask or helmet, which they are obliged to wear as a mark of punishment and degradation for every petty offence." Roumania, you will remember, was one of those down-trodden nationalities of whose wrongs we have heard so much. In the French Basque country, in 1802, the Gypsy bands around Bayonne and Mauléon were caught by night as in a net, huddled on shipboard, and landed presently on the coast of Africa. And in Germany, for two whole centuries, the Gypsies were hunted down like wild beasts. In 1720, in the day's "bag" of one Rhenish potentate, among deer, wild boars, and other game, occurs this entry :—"*Item.* a Gypsy woman, with her sucking child."

In startling contrast to this persecution, the Gypsies have, during five centuries, been often countenanced by persons of the highest rank. On the Continent, they received letters of protection more than once from Pope and Emperor ; and to-day in Austria, the Archduke Joseph is a prince among Romany Ryes (or "Gypsy gentlemen"), as Gypsies call the lovers of their race. In England, about 1518, Thomas, Earl of Surrey, entertained "Gyptians" at Tendring Hall, Suffolk ; in Scotland, in

1540, James V. entered into a formal league or treaty with his "lovit John Faw, Lord and Earl of Little Egypt," granting him authority to execute justice upon his company and folk, conform to the laws of Egypt. There, too, in 1559, as he was riding one day from Edinburgh to Roslin, Sir William Sinclair "delivered an Egyptian from the gibbet in the Burgh Moor, ready to be strangled. On which account," adds good Father Hay, "the whole body of Gypsies were of old accustomed to gather in the marshes of Roslin, where they acted several plays during the months of May and June. There were two towers which were allowed them for their residence, the one called Robin Hood, the other Little John." I might multiply similar instances; enough, that in 1750 the then Prince and Princess of Wales drove to visit the Gypsy queen, Bridget, in Norwood Forest; and that Prince Victor of Hohenlohe has sat in the Gypsy tent of Lazarus Petuléngro at the Liverpool Exhibition of 1886.

Now, how are we to reconcile this contradiction, that the Gypsies should thus have been persecuted with the one hand, and caressed with the other. Well, I have no hesitation in affirming that the persecution was largely due to the imputation of crimes, of which the Gypsies are not, were never, guilty. You yourselves will have heard that they are kidnappers, stealers of children. It is an old charge, older than John Bunyan's days, who likens his feelings as a sinner to those of a child carried off by the Gypsies. Chief Justice Popham, who was born in 1531, is said, while quite a child, to have been stolen by a band of Gypsies, and for some months or years—on this point authorities differ—to have been detained by them. It is further alleged that they disfigured him, and burnt on his left arm a cabalistic mark. In a Scotch witchcraft trial of 1586 there is mention of a Mr William Smith, who, besides being the king's smith, was also a 'great scholar and doctor of medicine.' He, it seems, had, when eight years of age, been 'taken away by an Egyptian into Egypt, which Egyptian was a giant, where he remained ten years, and then came home.' At the time of the trial he was away again—this time with the 'good neighbours,' or fairies. Or there was the famous Adam Smith, author of the *Wealth of Nations*. He, too, as a boy is said to have been carried off by Gypsies, and not to have been recovered for several hours. Or there was the alleged abduction of Elizabeth Canning, which made such a stir in London in 1759; or that of Elizabeth Kellen in 1802: or that of Anna Böckler in 1872. The last was the only child of a rich Pomeranian farmer, and no fewer than forty-seven German Gypsies were imprisoned on suspicion of having kidnapped her. A twelvemonth later, as luck would have it, her corpse was discovered in one of her father's barns, where the farm-boy, her murderer, had buried it. That case is typical of many more. Elizabeth Canning turned out a rank impostor; so, too, did the other Elizabeth. Indeed, my investigations of every alleged instance of kidnapping have always resulted in a verdict of acquittal, or, at most, in a 'not proven.' Gypsies have too many children of their own to trouble themselves with other folk's brats. But in almost every Gypsy family, the purest even, there will be one white sheep; one child of the dozen will be comparatively fair, will bring out some far-away strain of Gentile blood. And strangers noticing this child have jumped to the conclusion that a fair Gypsy is a rarer fowl than a black swan. "They must have stolen it," is the cry; and hence, in all likelihood, arose the myth.

A yet more monstrous charge has been that of cannibalism. In the old edition of Chambers' *Encyclopædia*, it was gravely stated that Gypsies "were or are wont to eat their parents;" and in 1782, little more than a century since, forty-five Gypsies, men and women, were beheaded, broken on the wheel, quartered alive, or hanged for cannibalism. Among them were their Bishop and their "Harum Pasha," the ornaments in whose cap were valued at £600. The manner of their detection was thus: Arrested first by way of wise precaution, they were racked till they confessed to theft and murder; then were brought to the spot where they said their victims were buried, and, no victims forthcoming, were promptly racked again. "We ate them," at last was their despairing cry; and straightway the Gypsies were hurried to the scaffold; straightway the newspapers rang with blood-curdling narratives of Gypsy cannibalism. Then, when it all was over, the Emperor sent down a commission from Vienna, the outcome of whose investigations was that nobody was missing, that no one had been murdered—but the Gypsies. This was in Hungary, but even in England, in 1859, a judge seems to have entertained a similar suspicion. In that year, at the York Assizes, a Gypsy lad, Guilliers Heron, was tried for a robbery, of which, by the way, he was innocent. "One of the prisoner's brothers" (I quote from the *Times*) said they were all at tea with the prisoner at five o'clock in their tent; and when asked what they had to eat, he said they had an *urchin* cooked. His Lordship (Mr Justice Byles): "What do you say you had—cooked urchin?"

Gypsy : "Yes, cooked urchin.   I'm wery partial to cooked urchin."
His lordship's mind, says the reporter, seemed to be filled with
horrible misgivings, until it was explained to him that *urchin* was a
provincialism for "hedgehog," and that hedgehogs are a favourite
Gypsy delicacy.

I am not here to hold a brief for the Gypsies.   I do not
pretend they are immaculate.   Crimes of violence *have* been
rare among them ; murder almost unknown.   And I could give
you some striking instances of Gypsy honesty, for Gypsies are
trustworthy, in proportion as they are trusted.   But I freely own
that there still are Gypsies who are " light-fingered, and use
picking," even as there were when Andrew Boorde wrote about
them, and that was two hundred and fifty years ago.   Then, too,
the older Gypsies would sometimes make off with another man's
halter, and the other man's horse at the end of it—a crime,
however, now obsolete in these days of telegraphs and the rural
police.   And there is fortune-telling, with which Gypsies still
delude the credulous.   I certainly am not going to say one word
in defence of fortune-telling ; it is quite as silly, if not quite so
mischievous, as table-turning ; silly, although an African traveller
of my acquaintance is firmly persuaded of its truth.   Years ago
he had the lines of his hand read by a Gypsy girl near London.
He was not a doctor then, he had no idea of ever becoming a
traveller, yet she told him (so *he* tells me) that a doctor he was
to become, that he was to cross the seas, and wander in strange
lands, was to be in peril of his life, but should come safe through,
return, and marry, and so forth.   And once in the heart of Africa
he *was* in deadly peril of his life, for he stood with a noose round
his neck, in a crowd of infuriated savages ; but he thought of the
Gypsy girl's words, and how all she had said had come true, and
he laughed, feeling sure of his safety.   And seeing him laugh,
they released him ; they dared not harm a man so resolute.   So,
at least, my friend told me, a few weeks since, at our club.   In
return, I told him another fortune-telling story of another friend
of mine, an artist, who visited some Gypsies at Dunbar.   They
told him his name, and where he came from, though he had only
just landed a week before from Melbourne.   He was greatly impressed with their powers, was quite certain there *must* be something in palmistry.   However, a few months after, he met the
same Gypsies in Fife, and, of course, he again consulted the
oracle.   " Look here," he said to Mrs Petuléngro, " that first
time you told me my name, and I gave you five shillings ; now

this time, I'll give you ten if you'll let me into the secret of your power." " You will, my gentleman ? " Certainly he would. "Well, then, my gentleman, don't you remember coming into the tent, and sitting down a bit ; then you got up, and went outside with one of the boys to have a look round the camp, but you left your umbrella behind, with your name and address on it ? " So there was *that* mystery solved ; but to think he had never hit on the solution !

Gypsies never offer to tell me my fortune ; once, indeed, I took a young lady to have hers told, and my Gypsy friends were half indignant with me. Didn't I know better, they asked, than to go and encourage such foolishness. Mere foolishness often it is, a passing jest ; but fortune-telling, or rather fortune-seeking, has sometimes assumed a very much darker form. Thus, in the trial, three hundred years ago at Edinburgh, of Lady Fowlis for witchcraft, incantation, sorcery, and poisoning, we learn that she had sent one of her servants to the Egyptians, to have knowledge of them how to poison the young Laird. The errand must have miscarried, since the poison was got from a merchant in Aberdeen. And in the *Times* for February and March 1862, there was a long account of a police case against a Gypsy woman, Georgina Lee, twenty years old, who appeared in the dock with a baby in her arms. She and her husband camped, it seems, on Hounslow Heath, and one day she called at a gentleman's house near by. She got telling the servant-girls' fortunes, told the cook what she knew to be true, that she was to marry a Marquis. Then the drawing-room bell rang ; the lady too wanted to have her fortune read, wished to know if she should be married again within the twelvemonth, and finished by offering Georgina a sovereign for something that would kill her present husband. So, on Friday, Georgina returned with a powder wrapped up in a paper, and the lady then told her that, if it did any good, she would give her ten shillings. But Georgina wanted cash down, and, the lady refusing, got hustled out of the house. In the middle of which hustling, the happy husband comes upon the scene, and gives Mrs Lee in charge for attempting to obtain money on false pretences. False they undoubtedly were, for the powder turned out to be nothing but harmless chalk. So, after a fortnight of remands, Georgina Lee was sentenced to three months' hard labour ; the lady got—nothing.

Yes, fortune-telling has brought the fortune-tellers into trouble as often as favour. But the Gypsies have higher claims on our consideration. *Imprimis*, they are excellent company, able to converse with prince or peasant, and to give a good answer to each, for they have seen much, and know how to describe what they have seen. Secondly, to the Gypsies we are indebted for, it may be, three-fourths of our fairy tales. M. Jourdain, you will remember, was surprised to find that all his life long he had been speaking prose without knowing it. You also may be surprised to learn that from earliest childhood you and your grandmothers (especially your grandmothers) have been hearing or telling Indian fairy tales. Yet, according to some very high authorities, our most familiar nursery stories—*Puss in Boots, Cinderella*, and all the rest of them, are as certainly Indian in origin as is the Romani or Gypsy language. No, says Mr Lang, that cannot be ; it is impossible that stories which orginated in India can have reached Siberia, and Europe, and Africa, and America, by oral transmission, and within the historical period. Impossible, quotha. The Gypsies came originally from India, and even during the two last centuries we find large bands of Gypsies journeying from Poland to China, from Turkey to Sweden, from Hungary to Algeria, from Corfu to Liverpool, from Portugal to Brazil, and from England to the States, New Zealand, and Australia. And these ubiquitous, much-wandering Gypsies possess versions of all our familiar fairy-tales, only versions often much better than our own. In Turkey, Gypsies have long filled the *rôle* of professional story-tellers ; nor even in London is that *rôle* unknown to them, for it was in St James's Street that Mr Campbell of Islay picked up two Gypsy tinkers, from whom he and Sir George Dasent extracted eight good folk-tales, all about princesses, magic hats and sticks, castles of copper and silver and gold, and such-like. Now, one of the Gypsies, Mr Campbell informs us, played the fiddle by ear, and was commonly sent for to wakes, where he entertained the company with stories, which comes very near the professional story-teller.

Thirdly, the race has a marvellous faculty for music. Some of you very likely have heard the Blue Hungarian Band. That band consists wholly of Gypsies. The Abbé Liszt—a high authority—ascribed to the Gypsies the creation of Hungary's national music, and certain it is that over all South-Eastern Europe, every musician is almost certainly a Gypsy, and every Gypsy is certainly a musician. That is only partially true in England. I know an estate in Norfolk, where there were great rejoicings when the son and heir came of age, and his father,

Lord Omnium, promised a sovereign to every Gypsy fiddler who should put in an appearance. Twenty appeared, each man with his violin, and a grand show they made as they played all altogether, standing in a semicircle. " But," one of them told me years afterwards, "there were only twelve on 'em really knew how to fiddle; the rest of us had soaped our fiddle-strings, so as not to make no noise when we drew the bow over them. But we each got the sovereign." Welsh Gypsies, as a rule, are more musical than their English brethren, and many of the celebrated Welsh harpists are Gypsies, whilst the Gypsy Allens were the most famous of the Border bagpipers.

Playing cards again, are by some supposed to have been brought into Europe by Gypsies from the east. The tented musicians, refugees from Hungary and Lorraine, who about 1555 discovered the Stourbridge fire-clay, were very possibly Gypsies. To Gypsies also have been ascribed the saddler's craft, and the introduction into Europe of gunpowder. But, even though we concede to the Gypsies the credit of having introduced folk-tales, the *czardas*, playing cards, glass-making, saddlery, and artillery, yet we may not have half acknowledged our full indebtedness.

To the Jewish race, now so dispersed, so despised, you owe religion—all your hopes for the life to come. What if to the Gypsy race, similarly dispersed, and ten times more despised, you owe all, or well-nigh all, that renders this present life liveable—a knowledge of the metals? Without the metals life would now seem impossible. Every mouthful of bread we eat, every article of clothing we wear, the house we live in—these all have in some way or other demanded the use of metal. Yet we know that three thousand years ago the dwellers here in Great Britain had absolutely no knowledge of the metals, had no better implements than tools of stone. Then, says Sir John Lubbock, the art of working in bronze was introduced into Europe from the East by a small-handed race like the Egyptians or the Hindus—a nomade race, too, who practised the self-same methods in different lands, and who, whether acquainted or not with iron, were exclusively workers in bronze. What race this was he leaves an unsolved problem, except that it certainly was not the Phœnicians. But several foreign archæologists have been led independently to the conclusion that this unknown race, small-handed like the Gypsies, nomade like the Gypsies, and, like the Gypsies, immigrants from the East, was indeed none other than the Gypsy race. It looks at first a daring paradox, but, examined closer, the paradox sensibly diminishes. To begin with, we know absolutely nothing of the date of the Gypsies' first appearance in Europe. It may have been one thousand years ago, it may have been three thousand; all we can say is, that history is silent, and that its silence speaks for a *pre*-historic arrival of the Gypsies. Secondly, at the present day, the Gypsies in South-eastern Europe may be said to monopolise the blacksmith's craft and the coppersmith's. In Transylvania, for instance, if you want your horse shod, you have to send him to a Gypsy farrier; if your kettle has a hole in it, you get it mended by a Gypsy tinker. Indeed, so exclusively is the smith's a Gypsy (and therefore a degrading) trade, that in Montenegro, when in 1872 the Government established an arsenal, no native Montenegrins could be induced to fill its well-paid posts. And a traveller tells me that in Asia Minor it is just the same: the Gypsies have still a like monopoly of metal-working, the native shoeing-smith being no true smith in our sense at all. He is supplied by Gypsies with horseshoes of various sizes, and merely hammers them on. Now, it is hard to conceive how the Gypsies could have usurped so all-important an industry, far easier to imagine that it must have been always theirs. Thirdly, even at the present day, the Gypsy coppersmiths of South-eastern Europe will forsake the land of their birth, and for seven years wander all over Europe, everywhere manufacturing copper vessels. Even now they must often arrive at remote country places where the methods of working in copper are clean unknown; as it is now, it may well have been two thousand, three thousand years before. Fourthly, nearly all the early notices of Gypsies refer to them as metal-workers. Thus, an Austrian monk wrote of them almost seven centuries ago as "cold smiths," workers, that is, in the cold metal. "They have no home or country," he says; "everywhere they are found alike; they wander through the world, abusing people with their knaveries." Again, in the old Byzantine writers, we light on mention of certain so-called *komodromoi* (roamers, that is, through the villages). These *komodromoi*, it appears, were both copper and goldsmiths, wandering through the country, and using bellows made of skins, like those of some Greek Gypsies described by a German traveller in 1497. Now, if these *komodromoi* were Gypsies, as there is every reason to suppose they were, they are strangely connected by tradition with the central event in the world's history—the Crucifixion. For, according to a Greek apocryphal gospel, as also to a legend still current in Montenegro, it was a *komodromos* or Gypsy who forged the nails for the Crucifixion; wherefore the whole race has been thenceforth accursed of heaven. The Gypsies of Alsace and Lithuania have a tradition of their own, opposed to, and in all likelihood devised expressly to refute, this legend. How there were two Jew brothers, Schmul and Rom-Schmul. The first of them exulted at the Crucifixion; the other would gladly have saved our Lord from death, and, finding that impossible, did what little he could—stole one of the nails. So it came about that Christ's feet must be placed one over the other, and fastened with a single nail. And Schmul remained a Jew; but Rom-Schmul turned Christian, and became the founder of the whole Rómani race. This Gypsy legend offers a plausible explanation of what has long puzzled antiquaries, that in the most ancient crucifixes there are always four nails, in later ones only three. The earliest known example of this daring innovation is a copper crucifix of Byzantine workmanship, dating from the close of the 12th century. Now, if Gypsies had then, as now, a practical monopoly of metal-working in South-eastern Europe, this crucifix must have been fashioned by a Gypsy, when the *three* nails would be an easily intelligible protest against the Gentile libel that those nails were forged by the founder of his line.

Be that as it may, I have shown that the Gypsies have possibly been greater benefactors to the Gentiles than even was Watt or Stevenson. I have shown, too, that the Gentiles rewarded them —as benefactors often are rewarded—with persecution. For surely any wrong-doings of the Gypsies fade into insignificance by the side of the wrongs that were done them. How, then, have the Gypsies emerged from that persecution? None the better for it, of that one may be positive. Still, as they possess no written histories to preserve the recollection of their wrongs, so to-day their feeling towards Gentiles is one more of contempt than of hatred. The Gentile seems to the Gypsy less clever than himself, a poor, credulous fool, who believes in fortune-telling, and who can generally be done in a horse bargain. Indeed, this odd sense of superiority is latent (or blatant) in even the poorest Gypsies.

They are not patriotic—why should they be? During last century many were impressed, but they do not make good soldiers or sailors. In a Spanish campaign years ago, two soldiers dropped out of the opposing ranks, and the tide of battle rolled by them. Presently one half rose from the ground, and espying the other's corpse, as he fancied, crept forward to plunder. But the other dead fox was not to be caught like that.   He, too, rose, and then suddenly there were cries of recognition—"Zincalo!" "Rómani chal!"   For the one was a Spanish, the other an Austrian, Gypsy.   Five minutes later they were sharing a flask of schnaps, and drinking damnation to the Spanish and Austrian services.

   Still, the Gypsies are no cowards when they have got to fight for themselves.   They have shown that often, from Tom Winter's day down to Jim Mace's.   But if you want Gypsy fights, you must go to George Borrow.   There is the one, described to him by Jasper Petuléngro, between the Bow Street runner and the Gypsy. The runner knew that his man would pass through a certain lane, so he posted himself there one cold, moonlight night.   And, after long waiting, he "heard a gate slam, and then the low stamping of horses; and presently he saw *two* men on horseback coming towards the lane through the field behind the gate.   The man who rode foremost was a tall, big fellow, the very man he was in quest of.   The other was a smaller chap, not so small either, but a light, wiry fellow, and a proper master of his hands when he sees occasion for using them.   Well, brother, the foremost man came to the gate, reached at the hank, undid it, and rode through, holding it open for the other.   Before, however, the other could follow, out bolted the runner from behind the tree, kicked the gate to with his foot, and, seizing the big man on horseback, 'You are my prisoner,' said he   The Gypsy clubbed his whip, and aimed a blow at the runner, which, if it *had* hit him on the skull, as was meant, would very likely have cracked it.   But the runner received it partly on his staff, and then, seeing what kind of customer he had to deal with, dropped his staff and seized the Gypsy with both his hands, who forthwith spurred his horse, hoping, by doing so, either to break away from him, or fling him down.   But it would not do; the runner held on like a bull-dog, so that the Gypsy, to escape being hauled to the ground, suddenly flung himself off the saddle.   And then happened in that lane such a struggle between those two—the Gypsy and the runner—as I suppose will never happen again.   But you must have heard of it; every one heard of it; every one has heard of the fight between the Bow Street runner and the Gypsy."

   "No," says Borrow, "I never heard of it till now."

   "All England rung with it, brother.   There never was a better match than between those two.   The runner was somewhat the stronger—all those runners are strong fellows—and a great deal cooler, for all of that sort are wondrous cool people. He had, however, to do with one who knew full well how to take his own part. The Gypsy fought the runner, brother, in the old Roman fashion. He bit, he kicked, and screamed like a wild cat, casting foam from his mouth, and fire from his eyes. Sometimes he was beneath the runner's legs, and sometimes he was upon his shoulders. What the runner found most difficult was to get a firm hold of the Gypsy, for no sooner did he seize him by any part of his wearing apparel, than the Gypsy either tore himself away, or contrived to slip out of it, so that in a little time the Gypsy was three parts naked; and as for holding him by the body, it was out of the question, for he was as slippery as an eel. At last the runner seized him by the Belcher handkerchief, which he wore in a knot round his neck, and, do what the Gypsy might, he could not free himself. And when the runner saw that, it gave him fresh heart, no doubt. 'It's no use,' he said, 'you had better give in. Hold out your hands for the darbies, or I'll throttle you.'"

"And what," asks Borrow, "did the other chap do who came with the Gypsy?"

"I sat still on my horse, brother."

"You!" says Borrow; "were you the man?"

"I was he, brother."

"And why didn't you help your comrade?"

"I have fought in the ring, brother."

"And what had fighting in the ring to do with fighting in the lane?"

"You mean not fighting. A great deal, brother; it taught me to prize fair play. When I fought Staffordshire Dick, t'other side of London, I was alone, brother. Not a Gypsy to back me, and he had all his brother pals about him. But they gave me fair play, brother, and I beat Staffordshire Dick, which I could not have done had they put one finger on his side the scale, for he was as good a man as myself, or nearly so. Now, brother, had I but bent a finger in favour of the Gypsy, the runner would never have come alive out of the lane, but I did not, for I thought to myself, fair play is a precious stone."

Are Englishmen and Gypsies changed since then? It seems that Englishmen are.[1]

---

[1] This was written just after the prize fight in Belgium between Slavin and Smith, when the Australian was brutally mauled by English roughs.

Here in London there must be hundreds of Gypsies ; here in London there must be hundreds, thousands of cage birds. As the caged lark to the free, wild lark, so is the city Gypsy to his country brother. The former may have some smattering of book-learning, the latter not know big B from a bull's foot ; else the life-long tent-dweller in quiet lanes has small cause to envy the Battersea hawker. It is easy sneering at the " noble savage," but an open-air life *does* possess an ennobling influence. And though a Gypsy boy may know nothing of the three R's, and even less of all your schoolboard 'ologies, he can give you the (unscientific) names of every bird that flies, and every herb that grows, which knowledge Solomon himself was proud of. To step out of one's tent right into the star-lit night, to fall asleep to the murmur of a brook, all one's life long to lie in nature's bosom—that life, with few cares about Heaven, is Heaven already. But, like other wild creatures, our country Gypsies are threatened with extinction. Enclosure acts have struck a deadly blow at English Gypsydom, driving the wanderers from grassy hedgeside and breezy common to the dingiest purlieus of our dingiest towns. A pity for them ; a pity, too, for poet and painter. One morning, some years ago, a poet was crossing Snowdon with a friend. "She was not what is technically called a lady, yet she was both tall and, in her way, handsome, and was far more clever than many of those who might look down upon her, for her speculative and her practical abilities were equally remark-able. Besides being the first palmist of her time, she had the reputation of being able to make more clothes-pegs in an hour, and sell more, than any other woman in England. The grandeur of that Snowdon sunrise was such as can only be seen about once in a lifetime, and could never be given by any pen or pencil. 'You don't seem to enjoy it a bit,' was the irritated remark of the poet to the Gypsy woman, who stood quite silent, and apparently deaf to the rhapsodies in which *he* had been indulging. 'Don't injiy it, don't I?' said she, removing her pipe. 'You injiy talkin' about it. I injiy lettin' it soak in.'" No London Gypsy may hope to look upon a Snowdon sunrise.

I should have liked to tell you more about Gypsy life, that life which the song says is a merry one. And so it is ; but even Gypsies die, and, therefore, their life is not without its sorrows. Eight years ago come May, a letter reached me in Edinburgh from old Lementina Lovell. There is never very much in Gypsies' letters beyond loves and greetings, and such-like. This letter was no exception; it ended thus: "Lancelot [her youngest son] sends his duty, and would take it very kind in you to look in, if so be as you are round this way, for he is dying." As luck would have it, I had nothing just then on hand, and was wanting a holiday; so I started that night for Loamshire. Next morning, exactly at sunrise, I reached the little roadside station, from which I had twelve miles to walk to the Lovells' encampment. It was a delicate, clear morning, sweet with the scent of hawthorn and hyacinth, and as I walked, I heard my first cuckoo on the right hand—sure omen of coming good. My way took me down into the valley, where lies the sleepy little town of Clun, and up out of the valley on to the hills which separate England from Wales, and on which, as I knew, the Lovells were encamped. I had still half a mile to go, when a Gypsy child met me—little Anselo Lovell, nephew to Lancelot. I have said that all Gypsies know the Gypsy language. This child is the one exception—*he* is deaf and dumb. Yet already, at six, he had invented an odd sign-language of his own; its sign for me the twirling an imaginary moustache. And now in that strange sign-language he tried to acquaint me with his uncle's state, then ran on ahead to tell them I was coming. At the camp I found a multitude of Gypsies, for all Lancelot's brothers and sisters, with their wives, and husbands, and children, had gathered from every airt to see him go. All through that day they kept coming, the last the grandmother, a little old, old woman, who had journeyed a hundred miles. She came into the tent where Lancelot lay, sat down on the earth, and, covering her head with her mantle, said: "*Kíno shom, chawollé*" (Little children, I am weary). And all that day lay Lancelot, dreamy, but conscious, wholly free from pain. Towards evening he said to his elder brother, Pyramus: "Play to me."

How well I remember the scene.

The tents were pitched upon the western hill-slope. Beside them ran Offa's Dike, reared centuries before to keep out the Welsh marauders; the silver Tame flowed beneath; and beyond stretched the beautiful Welsh country, all shimmering through the soft blue wood-smoke of the fire that smouldered outside. Some sat within the tent, but more on the turf without—the children awe-struck, puzzled. The sinking sun slanted through the tent-opening, and lighted up Lancelot's face, which was lighted up, too, by happy recollections. For Pyramus, the cunning fiddler, was playing the dear old Welsh melodies. First, the

" March of the Men of Harlech," and then from its stirring tones he slid imperceptibly into the tender "Shepherd of Snowdon." And as he played he wept, the big, strong man. " Play that again, my Pyramus," said Lancelot. And Pyramus did play it again, but not quite to the end, for, as the last bar opened, Lancelot died. Then there was lamentation in the tents of Egypt.

Printed at THE EDINBURGH PRESS, 9 *and* 11 *Young Street.*

INDEX.

PRINTED AT THE EDINBURGH PRESS, 9 AND 11 YOUNG STREET.

www.ingramcontent.com/pod-product-compliance
Lightning Source LLC
Chambersburg PA
CBHW032309280326
41932CB00009B/758